THE OMNIPOTENT MAGICIAN

THE OMNIPOTENT MAGICIAN

Lancelot 'Capability' Brown, 1716–1783

Jane Brown

Chatto & Windus
LONDON

Published by Chatto & Windus 2011

2 4 6 8 10 9 7 5 3 1

First published in Great Britain in 2011 by
Chatto & Windus
Random House, 20 Vauxhall Bridge Road,
London SW1V 2SA
www.rbooks.co.uk

Addresses for companies within The Random House Group Limited can be found at:
www.randomhouse.co.uk/offices.htm

The Random House Group Limited Reg. No. 954009

A CIP catalogue record for this book
is available from the British Library

ISBN 9780701182120

The Random House Group Limited supports The Forest Stewardship
Council (FSC), the leading international forest certification organisation. All our titles
that are printed on Greenpeace approved FSC certified paper carry the FSC logo.
Our paper procurement policy can be found at www.rbooks.co.uk/environment

Mixed Sources
Product group from well-managed
forests and other controlled sources
www.fsc.org Cert no. TT-COC-2139
© 1996 Forest Stewardship Council
FSC

Typeset in Bembo by Palimpsest Book Production Ltd,
Falkirk, Stirlingshire

Printed and bound in Great Britain by Clays Ltd, St Ives plc

CONTENTS

A note on currency values. The National Archives Currency Converter website gives equivalents, (a) in 1750 Lancelot's £25 per annum equalled £2,129; (b) in 1770 his accounting sums of £1,000 equalled £63,690. Thus multiplying the sums given throughout the book by 60 will give the reader a fair match for modern money.

A note on dates. Until 1752 the new year began on 25th March. As the point of change from the Julian calendar to the Gregorian in September 1752 was approximately in the middle of Lancelot Brown's life, I have corrected the dates to New Style from the start, taking the New Year as 1st January.

LIST OF ILLUSTRATIONS

Illustrations in the text

Lancelot Brown Family Tree

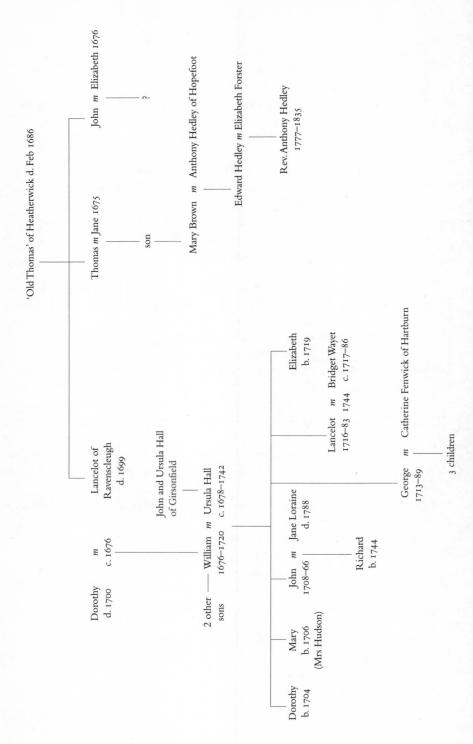

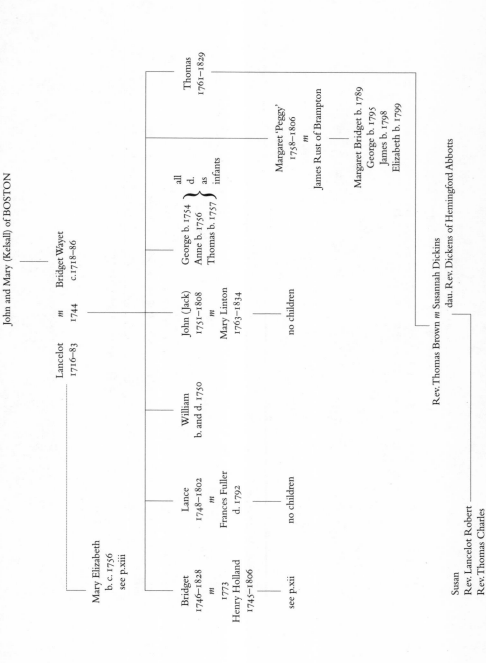

John and Mary (Kelsall) of BOSTON

Lancelot *m* 1744 Bridget Wayet
1716–83   c.1718–86

Mary Elizabeth b. c. 1756 see p.xiii

Bridget 1746–1828 *m* 1773 Henry Holland 1745–1806 — see p.xii

Lance 1748–1802 *m* Frances Fuller d. 1792 — no children

William b. and d. 1750

John (Jack) 1751–1808 *m* Mary Linton 1763–1834 — no children

George b. 1754, Anne b. 1756, Thomas b. 1757 } all d. as infants

Margaret 'Peggy' 1758–1806 *m* James Rust of Brampton
Margaret Bridget b. 1789, George b. 1795, James b. 1798, Elizabeth b. 1799

Thomas 1761–1829

Rev. Thomas Brown *m* Susannah Dickins dau. Rev. Dickens of Hemingford Abbotts
Susan, Rev. Lancelot Robert, Rev. Thomas Charles

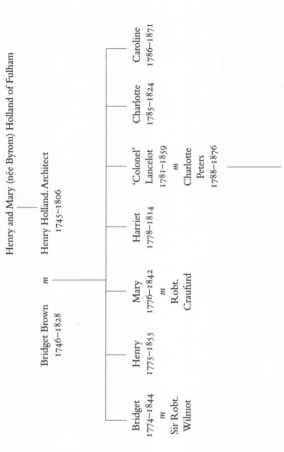

Henry and Mary (née Byrom) Holland of Fulham

Bridget Brown   *m*   Henry Holland. Architect
1746–1828   1745–1806

Bridget
1774–1844
m
Sir Robt.
Wilmot

Henry
1775–1855

Mary
1776–1842
m
Robt.
Craufurd

Harriet
1778–1814

'Colonel'
Lancelot
1781–1859
m
Charlotte
Peters
1788–1876

Charlotte
1785–1824

Caroline
1786–1871

15 children, of whom Henry 1808-93 was Governor of Bank of England 1865.

Henrietta 1829–1912 *m* Henry Wise, descendant of Royal Gardener Henry Wise 1653–1738.

The name Lancelot persisted down the generations.

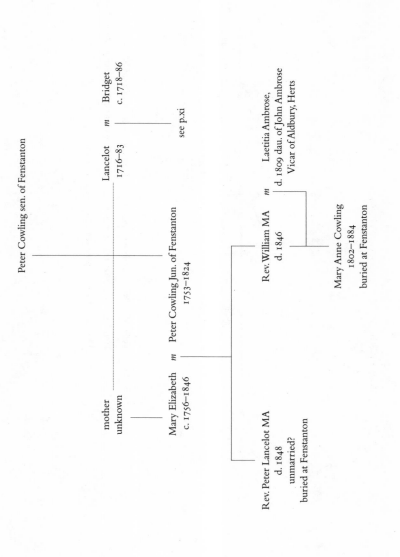

Peter Cowling sen. of Fenstanton

Lancelot *m* Bridget
1716–83   c. 1718–86

see p.xi

mother .... *m* Peter Cowling Jun. of Fenstanton
unknown   1753–1824
Mary Elizabeth
c. 1756–1846

Rev. Peter Lancelot MA
d. 1848
unmarried?
buried at Fenstanton

Rev. William MA *m* Laetitia Ambrose,
d. 1846   d. 1809 dau. of John Ambrose
                 Vicar of Aldbury, Herts

Mary Anne Cowling
1802–1884
buried at Fenstanton

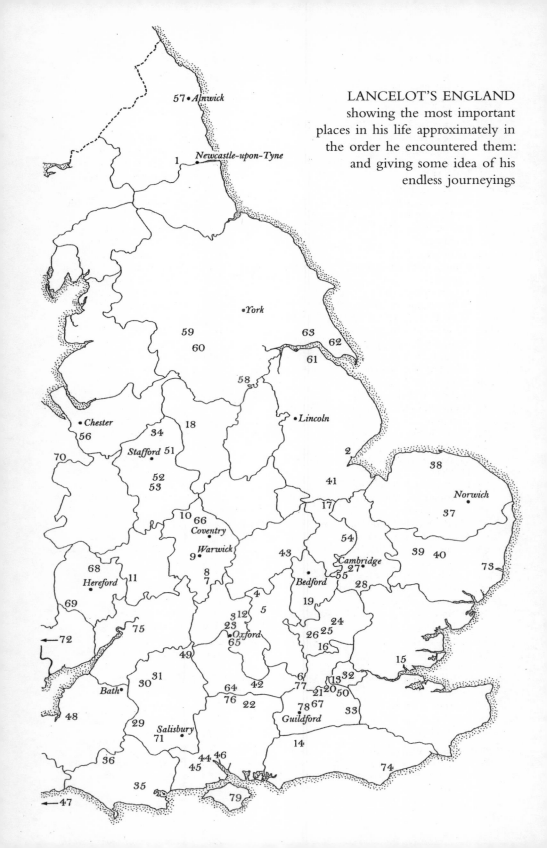

LANCELOT'S ENGLAND
showing the most important
places in his life approximately in
the order he encountered them:
and giving some idea of his
endless journeyings

57 • Alnwick

1 • Newcastle-upon-Tyne

• York

59
60

63
62
61

58

• Chester
56

34   18

Stafford 51

52
53

70

• Lincoln

2

38

41

• Norwich
37

17

10
66
Coventry

9 Warwick

8
7

54

43

Cambridge
27
55   28

39   40

73

68
Hereford   11

Bedford

69

75

4

19

5

72

3 12
23
Oxford
65

49

30 31

Bath •

64

76   22

29
Salisbury
71

36

44 46
45

35

48

24
26 25
16

15

6
77
13 32
21 20 50

78 67
Guildford   33

14

74

47

79

1. Kirkharle, Wallington (NT), Cambo and Rothley
2. Boston, home of Bridget Wayet
3. Kiddington, Oxfordshire, his first lake
4. Stowe (NT) and Wakefield Lawn
5. Wotton Underwood, Buckinghamshire
6. Stoke Park, Stoke Poges, Buckinghamshire
7. Compton Verney, close to Radway and Edge Hill
8. Charlecote Park (NT)
9. Warwick Castle (open daily)
10. Packington Hall
11. Croome Court (NT) and Pirton demesne
12. Kirtlington Park
13. Hammersmith, the Brown family home 1751–64
14. Petworth Park (NT)
15. Belhus (Country Park)
16. Moor Park, Hertfordshire (part public)
17. Burghley House (open regularly)
18. Chatsworth (open regularly)
19. Wrest Park (English Heritage) and Ampthill Park (public)
20. Syon House (open regularly), Kew, Richmond Park
21. Hampton Court (home 1764–83) and Hampton
22. Stratfield Saye (open regularly)
23. Blenheim (open regularly)
24. Luton Hoo (Hotel) and Luton Walled Garden
25. Beechwood, Hertfordshire
26. Ashridge, Hertfordshire, (Golden Valley NT woodlands)
27. Madingley Hall and Cambridge (St John's College wilderness)
28. Audley End (English Heritage) and Shortgrove
29. Longleat, Wiltshire (open regularly)
30. Corsham Court (open regularly)
31. Bowood (open regularly)
32. Queen's House, now Buckingham Palace and St James's Park
33. Gatton Park
34. Trentham, Staffordshire (open regularly)
35. Milton Abbas, Dorset (Milton Abbey School
36. Sherborne Castle, Dorset (open regularly)
37. Kimberley, Norfolk
38. Melton Constable, Norfolk
39. Euston Hall, Suffolk (open as advertised)
40. Redgrave, Suffolk
41. Grimsthorpe Castle, Lincolnshire (open as advertised)
42. Caversham Park, Reading
43. Castle Ashby, Northants (open as advertised, lakes public access)
44. Broadlands, Hampshire (open as advertised)
45. Paultons Park, Hampshire (amusements park)
46. North Stoneham (public park)
47. Ugbrooke and Mamhead, Devon
48. Burton Pynsent, Somerset
49. Tottenham Park, Wiltshire
50. Wimbledon Park (part public park)
51. Ingestre, Tixall and Shugborough
52. Weston Park, Tong and Chillington
53. Patshull Park
54. Fenstanton and Hilton, Huntingdonshire
55. Wimpole Hall (NT)
56. Eaton Hall, Cheshire
57. Alnwick Castle (open regularly)
58. Sandbeck Hall and Roche Abbey (abbey English Heritage)
59. Harewood, Yorkshire (open regularly)
60. Temple Newsam, Leeds (open regularly)
61. Brocklesby, Lincolnshire
62. Burton Constable, Yorkshire East Riding (open as advertised)
63. Sledmere (open as advertised)
64. Sandleford Park near Newbury (St Gabriel's School)
65. Nuneham Courtenay
66. Coombe Abbey (Country Park)
67. Claremont (School has house and park)
68. Berrington Hall (NT)
69. Moccas Court
70. Wynnstay
71. Old Wardour Castle, Wiltshire
72. Dinefwr. Llandeilo Dyfed (NT)
73. Heveningham, Suffolk
74. Ashburnham, Sussex
75. Woodchester Park, Gloucestershire (NT)
76. Highclere Castle, Hampshire
77. Langley Park, Buckinghamshire
78. Clandon Park, Surrey (NT)
79. Appuldurcombe, Isle of Wight (English Heritage

Author's note. A list of commissions complied by John Phibbs will be found in Roger Turner's *Capability Brown and the Eighteenth Century English Landscape*, 1999 or the reader is referred to the most recent county volumes of *The Buildings of England* www.pevsner.co.uk

L ANCELOT BROWN AND HIS WORKS entered my life a long time
ago; as a ten-year-old I was taken to Longleat for a day of unbe-
lievable wonders after the privations of wartime. The view from
Heaven's Gate (sadly, no longer the approach road) seemed just that,
down into the huge, dipping bowl of green set with magnificent old
trees, and in the centre a domed and pinnacled palace, such as I had
never seen before. The house smelt strongly of a musky scent, and the
portraits of Elizabethan children with dolls' faces haunted me. I still have
the antiquated guide book written by the Marchioness of Bath, signed
with a magisterial 'Bath' in pencil by the 6th Marquess, which I read
from cover to cover, and found that in the 'splendid and extravagant days'
of the 1750s Lord Weymouth had called on 'the services of Lancelot
Brown, nick-named "Capability" because of his habit of optimistically
telling prospective employers that the scene held "great capabilities".
William Cowper's *The Task* was then quoted – 'Lo! He comes, The
omnipotent magician, Brown appears' – and Cowper's satirical intent was
waved away, as it has been many times since. I certainly believed in the
'omnipotent magician Brown' as someone on a par with Merlin and the
Fairy Godmother. The view from Heaven's Gate and the idea that a man,
or even a woman, might do wondrous things with parks and woods and
fields dozed in a far corner of my brain, and it was a long time before
it was awakened.

In 1970 I was a mother of two young children and wanted to write,
but my desired subject – 'the landscape' – was elusive and difficult. The
gods were kind, for that year two great books were published that gave
me abundant pointers, Brenda Colvin's *Land and Landscape* and Nan
Fairbrother's *New Lives, New Landscapes.* Colvin's battle-cry for the 'new'
profession of landscape design had first sounded in the meagre post-war
air of 1947, but the 1970 edition was respectably weighty, and the challenges crowded every page. Colvin is gloriously lucid and grandly angry:
'We know ... that man can ruin his surroundings and make them

unsuitable for future generations . . . but we continue to act as if we did not know it'; 'we should think of this planet, Earth, as a single organism, in which humanity is involved. The sense of superior individuality which we enjoy is illusory'; 'the visual degradation of the landscape is a warning of peril not to be disregarded'. Nan Fairbrother is more grounded, though passionately so, in the solutions for our everyday landscapes; she courageously takes head-on that great British bugbear, nostalgia: 'The choice then is not between the old and new but between good landscape and bad. But it *is* a choice, and even though it is sad that the old must go (as it always has been), the true tragedy is not that the old must go but that the new should be bad.'

Colvin and Fairbrother found common cause in the necessity of learning from the good landscapes of the past, the polishing of ancient skills and understandings adapted for the present; thus landscape history was essentially a component of modern landscape architecture. For both my heroines the eighteenth century was the golden age, not in any nostalgic way, but simply because the lessons to be learned there were of greatest value. Colvin writes:

> It was in the eighteenth century, in England, that garden and landscape first came together and were seen to be in relationship. The idea of designing gardens as part of the wider landscape, and the wider landscape as a garden, was new, and was not fully grasped even in the eighteenth century. Now that we become aware of the need for conscious design on a far broader scale than ever before, the history of landscape and of gardens may be seen as two entwined threads of one theme.

'The idea of designing gardens as part of the wider landscape, *and the wider landscape as a garden*' (of essential use in the design of housing and recreational landscapes, schools, workplaces, farmland and forestry), was both professionally and popularly embodied in the works of my old friend, Mr Brown. After his death in 1783 he had been eclipsed by Repton, Loudon, Paxton and the great Victorian gardeners, and it was only in 1940 that Dorothy Stroud began collecting material on him, 'whose name was frequently turning up in writings on houses and gardens, but only in the vaguest way', as she explained in her foreword to *Capability Brown*. Her book, held up by the war, was first published in 1950 and sailed on through several editions; Stroud resurrected Brown, and none of the hundreds of thousands of words that have followed – including mine – could have been written without her. (Is it mischievous to suggest that the architectural historians, the big guns that surrounded her, like

Sir John Summerson and Christopher Hussey, happily let a woman deal with the gardener? If so, she turned the tables and triumphed.) My only regret is that she (or her publishers) used the title *Capability Brown*, for I have found no use of the term 'Capability' during his lifetime: the nickname has inspired ridicule, and was not given as a compliment, and I will call him by his baptismal name, Lancelot.

In the summer of 1983 the bicentenary of his death was marked by the opening of a small but notable exhibition, *Capability Brown and the Northern Landscape* at the Laing Art Gallery in Newcastle (which I reported on for *Building Design*). This exhibition evoked vivid and tangible connections to his life's work, but all too soon afterwards his reputation tumbled again. He was assailed by detractors, and by the champions of his newly revealed rivals, accused of destroying old gardens and living villages and, worse, of being a 'contractor' who systematically larded the face of England with his 'boring' lakes, clumps and plantations. On the other hand, the places where he was proved to have worked multiplied into the hundreds – just a sampling will include Stowe, Charlecote, Burghley, Longleat, Croome Court, Milton Abbas, Petworth, Broadlands, Bowood, Corsham Court, Sherborne Castle, Syon, Claremont, Sledmere, Harewood, Alnwick Castle, Audley End and Chatsworth, to name, as they say, but few. At the least, he made a considerable part of the heritage that our tourist industry relies upon; at best, he held up a mirror to the English landscape, cannily persuading his aristocratic clients to pay for lessons in the remaking of England that would fit her for modern times. In either case, and both, the question remains: how did he do it? This is the motivation for this book.

Lancelot Brown made a distressingly public end, collapsing in a Mayfair street on a winter's evening in early 1783. He had dined with his old acquaintance, Lord Coventry, at Coventry House in Piccadilly (now no. 106), and only had to walk around the corner to his daughter's, Mrs Holland's, in Hertford Street where he was staying: but, for whatever reason, he fell – and, being a big man, fell heavily – and being Lancelot Brown, the King's Master Gardener and a familiar figure, he was soon surrounded by willing helpers. Tradition has it that he fell outside Lord Sandwich's house, also in Hertford Street, where the footmen knew him well, and so in safe hands he was carried home to his daughter's house. There he was made comfortable, and the next morning – for he would have no undue fuss – his wife Biddy was fetched from their home at Hampton Court, and his lawyer Mr Edison was summoned so that he could dictate and sign a codicil to his Will. That evening, Thursday, 6th February 1783, at about nine o'clock he died.

The news travelled fast. 'Your Dryads must go into black gloves, Madam' was the pretty phrase that Horace Walpole used to Lady Ossory, rather spoiling it in his waspish way. 'Their father-in-law, Lady Nature's second husband, is dead.' He later tidied his thoughts into a suitable epitaph:

> With one Lost Paradise the name
> Of our first ancestor is stained:
> Brown shall enjoy unsullied fame
> For many a Paradise he regained.

Tributes were paid to 'his great and fine genius', and to his 'uncommon degree of fortitude and good spirits', for it was well known that he suffered from asthmatic attacks, the legacy of a serious illness when he was in his thirties. Lord Coventry spoke openly of his loss, of the ideals and ambitions that they had shared for more than twenty years in making his country home at Croome in Worcestershire: he later placed a Coade-stone casket beside Croome's lake, with the inscription:

> To the Memory of
> Lancelot Brown
> Who by the powers of
> His inimitable
> And creative genius
> Formed this garden scene
> Out of a morass.

Far across the country, at Burghley House outside Stamford, where Lancelot had worked happily for more than twenty-five years, Lord Exeter had Brown's portrait by Nathaniel Dance placed in the Pagoda Room. It hangs there still. The King, George III, was less gracious: when he met his Richmond gardener, Michael Milliken, Lancelot's protégé whom he brought south from Chatsworth into thirty-five years of comfortable royal service, he is reported as saying, 'Brown is dead! Now Mellicant [*sic*] *you* and I can do *here* what we please.' Walpole thought this story 'worth a million'. In his home country, which Lancelot had left forty-five years before, the *Newcastle Courant* reported his death 'of an apoplexy', identifying him as Head Gardener to His Majesty at Hampton Court 'and uncle to Richard Brown, Esq. of this town'. Richard was the only child of Lancelot's eldest brother John Brown and his wife Jane, the daughter of Sir William Loraine.

The following year, 1784, François de La Rochefoucauld visited England and caught a fresh memory: he wrote in his *Mélanges sur Angleterre* that 'Le Brun' had so quick and sure an eye that, after riding around a park for an hour, he could conceive a design, for the whole, which he had marked out in an additional half a day. 'Le Brun' did one French design but had no ambitions there, and when he was offered £1,000 by the Duke of Leinster to go to Ireland, to Carton in County Kildare, he replied that 'he had not yet finished England'. Sadly he could not finish England: but he had perfected a phenomenon of cultural design, the natural English Landscape Garden, which was dubbed '*le jardin anglais*' in Europe, and which carried its implicit vision of England into worldwide and lasting fame.

In the Hollands' house in Hertford Street all was quiet. As Lancelot and Bridget lived in a tied house at Hampton Court, their only home of their own was the small Huntingdonshire manor of Fenstanton, which Lancelot had acquired just fifteen years earlier, thinking of his retirement. After a few days the cortège set out, just the men as was the custom, led by his eldest son Lance and his son-in-law Henry Holland, on the sombre journey northwards, along the old road through Hoddesdon and Ware to Royston. After milepost 44, in Cambridgeshire, they passed along the boundary of Wimpole Park, where Lancelot had so recently been, and hopefully the estate workers were there to salute his passing. Soon after milepost 53 at Papworth St Everard (as it was then called), they left the road the Romans had called Ermine Street and struck off along the low-lying and muddy track towards Hilton; they may have taken shelter at Lance Brown's house at Elsworth on the hill, and carried on northwards to Fenny Stanton. The 'fenny' is the clue, for the low road through Hilton and across the green to Fenny Stanton was very wet, a fraught passage for a heavily laden coffin cart across running rivulets and rickety bridges.

They brought him, almost a stranger to a strange land, to a place he had hardly visited, but where he was laid to rest: and here, in the little church of St Peter and St Paul beside the green at Fenstanton, the mysteries begin. In the church register his burial date is 16th February, which was a Sunday, and most unlikely, but for an error or some mishap – perhaps simply the muddy roads, which made the cortège late. For many years the churchwardens of Fenstanton have puzzled over the location of their most famous grave, a matter much debated. Some people have said that Lancelot is not buried here at all. On the chancel wall is that most quoted of epitaphs:

Ye Sons of Elegance, who truly taste
The Simple charms that genuine Art supplies,
Come from the sylvan Scenes His Genius grac'd
And offer here your tributary Sighs.
But know that more than Genius slumbers here,
Virtues were his which Arts best power transcend.
Come, ye Superior train who these revere
And weep the Christian Husband, Father, Friend.

This was written by the Reverend William Mason, author of a long poem *The English Garden* and friend of Thomas Gray, and both Gray and Mason had been familiar with Lancelot and his works for many years. Mason, who at Lance Brown's request was consulted by Lord Coventry over the epitaph, easily made the connections between Gray's *Elegy* and the remote, uncelebrated scene at Fenny Stanton, where:

. . . with dirges due in sad array
Slow thro' the church-way path we saw him borne.
Approach and read (for thou can'st read) the lay,
Grav'd on the stone beneath yon aged thorn.

Lancelot had intended Fenstanton to be the family's home, though he had never lived there himself. His wife Biddy died in the summer of 1786, and she was buried beside him. Shortly afterwards their daughter Peggy married James Rust of Brampton, and Lance Brown and his brother Jack, when he retired from the navy, and the youngest brother Thomas, all lived in the Huntingdon area. This quiet little countryside became home to Lancelot's descendants for many years to come.

NORTHERN PERSPECTIVE

The breath of Spring is gratefu', As mild it sweeps alang;
Awaukening bud an' blossom, The broomy braes among;
And wafting notes of gladness, Fra ilka bower and tree;
Yet the bonnie Redesdale lassie, Is sweeter still to me.
'The Bonnie Redesdale Lassie', contemporary ballad

THE FACTS OF HIS BEGINNING ARE BARE. Lancelot, son of William Brown, was baptised in the church at Kirkharle in Northumberland on Sunday 30th August 1716, as the vicar, Richard Ward, recorded in the register. No date was given for his birth and no mention made of his mother.

Kirkharle, in the Wansbeck valley west of Morpeth, was the demesne of the aged Sir Thomas Loraine and home to something over two dozen families in farms and cottages. William Brown was a newcomer, but had proved himself reliable as Sir Thomas's steward or estate manager. Even so, for a baby destined to cut a glorious swathe across England and dine with dukes, Lancelot's was a modest birth, and subsequent historians had to excuse this apparent disconformity of the social order by suggesting that he was an aristocratic by-blow. This was romantic nonsense, typical of the Victorians; better by far to search for his mother and William Brown's forebears in the Northumbrian landscape that nurtured them all.

From the south and Corbridge, the road the Romans made breaches the Wall at the Port Gate, at milecastle 22, and strikes bravely northwards into the wild and chilly uplands. After 1½ miles it attains Beukley top, and at a glance it can be seen lurching relentlessly northwards, heading for Jedburgh in leaps and bounds across half of Northumberland. To the west the majestic North Tyne makes its brown and bubbling way down from Liddesdale, and in the northern distance is Redesdale, where the Brown forebears are most likely to be found. This panorama is Lancelot

Brown's native landscape in its largest guise, the country between the Wall and the Border, which in the early eighteenth century had more in common with lowland Scotland than with any English county. Oatmeal was the staple diet, about one-third of adults were able to read (more than in many an English shire) and available books and newspapers were more likely produced in Edinburgh than in London: 'Northumbrians and Lowland Scots even tended to look alike, with the same raw, high-boned faces and the same thin, angular physiques'.

Redesdale presents a brown, peat-stained countryside, where 'brownt' was synonymous with burnt, where the Burns and the Milburns were infamous reiver clans, and where names called across the heather were as variable as the winds, until they were finally fixed and written down. These men of the hills wore brown clothes, the wool was naturally browned and made good camouflage for their nefarious deeds amongst the brakes of bracken. The name Brown was thus easily acquired. One early Brown was a wily lawman in the fifteenth century; another worked for Queen Elizabeth's spymaster Lord Walsingham; yet another, the leader of a gang of rustlers named Geordie Brown, was captured and saved by the 'fyrebrande' Robert Kerr, 1st Earl of Roxburgh, only to be recaptured and hanged in 1596. The name is not common in the sparse records of the time, and Browns were easily outnumbered by ranks of Hedleys, Elliotts, Reeds and Robsons in Redesdale, and by Fenwicks, Ridleys and Forsters farther east. Elsdon is traditionally the capital of Redesdale (Otterburn had no church or church conformity until the 1870s) and the registers begin in 1672 – though in such a damp and musty vestry, in such wild and rough country, their veracity cannot be absolutely trustworthy, nor the efforts to get to the church for baptisms and marriages too urgent. There were many common-law marriages, and itinerant priests of the Catholic and Dissenting kinds who administered to the scattered cottages in the hills, and many good reasons why the Brown ancestors are inevitably elusive.

The first Elsdon church register, of a brief seventeen pages with the bottoms lost to the damp, reveals likely seventeenth-century Browns of 'Hadderwyk' – Heatherwick, the gentle fells crossed by the Heatherwick burn, which flows into the Rede, just south of Otterburn. In the middle of winter, in late February 1686, the body of 'Old Thomas' Brown was carried from his home 7 miles into Elsdon, for burial and entry into the Rev. William Mitford's register.* 'Old Thomas' was a weaver who lived out his days on the green and heathery fells, where sheep and goats were

---

* Vicar of Elsdon from 1674 to 1715.

kept for their wool. He is a good beginning, and at least three of his sons are known by their names: the eldest Lancelot; then Thomas, also a weaver and outworker for the Otterburn mill, who had married Jane in 1675; and John, who married Elizabeth in 1676. After their father's death there was weaving work for Thomas the younger, but his brothers had to seek their livings elsewhere.

The Elsdon registers show the Browns, brothers and cousins. The customary family names are Thomas, John and William (though Lancelot is rare), with Dorothy and Mary for the girls. They peopled the hills around Otterburn, filtering to Corsenside and Overacres – home of the Howards, the lords of Redesdale – and to Raylees and Ravenscleugh. Northumberland's great historian, the Rev. John Hodgson, who knew this countryside so well, believed that Lancelot, Old Thomas the Weaver's eldest son, became 'of Ravenscleugh', his name appearing in the Hedley family records by virtue of the marriage of his niece Mary Brown to Anthony Hedley of Hopefoot. From Ravenscleugh, a hamlet deep in the hills about 5 miles south of Elsdon, he moved south to Kirkharle, where his burial is recorded, *Lancelott Browne,* on 26th August 1699, the entry sadly and shamefully marked that the dues were not paid; such a contrast to the seemly obsequies on Old Thomas's departure. Dorothy, 'his relict,' lasted hardly another year and was buried on 3rd August 1700.

Lancelot and Dorothy had at least three sons, and two of them had moved into the countryside around Kirkharle, but William Brown was still in Redesdale. In the spring of 1701 he was married in Elsdon church, to Ursula Hall: they were 'both of this parish'. Ursula's parents were John and Ursula Hall of Girsonfield, and her father was directly descended from one of the most formidable of the Border reiver clans, the famously 'fause-hearted Ha's' whose exploits are recalled in the Border ballads. Girsonfield was no longer their fortress as of 200 years before, but was tamed into a comfortable farmhouse, although the family still reared strong characters of consequence in Northumberland, and undoubtedly William Brown had made a good marriage: his bride could hold her head high in any company, and was to impart that edge of pride to her sons.

William and Ursula were a well set-up couple, both in their early twenties, but they knew there was no future for them in Redesdale; there were no schools for their children, the only work was shepherding or farming in a remote steading, and after a hundred long years of settlement, which had come about when James VI of Scotland became James I of England, the holdings had grown ever smaller and the land played out. When the Howards sold the lordship of Redesdale to the Duke of

Northumberland in 1750, it was valued at a mere £350. A spate of improvements and enclosures was coming, but not in time for the young Browns, and it was necessary for them to leave. Was it a message from William's mother, the failing Dorothy, that had alerted William that work and house awaited him at Kirkharle?

Their way south along the old drove road* led them for five high and open miles over Ottercops Moss, across a seemingly endless country of hills and crags, suddenly and surprisingly transformed into a flat mead-owland with many streams when they reached ancient Kirkwhelpington. Here the streams form themselves into the infant River Wansbeck, which they could easily follow for a few miles of level journeying into the Kirkharle demesne. Their new home was in this gentle valley of lazily rolling meadows and big trees, with the gathering of grey stone cottages beside the burn, all watched over by the church dedicated to St Wilfrith, or Wilfrid, the seventh-century monk of Lindisfarne.

St Wilfrid's Church, Kirkharle where Lancelot was baptised in the summer of 1716, from Hodgson's *Northumberland*, 1827.

As Ursula Brown did not become pregnant with her first child until the autumn of 1703, a good two years after their marriage, it seems that William might have travelled alone to secure his job and home from Sir Thomas Loraine. Ursula was clearly a young woman who knew what she was doing, and their first child, a daughter named Dorothy, was born on 18th May 1704 and baptised in Kirkharle's church three weeks later. Dorothy was followed by Mary, on 22nd August 1706 (baptised on 12th

* Substantially the route of Thomas Telford's road, the present A696.

September), and then John, baptised on 3rd February 1709. Then a space, which may indicate a miscarriage (though there is no entry for an infant burial), until George, 'Geordie', was baptised on 29th October 1713, followed by Lancelot, who was born in the summer three years later.

Lancelot was seemingly named for his grandfather, but knowing how mothers make romance out of their sons' names, there are other possibilities, not least that Ursula was bewitched by the balladeers' rendering of Arthurian stories, and of the greatest and most thoughtful (if not the most perfect) of the knights Sir Lancelot, whose castle of Joyous Gard was believed by Northumbrians to be at Alnwick or Bamburgh. The assiduity of their children's baptisms, dates of more importance than their actual birthdays (which are not recorded for John, George and Lancelot), reveals how the Browns chose to conform to ordered English society. It was less than a decade after the Union of 1707, and Lancelot was to be their first baby born into Hanoverian Great Britain; even so, their hearts may have told them differently, especially when the call came across the countryside to join the gathering at Green Rigg on 6th October 1715 to ride in support of the Pretender's claim. The country rose almost to a man, led by Charles II's grandson James, the Earl of Derwentwater, the Member of Parliament Thomas Forster and sundry Widdringtons, Thorntons, Shaftos, Charltons and Swinburnes. Ursula's kinsman (possibly her uncle), Judge Jack Hall of Otterburn Tower, was with them. Did William Brown ride? Or was he excused by Sir Thomas Loraine's plea of age and infirmity, just as Sir Thomas (nearing seventy) excused himself, and so did their neighbour Sir William Blackett at Wallington. Sir William found it politic to attend to his interests in 'Geordie' (for George I) Newcastle. All that winter, when Ursula's latest pregnancy began (it is possible that the unwarlike William did ride, and that Lancelot was conceived as the result of his early and safe return), the country was alive with news of the rebels' doings, and especially of how Lancelot Errington, having 'taken' Holy Island for the cause, had to hide amidst seaweed and rocks to escape the soldiers from Berwick; soon captured, shot and wounded, he still managed to escape, hiding in a pea stack and succoured by the local people until he took ship to France.*

There is every reason to believe that William and Ursula Brown's fifth child and third son – they were Jack, Geordie and Lancie (or Larnie) as children, but John, George and Lancelot when grown – had a good and

---

* Derwentwater's other supporters who rode south were routed at the Battle of Preston. The rising was over, and Derwentwater was hanged on Tower Hill in February 1716. Lancelot Errington died in his bed at Beaufront Castle in 1746, broken-hearted at the defeat at Culloden.

loving upbringing at Kirkharle. The Loraine estate was a small world, an estate of about 2,000 acres, about a quarter of that being dry pasture, with meadows and moorland crossed by the Kirkharle burn and Swildur-burn, all on the south side of the River Wansbeck. The Thorntons farmed the land to the north, the Swinburnes were at Capheaton and Bavington to the south, and the Blacketts' Wallington estate lay to the east. In the dozen or so years since his arrival William Brown had proved himself to be fair and honest and hard-working, and had confirmed his place in the small community.

The Loraines had been at Kirkharle since about 1430; their baronetcy was a gift from Charles II in 1664 for services rendered to his father, but though their hearts were Stuart, they saw the wisdom of seeming Hanoverian. With the death of Sir Thomas, who was buried at Kirkharle on 14th January 1718, the estate was inherited by his grandson William Loraine, a London lawyer and politician in late middle-age. For several years Sir William had been much at Kirkharle minding his inheritance: his first wife had lived only three years after their marriage (she was Elizabeth Lawrence, daughter of the Mayor of London in the Plague year of 1665), but he had her fortune, plus another from his second wife, Anne Smith from Buckinghamshire, the daughter of another family of loyalist lawyers who had benefited at Charles II's restoration. Anne brought him five sons and four daughters, and fifty years of married life. His scholarly turn of mind had made him 'competent in Judgment of Architecture and Physick, exemplary in Planting and Enclosure' and he was keenly occupied in building new farmsteads, 'draining Morasses, clearing the Lands of ponderous, massy, and hard Stones, to prepare them for Tillage'. In other words, Sir William was a pioneering improving landowner, whose knowledge and experience were to benefit the three Brown boys. The shadow on this happy valley was that he had taken the opportunity of buying some of the land forfeited by the Swinburnes of Capheaton for their support of the Earl of Derwentwater, which caused a rift between Kirkharle and its southern neighbour.

The Brown boys grew sturdy and strong, the Northumbrian way, on breakfasts of bread, beer and salt fish, dinners of roast pike or mutton, the eternal mutton broths and casseroles, all sweetened with 'Singin' Hinnies' – griddle scones thick with currants. Local tradition has it that the young Lancelot went to school at nearby Cambo, but it seems certain that he started in the small school at Kirkharle, with an itinerant or dame teacher; someone – and it could well have been their mother Ursula – gave all three brothers the foundation of a good strong writing hand and the means of self-expression. Not to be despised was the inescapable reiver genetic inheritance: Lancelot's brothers would have put him on a pony almost as soon as he could walk; he soon became an accomplished rider, and it would form the basis of his life. Instinctively they practised fellcraft: the ability to smell the landscape, looking to the skies for the coming squall, sensing the dangers of a sucking bog, the way to hide in and escape from a gorse thicket, skills once practised in bloody earnest, which were now boys' adventures and games. It was a frugal, energetic childhood, in the open air in all weathers, running errands, fishing in the burn pools, snaring a hare for the pot, or a marten or wild cat for the church-warden's bounty penny.

William and Ursula's youngest child, Elizabeth, was christened on 5th November 1719. Then, the following spring, this prospering little house-hold was hit by the death of their father William Brown, hardly into his mid-forties, who was buried in the churchyard on 4th April 1720: the register styled him 'William Brown of Kirkharle', which spoke of the respect he had earned. Whether it was pneumonia or some chest infec-tion that took him, or a farm accident, is unknown, but it must have been a desperately sad time, hardly understood by the four-year-old Lancelot. John Brown, the eldest brother, was just twelve, and his child-hood probably ended as he was pushed to fill his father's shoes; Dorothy and Mary, sixteen and fourteen, had quite possibly to become appren-tice cooks or seamstresses, but such is the silence of domestic history that we shall never know. What is certain is that John and seven-year-old George took especial care of Lancelot, and looked out for him and taught him all they knew, and more.

One other event of these years can be identified, when the occupants of Kirkharle's street turned out onto the green slope just beside their customary path to church, for the unveiling of Sir William Loraine's new memorial: 'In Memory of Robert Loraine his Ancestor who was Barbarously Murdered in this place by the Scots in 1483 for his good service to his Country against their thefts & Robberys As he was returning Home from the church Alone where he had been at his private Devotions'.

This perhaps reminded them all that the peace of Kirkharle had not always been, and was hard-won.*

Once again, tradition has it that Lancelot Brown remained at school until he was sixteen, in 1732, when he was launched on his seven-year apprenticeship in the Kirkharle estate workshops. This was a long schooling

---

* The year was 1728; the stone is still there.

for those days and invites many questions: the fate of all three brothers may provide some likely answers. At the gathering around the memorial in 1728 John, the eldest, was in his twentieth year, and with the encouragement of Sir William Loraine he was well on the way to becoming an accomplished surveyor, which fitted him for managing the Kirkharle estate and, before he was much older, for the additional roles in road-building and other engineering projects that were fast improving this countryside. George, at fifteen, was a gentler character, home-loving and good with his hands, and was an apprentice stonemason on the neighbouring Wallington estate, where he was to remain all his life. There was a schoolhouse at Cambo, the Wallington estate village just 1½ miles by footpath from Kirkharle, which merited a full-time schoolmaster, where both George and Lancelot could well have had their later education. The two estates, Wallington and Kirkharle, worked in neighbourly harmony, and all three Brown brothers were well regarded at Wallington; John was a close friend of William Robson, the Wallington agent, who was later godfather to John's son. George's schooling finished when he was twelve, as was customary, whereas Lancelot − with the benefit of being the youngest, and an attractive and curious boy − may have earned his extra years as a country scholar at Morpeth Grammar School: if Sir William Loraine had sponsored John's training as a surveyor, he could easily have helped Lancelot to the grammar school, for he had great influence in the town and was a Member of Parliament in the county interest.

And what of their mother, the widow Ursula Brown, who makes no recorded appearances in the later stories of her sons? She was only in her early forties when she was widowed, and it seems most likely that she would have married again. Searching the registers once more for her unusual first name, the only possible mention is of an Ursula Elliott, who was buried in 1742 in East Woodburn, a hamlet tucked into the foothills and beside the Rede, an exquisite, remote place. Had she seen her daughters Dorothy and Mary and her three boys settled, then taken her youngest daughter Elizabeth back into Redesdale? At the time she died, John was about to make an interesting marriage, George was settled at Cambo, and Lancelot was far away, at Stowe.

The Apprentice

At the end of his schooling Lancelot had grown into an attractive youth, tall and long-boned in the Northumbrian manner, with amused blue eyes and thick, wavy brown hair. It seems strange that such a personable young man did not leave for Newcastle and some smart architectural or engineering apprenticeship, but his tendency to racking coughs and chest complaints that marked his later life (and that of his brother John) suggested that the dust and pollution of the city's airs would do him no good, and that he was better in the open air. Besides, he loved his home countryside and had, as yet, no desire to leave; he had the airy confidence of his Redesdale forebears, a rich inheritance, as judged by Iris Wedgwood in her descriptions of Redesdale shepherds, 'with the manners and bearing of gentlemen and a store of knowledge far beyond farming matters'; from their long winter evenings reading, the shepherds tended to sturdy independence in their opinions, not aping their landlords and 'certainly not cowed by marquess or duke'. This was a heritage that Lancelot absorbed; he had something of this opinionated, mischievous spirit, albeit overlaid with charm, and needed plenty of space. Also, the Redesdale connection was still tainted by an Act of the Merchant Venturers of Newcastle (made in 1554, but in force until 1771) that they would take no apprentice 'borne or brought up in Tyndall, Ryddisdall or any other such lyke places'.

So it was to be an apprenticeship at home, at Kirkharle with Sir William Loraine's head gardener, whose name is not recorded, and under brother John's eye. The ancient 'trade crafte or misterie of Gardening' was endemic in country life, and was influenced by the Company of Gardeners' syllabus for apprentices to learn 'planting, grafting, Setting, sowing, cutting' and every attention due to trees and 'Plantes, herbes, seedes, fruite trees, Stockes [and] Settes'. Sir William had spent much of his life in London, and it was amongst the City's guildsmen and seedsmen that he formed his own gardening ambitions, which were to shape Lancelot's future; the patient tasks of the kitchen garden and propagating yards were the basis, and Lancelot learned enough of these domestic skills to know when and where to employ them, but he was also plunged into the midst of Sir William's more robust schemes. Sir William 'planted of Forest-trees, Twenty-four thousand, and of Quick-Sets above Four Hundred and eighty-thousand; and being skilfull in the Fruit-Garden, planted of Fruit Trees Five hundred and eighty'. Hand in hand with the planting were the necessary improvements, drainage and enclosure works with hedges and fences, paths and drives, and it is surely no accident that Richard Welford, in reporting these details in *Men of Mark 'Twixt Tyne and Tweed* (1895), gives the completion date most definitely 'to 1738 inclusive'. At this time Lancelot would have completed his term, and as Sir William was by then almost eighty years old, a good, strong amanuensis had clearly been essential for all these works. Lancelot's grounding in the basic skills of his life's work – land drainage, setting the line of a hedge or an avenue, the propagating and planting of trees – was thus acquired in his beloved home landscape.

It was perfectly in the paternalistic tradition that Sir William would take an interest in this willing pupil, for he had most likely been present at his baptism and had watched him grow. The term 'amanuensis' is not too strong, and caused jealousies perhaps in the rank-and-file gardeners, the kind of envy that spawns rumours about favouritism and sons born 'the wrong side of the blanket'. This was most unlikely at Kirkharle. (It was actually Squire Blackett at Wallington who had the reputation for liberally fathering about the countryside, though this was equally unlikely in Lancelot's case, and an insult to the integrity of William and Ursula Brown.)

The Loraines were of that cast of gentry who found serious solace in the planting of trees, especially royal oaks, the Boscobel oak being the saviour tree of Charles II. (Their arms were crested by a 'couped' and sprouting laurel, with a red belt edged and buckled for a Civil War battle honour, as an additional mark of their interests and loyalties.) Interestingly the growing of fruit trees, Sir William's particular passion, was also polit-ically symbolic – stemming from Oxford nurseryman Ralph Austen's *Treatise* (1653, 1657, 1665) on fruit-growing and cider-making as a national restorative; not to be outdone, Sir Thomas Sclater, a Cambridge man, kept an orchard diary from the autumn of 1674, detailing his absorbing interest and enthusiasm, which led to a proposal to the Royal Society for the encouragement of scientific fruit-growing in both universities as an example to gardeners and landowners in general. Lancelot's expertise and interest in fruit production in orchards and walled gardens remained with him always.

The 'favouritism', and consequently access to Kirkharle Hall, allowed to John and Lancelot meant that opportunities to read the books in Sir William's library gave Lancelot his ideas about the world beyond the fruit garden. Sir William's competence 'in Architecture and Physick' came from his own ability, but also from the company he had kept in London; his first father-in-law was the Mayor of London, Sir John Lawrence, who had employed Robert Hooke to survey the fire-damaged streets of the City, and who continued to be involved in Wren's and Hooke's rebuilding plans. Sir William may well have had Hooke's fantastic *Micrographia* (published by the Royal Society in 1665), with his astounding drawings of the monstrous flea and the barbed nettle as seen through his single-lens microscope: he would have known how Hooke had elevated the skills of surveying by his 'swift, faultless arith-metic', his calculations of the strain on a load-bearing wall, of the support needed for a tall building, of the compensation due for land taken for road widening. This was a professional expertise that appealed to both John and Lancelot, the latter finding a particular challenge in building tall structures.*

Another influential earlier work was John Evelyn's *Sylva, or, A Discourse of Forest Trees* (published by the Royal Society in 1664), also urging the patriotic duty to grow timber, and annexed to *Pomona*, concerning fruit trees and cider. *Sylva*, with its affectionate portraits of personable oaks, elms, chestnuts, rowans, maples, limes, birch, alders, larch and Scots pines (the signature tree beloved of royalists) and its sound techniques of woodland management, remained valid throughout Lancelot's career. It introduced Lancelot to the aesthetics of trees in the landscape: 'Nothing could be more ravishing' than a spreading oak at handsome intervals in the wood; elms for avenues he described as 'a tree of comfort, sociable and so affecting to grow in company that the very best I have seen do almost touch one another'; of the beech, 'spreading trees, and noble shades with their well furnished and glittering leaves'; and of the enigmatic ash, the provider of poles for garden work, for arbours and espaliers, companion to the carpenter, wheelwright, cartwright, cooper, turner and thatcher, 'there is money – a small and pleasurable industry for 40 years – in planting ash'.

A flattering title ensured a place in a gentleman's library, none more so than Stephen Switzer's *The Nobleman, Gentleman and Gardener's Recreation* originally published in 1715, with a major enlargement into three volumes as *Ichnographia Rustica* in 1718. Switzer was enough of an iconoclast to attract a young man's attention, and time and again in Lancelot's working life echoes of Switzer's philosophy appear. Switzer was an advocate of the *ferme ornée*, where 'Planting, Agriculture, and the other Business and Pleasures of a Country Life' were as pretty as a garden; he was the slayer of the 'loathsome burden' of vast and expensive formal gardens; he was sufficiently well travelled to describe French ideas for a ditch, *la fosse* – the term from siege warfare that was so deftly adapted to the 'ha-ha'. Lancelot frequently used the word *fosse* in later life, and only rarely 'ha-ha'. And Switzer wrote so appealingly:

> Surely happiness would be the lot of the rural gardener if his Grounds were handsomely divided by Avenues and Hedges; . . . and if there were Trees for Shades with little Walks and purling Streams, mix'd and incorporated with one another, what cou'd be more diverting?

* Lancelot advised on the building of the Gibside Column of Liberty, see page 58; his Burton Pynsent tower in Somerset, designed and built for Lord Chatham in 1765, can be cited as Robert Hooke's influence, a younger and smaller 'cousin' of Hooke's Monument to the Great Fire of London.

And why, is not a level easy Walk of Gravel or Sand shaded over with Trees, and running thro' a Corn Field or Pasture Ground, as pleasing as the largest Walk in the most magnificent Garden one can think of?

Besides as these Hedge Rows, little natural Coppices, large Woods, Corn Fields, &c. mix'd one amongst another, are as delightful as the finest Garden; so they are much cheaper made, and still cheaper kept . . .

And more than all, the careless and loose Tresses of Nature, that are easily mov'd by the least Breath of Wind, offer more to the Imagination than the most delicate Pyramid, or . . . most elaborately clip'd Espalier . . .

Again, why should we be at that great Expence of levelling of Hills, or filling up of Dales, when they are the Beauty of Nature?

Sylva and Switzer, and Batty Langley's *New Principles of Gardening* – first published in 1728 with straightforward directions for the making of aesthetically pleasing 'Walks' and 'Groves' – were the most widespread and obvious sources for Lancelot's interest in gardening on the larger scale. To a young man who had seen so little of this world, who had perhaps travelled as far as Newcastle and seen the formal garden of Anderson Place belonging to the Blacketts, who had enjoyed summer jaunts when all the countryside turned out for the August Stagshaw Fair, these books introduced the fabled and far-away names of Stowe, Blenheim, Grimsthorpe and Castle Howard.

Sir William Loraine's formal gardens with their avenues, walks and even a fountain were much admired in their day, but these gardens where Lancelot worked out his apprenticeship have disappeared. From the scant archival information and from evidence on the ground, the landscape architect Nick Owen has suggested their layout in the accompanying sketch. The Kirkharle Hall that Lancelot knew has been in part demolished, but stood on the axis of east–west avenues stretching along the valley: these were most likely elm avenues, for the ground was wet, but there was also a beech avenue to the south, on the rising ground towards Capheaton. Kirkharle Hall had large walled gardens close by, home to the favoured fruits, flowers and most likely the fountain, which was part of the garden's water supply – the water piped from ponds linked by the Kirkharle burn on the western slope, which would have given sufficient head of water for the fountain. Also on this western, and south-facing, slope and behind the row of cottages where the Browns lived was a pleasure ground, well planted and screened with copses of trees. The vast numbers of hawthorn quicksets that Sir William is credited with planting were undoubtedly for the hedges to enclose his fields.

★   ★   ★

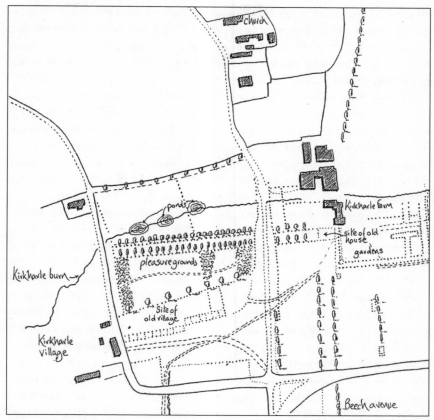

Kirkharle demesne as it was during Lancelot's apprenticeship, constructed from evidence on the ground by Nick Owen.

Lancelot's brother George kept him in touch with the excitements of new money at Wallington, next door, where the Blackett of the day was now Sir Walter Calverley Blackett, who had rather come in by the side door. He was born Walter Calverley of Calverley in the Aire valley, and his mother was Julia Blackett, who inherited a substantial part of the fortune of her brother, Sir William Blackett, 2nd Baronet, on his death in 1728, on condition that her son married Sir William's illegitimate but much-loved daughter Elizabeth Ord, and took the name of Blackett. This had duly happened, and the new Sir Walter Calverley Blackett found himself with the newly built house at Wallington and a considerable income from lead-mining interests in Hexhamshire, all carefully counted and docketed by an army of cashiers and clerks in Newcastle, to spend on his estate. (Sir William Blackett had originally bought

Wallington and lead mines in Allendale from Sir John Fenwick of colourful reputation; it was Fenwick's confiscated horse White Sorel that tripped on the molehill at Hampton Court and despatched his rider King William III, thus making way for Good Queen Anne – a much-prized story hereabouts.)

George Brown was prospering, the epitome of Sir Walter's reputed dictum: 'Every man carries his honour in his own hand . . . origin is nothing, it shall never have weight with me.' George became firmly established at Wallington, and graduated from mason to mason-architect (his signed drawings for kitchens and service buildings of the 1760s are in the house), and worked with the architect Daniel Garrett, who came to Wallington in the mid-1730s. Garrett designed the Hall's coach house and clock tower and the sloping green court that connects them, and all the estate buildings in Cambo, which George Brown built (including George's own house, where he was to live on his marriage to Catherine Fenwick of Hartburn and for the rest of his life).

Daniel Garrett was a figure of no mean interest: some twenty years older than Lancelot, he was of humble, northern beginnings and had been taken up by Lord Burlington as the lowliest of appointees to the Office of Works in 1727. He was a Labourer-in-Trust or foreman, where Henry Flitcroft was Clerk of Works and William Kent was Master Carpenter. Garrett must have been an attractive character, for he progressed to being Lord Burlington's 'personal clerk of works and draughtsman', and so had acquired the habits and proportions of the Palladian revival and was familiar with Lord Burlington's Chiswick House and its gardens. He built the cathedral library in Newcastle for Sir Walter Blackett in 1736. Other places where Garrett worked, in the North at Gibside for George Bowes and at Nunwick for Lancelot Allgood, and farther south in the Midlands at Warwick Castle and Kirtlington, soon become connections of Lancelot's early career, suggesting that he was encouraged by Daniel Garrett; in Garrett's work at Wallington, Lancelot glimpsed for the first time a way of working that he might make his own. The most obvious difficulty was that Garrett had progressed partly by his ability as an architectural draughtsman, an accomplishment that Lancelot had no means of acquiring in those early years.

History is so definite on the date 1738 for the ending of Sir William Loraine's gardening enterprises that Lancelot's twenty-second summer becomes his time of decision: if his had been an ordinary apprenticeship he would have taken his presentation tools, his status as a journeyman and gone to a position as a gardener that he had learned of via the grapevine. Gardeners, or at least those with ambition, were expected to travel long distances, to leave room for the young apprentices, and perhaps

Points from Batty Langley for Apprentice Brown:

1. That the grand Front of a Building lie open upon an elegant Lawn or Plain of Grass, adorn'd with beautiful Statues, terminated on its Sides with open Groves

2. That such Walks, whose Views cannot be extended, terminate in Woods, Forests, mishapen Rocks, old Ruins, grand Buildings, &c

3. That shady Walks be planted from the End-Views of a House, and terminate in those open Groves . . . and thereby you may enter into immediate Shade, as soon as out of the House, without being heated by the scorching Rays of the Sun

4. That Hills and Dales, of easy Ascents, be made by Art, where Nature has not perform'd that Work before

5. That all Walks whose Lengths are short, and lead away from any Point of View, be made narrower at their further Ends than at the hither Part; for by the Inclination of their Sides, they appear to be of a much greater length than they really are;

6. that the walks of a Wilderness be never narrower than ten Feet, or wider than twenty five Feet; and these walks be so plac'd as to respect the best Views of the Country

7. Observe, at proper Distances, to place publick and private Cabinets, which should be encompass'd with a Hedge of Ever-Greens, and Flowering Shrubs next behind them, before the Forest-Trees that are Standards [*nb interpreted as layering*]

8. All Grass-Walks should be laid with the same Curvature as Gravel-Walks; for, by their being made flat or level from Side to Side, they soon settle into Holes in the Middle; the Proportion for the Heights of the Crown, is as five is to one, that is, if the Walk be five Foot in Breadth, the Height of the Middle, above the Level of the Sides must be one Inch; if ten Foot, two inches &c

9. Distant Hills are beautiful Objects when planted with little Woods; as also are Valleys, when intermix'd with Water and large Plains; and a rude Coppice [*clump*] in the Middle of a fine Meadow, is a delightful Object

10. In the Planting of Groves, you must observe a regular Irregularity; not . . . like an Orchard . . . but in a rural Manner, as if they had receiv'd their Situation from Nature itself; plant in and about your several Groves good store of Black-cherry and other Trees that produce Food for Birds, which will not a little add to the Pleasure . . .

11. The several Kinds of Forest-Trees make beautiful Groves, as also doth many Ever-Greens, or both mix'd together; but none more beautiful than that noble Tree the [Scots] Pine [*to which the Cedar of Lebanon is soon added*].

Notes applicable to Lancelot's training, from Batty Langley's 'General Directions,' *New Principles of Gardening, 1728.*

try one new position before they settled into a marriage and a headship, which brought a desirable house. A typical example and friend of Garrett's was the redoubtable Thomas Knowlton, Lord Burlington's head gardener at his estate at Londesborough in Yorkshire since 1726, who was settled for life, with a good house, many perquisites and a respected position in the community. But, even before he left home, Lancelot had rejected the idea of a journeyman's position in a conventional flower-and-vegetable garden, and this was a situation he always avoided.

One day towards the end of his apprenticeship George Brown came home with the news of another arrival at Wallington, a man named William Joyce who was surveying for improvements to the grounds and

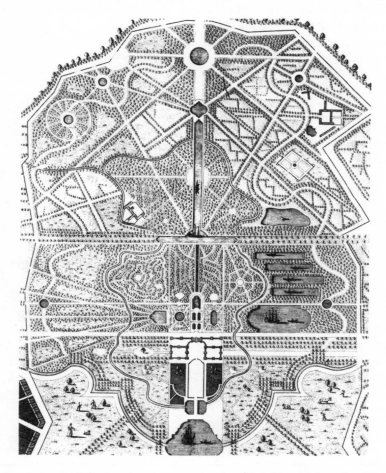

Stephen Switzer's ideal of rural gardening, promoting the fashion of the early eighteenth century, from *Ichnographia Rustica, 1718*.

the woods. Joyce was a southerner, an itinerant layer-out of gardens, a disciple and acquaintance of the very same Stephen Switzer whose books Lancelot had seen. At this time, in 1737, Joyce had placed an advertisement in the *Newcastle Courant* offering himself as 'being qualified and fitted with proper instruments for describing and surveying land and maping [*sic*] gentlemen's estates'.* An exercise in surveying the Wallington grounds using the 'proper instruments' had all the appeal of a celebrity masterclass, for a surveyor's theodolite was a rare and expensive instrument, which neither Sir Walter Blackett nor Sir William Loraine possessed. All the surveying and measuring at Kirkharle, and Wallington, had hitherto been a painstaking process of playing out the Gunter's chain (of 66 feet), placing the marking rods, measuring the offsets and listing the measurements in the field-book. To observe the use of a plane-table and compass in making a plan of the grounds, and the use of the Wheel or Perambulator that measured distances, even in the absence of a theodolite, was a scientific demonstration, to be talked of for days to come.†

William Joyce offered an even more vivid image of what Lancelot might be, a travelling 'describer and surveyor', laying out grounds: 'design' was not a word much used at the time. At first it seems Lancelot looked for work in his home country, though the evidence is almost nonexistent (for who would record the doings of a nonentity of a young gardener?), but the strong local traditions cannot be completely ignored. At the Swinburnes' Capheaton Hall he is accused of destroying a 'beautiful formal garden' shown in a drawing by Robert Crossby of the 1670s, substituting Switzer-style walks in natural copses and alongside a 'purling' stream, which were 'much cheaper made, and still cheaper kept'. Lancelot is also supposed to have worked at Benwell Tower, the Newcastle terminus of the Wall and the home of 'Bonnie Bobby Shafto's' family; he was later to be claimed by one of the family as an old friend when they met in London. That he worked at the Charltons' Hesleyside had long been mooted on the strength of a plan that William Charlton mentioned in 1776, but this has been investigated and discounted by Professor Brian Hackett. Perhaps because of the connections with Daniel Garrett and William Joyce, it is said that Lancelot applied for work at Nunwick, but this has never been proved. But, nearer home, at Hartburn, about halfway

---

* He had worked at the Allgoods' Nunwick on the garden for Daniel Garrett's house, which was sited dramatically overlooking the North Tyne a few miles north of Milecastle 29 on the Wall.

† A theodolite was acquired much later for the Wallington estate and was shared with Kirkharle; Letter Book 1764–76, NRO 672/2/48, 10th October 1769. An instrument of about 1760 made by Thomas Heath 'at the sign of the Hercules and Globe' in the Strand, London, and another by Heath of about 1730, are in the Science and Engineering Collection of Tyne & Wear County Museums, Newcastle.

between Cambo and Morpeth, the Hart burn flows beside a steep and prettily wooded river-cliff, where 'pleasant and romantic' walks were planned and made by Archdeacon Thomas Sharp at some time in the middle of the eighteenth century. It is perfectly possible that Lancelot gained some work experience here at the very outset of this project: Hartburn Glebe traditionally belongs to, and is maintained by, the people of Hartburn. Most intriguing of all is the story that he worked for the feisty, musical, coal-rich George Bowes, who was making his vast garden beside the Derwent at Gibside in County Durham, though if this was true, then Lancelot did not stay at Gibside for any length of time.

All these failed efforts and false starts were in the months after his twenty-second birthday in the summer of 1738, when the circumstantial evidence points to some disruption in the happy life at Kirkharle. The completion of Sir William Loraine's garden and park layout meant the removal of the 'street' of cottages where the Browns and their fellow estate workers lived (as shown on the plan on page 19), and the building of a group of new houses on the higher land to the west of the park. As Sir William was a benevolent landlord, this was hardly the brutal ejection that marked this process in other places; it was gradual, but nonetheless disturbing: was it the dilapidation and promised destruction of her home that decided Ursula Brown to accept Mr Elliott's offer of marriage and return to Redesdale, with the youngest Brown, Elizabeth, who was nineteen? The older sisters, Dorothy and Mary, were both in their thirties and were married with houses of their own; George, a fully fledged stonemason, was committed to his life and work in Cambo.*

With John Brown, aged thirty, an interesting situation had arisen. John had become Sir William Loraine's valued right-hand man in farm and estate matters, virtually his agent or steward. Agents were important figures in Northumbrian country life, the go-between a landlord and his employees and neighbours – customarily taciturn souls, keeping everyone's secrets. The agent went in at the front door at weddings and Christmases, and on working days he was found in the estate office or business room in the house, with its comfortable leather chairs, rent table and plan chest (having entered through the gun lobby). He was almost, though not quite, one of the family, and this closeness had turned John's life into a romance, as he won the heart of the Loraines' daughter, Jane. Little is known about Jane, except that she was in her late thirties, the youngest of nine siblings,

---

* In Barbara Charlton's *Recollections of a Northumbrian Lady 1815–66*, 1989, p. 123, there is mention of Miss Catherine Fenwick, born in 1756, kinswoman of the Catherine Fenwick married to George Brown of Cambo – a lady who, at eighty-three, spoke in broadest Northumbrian singsong 'like a cook', though she looked like a duchess!

was fond of children and made herself useful to her married sisters and brothers; she was certainly held high in the family affections for the rest of her long life, with allowances for her welfare mentioned in her mother's and other family wills. Jane and John were very sure of their love, and were to have a good and enduring marriage, producing a fine son, Richard Brown, though they did not marry until 1743, after Jane's father's death. But even their contemplated marriage made the housing situation sensitive, for Jane Loraine could not possibly move out of Kirkharle Hall to live in a village cottage, nor perhaps even in the best of the new-built Kirkharle houses that was marked for the agent.* In all this upheaval and uncertainty it must have seemed timely for Lancelot to leave. Jane's mother, Dame Anne (an address she preferred to 'Lady Loraine'), came to his rescue, saying she would give him letters of introduction to her relatives, the Vyners in Lincolnshire, whom she knew were moving to a new estate, and to the Smiths in Buckinghamshire.

To Lancelot, the concepts of 'Lincolnshire' and 'Buckinghamshire' were necessarily hazy: Sir William's maps were probably acquired in the days when he travelled a great deal, some thirty years before, but still served, and William Camden's *Britannia* – in one of many seventeenth-century reissues, or the splendid 1695 folio published by Robert Morden – revealed the English counties in their separate and eccentric glories and combined them into an atlas. There were reissues of John Speed's *Theatre of the Empire of Great Britain* in 1710 and 1713. (The enduring popularity of the Jacobeans Camden and Speed indicates a lull in English map-making in the years when Lancelot began his travels, but the glorious flush of famous names – the atlases by George Bickham (1743), John Roque (1746), Thomas Kitchin (1749) and Emanuel Bowen (1767) – soon materialised.) As for finding his way south, if he was fortunate Lancelot acquired John Ogilby's *Britannia,* the ribbon-maps first published in 1675, but latterly reduced into a traveller's *Pocket Guide* bound in calf and of a handy size for the saddlebag. These maps marked the route with every bridge, crossroads, hamlet, town and many landmarks, as well as the unfailing compass points; the first sequence was for the road from London to Aberdeen, easily read in reverse for the southwards journey. Emanuel Bowen's and John Owen's version of Ogilby, *Britannia Depicta, or Ogilby Improv'd,* first published in 1720 and in twelve subsequent editions to 1764, gave him copious information and road directions for every county. In a very real sense the skills of the English map-makers made Lancelot's

---

* This house is prominent and marked as belonging to 'Mr Brown' on Armstrong's map of 1769, though by that time it was Richard's.

career possible: he knew nothing of England when he set out from his northern fastness in early 1739, he rode his saddle-horse into a land full of strange sights and even stranger people, on his first of many voyages of discovery.

CHERCHEZ LA FEMME, OR LANCELOT'S BRIDE

The old mayor climbed the belfry tower
The ringers ran by two, by three;
'Pull, if ye never pulled before;
Good ringers, pull your best,' quoth he.
'Play uppe, play uppe, O Boston bells!
Ply all your changes, all your swells,
Play uppe "The Brides of Enderby".'

—Jean Ingelow,
'High Tide on the Coast of Lincolnshire, 1571', 1863

THE TWO YEARS FROM Lancelot's leaving Kirkharle in early 1739 until he started work at Stowe in early 1741 are almost lost years, with few clues as to his whereabouts; but during these two years he met and won the woman who was to be his wife, and gained a great deal of experience in water engineering and the making of lakes, the key to his later successes. It is clearly worth detecting his progress.

I think that he went on his way via William Joyce, who was based in Gateshead, perhaps to acquire some polish to his surveying. Joyce, apparently pessimistic about his own future in planning gentlemen's estates, despairing that so many northern landowners were more interested in developing their coal mines than their parks, was starting his own nursery. Nurseries were prospering on sheltered sites on the south bank of the Tyne, conveniently placed for the excellent coastal transport of plant stock. Master John Strandrick of the *St Michael* and Mr Jonathan Weldon of the *William of Newcastle* both carried bundles of cherry, damson, medlar trees and sweetbriars from Henry Woodman's nursery at Strand on the Green on the Thames. Plants did not mind rough weather and were good trade in winter, suiting both the lifting and planting seasons and making way for the human cargo in better weather after the spring storms. William Joyce was soon advertising fruit trees, shrubs and seeds 'at Gateshead as cheap as in London', and his nursery was to flourish, becoming one of the most important in the north. There is just a chance that Joyce did arrange for Lancelot to meet Stephen Switzer, for Henry Woodman had written just a few years earlier, 'I am not att all surpris'd [that] Mr Switzer has been with you & all in your Neighbourhood seeing he has nothing else to recommend him (having not a foot of Nursery ground & what he sells must take of others) but his elaborate draughts & designs.' Woodman, an influential Thames-side nurseryman, clearly thought little of itinerant designers and had continued: 'as every man is to be commended for his diligence & Industry I would not here be thought to say any thing illnatur'd of him but confess 'tis a practice I was always asham'd of to thrust my selfe [forward]'.

Switzer was in his late fifties at this time, and had worked for Henry Ellison at Gateshead Park, but as a younger man had worshipped John Vanbrugh and followed him everywhere, and it was his interest in Seaton Delaval Hall that brought him to the north. Seaton Delaval was Vanbrugh's last great mansion, left unfinished at the architect's death in 1726; memories, especially country memories, were long-lasting in the 1730s, and 'Glorious Van' – Sir John, the ex-soldier, ex-spy and playwright who had prodigiously upped and built his first house, Castle Howard, thereby becoming a famous architect, who was never known to design a garden but was appointed Surveyor of the Royal Gardens and Water Works – was an attractive hero. Whether Lancelot saw Seaton Delaval with Switzer cannot be known, but some Vanbrughian notions were deeply ingrained into his earliest ambitions: a shared passion for battlements and crenellations is easily accounted for, but only someone with an insider's knowledge could have told him that the architect Vanbrugh saw no necessity for drawing, but had an indispensable 'organizer, draughtsman and designer' in Nicholas Hawksmoor. Ambitions, it seemed, could be freely chosen by an ambitious young man.

Enter Miss Wayet

Whilst he was with William Joyce at Gateshead it became abundantly clear that the easiest, and most usual, way south was by sea, taking passage with his horse, on one of the coasters calling at Boston, the second-busiest port in England at that time, and closest to his Lincolnshire destination. Joyce perhaps pointed out that the fenland of Lincolnshire was also the proving ground for the latest technology in water engineering and dam-building, knowledge that Lancelot knew he needed to acquire.

How is it possible to say what happened next without a little imagining? For, in Boston, Lancelot met his happy fate; it could well have been a meeting at a Bostonian social gathering, for he was surely equipped with introductions to like-minded professionals in the town; or was it simply the magic of a fine spring morning in 1739? Burly, upright Mr Brown, surveyor and would-be landscape improver, was walking out, wearing his dark-green worsted jacket with a high collar and large pockets, which became his uniform, with a snow-white stock and felted tricorne hat, which he perhaps raised when he met Miss Wayet? Miss Bridget Wayet, who was tall and fair with a prettily pointed nose and demure dress, lived in South Square and walked almost daily past the neat seafarers' houses and the quays where the ships docked, on her way to the flesh- and fish-markets in the Town Square.

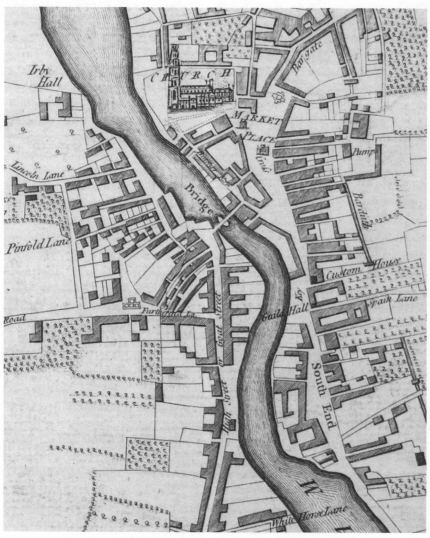

Boston, from Captain Armstrong's *Lincolnshire*, 1779.

Boston was a town of about 3,000 souls, a town divided by the outfall of the great and temperamental fenland river, the Witham. The Wayets or Waites were traditionally collectors of the tolls on the town bridge, and had interests on both sides, so to speak: on the harbourage and especially the embankments; consequently they had evolved into professional surveyors and engineers. Bridget's father, David Wayet, an Alderman and chosen for the mayoralty on May Day 1711, was 'of respected memory' for securing an Act of Parliament for a fresh-water supply to the town from the West Fen, and for building the mill called the Waterhouse. Alderman Wayet had married Mary Kelsall in 1702, and Bridget appears to have been their youngest child, born in 1717. Now, at twenty-two, a mature and capable young woman, she was also a woman of property from her father's legacy of a land-holding. She lived with her eldest brother John Wayet and his wife Mary, who had been married for about seven years, in their handsome house, built by their father, of five bays with modern sash windows and three storeys, at no. 13 South Square.* Their neighbours were the most distinguished Boston families, the Fydells, Ingelows and Sleaths, who lived beside their warehouses along the quays.

The antiquary William Stukeley, who settled here as a young doctor, called Bridget's Boston 'busy and smelly', but distinguished by the Stump; the town was dominated by St Botolph's and its tower, the Stump, which came into view at every turn, even in the midst of a forest of masts and windmills. Built out of medieval prosperity, begun about 1425, finished about 1520, it is something of a miracle that such a tower, 272 feet high, could be so wondrously supported to stand straight on mud and sand and, presumably, vast amounts of wool. St Botolph's, named for the saint of seafaring men, guards the town and the seafarers with its lantern tower, the highest and noblest in Europe, seen easily from 40 miles around on land and sea. St Botolph's was an important part of the Wayets' life, for they were undoubtedly regular worshippers, and Mary and John (who was to be Mayor in 1755 and 1767) lived into a dignified old age and are commemorated in a handsome monument in the church. It was the custom for family weddings to take place here.

The tidal Witham, measured at the Stump, was 83 feet wide at high water, and lost almost 20 feet at low water (reaching 65 feet). The great slurpings of sand and mud that came and went with the tides were elemental forces in the turbulent history of fen drainage; consequent upon the dangers, Boston was a town of powerful guilds and factional

* The house survives.

interests, and saw invasions of landowners who swarmed like vultures with every fresh drainage initiative to acquire 'new' land. Conflicts were endemic between those who wanted dry land for agriculture and the 'lawless fenmen' who revelled in a watery heaven. At this time, as Nicolas Kindersley reported in 1736, the ancient navigation between Lincoln and Boston was useless, a tidal slough of broken embankments and sprawling mud. Ostensibly there was work here for a keen young man to learn about bridge-building and embanking, but perhaps the situation in the town was too chaotic, and the vested interests too inflexible.*

Boston and the surrounding flatlands were vulnerable to devastating storms and floods; 'The Brides of Enderby', quoted above, commemorates the women of the hamlet of Mavis Enderby, who celebrated the installation of Boston's bells in the sixteenth century, which rang their warning to those on land, with their menfolk at sea, for ever afterwards. The connection between the town and the villages of the old coastline, about a dozen miles inland across West Fen, remained close, and successful Bostonians sought fresh country air (and firm, dry land) in the countryside between Horncastle and Spilsby; the Wayets were no exception. Also, Joseph Banks II of Revesby – rich in land and money, a man of poor education, rough manners and a warmly philanthropic heart – owned a large area of marshland south of Revesby and Mareham, which he planned to drain and enclose. This was a private matter of enclosure, managed by his second son William Banks for the parishes of Tumby, Mareham and Revesby, in which the Langtons, who were cousins of the Bankses, had an interest.

Bridget's brother John Wayet was also involved in this scheme in 1739 because he owned property at Mareham and Tumby, and their joint needs were for a road and a drain running southwards to Boston, the drain to enter the Witham near the present Anton's Gowt or Cowbridge. It seems that Lancelot was working here in the autumn of 1739, for in the December the Rev. Bennet Langton wrote from Cavendish Square (he could not persuade his wife and daughters away from the pleasures of London) to Joseph Banks II that 'Upon my going to Mareham a little before I left the country I had some discourse with Mr Brown concerning inclosing the several [walks], who was satisfied that it would be of the greatest benefit imaginable to the town in general and to all our interests in particular.' This sounds so like a conversation with Lancelot. The land around Mareham le Fen is still distinctly marked with drain channels as crisply as medieval strips, and with dry footpaths for the villagers, which Lancelot

---

* The Witham was not to be tamed until the advent of steam pumps in the later eighteenth century and the work of engineers John Grundy junior and John Smeaton.

The landscape of Mareham le Fen from Armstrong's *Lincolnshire*, 1779. Were these the 'walks' that Lancelot made in 1739?

dignified as 'walks'. The land was so fertile that Mareham saw great subsequent prosperity, with the development of varieties of potato and commercial production of daffodils and tulips; to this day Mareham has a local distinctiveness. These fields and watercourses served for a preliminary practice, with John Wayet's help, in embankments and sluices and the wilful ways of flowing water, but it seems unlikely that Lancelot found any satisfaction in working here, other than to please Miss Wayet.

The Langton-in-Partney home of the Langtons was another kind of prospect altogether; tucked into the foot of the Wolds just north of Spilsby, the Langton landscape is exuberantly hilly, as if it has escaped from the sea and is lurching and laughing in delight. The gabled Jacobean Old Hall that Lancelot would have known was bowered in trees, its huge and glittering windows gazing southwards across a blue infinity of fen and sea. These hills and dales of Langton offered a challenge that he perhaps

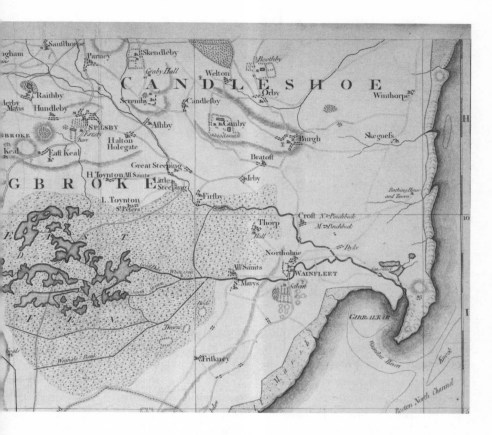

dismissed with a laugh, a volatile landscape too nearly reflecting the fey eccentricities of the good and honourable Rev. Bennet Langton, with the play-loving wife and giddy daughters whom he found such a handful, so that nothing was ever settled or straight-running. But Langton senior (as well as his son, also Bennet Langton, who was to be Dr Johnson's friend, but was still a child in 1739) was known as a keen agriculturist and tree-planter. His mother had come from Langley Castle in the South Tyne country, and so they were certainly known to the Blacketts at Wallington.

The Vyner family, the relatives of Dame Anne Loraine to whom Lancelot had been directed, had made their fortune as goldsmiths in Restoration London, and were in the process of moving from old and damp Tupholme, a lonely Cistercian site on the Witham marshes, to Gautby between Bardney and Horncastle. Gautby has a wonderful site, and extensive brick-walled gardens were being built at this time, in 1739–40, but the Vyners seemed in no hurry. The house and the church were their building priorities for the next half-dozen years and they were unlikely to have been persuaded into laying out their park. Mareham, Tumby, Langton and Gautby, were these all Lancelot's attempts at finding work in Lincolnshire? Did Bridget Wayet, or anyone else for that matter, understand just what he wanted to do, and that the building and managing of a traditional walled kitchen garden, or even of productive market gardens, was not for him? Enough perhaps that in that romantic countryside of the foothills of the Lincolnshire Wolds, through the Enderbys, Somersby and Horncastle, Lancelot and Bridget had time to learn about each other and find that they wanted to spend the rest of their lives together.

Lancelot then decided to try Dame Anne Loraine's other introduction, to her father Richard Smith of Preston Bissett, just south of Buckingham. It was a long trek across the shires, his first real taste of the endless journeyings of his life, but he travelled with purpose and hope. Heading inland to avoid the fens, he could have reached Grantham on a good day's going, then Melton Mowbray and Market Harborough, and so into Northampton at the end of a third exhausting day's ride. From there it was an easier 25 miles or so south; coming out of Whittlebury Woods, he would have seen the landmark of Stowe castle, but he continued through Buckingham to the village of Preston, where he found an old gentleman nearing ninety.

However, tradition has it that Squire Smith had found him a job, though Lancelot had to ride for another day westwards, to the Cherwell valley – a country he would come to know very well – and on to the tiny Oxfordshire hamlet of Kiddington. The evidence comes from John Penn, the later owner of Stoke Park at Stoke Poges in Buckinghamshire; Penn had found a plan of Stoke attributed to Brown in the house, and was thus interested in Lancelot's career. Penn wrote in 1813, 'It has been said that the first piece of water he formed was at Lady Mostyn's in Oxfordshire.' In 1739, the date Penn gives, Kiddington was the home of Sir Charles Browne (2nd Baronet, who died in 1751), whose granddaughter and heiress married Sir Edward Mostyn. According to Penn, Barbara Mostyn would have been ten years old at the time, and as everything at Kiddington is on a very small scale, to this clearly bright and observant child the 'arrival' of a lake where none was before, within easy sight of the house windows, was a great event.

Kiddington is on the River Glyme about three miles north of Blenheim's park-pale; some explanation of this prodigy lake, Lancelot's first, is given by Thomas Hinde (1986), who has paid particular attention to eighteenth-century water engineering. Hinde finds Penn believable, for:

Kiddington still looks like a Brown garden. Grassy slopes fall below the house to the south and west, where the little river Glyme has been dammed and turned into a modest lake. More grassy slopes rise fairly steeply on the further side where there are new clumps of trees as well as the stumps of much older ones. True, the valley's shape made the river easy to dam, and its slopes invited lawns and trees, but that is all the more reason for thinking that Brown may have seized the opportunity to make a garden which has most of the features of his numerous later ones.

This almost sacred spot retains a very real magic. A telltale cedar of Lebanon marks the turning off the main road between Woodstock and Enstone, into an older world of pretty cottages fronted by humpy hedges and cottage gardens, with the bridge over the Glyme and the drive to the hall presiding over its sleepy valley. The little Glyme gave itself so easily to make Lancelot's early dream come true — was he pleased when he realised the effect of his very first lake? Kiddington provided a text-book opportunity for the authoritative John Taverner's preferred way of making 'a water' — that is, 'with a head (i.e. dam) in a valley between two hills, by swelling of the water over grassie ground, not in former times covered with water'. Taverner, though he had died in 1606, was still the authority; he was Surveyor-General to the King's Woods south of the Trent, in succession to his father, also John Taverner, and had published *Certaine Experiments Concerning Fish and Fruite* in 1600, which was full of technical advice and was the source for such writers as Batty Langley and Stephen Switzer. Taverner's careful instructions held good: 'if you meane to make your head ten foote high, it had need to be ten foote broade in the top, and thirty foote broade in the bottome', built of 'only earth being broken very small, and watered with water often times as you raise it: for that will cause it to bind closer and surer than any ramming or timber worke will do'.*

There was another omen at Kiddington, and a thunderous one, in that Sir Charles Browne was married to Mary Pitt, the daughter of George Pitt of Stratfield Saye, godfather and cousin to William Pitt, the future Earl of Chatham. The Pitt family networking, in Lancelot's favour, had begun.

I doubt that Kiddington retained him long in the early months of 1740, but he had discovered that, within a few square miles of Oxfordshire and Buckinghamshire, there were almost a dozen places where he might work. His presence at Kiddington made his name known locally; he may

---

* Lancelot used this 'homogenous' construction in his next dam, at Wakefield Lawn in 1751.

have had a promise of Wotton Underwood from the Grenvilles, and perhaps set his sights on Stowe or Blenheim, but as nothing was immediately forthcoming he returned eastwards to Bridget.

He wanted to give Lincolnshire one more chance, and there was a slim hope of work at Grimsthorpe Castle, the home of the Berties – elevated into the company of Castle Howard and Blenheim, in grand gardening terms, by the attentions of Sir John Vanbrugh, with Stephen Switzer in his wake. In 1715, when the Berties had acquired their dukedom and their kinsman Vanbrugh was on the lookout for a job, they commissioned him to encase their plain old house with monumentally baroque façades. Though much was intended, by the time Vanbrugh died in 1726 the work was stopped, with only the north front, its 'fortress' pavilions and courtyard completed. This was built of Ancaster stone, leaving quarries – invariably landscaping opportunities – in the park. Switzer's evocation of 'The Manor of Paston' in *The Nobleman, Gentleman and Gardener's Recreation* and its subsequent editions, which Lancelot knew, was the thinly disguised Grimsthorpe, on which he had wished his ideas of the *extensive garden,* 'woods, Fields and distant Inclosures' having the attention of the industrious plantsman, and the garden being thrown 'open to all View to the unbounded Felicities of distant Prospect, and the expansive volumes of Nature herself'. Switzer's drawing of his rural garden approaches the fantastic, with east–west and north–south vistas springing from the house in the old formal way, but all the land in between filled with 'serpentine twinings' of paths and drives, writhing their way through woods, 'cabinets and bosquets', with many a piece of water. If the reigning Bertie, Peregrine, 17th Baron Willoughby de Eresby and 2nd Duke of Ancaster and Kesteven, was ambitious to this scale, there was a great landscape to be made and planted.

However, English dukes are unlikely slaves to imaginary schemes. When Lancelot arrived in 1740 he found some large pieces of water in the park, rather straight-sided and confined and looking like fishponds: the 2nd Duke was discussing the possibility of building a dam, with thirteen rocky arches as a sham bridge to make an extended water, and additional dams and sluices that would connect the Great Water and the Red Bridge Pond and make them appear as one. It is possible that Lancelot spent some weeks at Grimsthorpe discussing and surveying the possibilities of these great plans, but I fear he discovered there was no place for him, an outsider and a north-country man. The Duke had conservative ways; having considerable interests in the fens, he was knowledgeable on drainage matters and was inclined to favour the well-tried, if technically stilted methods of proven worth, rather than the novel. However nearly he was persuaded by Lancelot, it was not quite enough, and Lancelot could not have known that he had a rival. The Berties were politically powerful in Boston, and his Wayet connection – if it was firm enough – may have counted for him, but the town of Spalding was nearer to Grimsthorpe and this was a town full of remarkable talents, notably within the famous Spalding Gentlemen's Society, which attracted a rich gathering of scientific minds. The Society had a respected engineer, John Grundy, who had come into the area as a surveyor for the 2nd Duke of Buccleuch's lands, had presented a fine map of Spalding to the Society, settled in the town and taught mathematics at the grammar school, and was now occupied in planning improvements to the River Welland navigation. Grundy – a worthy pioneer and sound engineer – was known to the Duke of Ancaster and his kind, and the Duke would have looked no farther. Grundy was forty-four and had led an arduous life, but had given his son John, who was three years younger than Lancelot, a thorough and wide-ranging training. When the Duke of Ancaster started his park improvements in 1740 by removing a hillock of land that spoiled the view of the castle's north front, quite naturally Grundy senior suggested his son for the work: John Grundy junior removed the hillock, built the dams for Grimsthorpe's lake and remained working at Grimsthorpe for the next twenty years. Lancelot had to wait all that time, and more, for his chance.

The Brown boys, all three, seem to have been level-hearted and emotionally adept; they all made apparently happy and lasting marriages. We know nothing of Lancelot's 'wild oats'. Like both John and George, he aimed slightly above himself, aspiring to a young lady of comfortable middle-class origins (if Bridget Wayet has to be categorised), well educated and used to civilised living. The rooms in the Wayets' house in Boston's South Square were panelled, filled with well-polished and solid furniture, pictures, china and silver, and there were maids for the scullery and laundry, even if Bridget's sister-in-law Mary Wayet supervised the cooking herself. Everything pointed to the Wayets' hopes that Lancelot would join the family in Boston, where he would have been assured of a successful living. Fortunately he had his pride and belief in his own destiny and refused to be a comfortable nonentity, but there was no question of asking Bridget to marry him until he could provide a sure income and comfortable home. After his painful rejection at Grimsthorpe he returned to Buckinghamshire.

For a while he seems to have worked at the Grenvilles' Wotton Underwood, some 8 miles west of Aylesbury in well-watered countryside, where there were the makings of a beautiful park around Charles

Bridgeman's formal garden; Wotton, however, was never likely to be as famous as Stowe, which belonged to the Grenville brothers' uncle, Lord Cobham, and so when word passed around that the Stowe head gardener, William Love, was retiring, Lancelot took notice. John Penn has informed us that Love's replacement had to be 'able to converse instructively' on Lord Cobham's favourite pursuit, but be 'free from vanity and conceit which had rendered his former assistants disinclined to alterations upon which he had determined'. For Stowe, Lancelot was prepared to be circumspect, at least for a while. His application was successful – his moment had come.

3

THE KINGDOM OF STOWE

Sincerest Critic of my Prose or Rhyme,
Tell how thy pleasing Stowe employs thy Time.
Say, Cobham, what amuses thy Retreat,
Or Schemes of War, or Stratagems of State?
        William Congreve, 'Of Improving the Present Time', 1728

LANCELOT WOULD HAVE BEEN a dull dog if he had not already scouted Stowe, but even so it was an intimidating prospect; indeed, with doubled intimidations: the place and its owner. The estate extended over 5,000 acres, an island cut in green, an island of the fantastick and curious, many of the local people would have said, and quite mad. From Buckingham, Lord Cobham's pocket borough, its church steeple the springing point of the Stowe layout, Lancelot rode out along the 3-mile, tree-lined drive northwards. On this relentless road with wide verges a man on a horse must feel like a flea on a mouse, but at least there was plenty of warning of the coming of his lordship's coach and galloping team, which would give way to no one. The drive breasted the hill, the Corinthian Arch was not yet built, from where the rider gazed on the sparkling waters and green acres, the south façade of a giant mansion – and beyond, for miles, the avenues and rides stretched into the wooded distances of Whittlebury and Silverstone.

When Lancelot arrived on a February day in 1741, ringing the bell at the gate beside the Lake Pavilions, the strangers' entrance with attendant gardener, the kingdom of Stowe was intact – a fortress cut in green, a soldier's garden in the military manner, as Congreve had divined as he further addressed Cobham:

Dost thou recall to Mind with Joy or Grief
Great Marlborough's Actions, that immortal Chief,
Whose slightest Trophy raised in each Campaign

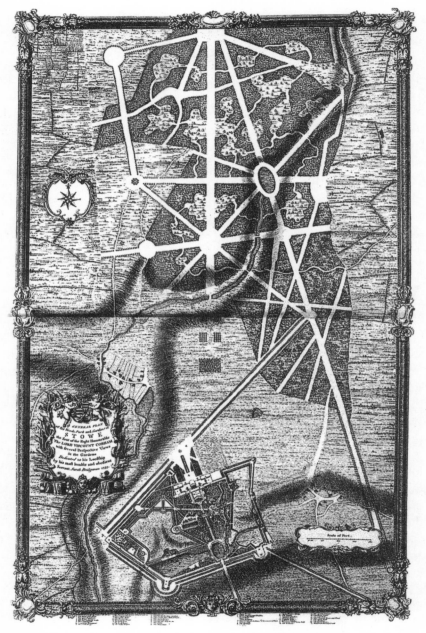

The Kingdom of Stowe, the map published by Sarah Bridgeman, 1739, showing the 'fortress' garden laid out by Charles Bridgeman, with the rides extending north to Silverstone. At the foot of the plan the Buckingham avenue has been fore-shortened but extends southwards for about two miles to the town.

More than sufficed to signalise a Reign?
Does the Remembrance, rising, warm thy Heart
With Glory past, where Thou thyself hadst Part,
Or dost thou grieve indignant, now, to see
The fruitless End of all that Victory?

Stowe's spiky outworks, like so many sharp elbows firing out into the sleepy countryside, were still much in evidence − it was a hero's garden. The fashionable and the curious had made it famous, and visitors had streamed through its walks for more than twenty years, the cleverest (like Congreve and Alexander Pope) immortalising the experience in rhyme. Pope's 'Epistle to Burlington' of 1731, whilst commending the virtues of his lordship's garden at Chiswick House, slides tangentially into praise of Chiswick's rival at Stowe:

To build, to plant, whatever you intend,
To rear the Column, or the Arch to bend,
To swell the Terras, or to sink the Grot;
In all, let Nature never be forgot.
But treat the Goddess like a modest fair,
Nor over-dress, nor leave her wholly bare;
Let not each beauty ev'ry where be spy'd,
Where half the skill is decently to hide.
He gains all points, who pleasingly confounds,
Surprizes, varies, and conceals the Bounds.

The secret was to 'Consult the Genius of the Place in all' − the 'genius', in one sense, implying the pagan gods of fields and woods (an allusion to Lord Cobham's known agnosticism); in a second sense, the 'genius' was the character of the countryside, as Pope had explained three years earlier: 'In laying out a garden, the first and chief thing to be considered is the genius of the place. Thus as [Richings], for example, Lord Bathurst should have raised two or three mounts because his situation is all a plain, and nothing can please without variety.' Stowe, set in a countryside of greater integrity than the 'plain' of Richings (at Iver in south Buckinghamshire) or the fields of Chiswick, inspired the greater accomplishment:

Nature shall join you, Time shall make it grow
A Work to wonder at − perhaps a Stow.

This dalliance in phrases and rhymes concerning politics and gardens amused a considerable spectrum of the reading and travelling public, for whom the great houses and their gardens were the chief attractions of the countryside in summer. Joseph Addison's imaginative rovings in 'the wild Fields of Nature', and his suggestion 'why may not a whole Estate be thrown into a kind of Garden' in *The Spectator* (no. 414, 25th June 1712), had diverted the fashion from the gods of war to those of nature, inspiring this new cult, which Stephen Switzer and Batty Langley, amongst others, were adapting into garden-design theories. Lancelot, becoming familiar with the theories, needed to be aware of all the levels of Stowe's celebrity.

Richard Temple, Viscount Cobham was a formidable employer, and it says much for Lancelot's nerve and ambition that he grasped the opportunity; it was to be a masterclass in dealing with a difficult lord. His lordship's portrait had recently been painted (1740) by Jean-Baptiste Van Loo, showing him, at sixty-five, lean and apparently fit from an active life, arrogant of bearing, his mouth the most telling feature of his face, compressed into a sardonic glimmer of a smile above a determined chin – a man who is master of himself, and everyone else. One of Marlborough's senior generals, he was a soldier through and through, subscribing to the idea of a regiment as 'a property owned by an unlimited company of which the commanding officer was managing director'; as he ran his regiment, so he ran his estates. In peacetime he loved gardening, as so many generals did, and he loved his former comrades, many of whom – including Colonel Samuel Speed, who oversaw the estate accounts, and Steward William Roberts, as well as sappers and engineers-turned-gardeners – were pensioners at Stowe. Lancelot was one of the few, possibly the only one in a senior position, without a military background; he was on six months' trial.

The Temple family had prospered as sheep farmers at Burton Dassett in Warwickshire, extending their holdings into the rolling countryside north of Buckingham in Queen Elizabeth I's days, and buying a knighthood and then a baronetcy to go with their increasing acres. The 3rd Baronet, Sir Richard Temple, having recouped the family fortunes largely out of being MP for the rotten borough of Buckingham for forty years, built a pretty brick house at Stowe, with a look of Wren about it, employing some of Wren's craftsmen. It was seen by Celia Fiennes in 1694, standing 'pretty high; you enter into a hall, very lofty with a gallery round the top, thence through to a great parlour that opens in a bellcony to the garden . . . gardens which are one below another with low breast walls and terass walkes', and with orchards and woods beyond. These terraced 'rooms' walled with hedges, with arbours and decorative topiary, were called Sir Richard's 'Parlour Garden'.

Sir Richard Temple had married his cousin Mary Knapp, and they had three daughters and an only son, Richard, born on 24th October 1675 and destined for the army. After spells at Eton and Cambridge (Christ's College), in his twentieth year he joined Captain Ventris Columbine's Regiment of Foot; he was present at the three months' siege – 'undoubtedly ye Most desperate that had been made in ye memory of Man' – and ultimate capture of the fortress of Namur. (Namur was the horrific siege redeemed by Uncle Toby and Corporal Trim in their garden-making described in Laurence Sterne's *Tristram Shandy*.)

In 1697 Richard had inherited Stowe and his father's parliamentary seat of Buckingham in the Whig interest. His military progress was equally speedy; he had his own Regiment of Foot in 1702, and he served through the gruelling marches and sieges of William III's and Marlborough's Flanders campaigns; he was at the siege of Lille, and with Marlborough at the 'last great set-piece victory' at Malplaquet near Mons in September 1709, 'though bought at so great a cost that it hardly deserves to be called a victory'. The following year he was appointed one of only five lieu-tenant-generals of the army in Flanders, and then kicked his heels uncom-fortably around Vauban's great fortresses of northern France until the politicians had argued their way into the Peace of Utrecht, signed to great bell-ringings and bonfires blazing in England in April 1713. With the Tories and Robert Harley in charge, Temple was stripped of his regi-mentals, only to find himself returned to favour with the coming of George I in 1714: the new king gave him a barony and he took the title of Cobham, under attainder from 1603, from his rather distant kin in Kent. The following year he married Anne Halsey, heiress of Stoke Park in Buckinghamshire, a brewer's daughter with £20,000. In 1718 he was made Viscount Cobham, a new title that he did not despise (though 'a miserable compromise . . . a new and inferior rank', in the opinion of the Tory Harry Bolingbroke) and, with the restitution of his general's pay and his wife's fortune, he was freed to serious gardening at Stowe.

Cobham was clearly a man of strong temper and swift actions; but he was also a man of great attractions – for himself and his influences – and Stowe was always busy with friends and visitors. He had seen to profitable marriages for his sisters, Christian Temple to her kinsman Sir Thomas Lyttelton of Hagley, and Hester to Richard Grenville at Wotton; and although he had been intransigently opposed to Maria marrying his regimental chap-lain, Richard West, their son Gilbert, a brilliant young man, was soon a great favourite at Stowe. All the nephews were welcomed, as Cobham knew he would have no children of his own (he had arranged for his viscountcy to pass to his nephew Richard Grenville), which is sometimes said to be the 'fault' of Lady Cobham, but it is now known that he had been taking drastic remedies for venereal disease for many years.

The military garden, as at William III's own Het Loo in the Netherlands, the 'siege of Troy' topiary garden made for him at Kensington Palace, and the Duke of Marlborough's 'colossal polygon' with walks along its bastions at Blenheim represented an appropriate fashion for an age when the street talk was dominated by the war news from Europe. Naturally enough, Lord Cobham's gardening started in this vein; in 1716, fresh from working for the Duke of Marlborough at Blenheim, the popular garden-maker Charles Bridgeman had begun at Stowe, well able to design (as befits a soldier of sieges) the very image of a fort. Bridgeman extended the long southwards vista from the Parlour Garden to the stream, which was dammed to make the Octagon basin, with its attendant Doric Pavilions, marking the south entrance to the gardens. Next Bridgeman 'threw out', as sappers do, a salient or earth-bank to the north-west of the Octagon, enclosing a large piece of ground; the salient, though continuing north-wards, was interrupted by an angled bastion, the site of Vanbrugh's Rotunda, which overlooked another piece of formal water, the old Hog Pond trans-formed into Queen Caroline's Pond, with her statue presiding.

Once started, extensions proved contagious. The salient, Bridgeman's bank-and-ditch ha-ha, became a fort-within-a-fort as the bounds were extended twice as far again westwards; Bridgeman dug the tentatively natural Eleven-Acre Lake, bounded by his great fortified bank and ditch, or ha-ha, known as the 'Grand Terras', broken by the angled bastion that contained the Temple of Venus; the ha-ha continued northwards to the Boycott Pavilions, built at the west entrance to the park. Within the nearer garden, east of the south vista, where the ancient Stowe parish church was surrounded with trees (and the remaining cottagers moved to Dadford village), Bridgeman laid out the Elysian Fields, the setting for William Kent's Temples of Ancient Virtue and of British Worthies. Here, in the 'fields' of sunlit lawns and serene water, the military garden died; vanquished by the soft-skinned boy from Bridlington, William Kent, and 'Mr Kent's notion of gardening, viz., to lay them out and work without level or line'. Bridgeman, proud of his work, had commissioned a set of views of Stowe from the French artist Jacques Rigaud and the engraver Bernard Baron, and these were published by Sarah Bridgeman in 1739, the year following her husband's death.

The bell at the gate by the Doric Lake Pavilions summoned a gardener to conduct visitors around, but the new gardener Lancelot was directed to Lord Cobham's Steward, William Roberts: as he walked, he passed 'a long but Narrow Visto leading up to the front of the House', the Octagon basin

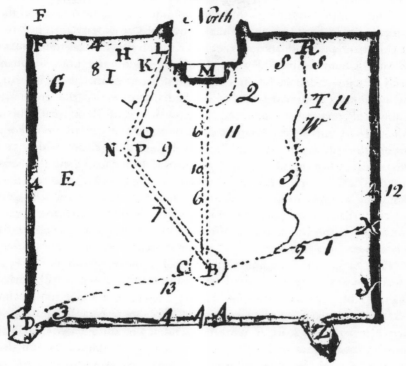

A Plan of Lord Cobhams Garden.

Stowe, 1742, diagrammatic plan drawn by an anonymous visitor showing the features that existed in Lancelot's time: these can be identified as follows:

A-A at foot, south of plan, the Lake Pavilions' entrance

B. Octagon Basin or Water, with C, a cascade.

D. Temple of Venus

E. Temple of Ancient Virtue 'rais'd on an Eminence'

F-F. The Boycott Pavilions

G. Vanbrugh's Pyramid

H. Temple of Bacchus

I. A small obelisk

K. A Saxon temple   L. A Roman temple

M. Stowe house

N. The Rotunda

O. 'His Present Majesty' George II on a column

P. Statue of Queen Caroline, 4 Ionic columns on a pedestal.

Q. The Temple of Virtue

R. A Hermitage

S. S two Shell temples

T. 'A 3-Arch'd Building'

U. 'An India house'?   W. Temple of British Worthies

X. A bridge   Z. The Temple of Friendship.

1. A Pebble 'house'

2. Congreve's Monument

3. 'the end of the River'

4. 4-4-4 'Grand Walks' i.e. boundaries at the time

5. a Cascade   6-6 the 'narrow visto' avenue

7-7 Walks   9. Dido's cave   10. The Sleeping parlour

11. 'a Witch house'   12. A Gothic Temple, on east boundary i.e. Gibbs's temple partly-built

13. The cold bath

with central rustic obelisk, failing to spout water 'for want of a due Supply', and west of the Octagon the 'long irregular form of water and cascade over several artificial Craggs and Rocks but only working for about 2 hours'. In its winter undress, and empty of belles in fluttering coloured silks and their scarlet-coated beaux, and in the rain, Stowe was at its least attractive.

But there was work to do. Lancelot's first job was to clear the remnants of Sir Richard Temple's Parlour Garden terraces, and Lord Cobham's walls of statue-filled niches, from the south front of the house, so that it lay open to a natural lawn: this still did not open up the great view southwards, except through the 'Narrow Visto' of Bridgeman's bosky Abele Walk, but it was progress towards the rural garden. To the east, beyond the Elysian Fields, the Hawkwell Field was grazed by sheep – 'a progression from the notion of Elysium to that of Arcady, an ideal *earthly paradise*' in literary terms. The architect James Gibbs was currently designing a large Gothic Temple to preside over the Hawkwell Field, so Lancelot had to prepare for this, and begin the enormous task of constructing the ha-ha around the east side of the garden, taking in the whole new area that was to become the Grecian Valley.

This ha-ha, its stabilising wall built of stone blocks two handspans square, owes its style of construction to the Roman builders of Hadrian's Wall; the blocks had to be split, and were rough-hewn not sawn, which was fine practice for more ornamental building. It was also good practice at managing a team of workmen, and at holding his own when the Stowe masons were inveigled away for work on buildings. The rhythms of digging and barrowing the soil, building the supporting wall and ramming earth behind it had to be well coordinated, whatever the weather. All of Stowe's garden was built with the age-old methods of men and barrows on planked runs, a system that, with the addition of horses and carts, lasted throughout Lancelot's career and beyond. As many gardeners did, he devised his own large tree-moving machine – an adaptable bucket on wheels – while at Stowe.

As for wages, Lancelot started at £12. 10s. for a half-year, with extra board wages paid six-weekly, this being indicative of his temporary status. After six months his position became clearer, and in the autumn of 1741 he was being paid additional amounts – 'new gardener's bills': large sums endorsed by Colonel Speed, indicating that he had negotiated a managerial way of working; he was paying for supplies of stone and materials and the wages of travelling artisan craftsmen, and keeping his own accounts. By Michaelmas 1742 he was officially head gardener, 'Mr Brown' – still at £25 a year, but with his allowances for contractors increased again. His extra board wages were £9 for thirty-six weeks and a permanent settlement.

Hopefully he was lodged with some rosy-cheeked pensioner's widow, as lucky gardeners were, for tragedy and bitterness were about to assault the Stowe community. Old soldier and Steward William Roberts, Lancelot's immediate superior, 'hanged himself because Lord Cobham had reprimanded him for mistreating, perhaps violently . . . the Mr D who had convicted a deer stealer'. 'Mr D' was a law officer, perhaps even a magistrate, so the matter was serious; but Roberts's misery and shame serve as chilling evidence of Lord Cobham's temper when roused, although he continued to support the Steward's widow and children.

Roberts was replaced as Steward by one Thomas Potts, who was soon at daggers drawn with a colleague, Leonard Lloyd, a lawyer who lived by the church in Buckingham and acted for Lord Cobham in political matters, and as Steward of the Burton Dassett estate. Potts and Lloyd, out to damage each other, poisoned everybody's working atmosphere, and then Potts vanished, as did the estate-office cash box, heavy with Michaelmas rent monies. A reward of ten guineas was offered for information as to Potts's whereabouts in the *Northampton Mercury*. Whether he was found we do not know, but Leonard Lloyd was vindicated, installed as Steward, and Mr Brown rose up one higher and became Clerk of Works.

Enter Jemmy Gibbs

This was an all-inclusive role, and Lancelot found himself responsible for workers on the wider estate, tasting the mixed blessings (the greetings and small gifts, as well as the catcalls and snowballs from hooting urchins) of becoming a well-known figure in Chackmore, Dadford, Silverstone, Whittlebury and the Lillingstones, as well as in Buckingham. He was endorsing his bills for the wages and expenses of carpenters, carters, sawyers, plasterers and masons' works, for stones from various quarries and for works on the Stowe library and chapel, as well as for garden buildings. His own words are 'heard' for the first time speaking up for 'the Helpers not charg'd Christmas which they say they wear always pay'd; if not approv'd [I] shall call it Back'.

Now, though some of the political and poetic undertones of Stowe's symbols may have passed him by, the importance of the architecture was borne upon him by the ponderous approach of James Gibbs. At Stowe, Vanbrugh, dead for fourteen years, was but a legend, though his 60-foot-high Egyptian pyramid, his memorial in the Home Park, was much in evidence. The ailing William Kent was rarely seen, for he had done most of his work prior to Lancelot's arrival. So now that Lord Cobham had called Jemmy Gibbs back to design big, important buildings – many to be supervised, brick by brick and stone by stone,

by Lancelot – here was an architectural opportunity that he was ready
to embrace.

Gibbs was in his sixtieth year, a man grown beyond professional jealousies, and was known to be 'courteous, moderate, humane and charitable'. With a famously classical portfolio behind him, including Pope's
villa at Twickenham, the church of St Martin-in-the-Fields, the King's
College Fellows' building and the Senate House in Cambridge, and the
Radcliffe Camera in Oxford, Gibbs lived and worked independently in
Henrietta Street, Marylebone, his only 'office' comprising one drawing
assistant and his library of architectural books. He was 'generally payed' 5
per cent of the total cost of a building, great or small, 'And if I goe to
the Countary I am allowed my Coach hire.' He charged one guinea for
a single drawing (say, for a bridge or an obelisk) and five to ten guineas
for sets of more complex drawings. Though Gibbs would have been paid
directly by Lord Cobham or Steward Lloyd rather than by Lancelot,
Lancelot was probably aware of these 'professional' charges. Gibbs was also
known to be on good terms with the craftsmen he encountered over and
over again, including the many who worked for the builders Smiths' of
Warwick, all of them familiar figures in the south Midlands shires. All
these things and more, and their shared northernness (though Gibbs was
more extreme, he came from Aberdeenshire and was educated at Aberdeen
Grammar School and by the Jesuits), indicate that Lancelot was deeply
impressed by Gibbs and his way of working, and took many of Gibbs's
habits for his own. (Was it from Gibbs that Lancelot first heard the name
of the trusty bankers, Drummonds of Charing Cross?)

Gibbs liked to teach; he had long realised the inaccessibility of the
vocabulary of classical architecture to the artisans and ambitious craftsmen
working in the countryside. His *Rules for Drawing the Several Parts of
Architecture,* first published in 1732, was reissued in 1738, priced at one
guinea, with loose sets in twenty-one weekly parts at one shilling each,
for those who could not afford the whole outlay at once. *Rules for Drawing*
may not have been found by Lancelot as yet, but he studied one of its
offshoots, recommended by Gibbs, *The Builder's Dictionary: or Gentleman
and Architect's Companion . . . faithfully digested from the Most Approved Writers
on these Subjects* (1734), containing 'a great deal of useful Knowledge in
the Building Business'. Lancelot studied this volume, making fifteen pages
of handwritten notes on the architectural terms and meanings that he
now needed to know (which were retained in the Stowe archives).
His point of practical reference was Gibbs's classical Temple of Friendship, designed at this time, built of fine golden sandstone (now in part-
ruins, revealing its brick-and-rubble core) and standing on Bridgeman's

Stowe, James Gibbs's Gothic Temple, for which Lancelot supervised the building, inspiring his love of castellations, from George Bickham, *The Beauties of Stowe*, 1750.

south-eastern bastion, of critical importance in the cross-views. Just to the east, and also by Gibbs, almost an 'end-of-term' building project, was the cubic Imperial Closet, with inside the alarmingly full-length figures painted by Francesco Sleter, of three Caesars: Titus, Trajan and Mark Antony.

Most interesting by far, and Lancelot's introduction to Gothic in a hands-on and defining experience, was Gibbs's innovatory, almost comic building dedicated 'to the Liberty of our Ancestors', which must have caused some guffaws amongst the builders. Set on Hawkwell Hill, with its pointed arches, churchlike windows, oddly angled castellations and towers (the tallest being 70 feet high), all in the strongest iron-stained east Northamptonshire stone, this stunning building of the Gothic Temple was impressed upon Lancelot's mind's eye for ever. It was still unfinished, merely an empty shell, in 1748, and we may imagine him examining it at his leisure in wintry dawns or on summer evenings, until he had marked and inwardly digested all the method of its curious design.

One more important building, erected under his clerkship, was the 'Lady's Building' (subsequently much altered and now called the Queen's Temple). Gibbs's original building had a rusticated and arcaded basement, with a pretty Venetian window for the first-floor room, intended for 'Ladies employing themselves in Needle and Shell-work' and 'diverting themselves with Painting and Musick'. This was Lancelot's first experience with the finesse of a Venetian window, a feature that he employed at his first opportunity at Croome.

The rather lackadaisical building programme, with too many new things started at once, gave an otherworldly atmosphere to the kingdom of Stowe. It was like a continuous *fête champêtre* or living on a stageset. These much-celebrated buildings, however, contained vital lessons about the siting of buildings in a landscape. The Queen's Temple (Lady's Building) and Lord Cobham's male preserve, the Temple of Friendship, answered each other across the length of Hawkwell Field, whilst the Gothic Temple on its eminence looked in from the east – each within its own space, but cohabiting in, as Samuel Richardson found, 'such a Scene of Magnificence and Nature display'd, the Fields abounding with Cattle, the Trees and Water so delightfully intermingled, and such a charming Verdure, Symmetry, and Proportion, every-where presenting to the Eye, that the Judgment is agreeably puzzled, which singly to prefer of so many collected Beauties'. Gibbs made Stowe Lancelot's 'university', and partly his Grand Tour, though more was yet to come.

A Marriage at Stowe

In all these five years since Lancelot left home there is little evidence of family matters. Did Lancelot see his mother Ursula again before she died in 1742? Did he go north for George's wedding to Catherine Fenwick of Hartburn the following year, or even for John's wedding to Jane Loraine in the spring of 1744? He certainly kept in touch with home and was surely there sometimes. Possibly he went as part of the same long journey that took him on his last visit to Miss Bridget Wayet in Boston, so that he headed north with the good news that she had agreed to marry him. They were married in the little church of St Mary's at Stowe on 22nd November 1744. Two years earlier 'the wal[l]s of the church were white washed and the Ld's Prayer creed and commandments painted on the Walls and the King's Arms drawn and fram'd and hung up in Mr Gabell's [vestry room]'. Lancelot and Bridget were married by Henry Gabell (vicar 1734–61) and signed his register in the vestry room. The five 'very tunable' seventeenth-century bells sang out.*

Lancelot had a home for Bridget, having persuaded Lord Cobham that they should live in the 'very good habitable House', as Defoe called

---

* In 1973 Simon Whistler engraved the signatures of Lancelot and Bridget, copied from the register, beside a window in the south aisle.

Two Pavilions at the Entrance to the Park.

Stowe, the Boycott Pavilions, as illustrated by Benton Seeley, 1750; the western pavilion, built c.1730 for a 'gentleman' was home to Lancelot and Bridget after their marriage in 1744.

it, that was the western of the two Boycott Pavilions; as Gilbert West explained in verse, this had been intended for Colonel Speed, Cobham's:

> Faithful Companion of his toilsome Days,
> (He led Thee on in Glory's noble Chace!)

This was truly a mark of Lord Cobham's regard for Lancelot and his bride, for West's poem continues:

> But shall the Muse approach the Pile, assign'd
> Once, for a Mansion to her much-lov'd Friend,
> And not bestow one sad, one tuneful Tear,
> Unhappy Speed! on thy untimely Bier?

The pavilions marked the western, Oxford entrance to Stowe, and were then joined by railings and gates. (These gates were subsequently moved farther westwards to the newer Oxford entrance.) In her miniature 'mansion' Bridget Brown was close to Nelson's Walk, named for the late foreman William Nelson, which led to the gate into the garden workshops and yards west of Stowe house, where Lancelot was often to be found. She was well secluded from the work gangs and from the constant stream of fine-weather visitors; but even so, one wonders what the former Miss Wayet from morally upright Boston thought of fashionably louche Stowe? She was isolated both physically and socially in a way she had not known before, for living in a garden might sound all very fine and romantic, but Lady Cobham and her ladies required a curtsey, and Bridget had to tolerate being patronised – albeit kindly – in return. One hopes she found at least one good ally amongst the wives of the household's senior staff. The estate farm and the farms at Boycott supplied her with milk, butter and cheese, but to reach the dairy she had to negotiate the ford at the Oxford Water; in the other direction it was almost 2 miles' walk to Dadford village. Gifts of venison and game came Lancelot's way, as well as his perquisites of vegetables and fruit from the gardens, but everything else had to wait for holiday jaunts to Buckingham's markets.

But Bridget was an intelligent and sober young woman, and she had invested her energies into Lancelot's well-being; it was more than enough to sit by the fire of an evening and hear his news, to sharpen his quills in a wifelike manner, to tidy his books and papers and talk of their dreams. Lancelot settled most happily into married life, and Bridget assumed her additional roles as his closest friend and most-desired companion, a situation that apparently never changed. His marriage was the rich and resourceful backdrop to his life and all that he did, the secret behind his quizzical smile and his ability to disarm the meanest and most critical of clients.

They were, in the old-fashioned sense, a Christian couple, and one wonders what Bridget made of Stowe, if – when walking out into the quiet garden on a fine evening – Lancelot dared introduce her to some of Lord Cobham's more risqué pagan indulgences: the walk to church through the Elysian Fields meant encountering so many graven images that one (anonymous) visitor had noted that 'unless the Influence of the Preacher is great indeed, More will pay there Devotions among the Antient Heathens than the Modern Xtians'. Lord Cobham fully intended the irony of having the Ten Commandments painted onto the church wall, yet being freely broken all over the garden: Cain was slaying Abel (near the Hermitage), the voluptuous Venus was disporting herself upon a pagan altar in the Rotunda, in Dido's Cave 'The Trojan Hero' Aeneas was ravishing 'the Tyrian Queen', while the Sleeping Parlour carried the exhortation 'Since all things are uncertain, indulge thyself'. In the Temple of Bacchus, 'The painted Walls mysterious Orgies spread', and not far away 'A cool Recess there is . . . Sacred to Love, to Mirth, and rural Play'. This Recess figures in Gilbert West's descriptive poem (1732) in the story of a pretty girl on a swing, startled by an ardent youth from whom she fled, 'swift away, more rapid than the Wind':

> And sought the Shelter of the closer Shade;
> Where in thick Covert, to her weary Feet,
> A Private Grotto promis'd safe Retreat:
> Alas! Too private, for too safely there

The fierce Pursuer seiz'd the helpless Fair;
The Fair he seiz'd, while round him all the Throng
Of laughing Dryads, Hymenaeals sung.

Venus, like a *madame* nodding her approval. Having escaped one, she fell
to a second pursuer (whom she thought a friend), popularly thought to
be none other than the previous vicar, Conway Rand – hence the Recess
was called the 'Randibus'.

Conway Rand, apparently good-natured enough to see the joke, was
also a former chaplain of one of Cobham's regiments, as well as the likely
guardian of Signor Fido, the Italian greyhound memorialised to the rear
of the Temple of British Worthies as the epitome of the virtues of Stowe:

> He was no Bigot,
> Tho' he doubted of none of the 39 Articles.
> And, if to follow Nature,
> And to respect the Laws of Society,
> Be Philosophy,
> He was a perfect Philosopher;
> A faithful Friend,
> An agreeable Companion,
> A loving Husband,
> Distinguish'd by a numerous Offspring,
> All of which he liv'd to see take good Courses.

'O Pitt! Thy country's early boast'

Stowe, in clement seasons and fine weather, was a crowded place, and
Lancelot soon learned that he had become a figure of interest, ever likely
to be drawn into conversation by visitors, or summoned by his lordship,
who came striding across the lawns dressed in fading regimentals (he
must have had closets full of uniforms that never wore out). He was
invariably accompanied by an adulatory string of ambitious young men,
his famous 'Cubs', and by poets like James Hammond, who wrote:

> To Stowe's delightful scenes I now repair,
> In Cobham's smile to lose the gloom of care;*

Lancelot never knew who would interrupt his morning's work with

---

* Or Paul Whitehead: 'Aske ye, What's Honour? I'll the truth impart, /Know, honour then, is
  Honesty of Heart. /To the sweet scenes of social *Stow* repair, /And search the Master's breast –
  /You'll find it there.'

some asinine, time-wasting question or other, for the house was always harbouring new faces. But there was soon one he learned to look out for: 'the tall, animated, commanding-looking Mr Pitt who talked a great deal and was it seemed much listened to'. William Pitt was arrogant and aloof, but — it helped that they were both tall and saw eye-to-eye — he was passionately interested in gardening, and invariably curious as to what Lancelot was doing, and in this way they came to an early (unspoken) understanding. Lancelot, with his reiver shepherd's genes, refused to be intimidated, and was unfailingly polite, and they became *convenable* with each other. Pitt was eight years older, a scion of a 'cockatrice brood of Pitts' thickly sprinkled in the landscape from Stratfield Saye in Hampshire through Dorset to Cornwall and 'that cursed hiding place' as Pitt called remote Boconnoc. Cobham's nephew, George Lyttelton, was his best friend, and together they were founder members of Cobham's Cubs, supporters of Frederick, Prince of Wales, and destined for bright political futures.

Pitt had been young Cornet Pitt in Cobham's regiment, and instead of kicking his heels in camp at Towcester or Northampton, he had formed the habit of escaping to Stowe and staying for weeks on end. Now Stowe was an essential stop in his inveterate ramblings around England, to hospitable houses with interesting grounds: to Ralph Allen at Prior Park in Bath, to his cousin John Pitt at Encombe in its own Dorset cove, to the Grenvilles' Wotton Underwood, to Gilbert West at West Wickham in Kent, to Sanderson Miller at Radway and to the Lytteltons at Hagley. Wherever he went he suggested garden improvements and was not averse to rolling up his sleeves and working at them. Because he was William Pitt, everyone was generously pleased at his taste.

In 1746 Pitt acquired a small estate of his own, on a ridge overlooking Enfield Chace, 65 acres beside the lane from Enfield to East Barnet, known as South Lodge. His venture was prompted by nostalgia, for soon after his birth in 1708 the family had taken refuge from a smallpox epidemic at Forty Lodge near Enfield, giving him an imagined fondness for Enfield Chace. He spent £1,350 on refurbishments to the Lodge, but the grounds were his real interest, where, according to Gilbert West, he had 'a little paradise opened in the wild', with the stream making two lakes with a wooded island, rustic bridge and a temple to Pan in the Doric style. It is possible that he 'borrowed' Lancelot to help with this, with Lord Cobham's blessing. Pitt was at his happiest working in his own garden, but — as with his febrile finances, which lurched from extravagance to pleading poverty — even these enthusiasms were short-lived, and he parted with South Lodge after five years. He would not have dreamed of paying Lancelot — nor perhaps would Lancelot have accepted payment, for he had a very strict code on such matters – and as they met as young men with futures to make, there seemed an innate equality (despite their differing fames) and their dealings were on the basis of an exchange of uncounted favours.*

In the autumn of 1745, when Bridget was heavily pregnant with their first child, the kingdom of Stowe was thrown into a panic by the news that Bonnie Prince Charlie and his Jacobite army were forging their way southwards: 'The country was greatly alarm'd on Friday with the rebels,' wrote Lord Fermanagh to the Verneys on 8th December:

> Ld Cobham pack'd up his arms and plate and the best things and sent them away, but where I don't know. This frightened people very much. They were carrying his things to Oxford but Mr Greenvill [Richard Grenville] stopt em upon the road and ordered them somewhere else. Ld Cobham was in town but Mr Dorrel [Lord Cobham's secretary] sent to the house and immediately they began to pack up and dismiss the workmen. 'Twas a simple affair and did hurt as it lower'd people's spirits.

The rebels got no nearer than Derby and then began to retreat; eventually this news filtered to Stowe and everyone relaxed, the house was returned to order and work restarted. In this atmosphere Bridget gave birth to the Browns' first child, their daughter Bridget, always to be especially adored and blest with a bright and happy future.

The Grecian Valley, 'not Taste or Judgment?'

The estate records for 1746 show another spurt of activity in the garden, the making of the Grecian Valley in the as-yet-unused north-east 'quarter', of about 60 acres, which Lancelot had enclosed with the ha-ha. In the winter of 1746–7 he spent much of his time walking and surveying what was still rough paddocks and farmland, now to be moulded into an ideal valley that the poets likened to 'the Vale of Tempe'. Lord Cobham was present as Lancelot supervised the men and their barrows as they wheeled and carted out almost 24,000 cubic yards of earth (spread over the northern park) to scoop out the dog-legged valley, which gave space to the naturalistic effect even more so than the Elysian Fields. Trees and evergreens were planted around the rim of the vale; paths were to wander through these, whilst the valley itself was intended as a piece of water. Lancelot was at last practising his favourite occupation, but was tactfully uncertain about the finishing, showing that he still respected his employer's

---

* An overgrown lake, relict wood and guardian cedars of Lebanon survive on the South Lodge site, amidst modern houses.

Stowe, the Grecian Valley *c*.1750, as Lancelot left it, with sheep grazing, the Temple completed (but not named for Concord and Victory until later) and Captain Grenville's column which was subsequently moved. From *The Beauties of Stowe*, 1750.

pride of ownership: 'as to finishing the Head of the Oval,' he wrote, 'I had never formed any other idea than what your lordship gave me "to Forme the Laurell Plantation with a Sweep under it and Concave to the Ovall" – that the Slope of the Head your Lordship thought might some time or other have statues put on it.' Work had come this far by February 1747 and Lord Cobham was away in London, and so Lancelot added his opinion that his lordship had given 'no absolute Orders to finish it and indeed I think it would be better not finished this season – thinking that a summer's talk and tryel's about it may make it a very fine thing'.

The summer's talk and trials, mocking-up effects for Cobham's approval, indicates the care that went into this pictorial landscape-making. The concave sweep up to the overhanging laurels, 'some time or other' to be dotted with statues, was a Kentish notion. At the opposite end of the vale there was to be a large building, looking down the vale and placed at an oblique angle, very much as Claude Lorrain set his buildings in many pastorals, for instance the *Landscape with Ascanius shooting the stag of Silvia*, of 1682 (now in the Ashmolean Museum, Oxford). Lord Cobham could have adapted this trick from Vanbrugh's and Kent's inspirations from stagesets, or from George Lambert's painting of Chiswick of 1742, the angled 'View from a balustraded platform above the cascade to the side of the villa and partially along the lake'. Equally Cobham could have seen Claude's *Liber Veritatis* (200 of his drawings) which was in the collection at Devonshire House in Piccadilly.

The Grecian Valley's building was started in 1747, and in a note attached to that year's accounts Lancelot explains, 'the plan of the Long Room will be sent by the next post. I should have sent it this post but could not get it finished'. On her visit six months later in the summer of 1748, Sophia Newdigate noted 'Noble Apartments' newly completed in the house, including the ballroom, gallery and chapel, all of similar 'long room' proportions; the 'foundation only' was laid on the 'prodigious building' that she was told was copied from Maison Carrée at Nîmes, in the new area of the garden. No one called the 'maison' a temple, and it could have been Lancelot's 'long room', and the timing suggests that he had been trusted with the construction drawing for the footing platform and therefore played a considerable role in its brilliant siting.*

Also in that summer of 1748 the Marchioness Grey visited Stowe, describing the embryonic Grecian Valley:

To preserve the Memory of her Husband.
Ann Viscountess Cobham,
Caused this Pillar to be erected in the Year 1747

Stowe, Lord Cobham's Monument, built by Lancelot two years before Lord Cobham's death in 1749.

---

* The building was not roofed until after Lord Cobham's death, and it has no named designer for the original; in the 1750s Cobham's heir, Richard Grenville, made alterations to it, and he is portrayed by William Hoare holding a model of it (the pun on his title of Earl Temple, inherited from his mother in 1752, cannot be discounted). It was dubbed 'The Temple of Concord and Victory' in 1763, in honour of the peace after William Pitt's great victories of the Seven Years War, in which the Grenville brothers had played some part.

there are now going on Improvements in the 60 Acres last inclos'd, which is a Fall and Rise again of the Hill on the Opposite Side behind that which is already finished. But even this by the Laying-out seems to have no sort of Variety. The Slopes bare like the Other Side with Walks up or round them; a Piece of Water is to be in the Valley below, and vast Buildings larger and mightier than all the Others upon the Sides: – Sure this is not Taste or Judgment!

Jemima Yorke, the Marchioness Grey, was the most top-lofty of aristocrats, mistress of her own Wrest Park, with its fine and ancient formal garden, and – by her marriage – of Wimpole Hall; it was not in her nature to approve of anything anyone else did, and though she was naturally suspicious of the new naturalism, she noticed Lancelot Brown and what he was doing, and approved.

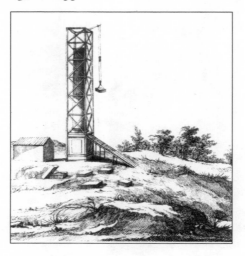

Gibside, County Durham: Lancelot had given George Bowes advice on the building, and work in progress was sketched by R. R. Angerstein, *Travel Diary 1753–1755*

The phrase 'Grecian diagonal', also in the 1747 accounts, refers to the vista from Lord Cobham's monument to the new building (Concord and Victory), another critical piece of siting. Lancelot was certainly in charge of the construction of the monument, a fluted octagonal shaft 104 feet high with a spiral staircase inside, built on Lady Cobham's orders, before her husband's death. Possibly Gibbs supplied the design, which Lancelot found he had to modify in the construction, because 'the Wind has a very great effect on Buildings that stand on so small a Base'. (The monument had to be additionally buttressed forty-five years later.)

His observation on the effect of the wind was written in a letter to George Bowes of Gibside, after Lancelot had left Stowe, when Bowes asked his advice, perhaps indicating that Lancelot was given the opportunity to return to work in the North. Columns entered his repertory of unusual building skills: it is possible to see the connection from Hooke's Great Fire Monument, seen in *Micrographia* in his youth (though not yet in reality), to Lord Cobham's monument and the Gibside Column, culminating in the Burton Pynsent Column built for Pitt in the 1760s. Once Lancelot had accomplished a project with success, he stored away the details for possible future use.

Lord Cobham died in September 1749, and was buried in the crypt beneath the Penyston chapel in Stowe church. There is no flamboyant monument in the church, nor apparently was there pomp and circumstance at his funeral, of which no account survives. Perhaps he felt his garden was sufficient memorial.

The Grecian Valley had been his lordship's final piece of garden-making. For Lancelot it was unfinished, for the intended water was never made. There were springs enough, and the ground lay wet in rainy seasons, but a lake would have needed a holding dam and puddled-clay lining, major works that he could not organise without express permission. Jealousy may enter the equation here, for Cobham's heir, his nephew Richard Grenville, had become increasingly impatient of waiting for his inheritance, ever since he had taken charge in the panic caused by the news of the approaching Jacobites in 1745. Grenville had used the rectory at Finmere, just west of Buckingham, as a base for keeping his eye on Stowe, and Lancelot worked there for him; a ha-ha, dell and trees, 'so disposed as to produce the effect of a long perspective and considerable space where there was really very little', survive at Finmere. But the Grenvilles soon made it clear that they would bring their own senior staff to Stowe with them, and Lancelot would have to leave.

Lady Cobham, her distress magnified by her love of Stowe and fears that her husband's legacy would be changed, turned to Lancelot to help her remove to her old home, Stoke Park at Stoke Poges in far south Buckinghamshire, inherited from her father Edmund Halsey. Soon after the move Anna Grenville, writing from London to her husband at Stowe, revealed the situation – she had seen the King, who asked if all the Stowe estate 'was to be put into gardens?':

I went to my Lady Cobham yesterday and she began in a violent manner

about the Sheep being put into the garden. I told her they look'd mighty
pretty and that everybody said it wou'd make the turf much firmer, but
if they did harm they would be taken out I suppos'd, but that I really
never disputed anything with you for I thought you knew much better
than I, and she said she shou'd scold you well when she saw you.

Now Lancelot became embroiled in the argument, as Anna Grenville
continues:

I knew what I was to meet with for she told Brown she had cry'd all
night and never slept a wink about it and raved and tore and said if my
Lord C could know how Stow was used how vext he would be, and he
said Lady Temple and Lady Hester [Richard Grenville's mother and sister]
were in an uproar about it too. They were both by when she begun with
me but they button'd up their mouths and said not one word. Now one
should imagine they might have tryd to stop her instead of setting her to
work considering you are a party concern'd. I wish you would ask Brown
what she said to him for I have not seen him . . . It happened at a bad
time for me for I was ill and low spirited and she worried me almost to
death, I fancy you will be tired enough with her and the less we see her
and have to do with her the better.

Not so Lancelot, who continued to visit Lady Cobham at Stoke Park,
and in the summer of 1750 made a plan for some garden alterations. He
found a huge brick-and-mullioned house full of Tudor glories with a
small park containing five fishponds, which he transformed into a long
piece of water. A consolation for the Grecian Valley from the kind Lady
Cobham? The water 'flowed' beside a wide lawn and was crossed by a
pretty three-arched bridge, with a Palladian topping. Referring to the
bridge John Harris has noted, 'if architectural historians mutter James
Gibbs they may not be wrong'. Gibbs and Lancelot may even have done
some of the work at Stoke *before* Lord Cobham's death, for the house
had been managed from Stowe ever since 1729 when Lady Cobham's
father had died, though it was usually let to friends or relations.

Lancelot was given time to arrange his leaving, and the Brown family
were not to be hurried out of their home: little Bridget was now
approaching her fourth birthday, their son Lance, baptised on 13th January
1748, was a toddler, and Bridget expected another baby in the spring of
1750. This was William, who was baptised in April, but soon died. Even
so, their Boycott Pavilion, intended for one widower gentleman, and fine
for a happy couple with their first baby, was now too small for them.

4

SURVEYING HIS FUTURE – LANCELOT'S GREAT RIDE

But as where Britain's Fair assembled shine,
The rays of beauty spread a light divine;
So here, where nature does her triumphs show,
And with majestic hand adorns a Stowe;
Description fails – all fancy is too mean,
They only can conceive it – who have seen!

Samuel Boyse, 'The Triumphs of Nature', 1742

THE SUMMER OF 1750 SAW the circulation of Thomas Gray's 'Elegy Written in a Country Church-yard'; the churchyard being under the windows of Lady Cobham's house at Stoke Poges, and Gray being a local young man. When Gray was not academically occupied in Cambridge, he spent his time with his mother and aunts at West End Cottage (now Stoke Court), less than a mile from the church to the north. Like Lady Cobham, the Grays were bereaved, Thomas's much-loved Aunt Mary having died the previous autumn, leaving his mother and one aunt at the cottage. However, in that summer they were all cheered; 'Lady Cobham was by all accounts delighted to learn,' writes Robert Mack, 'that the author of the *Elegy* then being shown and read in every fashionable London drawing room was even then residing with his mother and his aunt at their residence in Stoke Poges.' Lady Cobham's glooms were lifted by having a poet to lionise, and there were to be two happy outcomes: one that Thomas Gray and Lancelot Brown (who were the same age, thirty-four) met each other that summer; and, second, that Gray wrote a delightful farrago entitled 'The Long Story' of how the 'Amazons' – Lady Cobham, her companions Lady Schaub and Miss Henrietta Jane Speed (the daughter of the same Colonel Speed who was to have lived in Lancelot's Boycott Pavilion at Stowe) – made an 'assault' on the Grays' cottage to find him:

> The heroines undertook the task;
> Through lanes unknown, o'er styles they ventured
> Rapped at the door, nor stayed to ask
> But bounce into the parlour entered.
> The trembling family they daunt,
> They flirt, they sing, they laugh, they tattle,
> Rummage his mother, pinch his aunt,
> And upstairs in a whirlwind rattle.

The poet is eventually found, speechless, though not for long: 'The Long Story' was a relief to all after the anguish of the 'Elegy'. The inhabitants of West End Cottage and Stoke Park became the best of friends, and Lady Cobham lived on happily at Stoke for ten years, with interludes spent in livelier society in London or Hampton Court, where she had many friends, including the actor David Garrick and his vivacious circle. These 'Amazons', and their poet, became founder members of a company of Lancelot's well-wishers, people of all kinds and conditions (by no means all owners of large estates) who spoke of him warmly and forwarded his cause. This oiling of the social machinery, which in our time has been rationalised into business accounting as 'goodwill', is hardly documented at all in Lancelot's life, but often it is clear that whispers in the dark, or prayers, enabled the timeliness of his good fortunes. Thomas Gray, like William Pitt ('Honorary President' of the Brown well-wishers), was an inveterate rambler, and he and his great gardening friend, the Rev. William Mason, were watchers of Lancelot's progress.

It has long been known that Lord Cobham had 'lent' Lancelot to his friends and relations. He was sympathetically aware that Lancelot had to have a future that he could not provide, and allowed that meetings in the garden at Stowe might have consequences. The Denbighs, the 5th Earl and his wife Isabella, were garden visitors, the Cobhams' town neighbours in Hanover Square, and they had a house, Newnham Paddox, set in lovely Warwickshire countryside just south of where Watling Street meets the Fosse Way. In the spring of 1746 Lancelot had been to Newnham to plan and direct 'alterations of the grand canal, and carrying it on to the head of the pond in the park . . . with other work done in consequence of this'. Eighteen months later the joining of the canal and pond into 'the serpentine water' had been achieved, and Lancelot was levelling the banks, and cleaning the pond and 'laying it with hanging slopes'. At this point the Denbighs ran out of money.

Sanderson Miller to the Rescue

Another meeting in the garden was of even greater consequence. Sanderson Miller was a young gentleman-architect; his father, also Sanderson Miller, had been a prosperous Banbury merchant who lived at Boycott Manor, until Lord Cobham bought it around 1712, at the start of his territorially expansive gardening. Miller senior had moved westwards to Radway Grange, spectacularly positioned at the foot of Edge Hill in Warwickshire. Sanderson junior was Lancelot's age, but his education had included three companionable and enjoyable years at Oxford. He had inherited Radway in 1737, as the only surviving (though youngest) son, and, enthused by his Oxford friends, soon became a passionate improver, with a talent for designing buildings, mostly in the Gothic style. In 1746 he had married Susannah Trotman, who was related to the Temples, so he naturally gravitated to Stowe. He also kept a diary, and the entry for 5th November 1749 reads: at Stowe 'Walking in the Garden with the Com[pany] & Mr Brown & Dorrel', for five hours!

Five hours was time enough to get the measure of Lancelot, finding him refreshingly conversible on the nuances of lake edgings, dam pilings and the foundations for temples and columns. At some point Miller said that Lancelot 'really must see Radway' and, after the invitation had been repeated, Lancelot took him seriously. And so, when Bridget insisted that she had recovered from the birth and death of little William, and Lancelot had seen Lady Cobham settled at Stoke, he made plans for a long expedition, a ride to explore the heart of England and look for work. He could well be spared as all his labourers were busy in the fields, for garden improvements now gave way to farming priorities.

He set out at the end of the first week in August of 1750, his hack splashing through the ford and on to the Boycott Farm crossroads, where he turned north; he could see the Miller's old Boycott Manor across a small valley, and then his road was up and down through the harvest fields. Biddlesden was where the monks of the now-ruined abbey had first bridged the river Great Ouse, and there looked to be a tremendous opportunity for a lake, but no one to pay for it. The going was high and dry across Northamptonshire and, barring incidents, he could easily reach Banbury in time for supper. His first goal was out of the town north-westwards, on the old road through Drayton and Wroxton, which passed alongside the pale of Lord North's park.

Wroxton was Sanderson Miller's pride and joy; Miller was his lordship's gentlemanly provider of Gothic fantasies for the abbey and the park, and his Temple on the Mount was being built. Of greatest interest

Sanderson Miller's Gothic Tower on Edge Hill in Warwickshire, drawn by Barbara Jones for *Follies and Grottoes, 1953*.

were the 'irregularities' of the 70 acres 'finely diversified with wood and water'; Lord North had replaced his old formal gardens and canals with lawns and serpentine streams, wide enough for the pleasures of a rowing boat; the water was ingeniously drawn from the Sor brook, thus draining what had been a bog. He had naturalised the Great Pond into a 7-acre lake and planted a great number of trees, which were now casting delightful shadows on the waters; in addition he had a Chinese summer house, the venue for suppers of cold meats and ice cream. Wroxton was a fine example of how a courtier might indulge his private tastes and considerable talents in a home secreted down a country lane, somewhere in England. Francis North, later the Earl of Guilford, was in his late forties, a friend to both George II and Frederick, Prince of Wales; the latter was godfather to his son, named Frederick, who had grown up in 'a happy and devout family atmosphere' at Wroxton (a wise man kept both his children and his gardens from exposure to the great world). Frederick was now eighteen and down from Oxford; he and Lancelot would be easy acquaintances in later years.

Wroxton's innovations were interesting, but there was no work for Lancelot. Just over 4 miles farther on was Upton House, set high, with a long valley opening to the south, where the stream was being dammed to make a pool, the Temple Pool, and a hillside spring was being harnessed to fall in a cascade. The owner, William Bumstead, had dared to make an offer for Radway Grange, deeply offending San Miller. 'Pox take Bumstead and all fools who are your enemies,' wrote a consoling friend. There was no future there.

Sanderson Miller's Egge Cottage at Radway, where Lancelot dined on his visit in August 1750, drawn by Barbara Jones.

Stopping at Upton depended on how long Lancelot had loitered around Hornton, attracted by the dust clouds and crunching of the quarrymen's saws, for this was the home country of the coveted Middle Lias or Marlstone, the iron-stained golden stone that had been used for Stowe's Gothic Temple. Lancelot was ever the curious traveller, and so much of England was new to him; he stored sights and impressions for future use, but also as fuel for the stories he took home to Biddy and their children.

A short distance beyond Hornton he came to the hamlet of Edge Hill, dominated by San Miller's new Sham Castle or Gothic Tower, of the same Hornton stone. Finally, winding his way down into Radway, he found an entrancing village, its cottages and houses set well back in long gardens, and all seeming, as Alec Clifton-Taylor described, 'to soak up and store the sunshine within their rich tawny brown carapace'. That day, however, it was raining. San Miller recorded in his diary for 10th August: 'Wet', but that Brown 'had dined here'. Radway Grange, Jacobean and many-gabled, was at the head of the village street, with its land stretching up to the Edge Hill ridge; 'here' meant that they dined in Edge or Egge Cottage, built about six years earlier for just such purposes, as Miller's workroom and for entertaining his gardening friends. The papers on the workroom table revealed Miller's artistic approach, his practice of sketching his ideas for buildings; the masons worked from the sketches, managing without measured drawings.

That month Miller was celebrating the completion of his Tower with parties, and poetic appreciation from his friend Richard Jago in his poem 'Edge-Hill':

> Like a tall Rampart! Here the Mountain rears
> Its verdant Edge . . . thanks Miller! For thy Paths

That ease our winding steps! Thanks to the Rill,
The Banks, the Trees, the Shrubs, th'enraptured Sense
Regaling, or with Fragrance, Shape or Sound,
And stilling every Tumult in the Breast!

Lancelot – having climbed the verdant Edge, having praised every Gothic niche and painted window, every castellation and every step and turn of the curious castle – was, one hopes, blessed with a clear sunset so that he could see out over the vast battlefield plain. Miller never tired of describing the spectacle of some 25,000 men drawn up to fight on Sunday, 23rd October 1642, in the first major action of the Civil War and a royalist victory. He was holding his celebration for the Tower on 3rd September, the anniversary of Cromwell's death.

The following day, 11th August, Miller recorded, 'rode with him across ye Valley &c.', which meant following the foot of the ridge round to Arlescote, then across the valley (which now carries the M40) to where the land rises again and the hamlets of Avon Dassett and Burton Dassett are locked in vertiginous contours. Lancelot may have had an errand to fulfil at the Temples' estate of Burton Dassett, but their real goal was southwards, where the road climbs gently into the Farnborough demesne, the home of the Holbech family, and where Miller wanted to show Lancelot a new meaning of the word 'terrace'. Farnborough Hall was hardly more than fifty years old, built of the same glowing Hornton stone with Warwickshire grey ashlar trimmings, a lovely house, but hopelessly sited for a garden; the house was backed into the village and a hill, and looked out on a valley that wished only to be waterlogged. Hence the 'good and wise' William Holbech II was making a virtue out of this difficulty by building a wide green terrace, curving upwards and away to the south. This terrace was already half a mile long, but destined for greater length, like a linear park, driveable by phaeton or dog-cart, commanding views over the watery Vale of the Red Horse. Here is Richard Jago again, on the construction of the terrace:

. . . In sturdy Troops,
The Jocund Labourers hie, and, at his Nod,
A thousand Hands o'er smooth the slanting Hill,
Or scoop new Channels for the gath'ring Flood,
And, in his Pleasures, find a solid Joy.

Jago exaggerates, even for a poem of friendship, for although the local men and boys were undoubtedly glad of work in the lulls of the farming year, 100 would have been more likely than 1,000, who would have just fallen over each other and their barrows. As an essay in man-sculpted earthworks, Lancelot would have found this fascinating, as was the way Holbech had contrived the streams of the Hanwell valley into appearing an elongated lake.

Sanderson Miller was proud of having advised Holbech, and the buildings to ornament the terrace were to his designs. They were built, like Farnborough Hall itself, by Smiths' of Warwick, who had built the Radcliffe Camera for James Gibbs. Francis Smith had died in 1738, and his son William in 1748, but the firm was still a force in the Midlands, now managed by the mason-architects the Hiorn family of Warwick, who kept the talented company of Smiths' artisans together. William Hiorn was known to be working at Farnborough; was it here that Lancelot heard of the intended improvements at Warwick Castle?

Sanderson Miller had been kindness itself, but not wholly altruistic; he and his gardening friends, 'the warmhearted crew' he had met at Oxford, had their moments of enthusiasm for digging and planting, but were sensibly aware that their extensive plans depended upon really hard labours. Miller had purposefully 'educated' Lancelot into their tastes by letting him see Wroxton, Radway and Farnborough. Miller liked to keep his Gothic 'plums' for himself, but saw Lancelot as useful where the landscape challenges were great, and he mentioned his friends George William Coventry at Croome near Worcester, and Thomas Barrett Lennard at Belhus in Essex. If Lancelot was to extend his trip to Croome, then he really should see George Lucy's great deer park at Charlecote and Lord Brooke at Warwick Castle, and ride another half a day north to Lord Guernsey's Packington, before turning south.

Armed with names and directions, Lancelot continued on his journey. First he came to, and perhaps visited, Compton Verney, with a new façade by Smiths' of Warwick, but an old-fashioned, straight entrance drive. (He was not commercially minded enough to carry a trade-card, but proving himself to be the late Lord Cobham's Clerk at Stowe was recommendation enough for his name to be noted.)

Soon he reached Charlecote's gatehouse, close to the Stratford road at that time. He quickly learned that the Lucys had been at Charlecote for some 550 years, and that the many-chimneyed brick house glimpsed through the gatehouse's arch was built by Sir Thomas Lucy in Queen Elizabeth's golden days. The park was newly paled and stocked with deer, and was in the care of James Mounford, Keeper to George Lucy. Here he certainly had the opportunity to ride around the park and decide what he would do, if asked. He saw James Fish's fine 1736 map of the estate, which gave him his bearings, so that he could make a sketch of his ideas.

To the north of the house he found remnants of raised formal gardens and brick-lined canals, or long ponds for carp. George Lucy had built a new summer house overlooking these ponds, replacing the brick gazebo of sixty years before, so he was clearly in the mood for spending money on his gardens. Maturing avenues, some of limes, radiated across the park; it was a salutary thought that when Charlecote was built, it was prettily sited beside the sunlit glades of the Forest of Arden (hence the young Will Shakespeare being caught for poaching in what had become Sir Thomas Lucy's park). A hundred years later, in the mid-seventeenth century, it exhibited a bleak aspect, 'deserted on every side, shut off by hills and thickets from almost all light and society of man. Also it has a river by it, whose waters are at all times nearly stagnant, save that once in the year it washes the house itself, as the Nile washes Egypt.' In the ensuing fifty years the thickets had been cleared, and the house and park opened up to sunny fields and meadows beside the River Avon, which ran close by the west front of the house.

Charlecote had the air of a happy place, and George Lucy ranked high in the list of Lancelot's most amiable clients. He was two years older than Lancelot, had inherited Charlecote when he was thirty, in 1744, and looked exactly as Pompeo Batoni portrayed him, with a candid, fresh, if rather prissy face revealing his kind heart and 'simple shrewdness', as well as his passion for fine clothes and good food. He 'feared boredom, loved his dogs . . . and pretty women, abhorred marriage but constantly talked of it', and 'bumped all over Europe' in the meantime. Charlecote was ruled by a triumvirate of which Lancelot needed to be aware. George Lucy was good friends with the Dowager Countess of Coventry, widow of the 2nd Earl. Born Lady Anne Somerset at Badminton, she was in her seventies and lived in a tall house at Snitterfield, just north of Stratford. San Miller's poetical friend Richard Jago was curate at Snitterfield and was also her good friend. The Dowager Countess had had a sad life, her only son having died at Eton when he was nine, and she had long been estranged from the Coventrys at Croome (although Miller's friend George William Coventry, soon to be Lancelot's 6th Earl, was to amend the connection). The Dowager Countess 'did not think it was necessary for Mr Lucy to take so irrevocable a step as marrying to solve his servant problems', so she had found 'an excellent widow', Mrs Philippa Hayes, to come and live at Charlecote as Housekeeper. Mrs Hayes was the proverbial treasure, who ruled benignly whether her master was at home or not, and noted everything down in her Memorandum Book. It was Mrs Hayes who had requested the Batoni portrait; Mrs Hayes who relayed all the Charlecote news when George Lucy was on his travels; Mrs Hayes who dispensed the Cheltenham waters that he sent home for dosing the household; Mrs Hayes who welcomed weather-bound travellers, who chased the rats out of the upstairs bedchambers, who was passionately fond of her poultry – 'Fowls from the Tenants' and 'Fish taken out of the Old Canal' being essentials to their diet. Fortunately both the Dowager and Mrs Hayes took to Lancelot, who found enough encouragement on this first visit to make up his mind to return.

He found that Warwick was full of masons and carpenters who worked for the Smith firm; Francis Smith was a legend in the town for his part in the rebuilding after a great fire in 1694, and the building was continuing, notably the new Shire Hall to San Miller's design. Mr Collins, 'the best stone-carver' in Warwick, worked in Smith's Marble and Stone Yard in Theatre Street, a base for all the building gossip of the Midland shires. Warwick held another of the benevolent ghosts of Lancelot's career, that of the old royal gardener to Queen Anne and George I, Henry Wise, whose family remained at Warwick Priory, though he had now been dead for a dozen years. Very much alive was the enthusiastic 'little Brooke', Lord Brooke at the Castle, who wanted to naturalise his river bank and almost immediately set Lancelot to work, at least according to Horace Walpole in a letter written on 22nd July 1751:

The view [of the Castle] pleased me more than I can express; the river Avon tumbles down a cascade at the foot of it. It is well laid out by one Brown who has set upon a few ideas of Kent and Mr Southcote. One sees what the prevalence of taste does; little Brooke who would have chuckled to have been born in an age of clipt hedges and cockle-shell avenues, has submitted to let his garden and park be natural.

And so the greatest gossip of the age had discovered Lancelot Brown.

Packington and Croome

Packington was another 18 miles north via Kenilworth, but San Miller had enthused about the ambitions of Lord Guernsey (later the 3rd Earl of Aylesford). The park was enormous and undulating, well watered by tributaries of the River Blythe, and with remnants of ancient ponds; his lordship wanted a lake – perhaps lakes – with cascades, and he also wanted sport and profit, with a duck decoy and ponds for rearing fish, which he intended selling on the London markets. This was Lancelot's introduction to the commercial advantages of lake-making; Lord Guernsey's ideas were undoubtedly drawn from his relative's, Charles Jennens's (Handel's librettist for *Belshazzar* and *Messiah*), Gopsall in Leicestershire.

At Gopsall, John Grundy the Younger had recently (1749) planned a dam and cascade 300 yards long to contain a Great Pond, for fish-keeping purposes. This was a pioneering cement-cored dam construction, of some significance in the progress of water engineering. Whether Lancelot visited Gopsall is not known, but he came to some conclusions for Packington, sketching his ideas on the reverse of his sketch plan for Charlecote, and leaving it at Packington for Lord Guernsey's consideration. (Though Lancelot returned the following year (1751), the extent of his work is unclear; Packington is still owned by the Aylesford family, and the land-scape features extensive fishing lakes on a far larger scale than anything he designed.)

It was a good day's ride back through Warwick to Stratford, and a night stop, before taking the Alcester road. He noted Ragley Park, for these places were the geography of his life now, but had another hard day's journeying to Croome. The obvious way for a stranger to avoid the hazards of this watery land was to head for Evesham and take the Pershore road westwards, keeping the long shoulder of Bredon Hill on the left-hand horizon, then south from Pershore, crossing Defford bridge and so into the Croome estate. This eastern approach led him directly to the vast walled gardens, where he found direction; emerging through the gate in the wall, the whole western view to the distant Malverns was spread out before him, across a wide and wet plain divided into large fields and an area called 'Seggy Meer Common' ('seggy' meaning soggy). To the left the house nestled beside the church, with the remnants of formal courts and gardens at front and rear. It was, or could be, a splendid scene, but the air was tinged with sadness, which Sanderson Miller would have explained. The Coventry family had come through a time of rifts, and the 5th Earl and his wife Elizabeth Allen had inherited Croome from a distant cousin in 1719; although they spent more time in London, the 5th Earl had conscientiously improved his estate, looking forward to the time when his heir, Thomas Henry, Viscount Deerhurst, would take it over. Thomas Henry (born in 1721) and his brother George William (born in 1722) were like twins, inseparable through school and at Oxford, where they played leading roles in Sanderson Miller's 'warmhearted crew' of friends. Their mother, the Countess Elizabeth, had died in 1738; and then, unaccountably, Thomas Henry, Lord Deerhurst, died on 20th May 1744 – 'unhappy, Black day' – at the age of twenty-three. The Earl was never to recover from these blows. He had no heart for Croome and stayed in London, and in 1748 had settled the estate on his second son, George William, who still struggled with the loss of his brother:

I am so shocked that I know not what I say or do. If I could be severed into two and one part left alive and the other part taken away, the separation could not be greater. He was indeed the better half and therefore God thought fit the worthiest should be removed . . .

His friends encouraged George William to find solace in planting and directing the waters, which he had begun to do. 'Lord Deerhurst has conducted his river well,' Edward Turner of Ambrosden reported after a visit in 1748; but all too soon George William was losing heart. He could find no peace, and blamed his house: 'it has always been an Inn and always must remain so,' he grumbled to Miller in February 1750 when asking him to plan a retreat-house; 'the hospitality of my Ancestors exercised for some generations at Croomb [sic] makes it impossible for me to effect any privacy or retirement'. He wanted to build his retreat on Spring Hill, near Broadway, which was the farthest eastern extent of the enormous 14,000-acre estate. In March, Miller noted that he had started 'drawing a plan for lord D', but neither plans nor urgencies were Miller's forte; he knew it was not only Spring Hill, but that the rather frantic George William wanted major alterations to Croome itself – a new church and ornamental buildings, and a new, naturalistic landscape. Hence Miller's motive in sending Lancelot. Quite what Lancelot thought when George William asked him to take on these major architectural projects can only be imagined. He made one request, that his lordship have the park area surveyed and mapped by a professional surveyor (it was to be John Doherty), ready for his return.

Then Lancelot headed for home. His timetable had fitted into some fifteen days and he was back at Stowe before the end of August.

Kirtlington and Wakefield Lawn

In that autumn of 1750 or early in 1751, whilst still living at Stowe, he had two local jobs. Kirtlington was a ride of about 20 miles from Stowe westwards to the Oxfordshire border, and it belonged to the corpulent Tory baronet, Sir James Dashwood. His house, on the same generous lines, had been built by the 'Palladian' Smiths of Warwick, with some involvement by both Daniel Garrett and James Gibbs. Sir James had commissioned a plan for his park from George II's gardener, the elder Thomas Greening, who seems to have relied entirely upon Switzer and showed the house surrounded by woodland with 'wiggley paths and small clearings'.

Greening's approach was not entirely wrong, for the glories of the park were the plantations of great oaks dating from the fifteenth century.

Much less appealing was the flat ground. Sir James had sited his house upon the only hill, so that any appropriately grand view merely drained away into the misty distances. An afternoon spent patiently riding to and fro, examining the ground for an area where a lake could be excavated and a hill raised for a pair of lake pavilions à la Stowe, was the only hope. Lancelot was at Kirtlington several times during the 1750s, but the surest evidence is that Greening's plan was marked 'totally changed by Brown'. (The park has now been extensively redesigned into a spacious golf course.)

(Sir James Dashwood was cousin to Sir Francis Dashwood at West Wycombe, which invites speculation. In 1750 Sir Francis was forty-two, wealthy and well travelled, and lavishing his money and taste on West Wycombe house and grounds, for which he had a survey prepared by Louis Jolivet in 1751. Could the survey have been prepared for Lancelot? West Wycombe would have seemed a natural move from Stowe in terms of opportunity, except that Sir Francis was setting out to ridicule Stowe by exaggerating its carnal conceits into features of his own, the swan-shaped lake recalling Leda and her fate, and various mounds aping parts of the female anatomy. Lancelot's circle of acquaintance became very large, but an intriguing number – Bubb Dodington (later Lord Melcombe), Sir John Aubrey, John Montagu, 4th Earl of Sandwich, Charles Churchill, Edward Lovibond, and even the Earl of Bute – are names entangled with the shadowy doings of the Medmenham 'friars'. Among her very last words, Dorothy Stroud records that Thomas Cook, 'whose peculiar skill and taste is exemplified in the happy disposition of the pleasure grounds at West Wycombe', was one of Lancelot's assistants and 'pupils'. Cook worked for Lord Despencer, as Sir Francis Dashwood became, from the late 1760s until Despencer's death in 1781, when he left Cook an annuity.)

Wakefield Lawn was Stowe's neighbour to the east, a hunting lodge belonging to Charles Fitzroy, 2nd Duke of Grafton, whose principal estate was at Euston Hall in Suffolk. For Lancelot, this was a useful connection; for us, it offers a vignette of him at work.

The 'lawn' was a clearing, or park, of 245 acres surrounded by the plantations of Whittlewood Forest; the ducal entrance (Lancelot came in by the back door from Stowe) was from the east, from Watling Street at Potterspury, and the track continued along the side of the hill before taking a sharp left bend and dropping down to cross a stream, and then a sharp right to climb again to the old lodge on rising ground. The lodge entrance was into a long court lined with stables, to house a great many horses, which seemed to have almost equal comforts to the guests in the sixteen heated rooms. The views were to the north, across water to the grazed 'lawn' and woods, the scenes of the chase. The water, called the Great Pond, appears to be spring-fed, the source of a stream that falls eastwards, eventually joining the Great Ouse river. Lancelot's task was to dam the Great Pond, with a cascade into a lower, smaller lake – the dam to carry the road across, between the two pieces of water, to the lodge.

In a way the job at Wakefield was a gift from the grave; the old lodge was being extended to the designs that William Kent had made for the duke several years earlier. Kent had been unwell for several years and died miserably, 'of a Mortification in his bowels and feet', on 12th April 1748, aged sixty-three. But for his death, Wakefield Lawn would have had a version of the Elysian Fields: a drawing by Kent survives at Chatsworth showing an imposing Euston-like house on a hillside, with foreground water in a rocky gulch presided over by a lounging river god and a startled dog, which has the look of Wakefield. The 'dog' is not well drawn and could be a fox, or even Kent's idea of a badger – both fox and badger, the favourite beasts of the chase, being carved life-size on the saloon chimneypiece.

The immaculately ruled, written and folded worksheets of the Duke's foreman John Wade, record the detailed labours of his workforce of thirty, including six women, in the January chill – 'moving the islands out of the great pond taking out the mud in some part of it'; there are trees to be removed from the overgrown pond, their roots prepared for 'fireing'; in some places the pond has to be deepened, in other parts widened. There is a great deal of 'faggoting of wood' and 'making fagots', which are presumably the brushwood foundation for the dam, or the lake edgings, as well as the waste-not, want-not economy of the woods, producing battens and pins for building and thatching. In between are the more general winter tasks: 'sowing turnips in the pheasantry', mole-catching, hay-carting, and working around the stables and garden. The labourers' names become familiar: Will Walls is always in the garden, at one shilling a day rate, with his assistant Luke Bruff and John Ludgate 'looking after the teem' of horses, both paid ninepence a day. The general rate is ninepence a day, sixpence for the women; they work six days, but sometimes on Sundays. These are the groundlings, literally mudlarks, who are making the overgrown pond into a respectable lake; beside them another team is building the earth dam, 80 feet wide at the bottom, 'calving' or sloping up to 25–30 feet wide at the top, carrying the roadway. The dam is 700 feet long (and the contour line indicates a depth of 25 feet). Lancelot was supervising the course of the road, construction of the dam and finishings of the lake, as well as the planting of clumps of trees on the lawn; the estate accounts show that he received 'nine payments, usually £50 or £100 each', totalling £707. 10s. over a period from December 1750 to May 1755, for both 'Work' and 'the water'.

But the immediacy of the scene comes from John Wade's neatly written 'Account of Labourers and Other Persons employ'd . . . in the Servis of his Grace' at Wakefield in June 1751; Will Walls, Luke Bruff and John Ludgate are at their usual tasks, and:

> Will Wale (a lowlier being) helping Thomas Haloway in the Stables. The other Labourers helping in ye Stables when the Duke was here Cuting a wash and faggoting of wood where *Mr Brown* wanted ye new Road. Mowing weeds, watering Trees. Making a new Road in Haymead . . . carrying hay from the Pheasantry . . . Cleaning out the Reek Yard, Loosening of Earth about new planted Trees, Honing and Rakeing the Gravill yards . . .

With a deal less mud in the June sunshine, amidst the bustle of the Duke's visit, the labourers are caught in time, as if painted by George Stubbs; the countryside is at work and foreman Wade and Lancelot are laying out the course of the new road.

Lancelot's great Midlands gallop of August 1750 had extended his education. The journey to Radway, on to Warwick and Packington, and across to Croome, had led him through yet more unfamiliar country, across the entirety of Warwickshire and into Worcestershire, with glimpses of the River Severn and the Malvern Hills. He had covered more than 200 miles. From Thenford Hill above Banbury, he had seen the Cherwell valley laid out as on a map, and from Edge Hill it seemed that half of England hovered in the mist. Had he realised, this young man most familiar with a corner of bony Northumberland and a small patch of Lincolnshire, just how large lowland England was at her broadest hips, and how full of rutted lanes and boggy hollows, and worse pitfalls for a lone man on a horse? Did he imagine he could tame her? Or, on a fine morning or in a golden sunset, did he appreciate just how delectable was Mistress England: a flowering of stone-built villages and summer gardens, set amidst great oak trees, and of willow-edged riverside pastures and fields of neatly stooked corn? Any sober, sane man must ask himself if it was possible, or even desirable, to improve on this happy countryside.

West Midlands gardeners talked less of Stowe and more of Hagley Park and The Leasowes. The Lytteltons' Hagley influenced Lord Deerhurst's ideas for Croome, though Hagley had the advantage of a much more dramatic setting on the edge of the Clent Hills, north of Kidderminster:

There along the Dale,
With Woods o'er hung, and shagg'd with mossy Rocks,
Whence on each hand the gushing Waters play,
And down the rough Cascade white-dashing fall,
Or gleam in lengthened Vista thro' the Trees.

Thus the popular poet (another northerner) James Thomson, who had revised *The Seasons* at Hagley, had imagined George Lyttelton 'courting the Muse' in his park, in 'Spring'. Close by, on the outskirts of Halesowen, was William Shenstone's modest *ferme ornée,* his grazing farm of 150 acres, with open fields and planted, watery valleys, which was both productive and beautiful on £300 a year. Shenstone's The Leasowes was much admired and talked of, though rarely with such insight as in this verse 'written at a *ferme ornée* near B[irmingham] 1749' by his friend Henrietta Luxborough:

'Tis Nature here bids pleasing scenes arise,
And wisely gives them Shenston[e] to revise;
To veil each blemish, brighten ev'ry grace;
Yet still preserve the lovely parent's face.
How well the Bard obeys, each object tells;
These lucid meads, gay lawns, and mossy cells;
Where modest Art in silence lurks conceal'd,
While Nature shines so gracefully reveal'd;
That She triumphant claims the total plan
And, with fresh pride, adopts the work of man.

Hagley and The Leasowes were too far north to be reached on this first trip, but the fame of both was so entwined in the fashion for improvement, which drove so many of Lancelot's clients' desires, that he surely saw them soon.

The Brown family's move from Stowe was finally fixed for the early summer of 1751; their new baby John, always to be known as Jack, was baptised in Stowe church on 23rd April.

George William Coventry had become the 6th Earl, fully in control of the Croome fortunes, and seemed likely to fulfil every young professional's dream of a patron who gave both employment and introductions to his friends. On another visit, armed with John Doherty's survey of the whole area north and west of the house, Lancelot had given a visionary performance from the eastern hill, describing how the 'grave young lord's' artificial river would be extended on a romantic course through the whole scene; how the bowl-effect of the park would be emphasised by plantings around the rim; and how − if the new church were positioned on this very hill − his lordship's friends and relations would be presented with the whole glorious prospect upon leaving the west door on Sunday mornings. That his lordship wanted his house to have the look of Inigo Jones, for whom his ancestor, the 2nd Baron Coventry, had conceived a great admiration during the development of Covent Garden, was something that required thought.

The prospects of Croome, Charlecote, Warwick, Packington, Kirtlington, Wakefield Lawn, perhaps West Wycombe, and the promise of work for Lord Dacre at Belhus in Essex − these were enough security for Lancelot to venture on his independent career. He and Biddy packed up their belongings and said goodbye to their home in the Boycott Pavilion; never again would they have such a romantic building to live in, but they had truly outgrown it. They set out southwards; for all Stowe's faults and frustrations, they were leaving the enchanted garden, apparently never to return.

5

HAMMERSMITH, A STAGE
FOR MR BROWN

Which way, Amanda, shall we bend our course?
The choice perplexes. Wherefore should we choose?
. . . Say, shall we wind
Along the streams? Or walk the smiling mead?
Or court the forest glades? Or wander wild
Among the waving harvests? Or ascend,
While radiant Summer opens all its pride,
Thy hill, delightful Shene? . . .
Slow let us trace the matchless vale of Thames . . .

James Thomson, 'Summer', *The Seasons*, 1727

THE BROWNS WERE BOUND FOR Hammersmith in the summer of 1751. And why on earth Hammersmith? The practical answer is that someone, probably kind George Lucy of Charlecote, offered them a house for rent. The Lucys had a long connection with Hammersmith, had given land for the churchyard to St Paul's church, and still owned a house nearby. The Browns' house was on the Mall, facing the Thames, and it is hardly less significant to add that the lake-like qualities of the river, gazed upon in that first quiet dawn, captivated Lancelot – the Thames, flowing serenely, reflecting sailboats and trees, with softly shelving green banks that made it easy for horses to drink and boys to bathe; the Thames, curving graciously away into the distance or divided by a leafy eyot (or island), was immediately printed upon his mind's eye as the ideal 'river-stile' and serpentine water.

Hammersmith was a village of picturesque squalor, very pretty in the sunshine, and part of that celebrated riverscape that Daniel Defoe had declared 'surpassed anything that Danube, Seine or Po could muster'. Defoe had given James Thomson his cue, with praises of the 'distant glories' displayed from Ham and Hampton Court, Richmond, Syon, Kew

Hammersmith, J. Oliphant's view, c.1750, showing the riverside community where the Brown family lived from 1751–64. The houses in the Mall are shown in the middle distance.

and Chiswick, downstream to Fulham and Chelsea, Battersea and Lambeth and thence to Somerset House in the Strand, 'for one fine house that was to be seen then, there are a hundred; nay, for ought I know, five hundred to be seen now, even as you sit still in a boat'. Though Hammersmith is missing from his list, being more of a working village, Defoe goes on to explain why an ambitious gardener should be there, for 'the river sides are full of villages and those villages so full of beautiful buildings, charming gardens and rich habitations of gentlemen of quality' – the very seat of 'the strange passion for fine gardens which has so commendably possessed the English gentlemen of late years'.

Hammersmith was a companionable mix of houses and cottages cheek by jowl with nursery gardens, boatmen's cottages, sail-maker's yards and fields of lettuces and lavender. A modest community, it formed one 'side' of the parish of Fulham, between the third and fourth mile from Hyde Park Corner on the Kensington turnpike, and on the north bank of the Thames's great sweep between Chiswick, 'the cheese farm', and Fulham, residence of the Bishops of London. The Malls, lower and upper, were separated from one another by the Creek, a picturesque inlet spanned by a wooden bridge – the High Bridge. At the bridge four old footways converged, the Lower Mall and Aspen Place, the Upper Mall and Bridge Street. Lancelot's letters were addressed simply to 'The Mall'; the Browns most probably lived in one of the tall seventeenth-century houses that once stood beside the river, but the records that show the rates paid on these houses have been lost.

Hammersmith was ripe for business. Gardeners' gossip told Lancelot of the best nurseries, and of good men looking for work, and where to locate the help that he needed. If only for nostalgia's sake, it was but a short ride to the great Brompton nursery of South Kensington, once the home of ten million plants, which had supplied trees by the hundreds for Blenheim, and equal quantities of apples and pears, mulberries and peaches to Woburn, without any hint of panic. Their roles here as nurserymen had supported the careers of the legendary old formalists, George London and Henry Wise. Stephen Switzer, who described himself as 'Gardener, Several Years Servant to Mr London and Mr Wise', had admired both of them, and had inherited some of London's northern clients. Henry Wise, a steady bachelor-gardener of forty-two when he married the daughter of a Royal Master Carpenter, Patience Bankes, found himself with the all-powerful Office of Works' entrée into royal gardens, as well as a wife who supported him through another forty years – toasted rhubarb being a favourite remedy when he returned from long wet rides from Chatsworth or Longleat.

Lancelot's Biddy was capable of all the comforts (even toasted rhubarb, though that had gone out of fashion), but she had her hands full with their growing family. She may have written up Lancelot's accounts when there was no one else to do so, but she would not be emulating the childless Patience Wise in answering letters, directing work and placating angry clients in her husband's absences. Charles Bridgeman, successor to Wise as royal gardener, had found he needed other enterprises – he owned the famous Bell Inn at Stilton on the Great North Road – to support his travelling consultancy. Indeed, designing alone seemed a perilous living, even for a great architect; 'when Vanbrugh could hardly afford to pay for his mother's funeral, Wise was retiring to Warwick Priory, leaving £200,000 at his death'. Rich or poor, these were Lancelot's predecessors, his inescapable ghosts, from whom he asserted his right to practise on his own terms, and without running a nursery.

Lancelot had to find nurseries that would suit him now: Robert Furber's fashionable nursery was in Kensington Gore; Furber was nearing retirement (he died in 1756), and so Lancelot made the aquaintance of his assistant and heir, John Williamson, from whom he was soon ordering flowering shrubs. This connection brought him an introduction to Philip Miller, curator of the Chelsea Physic Garden, whose influence was extensively weblike, and his *Gardener's Dictionary* (1732) in accruing editions had biblical status. Furber and Williamson also had close connections with the Gray nursery of Fulham, where Lancelot found a treasure trove of his favourite cedar of Lebanon, which became his signature tree. These were a speciality 'because they are the most beautiful of the evergreen

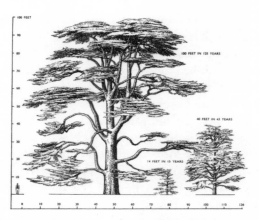

A cedar of Lebanon (*Cedrus libani*): the tree that Lancelot 'discovered' being propagated at Gray's Nursery in Fulham, and which became his signature tree.

race, and because they are the dearest; half a guinea apiece in baskets', in the opinion of the fastidious Horace Walpole. Christopher Gray advertised 'a greater Variety of Trees, Shrubs, Plants and Flowers cultivated in [the] nursery, than can perhaps be found in any other Garden for sale, not only in England, but also in any Part of Europe'. There were also 'scarce' arbutus 'at a crown apiece, but they are very beautiful' (not so the *Lignum vitae*, which 'stink abominably if you touch them and never make a handsome tree') and, as Walpole explained in a letter to George Montagu, 'cypresses in pots at half a crown apiece – [if] you turn them out of the pot with all their mould they never fail!'

With Williamson's and Gray's acquaintance, Lancelot made contact with the elite fellowship of Bartram's Boxes, a private trade in seeds and plants organised by a prosperous Quaker haberdasher in the City of London, Peter Collinson, and by the Pennsylvanian and Quaker farmer and botanist, John Bartram. Bartram would go botanising after his harvest was in, collecting seeds and seedlings, which were boxed and shipped with masters already carrying cargoes for the Collinson textile business. This box-scheme had been working for ten years, the packing and protection of seeds and plants in moss had been patiently mastered, and Collinson's effective organisation made sure that the boxes arrived safely, the plants 'as fresh and Lively as if that Minute taken out of the Woods'. From his office in the City, Collinson distributed the box contents, or a whole box, to his eagerly awaiting customers. He was shy of naming these, but there were about sixty: they included members of the royal family, Lords Bute and Petre, the owners of Longleat, Blenheim and Syon (all these were Lancelot's clients) as well as the participating nurseries: Williamson's, Gray's, John

Bush at Isleworth, James Gordon of Mile End and James Wood at Huntingdon. As Mark Laird has explained, this was the organisation responsible for the popularity of American plants, a craze that now soared to 'almost manic activity, rather as tulips had done one hundred years before'. Everyone wanted the colourful maples, thorns, robinias, ailanthus, red oaks, tulip trees and cornus, and Lancelot soon learned to use them.

Christopher Gray had the commercial coup of being able to propagate from the American plants growing in the garden of Fulham Palace. These were the first from the colonies, sent home to Bishop Henry Compton by his priestly collectors some fifty years earlier: the first *Magnolia virginiana* was shipped in a collection from Governor Nicholson of Virginia in 1698 for 'yr Lordsps paradise at Fulham'. Lancelot was able to explore this 'paradise', seeing for the first time 'the black Virginian walnut-tree, the cluster-pine, the honey-locust, the pseudoacacia, the ash-maple' and the curious cork-oak.*

The Thames was the life-blood of Hammersmith, the reason for its prized accessibility. The surrounding fields were fast converting from arable to strawberries, lavender and lettuces, as well as fruit and nursery stock to serve the London markets. The Thames was their supply route, as *The Spectator* had so delightfully discovered one fine August dawn when he 'fell in with a Fleet of Gardiners bound for the several Market-ports of London' – a cheerful crowd that amassed 'Ten Sail of Apricock Boats' at Somerset House landing stage. Grapes were grown in Hammersmith, and it was actually a rule of the parish workhouse that all spare land should be devoted to vines and the wine sold for its upkeep; the very name 'Vine' was a popular street and house name, as in Lee and Kennedy's Vineyard Nursery on Hammersmith's eastern boundary (the site of Olympia). Here, in James Lee, a fuchsia-mad botanist, and Lewis Kennedy (both in their thirties) Lancelot found contemporaries of consequence. West from Hammersmith was the nursery run by Henry Woodman at Strand on the Green, who traded by sea to William Joyce in Gateshead, and who had so derided Switzer for not growing his own plants. The now ageing and respected Woodman (who died in 1758) was also a past master at packing nursery stock plants for safe journeying, an unsung but necessary skill, explained by Thomas Hitt in his *A Treatise of Fruit-Trees*, of 1755.

---

* Bishop Terrick, vicar of Twickenham, became Bishop of London in 1764; he employed Stiff Leadbetter, surveyor to St Paul's Cathedral, to build 'Strawberry Hill' Gothic additions to the palace, and Bishop Terrick incorporated the exotic trees into a park, with meandering walks through orchard and meadows; he apparently wanted to 'employ' the Thames as his 'water' effect, but a moat and public right of way along the river bank prevented this. Fulham Palace garden, with its stately cedars of Lebanon, has always been remarked upon as being in the Brown style – was it not possible that the Bishop asked Lancelot's advice?

These were practicalities resolved, resources should he need them: in addition, two seeming gifts of fate confirmed the happiness of choosing Hammersmith. Lancelot discovered that nearby Twickenham was the home of Joshua Spyers or Spires, a respected churchwarden and 'draftsman', so described in 1749, who also supplied trees to Walpole for Strawberry Hill, and to whom Walpole paid two guineas for a survey of his Strawberry Hill estate. Joshua seems to have been near the end of his days, but his son, Jonathan, an accomplished artist, surveyor and plan-maker, shortly became Lancelot's most-valued travelling surveyor. He paid Jonathan Spyers for each survey and plan as it was accomplished, the fee varying according to the acreage surveyed and allowing for travelling and board expenses. Spyers's usual fee was £56. Lancelot also found his foremen from a pool of freelance travelling gardeners, with either surveying or nursery experience, who made good livings by being based in Hammersmith, part of the close professional networking. At this early stage of his career he was essentially on his own, with no permanent assistant; each workforce was controlled and paid by the foreman, and was drawn either from estate labour or directly from the locality.

The other 'discovery', whether made through a trip to Gray's Nursery or a visit to Fulham Palace, or through churchgoing – for All Saints at Fulham was the mother-church of Hammersmith's St Paul's – was the builder Henry Holland. Henry and Mary Holland had a house in Church Row, Fulham; he was a churchwarden at All Saints and they had a family of whom the eldest Margaret was nine, followed by Ann (seven), Henry junior (six), Mary (five), and Catherine was on the way. As families, the Hollands and Browns had much in common. In business terms, Henry Holland was a successful builder with a safe reputation, well regarded for his streets of town houses, especially in fast-developing Mayfair, and was apparently interested in extending into the country-house market. On the strength of Holland's promises, Lancelot decided that he could fulfil all of the Earl of Coventry's dreams and schemes for Croome.

The Croome decision made, and an immediate trip to Worcestershire planned, Lancelot then heard that George and Elizabeth Grenville at Wotton Underwood had given him a recommendation to her brother, Lord Egremont at Petworth House in Sussex. In late 1751, with the family all settled in the Mall house, Lancelot galloped off down the Portsmouth road into yet another county that was completely new to him, and within sight of Petersfield he turned eastwards onto the old road that follows the River Rother to Midhurst and Petworth. Petworth, he rejoiced, was to be a 'park' job, with the hope of a lake. But first he must tackle Croome.

Croome, 'the dusky Vale folorn'

Of his sculptural materials – earth, trees and water – Lancelot had the most fun with water. Water, given space, clearly enjoys itself, fresh river water tumbling in spate, ousted by the flood from its accustomed bed and running wildly like a naughty child, careering across fields, making bubbly, translucent cascades where it falls into a rut, and then curling and dancing its way by the shortest route back to the mother river. There was plenty of water to watch at Croome in the wet West Country, positioned as it was between two gentle hills which spawned the streams that fed the great rivers, the Severn to the west and the Avon to the east. Croome had always been wet and marshy, and Lancelot wondered why the Coventrys had put up with it since 1592, but habitation had bred their affection. Croome D'Abitot, the Elizabethan village by the church, had been named for Urso D'Abitot (D'Abetot), whom William the Conqueror had created hereditary Sheriff of Worcestershire (after his considerably violent progress across the country from the Sussex landings). In the sixteenth century the lawyer Thomas Coventry had bought that desirable Norman pedigree along with the open fields and pastures. Thomas Coventry had come from London with a fortune made by his kinsman John, a mercer and a friend of Mayor Richard Whittington.

Lancelot looked over Croome from the east hill; he looked down on a brick house of squarish proportions, of five bays and two projecting wings on the north front; the medieval church lay north-west of the house, and north and south of the house were the shadows of the extensive courts of seventeenth-century Croome, and the ghosts of onceglorious gardens. The Earl of Coventry's new, but rather short 'river' ambled across the scene from north to south, and from his eyrie Lancelot worked out the lines of the land drains that would channel surplus waters to fill a lake, and a longer 'river' flowing past the house to the south boundary of the park, where the holding dam would be built. The underlying geology was complicated – patches of clay of differing stickinesses overlaid with gravels – and so his careful planning of the drain lines was vital; some of these are 1½ miles in length, with a fall of perhaps 6 inches, others are dug as much as 8 feet down. The drain runs are sometimes of rubble limestone, and the larger drains and culverts are of brick (this is traditional technology that would be familiar to local labourers, for the pottery-tile drain did not come into use until later in the eighteenth century). The materials undoubtedly came from the courtyard walls that had been cleared, and the demolition of the old church. The Earl wanted a green landscape flowing around his house and decreed that the church

should be moved; perhaps it was Lancelot who suggested that the new
one could be built on the east hill to attract the eye from many points
around the park and the house's north-facing windows.

Sanderson Miller was still in close attendance, as no doubt Lancelot
wished (as he was soon to wish for Miller's advice at Burghley). The Earl
wrote to Miller saying, 'Whatever merits it may in future time boast it
will be ungrateful not to acknowledge you the primary Author' of Croome.
This in no way contradicts his frequent praise of Lancelot as the efful-
gent tamer of the 'morass', but it may explain how the three of them
came to decide upon the treatment for the house. Croome Court was
to be rebuilt on the foundations of the existing house, which lacked
length and presence. The new house at Hagley, so much admired by both
San Miller and George William Coventry, was being discussed and designed
by Miller, with detailed plans and elevations drawn by John Chute, a
sociable and talented amateur of the family at The Vyne near Basingstoke.
Chute's Hagley was a distinctive house, with four fronts of freestone, and
a tower at each corner rising higher than the main building. The strong
similarity between Hagley and the new Croome cannot be missed;
Hagley's 'Italian House', reminiscent also of Inigo Jones's work at Wilton,
was a combination of tastes that the Earl of Coventry could not resist.

The 'Hagley design' meant adding the four towers to the existing foot-
ings at Croome, giving the house the desired additional bulk and presence; while the 'Wilton effect' − the way Wilton is set low − made a
virtue of Croome's lowness. Lancelot, ever the perfectionist when it came
to understanding new concepts, and in need of physical confirmation of
the proportions, seems to have visited Wilton in early 1753. His visually
retentive memory was clear and accurate, and with measurements and
perhaps a trace from a drawing, he would have provided enough information for the builders' estimates, which almost entirely depended upon
a unit price multiplied out, with the 'near-guess' of experience for bulk
supplies, such as sand and lime. It was customary for the master masons,
master carpenters and other tradesmen to render their own estimates.
They were invariably supplied with only a 'draft' of the look of the
building, and made their own measured drawings for unusual details, such
as a string course or cornice moulding, and possibly for the Venetian
windows that were a feature of Wilton and Croome.

At Croome the old house was dismantled, leaving the centrally hori-
zontal chimney-range intact, and then built up again on the extended
plan, with the addition of the corner towers. Like (the much-better documented) Smiths' of Warwick, Holland's worked in the traditions passed
down from the medieval guilds, relying on the interlocking competences

of masons and carpenters. Each had his own patterns and experience, but after that 'much of the "designing" remained empirical, with details worked out, as building progressed', as Francis Smith's biographer Andor Gomme writes of the firm's craftsmen. Their materials – timber, brick and stone – had changed not at all, and even with the Palladian innovations the principles remained the same, and 'new classical mouldings were interpreted only as surface variations on structural techniques which had barely changed during the past six hundred years'. The purists' disdain for Palladianism was because they saw it as purely 'façade-ism'. Lancelot's experience as Clerk of Works at Stowe had equipped him well to manage both men and supplies, and he had mastered knowledge of the new architectural detailing. Proof that he was competent and likeable would seem to come from the fact that three master craftsmen who worked at Croome, each with his own team of labour – William Eltonhead the bricklayer, Robert Newman the mason, and John Hobcroft the carpenter – are all found working with him on many later commissions. Benjamin Read, who worked as his landscape foreman at Croome, was to work on Lancelot's largest and most important landscapes for the next twenty years.

Lancelot has been called the 'architect' of Croome, and in the subsidiary meaning of 'a person who brings about a specified thing', then of course he was; he was the visionary who saw the whole landscape *and the buildings in the landscape*, and he possessed the practical abilities to bring vision and ideas into existence. He was undoubtedly happier out in his park than on the building site. At Croome, it was in fact the house rebuilding that kept him there for long visits, but when the builders were busy he had time to examine the falls of the ground painstakingly and work out his drainage lines. Drainage was of critical importance to Croome, but it was also his opportunity to perfect vital skills. Thus Lord Coventry's appreciation that the beauty and comforts of his home derived almost entirely from its being lifted out of a 'morass' were just. That he called the green-clad and tall figure his 'architect', as he watched him moving across the meadows with his notebook and an assistant wielding the pedometer (the wheeled instrument for measuring distances), was entirely apt. Lancelot was working in the tradition of Henry Wise, Charles Bridgeman and William Kent, but it was a slim tradition and few understood his aims: measuring and mathematics were obvious preliminaries to building, but why would one want to measure grass? For the time being, and for Lancelot, there was no named role between the architect and that of the gardener – the latter firmly bedded down with the lettuces and pineapples.

Lancelot knew he was not an architect; he had not made the obligatory pilgrimage to Italy, nor studied at the feet of a drawing master. In

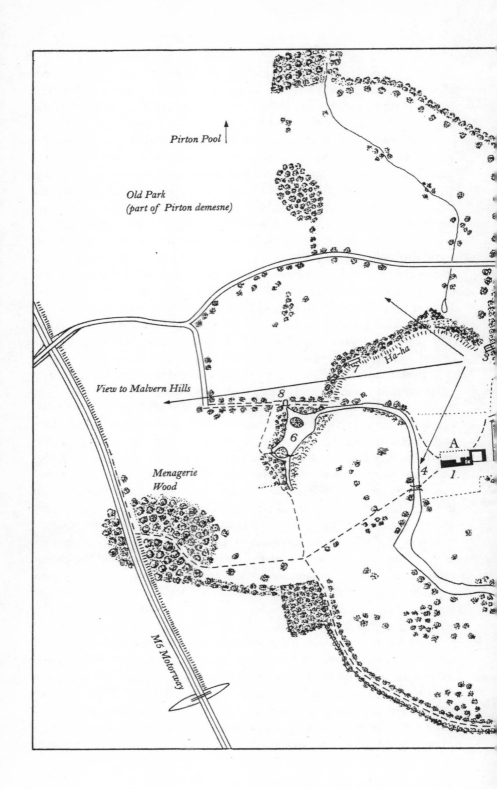

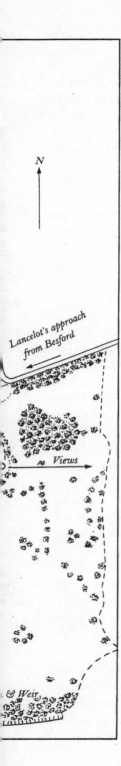

N

Lancelot's approach from Besford

Views

& Weir

Croome Court. Layout plan explaining Lancelot's taming of the 'morass' mainly 1751–65 for the 6th Earl of Coventry:

1. The house, rebuilt and extended at both ends, and adjacent stable court built to plans by Smith of Warwick; (area A shows site of Croome d' Abitot old church and walled garden courts).
2. Walled kitchen garden, a centre of activity at the time.
3. New church of St Mary Magdalene, built on the eastern hill, the view point for Lancelot's approach to the layout.
4. 'Short river' begun prior to Lancelot's arrival, with white wooden 'Halfpenny' bridge.
5. River-style lake extended to southern boundary, with dam and sluice on the park boundary.
6. North extension of watercourse and new lake, with two islands.
7. Robert Adam's Temple Greenhouse, shrubbery of exotics protected by ha-ha from grazing meadow.
8. Lancelot's Grotto.
9. Lancelot's Rotunda, with distant views; adjacent Shrubbery-planting to shelter path to the Church (and Ice-house).

his day 'architect' was an appellation grasped by the well-born, like Lord Burlington and the 9th 'Architect Earl' of Pembroke, and by the 'amateur' Sanderson Miller, or rewarded to the outrageously talented, like James Gibbs, William Kent or Robert Adam. A mason's apprenticeship, as Hawksmoor had had with Wren, hardly existed and was almost exclusively managed by the all-powerful Office of Works. Lancelot's life so far has made it perfectly clear that none of the above apply.

So there he was, out in the soggy meadows at Croome, working out his professional identity. He had little wish to design houses or build them, but felt honour bound to have the buildings in the right places for the good of his effects, knowing that he had to deal with the buildings to win his park commissions.

Croome was a good 100 miles from Hammersmith; how many times Lancelot made that trip can only be imagined, with the building and the drainage to be supervised, and the site for the Earl's new house at Spring Hill outside Broadway to be visited on the way out or back. Events, or an event, had complicated matters, in that the sober, handsome, musical, but humourless George William, Lord Coventry, a Groom of the Bedchamber, had fallen violently in love with a Beauty. This was none other than Maria Gunning, the eldest of the four daughters of Colonel John Gunning of Castle Coole in County Fermanagh and his wife Bridget Bourke of Mayo (of a family of famous beauties). Mrs Gunning had brought Maria and her equally beautiful sister Elizabeth to London for the 1751 Season, allegedly hoping they would become actresses or duchesses: Elizabeth was swept off her feet by James, 6th Duke of Hamilton, and Maria and Lord Coventry were married in early March 1752. Maria was vivacious and outspoken, a continual embarrassment to the Earl although he adored her, and she produced a stream of children, including an heir. The Countess did not appreciate the countryside, for she was much more Hyde Park than Croome Park, but Croome worshipped her, and every kitchen maid and garden boy and farmer's wife for miles around came under her spell. Lancelot was probably not immune. The Coventrys became great celebrities, and though the Earl wrote to San Miller in 1756 to say that Croome 'was a good deal altered since you saw it', he meant the house rather than the park, where Lancelot's improvements were of a lesser priority.

Croome's first phase ended with the death of the Countess, at only twenty-eight, her last illness supposedly aggravated by the lead poisoning from her lavish use of cosmetics. She was buried on the Croome estate at Pirton, and it is said that a crowd of 10,000 people, an astounding number in this almost deserted landscape, came to say their farewells. For the Earl, the old wound of his brother's loss was reopened, and he was desolate; he wrote a poem of mourning:

> Her noble Partner 'midst his Mansion Mourns
> Now treads at [evening] the dusky vale folorn
> Like Philomela pouring Plaintive Tones
> At night's pale Moon upon her lonely Thorn.

Warwick, 'a few ideas of Kent and Mr Southcote'

Walpole's verdict of 1751 on his view of Warwick's 'enchanting' castle, and the River Avon's cascade, 'well laid out by one Brown who has set upon a few ideas of Kent and Mr Southcote', was that of a connoisseur and critic. Of course Lancelot had learned from Kent's work at Stowe, but it is unlikely that he visited Philip Southcote's *ferme ornée* at Wooburn in Surrey. The gentlemen-aesthetes, like Walpole, had their own circles of favourites, but Lancelot was not of that world, nor did he follow predictable paths; his response was to the particular 'genius' of the place where he worked.

His work at Warwick Castle is difficult for us to judge, partly because it was so overlaid by changes in the nineteenth and twentieth centuries, but also because the castle is marketed as 'Britain's Greatest Medieval Experience' by its owners, Merlin Entertainments, who purchased it from the Greville family in 1978. Of course, for the castle's well-being this is a very good thing, but there is a disjointure between the pervasive atmosphere of dastardly deeds in dark dungeons (with the added bloodthirstiness, ghosts and demons beloved of armies of visiting children) and the civilised and serene setting beside the Avon that Lancelot contrived. His work is much appreciated, albeit summed up in the castle guide by facile phrases: 'It may look natural, but the curved sweep of the lawns down from the castle to the river is man-made. Specially chosen trees and shrubs were planted to create a frame for the castle and the landscape. The courtyard was also raised by several feet to give it a more classically balanced look.' When a second's thought is given to the implications of 'softening' the slopes of an impregnable fortress and converting its vast, rubbish-strewn bailey into a svelte green court fit for an Oxbridge college, then the soubriquet 'Brown the Magician' is not idly applied.

Lord Brooke had grown used to the Smiths, first Francis and then his son William, as overseers retained for making alterations and answering his lordship's whims. There were similarities between the genial Francis Smith, 'our honest builder', and Lancelot: both unflappable and notable for their integrity, and for dealing with their aristocratic clients with a polished deference. Now the firm of Smiths was in the hands of the Hiorn brothers, whom Lancelot had already made his allies, differentiating his outdoor works from the builders' sphere, so that they most likely provided craftsmen for the Warwick work when needed.

When Horace Walpole looked over the Banbury-road bridge in the summer of 1751 and saw the old mill and cascade and the 'natural' setting of the south side of the castle, work was only just beginning. (This bridge was not moved eastwards to its present site until after Lancelot's day.) Lancelot was allocated a number of workmen, a team of horses and a four-wheeled box-wagon to accomplish these Herculean tasks. The dourness of the work can only be imagined, with one gang of men digging and stone-heaving on the outer slopes of the motte, or mound, and along the riverside, using the rubble to make up the ground of the bailey inside, every cartload bumping over the roughened ground, up and down the slopes endlessly. They worked in all weathers, perhaps allowed into the shelter of the bailey in the bitterest cold. The bailey, with the surface of a well-trampled field – grown on 500-year-old layers of rubbish and slops, with haphazard levels that necessitated changes in steps and doorways – had to be raised, levelled and harrowed for seeding with fine grasses. It would be nice to think of an August 'holiday' (the best time for seeding) with the ox-drawn harrow, the oxen wreathed in corn marigold and daisies for their entry into the castle, levelling the barrowed soil, followed by the men raking, and the women and girls gathering baskets of couch grass and other undesirables. Then the seed would be broadcast, 'the cleanest hayseed' mixed with Dutch clover, to await the hoped-for rains. On the south side of the castle the River Avon, which divided around the long Castle Meadow, had its banks shaved and grassed, and planted with trees, so that it assumed the semblance of a double linear lake.

The intermediate phase of work at Warwick was in the 'park' across the Avon. Here, amid soggy and frequently flooded meadows, some seventeenth-century tree planting – the ghost of a formal wilderness – remained. This area was bounded on the east by the Banbury road, which Lancelot screened with a belt of planting. His chief work was in the drainage and damming of the Ram brook, which came from Myton in the east, to make a linear lake controlled by a sluice and dam where it joined the River Avon, with a road over this dam to connect what were now the two parts of the park. A number of clumps of trees were planted to assist the drying-out of the meadows, though these did not always please: 'I have undone many of the things [Brown] left me as I thought looking formal in the planting way,' grumbled Lord Brooke; '[he was] ever making round clumps that merit nothing but being very tame indeed'. However, he did not remove them all, for Thomas Hinde has observed that 'the clumps, twenty-one trees in the shape of a filled-in oval are planted with geometric regularity, each tree with the name of a member of the family beside it'. In addition to the emerald slopes and lawns of the castle surroundings – 'I must say he hitt off the slip of the garden ground well,' Lord Brooke later conceded – Lancelot's chief memorials at Warwick are the cedars of Lebanon and evergreen oaks (*Quercus ilex*), some of his favourite trees, of a majesty to match the castle.

Lord Brooke came to regard Lancelot as 'his old friend Mr Brown'. The final task at Warwick, for which Lancelot issued a contract of works that was agreed, was nothing short of 'excavating' the castle's massive stone walls, to create a series of family rooms out of dark cells. Thomas Gray, a friend to Lancelot, but not necessarily to Lord Brooke, saw the result soon after its completion in 1754 and was waspishly censorious of 'a little burrough in the massy walls of the place for his little self and his children, which is hung with paper and printed linen, and carved chimney pieces in the exact manner of Berkl[e]y Square or Argyle Buildings' (in Bath). In other words, shockingly nouveau. We can judge for ourselves, for these rooms, as redecorated by Frances 'Daisy', Countess of Warwick in the 1890s, for entertaining the Prince of Wales, are shown to visitors as the setting for a royal weekend party with the Warwicks, the Duke and Duchess of Devonshire, Winston Churchill and his mother Jenny, Lady Randolph Churchill, Field Marshal Lord Roberts and Dame Clara Butt. The rooms, furniture and costumes are authentic – only the flesh is wax. We know they also had a launch, built by the Great Western Railway Company, for trips on the lake and along the Avon.

In the context of the 1750s, it does seem curious that Sanderson Miller and his friends were busily sprinkling rocky knolls with sham castles, while here at Warwick, Lancelot was redeeming the violent history of a real fortress whose warring days were done.

During 1752 the smell of success made Lancelot reckless. Each new commission was enthusiastically accepted and, though surely he had the image of England in his head now, it was only afterwards that he considered the geographical implications. After his first exhilarating inspection, each new job had to be programmed into the sequence of current works. Neither lords nor labourers, it seems, understood that his work was not finite, like building, and that deadlines so easily became lost in mud and mire. By now all his first jobs were up and running. Petworth Park, for which he had requested a survey on his visit the previous year, was a most tempting prospect, but like the fairground juggler, Lancelot already had a number of plates to keep in the air. A tour of inspection might take him to the ladies at Stoke Park, who deserved his attention, and Lady Cobham liked to hear of Biddy's and the children's welfare. He might drop in at Wotton Underwood to see the Grenvilles for the same reasons (George Grenville was now a Commissioner at the Treasury and rising fast), and at Wakefield Lawn to check on progress (he finished there in 1755). Twenty-five miles farther north along Watling Street, at Newnham Paddox, Lord Denbigh's lake edgings were greening up nicely and the plantations had taken well. His lordship was in funds again and now considered rebuilding his house in the image of the new Croome.

Thinking about this as he rode, Lancelot crossed another 20 miles of country north of Coventry to Packington. Here the new Hall Pool, made by linking the old fishponds, was filling into 'a dramatic long sheet of water', and the extents of the belts and clumps of trees needed staking out, which could well amount to two days' work. Turning south for home, Sir James Dashwood of Kirtlington had recently paid him £100, and depending upon the progress of the ha-ha and the plantations, Lancelot might be able to ask for more.

His stays at home were never long, for he was either dashing west-wards again to Croome or, as he had promised to visit Lord Coventry's and San Miller's friend, Lord Dacre at Belhus, might head in completely the opposite direction, 20 miles or so beyond West Ham and into Essex. Lord Dacre was part of the Oxford coterie united by gardening, and grief: he had begun energetically four years earlier, planting 200 elms, some in a grove behind his house, others on his newly made south lawn; he had ploughed up 60 acres around the house 'to clean it thoroughly and lay it down quite smooth and fine', to which end he was 'preparing a Dunghill of Chalk marsh earth and Dung as big as my house to spread all over it'.

The Dacres' happiness was completely destroyed when their nine-year-old daughter Barbara died in March 1749; Dacre's letters to Miller and their friends had previously been concerned with the new-found inoculation against smallpox, brought from Turkey by Lady Mary Wortley Montagu, but it is unclear whether her death was related to this. The Dacres retreated to Italy in their grief, and commissioned Pompeo Batoni for a triple portrait, as if Barbara was still with them. On returning to Belhus in 1751, Lord Dacre wanted Lancelot to help forward his gardening schemes and grew quite tetchy that he did not come. He was always of a worrying disposition, nervous of his mother's known Catholicism, of being able to manage his newly inherited Belhus efficiently, and Barbara's fate only exacerbated this. Lancelot became the butt of his stinging tongue, but eventually of his generous praise.

★   ★   ★

In the early spring of 1753 Lancelot was at Petworth House. He returned home in time to put in his order for shrubs and trees to John Williamson at Kensington Gore, and this first order is dated 11th April 1753. The contract for the first phase of work at Petworth is dated 1st May.

Petworth enchanted Lancelot from the start. For a change, his work was close to a town, and one with comfortable inns; the house, 'with its elbows to the town' as Defoe quaintly put it, was approached through severe and substantial courts and offices, and it was all the more rewarding to break out onto the garden side. Here, the 6th Duke of Somerset's house, built some sixty years earlier in all the splendour of the master-craftsman–architect tradition of French influence, presented its 320-foot-long, many-windowed west façade to the park. To the north were pleasure gardens, thought to have been designed for the Duke by the formalist George London, with terrace, walks and an orangery garden.

Petworth's new owner, Charles Wyndham, 2nd Earl of Egremont, had not expected his inheritance, and he enjoyed beautifying his house and his grounds. Lancelot's first contract was for work on the formal pleasure gardens, which he by no means destroyed, but rather refreshed. He proposed 'to reduce and shorten the terraces, giving the ground a natural form in order that it blended properly with the Park and the level in front of the House'. Apart from this shortening of the terraces, he worked within the existing geometry. He became a flower gardener, proposing drifts of flowering shrubs to frame and unite the shapes of outgrown formal spaces, or *cabinets* (for small 'rooms'), including an oval garden for bay trees, and the orangery garden, now devoted to aloes in pots. The bays, *Laurus nobilis,* and the *Aloe vera* were both Mediterranean imports at home in Petworth's seaborne airs, the first aromatic, the second fleshly elegant, and both rare enough for comment, when gathered in numbers.

A wilderness of birch trees with straight paths criss-crossing it, 'the Birchen walks', dating from the early seventeenth century, was restored and apparently extended, with the addition of serpentine walks edged with flowering shrubs. The wilderness was to be contained, and protected from the park, by a flamboyant segmental sweep of ha-ha, 'A Foss to keep out the Deer Etc.' – a design idea that Lancelot had tried at Kirtlington, but now applied with greater verve. His plant orders to John Williamson, 'to be Charged to the Earl of Egremont', were for dozens of shrub roses, jasmines, lilacs, tamarisks, thorns, honeysuckles and holly-hocks. He also ordered the American imports that he had so recently seen in Fulham: the brightly coloured maples, 'Virginia Shumach'; *Rubus odoratus*, 'Virginia Raspberry'; and cloudy 'Smoke bushes' (*Cotinus*) – all the very height of fashion.

Collapse, and retrenchment, 1753 (aged thirty-seven)

Within weeks of signing the Petworth contract, however, in the middle of this first stage of work there, Lancelot drove himself to exhaustion and collapse. This seems to have been much more than an asthmatic attack, for he was laid very low for several weeks: a severe chilling, the result of too many wet and cold journeys, developed into something much more serious, perhaps a painful and feverish pleurisy. There was no shortage of doctors in Hammersmith, for there were many prosperous patients; opium was the panacea, and bleeding the all-too-frequent medic's remedy. The authority of the day was still Sir John Floyer's *A Treatise of the Asthma* (1698), with its emphasis on the benefits of cold baths. It is most likely that Biddy's nursing saved him, with gentler warm bathing and fomentations, poultices and liberal doses of beef tea and barley gruel. Small amounts of Indian tea and coffee were then regarded as restoratives. Lancelot's legacy from this illness was the frequent and retching cough, and gasping for breath, of the asthmatic, but like Dr Johnson (who consulted Floyer's *Treatise* as late as 1784) he was philosophic – this was 'only occasional and unless it be excited by labour or cold, gives me no molestation, nor does it lay very close siege to life'. There were many popular remedies, and Lancelot became something of a connoisseur of 'pectoral' lozenges containing camphor, balm or liquorice, or other concoctions, which he kept close by him. The pleurisy was, though, serious; in the sporting parlance of the day, a near-run thing, and he knew that Biddy had saved his life. If she was not already so, his wife now became the one woman who excited him to emotional extremes in the cause of loving gratitude.

The River Thames played a part in his convalescence; as his breathing eased, he sat at the window gazing out on the placidly flowing river, a soothing presence. Then he progressed to dozing in the sun outdoors, lulled by the slop-slop of the tide and the drift of chatter from passing boats. Everything London needed passed by the Mall at Hammersmith: coal and cattle and sheep, timber and bales of cloth, as well as the gardeners with their strawberries and flowers. Lancelot's view was from the top of the river's great loop around Castelnau and Barnes; this was not a long reach, but the westering sun, beyond Chiswick eyot (more prominent at the Hammersmith end in those days), turned it into a river of gold. In sun or misty rain, and frankly sometimes stinking, the great wash of water, combing its green banks and shingly beaches, overhung with trees that guarded sequestered paths on the opposite side, instilled its presence into his soul. In the quiet of evenings, washed with a fresh breeze and a passing sailboat or a punt or two, the Thames appeared as an elegant lake.

He had, unusually, time for his immediate surroundings. It was an easy stroll along Chiswick Mall and through part of the village to Chiswick House. Previously, his loyalty to Stowe made Lancelot jealous of Chiswick's fame, but it was now Chiswick in decline, and worth investigation. The immediate surround of the villa, with elegant stemmed-up trees shading the vases, urns and statues, was protected by iron railings, but the park was accessible at will. He could wander along the paths that snaked through the wilderness, and along the river that had lost its 'canal' formality and become gradually more serpentine, until at the far end it widened into a beautiful lake, with a newly made cascade. And such a convalescence would end in a holiday, and a boat trip for all the family upriver to Kew, perhaps to a picnic on the Green; there Lancelot could gaze beyond the busy Brentford ferry and note how the Thames settled into lakelike sinuousities as it flowed past Princess Augusta's Kew Garden and, on the opposite bank, had all the appearance of a lake as the foreground to Syon House.

His strength regained, serious thoughts were in order. He owed it to Biddy, who was not used to penury and worry, to acknowledge the precarious nature of his living. Taking a percentage of costs did not work for him as it did for architects, for landscape costs were a fraction of those for building, and completion was much delayed. His need to collect his monies, invariably paid late – £50 here, £100 there, and not paid at all if he did not collect – was too precarious, hopelessly insecure. His situation paled in contrast to that of his brothers. John and Jane Brown and their young son Richard were comfortably established in their home, Whitridge, on the Kirkharle estate, and John had recently been appointed clerk, treasurer and surveyor to the Alemouth Turnpike Trust. He was also surveyor for the eastern end of the Military Road from Newcastle to Carlisle, as well as the Ponteland turnpike. John's fellow trustees, with whom he was ranked a 'Gentleman', included representatives of the Ridley, Allgood, Blackett, Grey and Errington families – proof of his successful establishment.

George Brown and his wife Catherine were almost as comfortably settled in their house in Cambo, where George was responsibly involved with many of Sir Walter Calverley Blackett's property and mining interests. They may have urged their younger brother to come home? There is some evidence too that Biddy's brother, John Wayet, tried to persuade them to go back to Boston – after an earthquake in August 1755 he proposed to the Town Council that Mr Brown of Hammersmith might be paid a fee to inspect some of the council properties.

Petworth House. Proposals carried out for 2nd Lord Egremont, from 1753:

1. Petworth House, and the church and town to the east.
2. Shelter planting along road to Guildford (A283).
3. The 17th century 'Birchen Walks' restored and enhanced, with serpentine paths and sweeping segmental ha-ha.
4. The first lake, now the Upper Pond; the south end of the lake has been foreshortened, presumably when the new line of the road to Tillington and Midhurst (A272) was made.
5. Lancelot's second lake, now the Lower Pond.

Against this background, Lancelot applied the more businesslike way of working that he was trying at Petworth, with written and agreed contracts. Works would be detailed, with agreed down-payments of £200–300 on the quarter-days, so that he could pay his men working on direct labour on the job money from the client, and keep his own share. For really long-term works, as at Croome, he should be paid an annual retainer, though at the moment he did not want to impose this upon Lord Coventry and appear ungrateful to a generous patron. It was now that he opened his account at Drummonds Bank in Charing Cross, and it seems he did a little job for Andrew Drummond for the privilege, making a pleasant journey of some 10 miles over the green hills of Middlesex to Drummond's house at Stanmore. 'Old Andrew' (he was in his mid-sixties), the founder of the bank, had bought his estate – distinguished by the artificial 'Belmount' with a summer house on the top – in his first prosperity in 1729. He lived there 'in great style which he could well afford', a stout and rubicund gentleman with his intelligent spaniel, as painted by Johann Zoffany in his park – of which he was soon to be 'very vain', having had it 'dressed up' by Mr Brown.

In 1753 Drummonds Bank was in Angell Court at Charing Cross, now the corner of Whitehall, and across the road from Northumberland House. The bank liked its lordly customers, but Andrew Drummond had a kindness for artists and craftsmen too: he was treasurer for St Martin-in-the-Fields and the bank had managed the financing of James Gibbs's great church, which is how Gibbs came to be a Drummonds customer. The painters Johann Zoffany and Giovanni Battista Cipriani, the cabinet-maker Thomas Chippendale whose work-shop was in St Martin's Lane, and Captain Thomas Coram's Foundling Hospital all transacted their business in Angell Court. For the boy from Kirkharle, it was something of an arrival, to be the possessor of a bank account, and to become at home in the convivial surround-ings of the coffee- and chop-houses, the booksellers, instrument-makers and wig-makers and other delights of the courts along the Strand and around Covent Garden.

News of Lancelot's illness had spread. 'I am sorry to hear of your indis-position by Lord Egremont,' wrote Admiral Lord Anson, in his bold sailorly scrawl, on 26th September 1753. 'I am going to Moor Park today and shall be there till Sunday. The next week I shall go down on Thursday and shall not return till Monday by which time I hope and wish you may think yourself well enough to let me see you.' The Admiral, George,

Baron Anson of Soberton, victor of the 1747 action at Cape Finisterre and hero of his famous ship *Centurion*'s four-year circumnavigation of the world (which had included saving the city of Canton from fire and capturing a Spanish treasure-galleon), was clearly a force to be reckoned with, and Lancelot surely found himself well enough.

Moor Park in south Hertfordshire was a 'white Palladian palace' by the Italian architect Giacomo Leoni, finished thirty years before: it stood on a spur with views to Cassiobury Park and Watford to the north, and southwards to Uxbridge, and in a park 4 miles round, crossed by avenues of mature elms and walnut trees. Charles Bridgeman had reworked (or replaced) the older gardens on two faces of the house into an embracing hexagonal terrace, holding a long canal surrounded by 'wilderness' plantings of evergreens and fruit trees. The nature of the original ground, and phrases such as 'a harsh, offensive termination' and a 'sharpness of the edge' – used in contemporary descriptions of Bridgeman's gardens – make it clear that the terrace was composed partly of made-up ground (the soil cut away and moved to fill up the new level), and therefore subject to instability. Fashion and necessity decreed that Moor Park's surroundings were returned to the 'natural' landform. Work started at Moor Park the following year, 1754, and it was to be a very expensive operation. Horace Walpole mentioned that the Admiral had paid £6,000 after six years, for what Walpole despised as 'so many artificial molehills', but what a more generous visitor Thomas Whateley (1770) called 'hillocks' – 'not diminutive in size and [made] considerable by the fine clumps which distinguish them'. More recently, Alice Buchan (whose maternal grandparents, the Grosvenors, owned Moor Park) recalled Lancelot's work as a 'dullish piece of Hertfordshire [transformed] into a very fair imitation of Italy'.*

In the October of 1753 Lancelot went to Belhus, where his very appearance convinced the doubting Thomas, Lord Dacre. 'Brown has been here', he wrote to San Miller, 'and by what I find has realy been very ill . . . and upon the whole I begin now to think that he has not grown too Great to despise my little Businesses. He attributed to many hindrances his being so long absent, and says I ought to remember that for two months in summer I myself was not here . . .' To make up, Lancelot 'slaved at setting out the road and the rest of the Shrubbery all day', talked over plans all evening, 'and was in the best humour imaginable. Of his own accord [he] promised to come again next month.'

---

* Lancelot paid Nathaniel Richmond £3,122 – of the £6,000 – between 1754 and 1759; Richmond lived at Rickmansworth and supervised the work at Moor Park. He was clearly capable and ambitious, and keen on his independence, though ready to work with Lancelot when required, as he did on Syon Park and Sion Hill.

'The alteration of Burleigh'

Two visits in two months were most unlikely; most clients were content with two visits a year. There is no record of what happened to the promise, but Belhus was not forgotten, although it was nearly a year later that Lord Dacre reported to San Miller, 'Brown went with me about a month ago to Belhouse [*sic*] in order to give me his opinion about some plantations.' 'He tells me,' Dacre added, 'that he has the alteration of Burleigh and that not only of the Park but of the house which wherever it is Gothick he intends to preserve in that Stile.' So, Lancelot entered upon his third great commission of these earliest years of his solo career: Croome, Petworth and now Burghley, where on his own admission he was to have 'twenty-five years pleasure in restoring the monument of a great minister to a great Queen'.

Susceptible to effects, which were his stock-in-trade, Lancelot may be permitted a gasp at his first sight of the Cecils' wondrous palace, the many-pinnacled and chimneyed Burghley, glowing in the afternoon sun. It was almost exactly 200 years old, the house that Queen Elizabeth's Mr Secretary Cecil had started to build in 1555. And now he, Lancelot Brown,

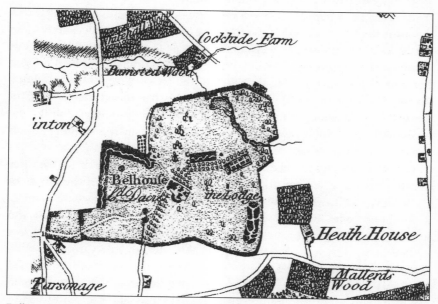

Belhus, Essex, extract from Chapman and Andre's *Map of Essex, 1777,* showing Lord Dacre's garden with the belts planted by Lancelot and the wet part of Bumstead meads where his lordship was eventually persuaded to make the lake. After many visits in the 1750s Lancelot gave up in exasperation, and Samuel Driver made Lady Dacre's flower gardens 1764–5, and Richard Woods completed the lake, 1770.

had the altering of it and its vast park – he may be further permitted a flutter of the heart and a sigh of anticipation, as he turned his horse to ride down into Stamford St Martin's.

He was already familiar with The George, at the foot of St Martin's Hill beside the River Welland, one of the most famous hostelries of the Great North Road. The George belonged to the Cecils, and much Burghley business was conducted there: it was one of 'the plums of the innkeeping trade', let with a 90-acre farm holding, which supplied meat and milk and the stables' needs for hay and fodder. One night at the inn, using his eyes and talking to the landlord Marmaduke Skurray, told Lancelot a great deal, especially about the Welland, which flowed by his window: the Welland, with a catchment area across half of England, and its tributary the Chater coming in from Rutland, just west of the town, sent torrents of muddy water pouring through Stamford in rainy seasons (as it still does). Next morning, depending on the mood of the river, Lancelot either rode along Water Street or climbed St Martin's hill directly, turning halfway up into the lane that ran along beside miles of Burghley's wall. He found the 'town' entrance into the park, and as he walked his horse eastwards realised that the benefit of the hill soon fell away. He came to the 'tipping point' – there was always a tipping point – the nodal from where his designer's eye assessed the scene, and realised that the great house actually sat (close to the 40-metre contours) perilously close to the water table of the Welland. It was all too evident: Burghley was surrounded by sparkling waters, by pools, basins and canals, and by the Great Pond on the south-east – all the result of the attempts of 200 years' labour 'to sett the house dry'. Generations of gardeners had found it 'sore work' in the beds, orchards and plantations, with all too often the refrain 'he say the holes wyll stand full of water do what he can' when the planting season came around. The cellars flooded too. Burghley clearly *needed* a lake.

On that first visit Lancelot found a house coming back to life after decades of deaths and misfortunes, making a fresh start in the hands of Brownlow Cecil, 9th Earl of Exeter, who was thirty, and his wife Laetitia Townshend, who brought him a dowry of £70,000 (or at least the interest at 3 per cent). Lancelot's relationship with Lord Exeter was direct – they only ever dealt directly with each other, and they took to each other: his lordship's 'bluff, blunt-featured, rosy-cheeked face and mild blue eyes' had more a look of Farmer Giles, but also 'the unquestioned self-assurance of a landowning potentate'. He also had a touch of vanity, and Thomas Hudson had just portrayed him in Vandyke costume, well stomached in a long, black silk doublet with slashed sleeves, his round face rising from a fluff of white lace.

For Lancelot, all Lord Exeter's personal qualities were enhanced by his love of Burghley; he didn't *own* Burghley, it was his sacred trust. He was 'an eminently peaceful potentate' who enjoyed the society of his Stamford friends and country neighbours, making only the shortest stays in London when necessary. The resources of the estates were considerable: 'the Home Manors', an array of villages in Lincolnshire and Rutland with well-wooded lands in Rockingham Forest (the Wood Books income averaged £1,000 a year in the 1750s), quarries of valuable building stones, the Yorkshire estate (£2,300 gross rental) and the London estate – Catherine Street and a 'shopping mall', the Exeter Exchange between the Strand and Covent Garden.

Stamford, of which the Cecils owned a goodly southern portion, was pre-eminently a stone town, the home of generations of master masons, their assistants and fixer masons who worked the products of the famous limestone quarries at Barnack, Ketton, Collyweston, Clipsham and Lyddington. Lord Exeter, only too aware of the way the estate was encumbered with the debts of his lavishly spending precedessor, the 5th Earl (who had spent £38,000 on travelling and collecting Italian paintings and furniture, and paying for the works of Antonio Verrio, Grinling Gibbons and the other craftsmen that filled the house), 'ran his estate in the style of an old-fashioned investment trust, geared to low-interest [and] semi-permanent loans'.

Before anything was done at Burghley, Lord Exeter commissioned 'An Accurate Survey of the House, Pleasure Grounds and Park' from John Haynes, a surveyor he knew from York. Haynes spent a good deal of time during 1755 on his scaled and annotated survey, which was accompanied by a series of architectural sketches of the house and garden features, making a detailed record. Lord Exeter was a careful steward.

Lancelot found Burghley with an array of avenues and cross-avenues, courts and orchards, laid out by his old familiar ghostly colleague, George London (possibly with additional work from Charles Bridgeman). London's last planting of 1702, Queen Anne's Avenue of 1,200 double-banked limes, stretched for a mile southwards from the house. Lord Exeter wanted this approach enhanced by enlarging the upper windows of the south front and raising the parapet, which was balustraded, to hide roof clutter; this jobbing mason's work was duly done. Lancelot was more concerned that a low stable block sat on the north-west corner of the house, spoiling the views to and from the park: Lord Exeter agreed that this block should be demolished, making the most of the clean gravel sweep of the north entrance court, and considerably enhancing the west façade with its gilded Tijou gates. A new stable court was built east of the house in a practical, no-nonsense pattern-book Gothic.

In his excited report to Lord Dacre, Lancelot mentioned 'the old Hall whose sides [are] now quite naked', the lofty Elizabethan banqueting hall with hammerbeam roof, which he thought might take some judicious Gothic ornament, but wished he had Sanderson Miller's opinion. It seems likely that he turned to the master carpenter William Halfpenny's *Rural Architecture in the Gothic Taste or Chinese and Gothic Architecture Properly Ornamented*, both of 1752.* Was there Gothic-arched panelling, reflecting the bays of the hammerbeam roof? We cannot know what Lancelot did, for it was removed when the present panelling and bookcases were installed in the nineteenth century.

A happier solution was found to Lord Exeter's request for ornamental ceilings in the Chapel and the Billiard Room: at Burghley, Lancelot is firmly credited with drawing his lordship's attention to the designs in *The Ruins of Palmyra,* published in 1753 and destined to become one of the most influential pattern-books of taste. It is a splendid large-folio volume and rare – was it a new acquisition that Lord Exeter wanted to show off, or was Lancelot left to amuse himself amongst the Burghley books? *The Ruins of Palmyra, otherwise Tedmor in the Desart* was a very superior pattern-book, to the credit of Robert Wood and James Dawkins, 'two gentlemen' whose curiosity had carried them more than once to Italy and who 'wanted to go farther' in 1751. Robert Wood, who had been travelling tutor or 'bear-leader' to the Duke of Bridgewater, was almost certainly known to Lord Exeter, who was himself a great Grand Tourist and collector. The lozenge designs for the Burghley ceilings, the work of a master stuccoist, are accurately taken from the exquisite engravings after Borra, by Foudrinier, Müller and Major, for this book. Palmyra ceilings became all the rage, a speciality of Robert Adam, who designed one for Osterley Park and another for the gallery at Croome.

Lancelot's supervision of these works at Burghley began in 1756: Lord Exeter paid him out of his private account £1,000 a year, £500 each June and December. The Countess Laetitia died that year, and there were no children; in her will she left the use of her £70,000 to her husband until he should marry again. The Earl then adopted his young nephew, Henry Cecil (the child of his younger brother who lived abroad), and brought him to live at Burghley, so that there was a future to work for. Lancelot grew familiar with the many 'short notes in lord Exeter's small round hand', which would arrange a meeting in London or ask him to call: he patiently attended to all these requests (which included scouting for a tenant for Lord Exeter's house in

* The Chinese bridge built at Croome of 1755 was taken from an illustration in Halfpenny's *Improvements in Architecture and Carpentry* of 1754.

Grosvenor Square), hoping for the day when he was allowed to start work on the lake.

Family life in the house by the river in Hammersmith Mall recovered from the shock of Lancelot's illness, but the toll had been heavy. Their fourth son, baptised George Stephen on 7th January 1754, did not live long. A daughter, Anne, was baptised in February two years later, but soon there was another sad little procession to St Paul's Church, where Thomas Rayne the curate met them for her burial. The little plots in the churchyard bound them to Hammersmith life, which they found comfortable and normally full of delights. Biddy Brown felt at home beside the water, for before being landlocked at Stowe, she had never known life without the jinglings of the breeze in sail riggings and the swish-swash of the tides. She found plentiful and varied shopping in King Street and close by, and in the summers she and the children walked to the local farm gates to buy strawberries and salads. Dame schools and teachers of singing and music and drawing abounded for Bridget (approaching ten), Lance (two years younger) and little Jack (four). Henry and Mary Holland and their family at Fulham were their close and companionable friends; young Henry was at school, but destined for his father's builders' business.

Sometimes they walked in the opposite direction, taking 'a delightful rural walk', as locally described, through the lanes to the village of Shepherd's Bush; or along by the Stamford brook to medieval Palingswick Green near Ravenscourt Park, or farther north to Wormholt Woods and the heathery 'scrubs' (much later corrupted to Wormwood Scrubs) and Old Oak Common, 'and from thence the eye commands beautiful and extensive views on the south' bounded by the far Surrey hills – Thomson's 'matchless vale of Thames',

> Fair-winding up to where the Muses haunt
> In Twit'nam's bowers, and for their Pope implore
> The healing God; to royal Hampton's pile,
> To Clermont's terraced height, and Esher's groves,
> Where in the sweetest solitude, embraced
> By the soft windings of the silent Mole,
> From courts and senates Pelham finds repose.

Most frequently they walked by the river, the companionable Thames, where their neighbours took the air, and as well as the boating there was plenty of fishing activity. Salmon and sturgeon were still being

taken out, though declining stocks made the sight of sturgeon something of an event. Eel-baskets were brought in from the river's bed;
there was the season for 'blenneting' for roach and dace with small drift
nets, which began each July; and there were barbel in plenty. Lancelot
was more than ever in thrall to the great river. So many people obviously enjoyed boating and fishing for pleasure, it seemed that, given a
stretch of water, everyone appreciated it. New lakes were in his proposals
for Croome, Petworth and Burghley, though even his best clients needed
persuasion, and with Lord Dacre at Belhus he was soon conducting a
campaign: 'I have had Brown down with me at Belhouse,' Dacre wrote
to San Miller, 'and am going to make a pool where now the run of
water is, in the lower part of my park . . . Brown and indeed my own
little judgment tells me that it will be a very great ornament.' With
Lancelot out of sight, Lord Dacre's courage failed, though he later rallied
and declared himself a 'Bold man' for deciding 'that all the rushy part
of Bumstead Mead will be converted into water' – 'nothing less than
a ten-acre pool'.

Pools, or lakes, suited the scale of Lancelot's working, for they were a
slow-maturing labour and a desirable fashion. From now on, no self-
respecting park owner could be found harbouring an old fishpond.

6

LANCELOT AND
'THE GREAT COMMONER'

My House! tis true, a small & old one
Yet now tis warm, tho' once a cold one.
My Study holds three thousand volumes,
And yet I sigh for Gothic columns,
Such as Sir Roger, learned Knight of Taste
At Arbury so well has placed,
Or such as Dacre, Gothic Master
Has introduced instead of Plaister.

Sanderson Miller, 13th December 1750

L ANCELOT HAD OBSERVED William Pitt's progress from the early days of their encounters at Stowe. In his first government post as Paymaster-General to the Forces – a post traditionally ripe for profits – Pitt had, 'to the astonishment of other politicians and the delight of a wider public', lodged the balance of the public money with the Bank of England and waived his personal commission. This had given people the idea that he was 'different from other politicians, less corrupt and self-interested'; these were the seeds of a growing adulation. Indeed, Pitt had little regard for money, and he was sometimes notoriously extravagant and at others pleaded poverty; when he had money, he was generous to his gardening friends, as Sanderson Miller continued:

With here a large Settee for sleep,
A window there to take a peep
Of Lawns & Woods and Cows & Sheep,
And Laurel Walk & Strawberry Bank
For which the Paymaster I thank.
The Paymaster well skilled in planting
Pleas'd to assist when cash was wanting.

He bid my Laurels grow, they grew
Fast as his Laurels always do.

Pitt had parted with his first house and garden, South Lodge at Enfield, in the early 1750s, and resumed his 'wandering Scythian life', his summer ramblings, giving his opinions and advice on other people's gardens. Even his closest friends and relations were in fear of failing him: 'It vexes me that you can't find fencing enough from all my father's wood,' wrote George Lyttelton from London to his cousin Molly West at Hagley, 'to enclose the plantation that Pitt marked out for the cottage. He will be much disappointed not to see it done, and indeed so shall I . . . I won't answer for Pitt's coming to Hagley at Whitsuntide, especially as there will be no cottage built nor trees planted there.' To his own cousin John Pitt, at 'dear unknown, delightful, picturesque Encombe' in its Dorset cove, Pitt exhorted: 'Throw about your verdant hills some thousands of trees – group away' (that is, clump them). His word was law and 'his wrath terrible', just as in the House of Commons, but Encombe was remote enough to be safe.

After five years as Paymaster-General, having set in train the strengthening of the navy and the army and underwritten future victories, Pitt collapsed (in the late summer of 1751) and was absent from politics for well over two years. The 'collapses', which became frequent, were attributed to gout; he was to be found dramatically swathed in flannel for an agony of his head, his stomach or his feet (though this is now understood to be manic depression, bipolar disorder, which took an awful toll on his body systems). In the midsummer of 1754 he was at Tunbridge Wells, taking the waters with Gilbert West, another gout sufferer, and more pleasantly occupied with the Wests at West Wickham (where he made suggestions for improvements), and with Elizabeth Montagu, who summered at Hayes Place nearby (whilst her husband Edward preferred Yorkshire). Mrs Montagu wrote of how 'we have been wandering about like a company of gypsies, visiting all the fine parks and seats in the neighbourhood'. They must have talked of Lancelot, for from this time she joins the ranks of 'Lancelot-watchers'; she was to observe from afar, and patiently, for many years.

At the end of July, Pitt resumed his rambling into Sussex, then north to Hertfordshire. The Sebrights of Beechwood Park, south of Luton at Markyate, were amongst his Hertfordshire friends, and Lancelot was working there. His commission followed the usual pattern, with a survey requested (1753), upon which he based proposals for generously sweeping plantations and huge clumps in a variety of 'amoebic' shapes in the park;

if these suggest that Pitt enthused Sir John Sebright, it would not be surprising. Beechwood's house was fronted by a formal terrace with bastions, removed in favour of a natural green sweep into the park, but retaining the 'copses' of wilderness planting that flanked the sweep.*

William Pitt rambled on from Beechwood to Stowe, all in 'continual rains', until he reached the small spa of Astrop Wells in Northamptonshire, one of his favoured cures. There he was 'lodged in a dungeon called the Manor House of King's Sutton', drinking the waters of St Rumbold's Well in the morning and riding 'in the dirt of Northamptonshire all the rest of the day', hoping he was leading a *healthy* life, 'for pleasure never found its way hither'. Astrop, in the Cherwell valley just south of Banbury, was the home of the lawyer and MP, Sir John Willes, the elderly Chief Justice of the Court of Common Pleas, for whom Smiths of Warwick had built a new house (1735–8) in Astrop Park. Pitt's 'dungeon' was Willes's old manor house. Within a few years (the late 1750s) Lancelot was also at Astrop (perhaps for cold bathing?), where he made a long, narrow lake from the stream flowing down from Astrop Hill and planted a sheltering belt of trees.

Still in 1754, William Pitt, 'well cobbled up by Astrop waters and the life of a post-boy, always in the saddle', changed his mind about his planned visit to Bath and Encombe, and took himself the much shorter distance back to Wotton Underwood. There he proposed to the thirty-four-year-old Lady Hester Grenville – she who had witnessed Lady Cobham's twittery about the sheep in the garden at Stowe, and whom Pitt had known for more than twenty years. They were married on 16th November that year and were to be blissfully enraptured with each other, and their children and gardens, for the rest of his life. Their honeymoon was spent at Mrs Montagu's Hayes Place near Bromley, which she was persuaded to sell, as both Mr and Lady Hester Pitt had fallen in love with it; on his earlier visit Pitt had wandered off, as usual, 'and found the most beautiful rural scene that can be imagined', and immediately ordered 'a tent, a picnic and tea'.

Hayes Place was an elegant villa, which the Pitts extended to twenty-four bedrooms, with stabling for sixteen horses, housing for four carriages, and the usual offices, dairy, brewhouse, laundry and a walled garden with peach houses and pineapple pits. While Hayes was being got ready for them, the Pitts spent four months at Chevening, about 8 miles to the

---

* In 1804 Arthur Young noted the fine and stately beeches, 'but the soil agrees with all sorts of trees; the cedars are immense; the oaks very large; the ash straight and beautiful; the larch, spruce and Scots fir equally fine, but the beech uncommon'. The Sebrights remained at Beechwood until well after the Second World War, but little is known of the history of the landscape, now mostly farmland, or of the fate of Lancelot's proposals.

south over Westerham Hill. This was the home of Philip, 2nd Earl Stanhope, whose mother Lucy was Pitt's cousin. It is said that Pitt designed Chevening's carriage drive, but Lancelot's name has also been suggested for this. Lancelot certainly became very familiar with Hayes Place. Pitt extended Hayes's 60 acres of fenced park by buying and renting fields in the adjoining parish of Farnborough. Hayes became (we have only the estate agent's description from 1789) 'pleasure grounds disposed with taste, fringed with rich plantations, timber scattered with pleasing negligence, [a] paddock refreshed with a sheet of water and the grounds adorned with seats, alcoves etc'. It became Pitt's refuge, prized for its seclusion; from love nest, it ripened into nursery as Hester's 'ever passionate husband', (as he signed himself) sired a yearly sequence of children: little Hester, John, Harriot, 'William the Fourth' and James.

While all this was going on, Lancelot had returned to Lord Egremont's Petworth, where work had been interrupted by his illness. (Petworth was now drawn into the Pitt networking, in that Lord Egremont's sister Elizabeth was married to George Grenville, now William Pitt's brother-in-law.) The leftover flower gardening from the first contract was completed, and shrubs planted to adorn the extended walks from the birch grove 'on through ye Laurels leading up to the Seat where the Dutchess of Somerset used to drink her Coffee as likewise through the Padock & on ye Side of [ye] new Terras, making at the same Time proper preparations for Flowers'.

And then, to bolster his new resolution, Lancelot went forward eagerly with the lake, all the works now carefully set out in contract form (1754). The first stage was the staking out, forming both the desired and practical outline and calculating the amount of earth to be moved 'for the lake in the park near the Half Moon Wood', where a pond existed. This followed Taverner's other, more risky way of lake-making: 'the one digged right downe into the ground by labour of man', with clay spread for the lining. The following summer, in June 1755, the work included 'the alteration of the Pond in all its parts viz the digging of all such parts out as are not deep enough, according to the stakes. The making of all the necessary clay walls. The levelling the bottom and making the slopes and for pitching the sides ... to prevent the cattle from damaging it'. A picturesque process this, with gangs of men spreading the clay, readily dug from the gault-clay strata nearby, and with endlessly processing horses and carts, as on an Egyptian tomb. The clay then had to be 'puddled', or tamped into a solid layer when wet, the best-known method being to drive a herd of sheep backwards and forwards, their little hooves making excellent tamps. A sheepsfoot roller was the more prosaic solution. There were subsequent hiccups, panics over leaks, but all were overcome; the following summer 'a further new lake' (now known as the Lower Pond) was ordered.

The Fox Letter

Unsurprisingly, if Lancelot can be said to have had any political allegiance, it was 'Pittian'. Pitt, observes William Hague in his biography of Pitt the Younger, 'would have called himself a Whig, the term Tory being largely pejorative and still heavily associated with suspected Jacobite sympathies . . . but [he] was usually distinct in his views from the great figures of the Whig aristocracy'. Lancelot, we suspect, had a small corner of his heart that was Jacobite, but then he was merely a gardener. At this time, 'Whigs seemed to hold no common ground. Every issue engendered new disagreements. Every Whig seemed to be a party in his own right, and what was worse, to glory in the fact.' William Pitt was certainly a party in his own right, and Lancelot was of his party; both were in sympathy with the 'Patriot' or 'Country Interest'. Lancelot was deeply patriotic with a small 'p': it was the inevitability of his profession and his daily communion with the soils and the very fabric of England. Like Pitt too, he could sometimes seem 'frankly Tory', being wary of the Hanoverian George II with his divided loyalties. Lancelot's clients reflected this ambivalence.

In the summer of 1755 the coffee-house gossips talked of nothing but Pitt and Henry Fox wrestling, at least verbally, each wanting to succeed the long-serving Duke of Newcastle as First Secretary (Prime Minister). George II did not like Pitt, but the people would have him; the King wanted Fox, but Pitt would not have *him*. The protagonists met in secret, seeking a compromise, but by early May they had fallen out entirely and it was said there would be no further communication between them. The Commons gave up the struggle and repaired to recess and gardening. An earthquake trembled over most of southern England on 1st August, causing considerable alarm. (It was later realised to be the advance tremor of the disastrous Lisbon quake of 1st November.)

Having heard of the warring, Lancelot was surprised by the arrival of a scrawled note from Kensington, dated 20th August, a scrawl redolent of the sweaty hands of a passionate and impulsive man: 'I am hard at work and digging gravel and have made a bargain for 500 loads of ballast which will move about 200 loads of earth – if you can come and put in a few stakes it would be a great guidance.' It was signed 'H. Fox'. Fox, variously 'an ambitious vain toad' or of a 'cunning, black, devilish countenance', lived in Holland Park with his wife Caroline Lennox, the eldest daughter of the Duke and Duchess of Richmond, with whom he had made a runaway – or at least a gallop across Mayfair – marriage. They were settled in a huge, decaying Jacobean mansion in the midst of the farms, cottages and gravel pits of Kensington, hence his 'bargain' in selling the gravel. Holland House occupied the whole rectangular block between Kensington and Notting Hill, with an ancient right of way, Holland Walk, cutting through on the east boundary. Did Lancelot go off to Kensington to give his 'great guidance'? Joshua Rhodes's survey of Kensington of 1766 shows an oval or round pond, rather in the manner of the pond in Kensington Gardens, with radiating avenues of trees springing from this; was this the pond Fox had dug? Did Lancelot peg out the shape and the lines of the avenues? It seems an un-Brownian feature, but then Henry Fox would have had his own way, and his wife's taste (Lady Caroline had spent long youthful hours helping her mother decorate the Shell Grotto at Goodwood) was for the antique fashion. Rhodes's survey also shows a boundary belt of trees sheltering a serpentine walk around Holland Park, so perhaps there was a little touch of the Brown style.

At some time in the late summer of 1756 Lancelot went to Madingley Hall outside Cambridge to discuss the making of gravel walks, lawns and a ha-ha with Sir John Hynde Cotton 4th Baronet, a man of his own age, a Member of Parliament and 'something in the City', who was enormously well connected in Cambridge and around. How they met is uncertain, but Sir John was related to the Yorkes (Lord Chancellor Hardwicke's family) at Wimpole, owned Shortgrove on the Cam near Saffron Walden (one of Lancelot's parks) and was connected to the Houblons of Great Hallingbury (another of Lancelot's clients) – a typical cat's cradle of connections. Lancelot was clearly happy about the work, Madingley Hall being a beautiful red-brick mansion of the time of Henry VIII, sited on rising ground with views over placid countryside, and he promised a contract to define the works and the costs.

By early October, Sir John was clearly thinking that he would soon have to leave Madingley for Parliament's return, and no start had been made on his walks and lawns, so he called at the house in Hammersmith Mall, only to be disappointed, for Lancelot was not at home. He was not far away and was full of apologies, expressed in a letter of 6th October, when he promised to be at Madingley well before Parliament reassembled in mid-November. Being Lancelot, he set out a little late, but was taken ill 'on the Road', and so returned home. Immediately Lance, aged eight, went down with scarlet fever, and Lancelot expected 'the other to fall every day' – poor Jack, just five – 'which renders it next to impossible for me to leave them till it is got over,' he told Sir John. Scarlatina was treated then with good nursing, a regime of bathing and throat poultices, a mild diet and cooling drinks, a time-consuming and exhausting task with two small boys. Lancelot was always known to be a good father, but here is a rare glimpse of him putting the family first.

The contract is dated 16th November 1756, and Lancelot eventually arrived at Madingley a week or so later. The works were not great; the contract has interesting details on the construction of a good, old-fashioned domed gravel walk – 7½ or 8 feet wide, 'laying a sufficient quantity of rubbish [i.e. rubble] under the gravel to keep it dry' – and reveals an extensive notion of 'lawns', all to be given 'a natural easy level' and turfed or sown, the quality of finish extended to all the grass in the near park. The contract is a model of economy of labour and materials, carefully guiding the work around the house, using excavated soil from the 'fosse' as necessary in the garden; and, it transpires, not digging the complete ha-ha, but 'only to remove as much earth as wanted in the garden & to make a Pattern of it to be done after & when Sir John pleases'. The agreed charge was £500, payable in three stages in 1757; only two payments (£200 in 1757, £100 in 1760) are credited in Lancelot's Drummonds bank account. It appears that he had to chase his money, but once again he was paid in other ways. A shaky hand, presumably Sir John's, has marked the contract: 'never executed nor any other but done upon honor on both sides & never repented by either'.

It was also in 1756, or possibly early 1757, that Lancelot first visited Stratfield Saye in the Loddon valley south of Reading, where he was to work for William Pitt's cousins, George and Penelope Pitt, for the next seven years. Stratfield Saye, more usually associated with the Dukes of Wellington (it was given to the Great Duke in 1817, two years after his victory at Waterloo), has never been thought of as a Brown park until Drummonds bank archives revealed that the Pitts paid him no less than £3,900. Gerald, 7th Duke of Wellington and an architect himself, clearly had no idea, for he wrote disparagingly of Lancelot's 'systematic' approach in general, and that 'he did not perceive that though it was natural for a stream to meander it was not natural for a sober man not to take the shortest, that is to say the straightest, line between any two given points'. He credited George Pitt (later Lord Rivers) with 'the prophetic eye of taste' and the reform of Stratfield's antiquated surroundings: 'he levelled the dreary garden walls and filled up the fish-ponds and by felling the avenues that frowned round the house he opened it to the cheering light of the sun'. The park was enlarged and planted 'with the truest taste which Mason or Walpole would have contemplated with delight'. As he wrote, the Duke was looking 'over the river to distant lawns well broken by large single trees which gradually accede into open groves and thence by a gentle transition into a depth of thick wood forming a varied and picturesque horizon, the wood in some places coming forward to the eye, in others retiring in large irregular masses'. All, presumably, Lancelot's works.

The Percy Connection

The invisible cord of Pitt's influence was strengthening, but Lancelot had his own good luck, a timeliness accruing in his career. He was lucky in the changing dynasties, the families where a younger heir invariably had ideas differing from those of his forebears. In these 1750s the young heirs had nearly all been on the Grand Tour, and they had all discovered *taste*. They had returned home to an almost general inheritance of played-out formal gardens, crumbling basins and canals, outgrown parterres and barren orchards, all seventy-plus years old and suffering from the dipping tides of fortune. The idea of reverting to the old-fashioned did not occur to them (the regressive and unnatural concept of 'restoration' had not yet been born). The instinct of the young was to make their own mark on the future.

Lancelot's good luck was nowhere more evident than in the case of the Percy inheritance. Charles Seymour, 6th Duke of Somerset (called 'Proud' even amongst dukes), and his duchess Elizabeth Percy (the 'Duchess', long remembered at Petworth for taking her coffee at her favourite seat beyond the laurels) were the joint heirs to all the Percy and Seymour estates. The Duchess died first, with everything reverting to her husband, and when the Duke died in 1748, their heir was their only son, Algernon, Earl of Hertford. Lord Hertford had earned his father's disfavour by allowing his only surviving child, the Duke's granddaughter, to marry 'beneath her', and so the Duke left his Seymour estates to his sister Catherine's son, Charles Wyndham of Orchard Wyndham in Somerset, who inherited Petworth and was made Earl of Egremont. The Duke could not stop Lord Hertford succeeding as 7th Duke of Somerset, or deprive him of his mother's Percy estates, which included Syon House, the Alnwick Castle estate and Northumberland House at Charing Cross. The 7th Duke, Algernon, was a tall, sandy-haired, asthmatic and serious man, already over sixty, and married devotedly for many years to Frances Thynne, the poet James Thomson's 'gentle Hertford'. They were both imaginative and practical gardeners, preferring their quiet life at home,

Richard Temple, Viscount Cobham
(1675-1749), by Jean-Baptiste van Loo, 1740.

William Pitt, Earl of Chatham (1708-1778),
by William Hoare, c.1754.

George Lucy of Charlecote (1714-1786),
by Pompeo Batoni, 1758.

George William, 6th Earl of Coventry
(1722-1809), by Allan Ramsay, 1765.

The matchless vale of Thames, an extract from Roque's
Middlesex, showing Hammersmith, the Brown family's
home 1751-64, amidst the productive landscape that
stretched from Kensington to Kew.

Wakefield Lawn, Northamptonshire, Paul Sandby, 1767,
showing the landscape setting Lancelot made for the 2nd
Duke of Grafton's hunting lodge, adjacent to Stowe.

Petworth, Dewy Morning, J.M.W. Turner, 1810, the view taken across Lancelot's first lake towards the west front of Petworth house.

laude, *Landscape with Hagar and the Angel*. everal landscapes by laude were in houses hat Lancelot visited d they influenced his aming of views and siting of buildings.

Croome Court, Richard Wilson, 1758: the view of Lancelot's landscape from the south-west, with the Court rebuilt in the Hagley style, Lancelot's rotunda to the right, his new church on the hill (not finished until 1763) and the William Halfpenny pattern-book white wooden bridge.

Burghley House, Frederick Mackenzie, 1819, from the west, showing Lancelot's three-arched bridge and his long lake. The coach has come via Lancelot's new south drive and will sweep around to the entrance court on the north side of the house.

Brownlow, 9th Earl of Exeter (1725–1793), in Van Dyck costume by Thomas Hudson. The Earl and Lancelot worked on Burghley together for more than twenty-five years.

Lancelot Brown (1716–1783), by Nathaniel Dance, *c.*1769

Elizabeth, Duchess of Northumberland (1716–1776), by Sir Joshua Reynolds: Lancelot's favourite duchess who championed his work at Syon House, Sion Hill and at Alnwick Castle.

Alnwick Castle, Northumberland. Vilet's view of workmen finishing the new castle approach under the direction of Lancelot's foreman, Cornelius Griffin.

Percy Lodge (more famous as Richings) at Iver in Buckinghamshire to any society. Sadly, all was brought to naught as the Duke died after only two years, in 1750, and Duchess Frances retired to Percy Lodge, which was hers for the rest of her life. Their daughter, Lady Elizabeth, and her husband Sir Hugh Smithson – to whom the Duke had already made over Syon House – now inherited Alnwick Castle and Northumberland House as well, becoming the Earl and Countess of Northumberland (to be created 1st Duke and Duchess in 1766).

So, having fared well at Petworth, it was quite natural that Lancelot should be called to Syon. This pleased him in many ways, especially as it was not much more than an hour's ride from home. Syon was not a large park, small in comparison with royal Richmond and Kew on the opposite bank of the Thames; it was formerly an abbey, and was confined by Brentford and the Bath road on the north, and by Syon lane, leading to the ferry, on the west. The rambling course of the River Brent formed the eastern boundary, and here planting was required to screen the growing development of wharves where it joined the Thames. Syon House, painted by Canaletto as Lancelot saw it, was distinctive, uncompromisingly four-square, castellated with corner towers; it gave the appearance of having been plonked on the land, probably high enough and far enough away from the river to be dry, but making no recognition of the presence of the Thames. The 6th Duke of Somerset had planted a double lime avenue on the north-west approach side, and the walled gardens extended on the north-east.

On the west side (the present entrance drive), comparison between a plan of 1747 and John Roque's *Middlesex* of 1754 shows that enclosures and terraces had recently been replaced by 'a landscape of lawns and open meadows . . . and a sinuous walk in a south-westerly direction from the house to Isleworth Church', known as 'the church walk wilderness'. The walk described by R. and J. Dodsley, 'in some places runs along the side, and in others through the middle of a beautiful shrubbery, so that even in the most retired parts of this charming maze, where the prospect is most confined, almost the whole vegetable world rises up as it were in miniature around you . . .'

Compare this image with Frances Hertford's description of 1747, of the walk they had made at Percy Lodge. Lord Hertford had made a long, narrow walk:

> into the resemblance of a wild lane in the country, and made it wider or
> narrower just as he had in mind to take in a great tree or fill up a vacancy
> with flowering shrubs. On the one hand there is for about forty or fifty

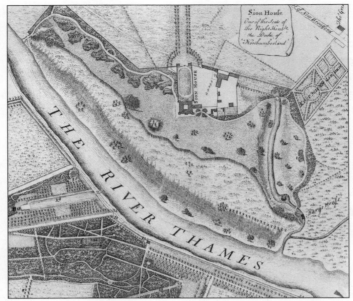

Syon House, Middlesex, from Roque's plan of Richmond, *c.*1765, showing the Church Walk Wilderness, the first of Lancelot's serpentine 'ambits' with 'edge of the cornfield' atmosphere, inspired by Lady Northumberland's mother, the Countess of Hertford.

> yards an open grove, through which you can see a corn field, with a turfed walk of about six foot wide around it, and bordered all round under the wood with roses, honeysuckles, Spanish broom, lilacs, syringas, etc.; and underneath these bushes cowslips, primroses, violets, foxgloves, with every flower that grows wild in the fields ... but there is nothing on the side next the corn to separate it from it.

The Hertfords were delighted with this walk, the latest of many naturalistic and pretty ideas for their garden; they were very close to their daughter Elizabeth (Betty) and their son-in-law, and it seems that when they gave them Syon in 1748, they also gave them the idea for the Church Walk Wilderness, with all its seclusion and charm. The Syon version, making use of trees and shrubs supplied by Lancelot's friend and colleague John Williamson from Kensington, included evergreen honeysuckles, Alexandrian laurels (*Danae racemosa*), lilacs, laburnums, shrub roses, syringas, viburnums and cherries; poplars, maples, planes, aromatic pines and six cedars of Lebanon were probably used as the background planting, for the Church Walk Wilderness was walled from the north and only offered views out through open groves on the river side.

Frances Hertford lived until the summer of 1754, and though she was

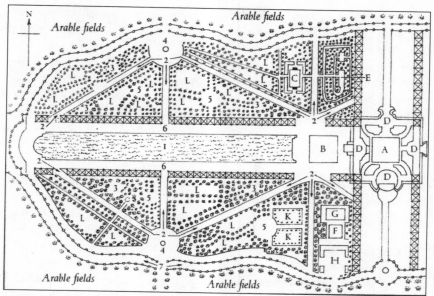

Richings, Iver, Buckinghamshire, Lord Bathurst's garden acquired by the Earl and Countess of Hertford and re-named Percy Lodge, where they made their serpentine flowery walk which overlooked the cornfields.

Key:
A, House;
B, Parterre;
C, Menagerie;
D, Terraces;
E, Labyrinth;
F, Gardener's house;
G, Melonry;
H, Stables;
K, Kitchen gardens;
L, (many) lawns and groves

1. Canal;
2. Cross paths;
3. Wildernesses;
4. Rond-points;
5. Fountains;
6. Lawn borders;
7. Footpath, or edge of the cornfield walk.

frail and reclusive at Percy Lodge, she was ever the keen and passionate gardener and would have made a considerable effort to visit Syon to advise her daughter (who was not such a great gardener). It is therefore just possible that Lancelot met her, and saw through her eyes the art of alternately (but not regularly) concealing and revealing the views from a meandering path through trees and flowering shrubs. Syon's Church Walk Wilderness, securely walled and treed 'at one's back' (the boundary concealed), became the pattern for many of Lancelot's meandering perimeter walks, with views into the park and the greatest sense of space – freedom alternated with the seclusion. If the 'park' is a cornfield, as it was at Richings, or even a hay meadow as at Syon, then gardening shifts subtly to art, the 'edge-of-cornfield' effects employed by Stubbs and Gainsborough.

At Syon (where he was first paid in February 1754) Lancelot elaborated the original Church Walk, and continued the effect on the east side of the house and around the eastern perimeter, the serpentine walk leading to the boathouse where the river barge was kept. In due time his beloved Thames was properly served; grading of the river bank is indicated on Roque's plan:

> a fine lawn extending from Isleworth to Brentford. By these means also a beautiful prospect is opened into the King's gardens at Richmond, as well as up and down the Thames. Toward the Thames the lawn is bounded by a ha-ha and a meadow; which his lordship ordered to be cut down into a gentle slope, so that the surface of the water may now be seen . . . the most beautiful piece of scenery imaginable is formed before two of the principal fronts [of the house] for even the Thames itself seems to belong to the gardens, and the different sorts of vessels which successively sail as it were through them, appear to be the property of their noble proprietor.

Syon, surprisingly, also acquired a lake. Or at least a linear river – the water (and fish) brought from the Thames and controlled by a sluice. The water appears to be taken upstream at Isleworth, through Syon Park by a long water crossed by the entrance drive and partly underground, before it is let out into the Thames by Brentford. A surviving sketch of the view from Syon House's entrance door, looking north to where the (then) drive crossed the water, indicates that Lancelot and Robert Adam discussed the position of the bridge. Today, the Syon reach is the only unembanked stretch of the Thames in Greater London, and so the lower slopes of the park are left as rough meadow and allowed to flood.

The Comet's Tail

Lancelot was forty in the summer of 1756; it was a summer of invasion scares, with the countryside running with rumours and alarms that enlivened his rides – his 'circuits', as he now called them – out into Essex, to Cambridge and Burghley, down to Sussex or out westwards to Croome. As the summer drifted into autumn, so Britain found herself at war, the backdrop of his work and conversations for the coming years. The 'Seven Years War', as it came to be called, was a transforming experience for England, and for the English. In 1756 there were overseas territories, chiefly the thirteen American colonies, 'Protestant and Anglophone'; after the 1763 Treaty of Paris the empire embraced Catholic Quebec and mystical (as well as mysterious) territories in West Africa, India, South-East Asia, the West Indies and the southern seas. Insecurity has often been suggested as a reason for the popularity of the English landscape style, and the need to acquire, fence and beautify a patch of England in case the great world became too unbearable.

The war began in governmental chaos – in fact, little government at all – hence the brief Pitt–Devonshire ministry (1756–7). (Lancelot would soon be working for the Duke of Devonshire at Chatsworth.) In the spring of 1757 publicly expressed anger forced vacillating ministers to action, and Admiral Byng was court-martialled for the loss of Minorca, and shot, despite Pitt's plea for mercy. Pitt was dismissed by George II, then called back again, becoming Secretary of State in uneasy alliance with the Duke of Newcastle. He was not so much a one-man party as a one-man war cabinet; the Duke and the Treasury ruled from Downing Street, while Pitt took over the running of the war from his house in the north-east corner of St James's Square (no. 12, now Chatham House) or from Hayes Place. He was apparently personally in contact with the commanders in the field in Europe and North America, with the admirals at sea and with that 'heaven-born general' Robert Clive, after his victory at Plassey in June 1757. And yet, in the midst of all this, Pitt found time to sanction a petition for Lancelot to have a royal appointment and pension.

Only Pitt could have quickly summoned the fourteen prestigious signatories to this petition, all of them his own friends and colleagues, and visitors to the house in St James's Square. There seem to have been two petitions, one of 1757 (lost in the crush of papers on Pitt's desk or between London and Hayes?) and another of March 1758. The petition was artfully drafted, asserting that:

> well-wishers of Mr Browne [*sic*], whose Abilities and Merit we are fully acquainted with, do most earnestly request the Duke of Newcastle to promote his speedy appointment to the care of Kensington Garden agreeable to his Grace's very obliging promises in that respect, the delay having already occasion'd great loss to Mr Browne in his Business and great inconvenience to many Persons for whom he is Employ'd.

Many of the amiable signatories are familiar: Admiral Lord Anson of Moor Park and First Lord of the Admiralty; Pitt's brothers-in-law, Richard, Earl Temple of Stowe, and George Grenville of Wotton Underwood; Pitt's friend Lord Ashburnham (for whom Lancelot was soon working); Charles Egremont from Petworth; Lord Coventry from Croome; Lord Exeter from Burghley; Lord Brooke from Warwick; and the Earl of Northumberland from Syon.

The remaining five are less predictable: the Duke of Ancaster, Viscount Midleton and three earls, Hertford, Holderness and Stamford. Lancelot had of course missed out to the Grundys at the Duke of Ancaster's Grimsthorpe Castle (did the Duke regret this?), but he was working at Ancaster House in Richmond at this time. George, 3rd Viscount Midleton, then MP for Ashburton in Devon and a Pitt colleague, was employing Lancelot at Peper Harow in Surrey (it is thought that plantings of cedars, oaks and beeches here are by him, but that Lancelot's widening of the River Wey and an island made in the process were lost; Lancelot was paid £450 in 1757–8). The new Lord Hertford at Ragley was a Seymour heir, and Lancelot passed close to Ragley on his way to Croome: Walpole reported on 20th August 1758 'Brown has improved both the grounds and the water though not quite to perfection', though nothing has been found at Ragley to substantiate this.

Robert D'Arcy (Darcy), 4th Earl of Holderness, is a unifying figure. Of steady character, Secretary of State, Pitt's ally and his sometime opposite number in the Northern Department, he was also a patron and friend of David Garrick, and the owner of Hornby Castle in Yorkshire and known to Lancelot's brother, John Brown, in his work as agent for the Duke of Portland. D'Arcy also owned Sion Hill House, a small park on the opposite side of the Brentford road from Syon House and beside the lane to Osterley Park. Lady Holderness was born Mary Doublet of Groeneweldt, and she had brought her Dutch gardener with her and 'kept a prodigious amount of kitchen gardening [in the] Dutch style'. Lord Holderness's expertise in the use of 'clean dressed hay seeds, white clover and trefoile', and as a grower of prize Newbury cabbages, was later praised by the travelling agronomist Arthur Young. Lancelot went to Sion Hill to make their pretty park, which was essentially two paddocks joined by a wilderness of woody shrubs and small trees, the whole surrounded by a wide perimeter belt of planting, trees and shrubs in clumps, sheltering a meandering walk. Lady Northumberland was a frequent visitor, and noted 'the walk round the field taken off with a rope & a border of flowers on ye country side', with prospects of the hayfield 'entirely rural and pleasing'. Frances Hertford's Church Walk Wilderness had clearly migrated across the road, courtesy of Lady Northumberland and Lancelot (who was paid £1,525 for work from September 1756 to April 1762).

The remaining name on the petition, Lord Stamford's, is enigmatic; he owned Enville, west of Stourbridge, set in a spectacular landscape between the Rivers Stour and Severn, with ravines, rocks and water enough to make a fantastically gothic garden. Lord Stamford was a gardening friend of William Shenstone and the Lytteltons at Hagley, and George Lyttelton would have taken Pitt to Enville. Perhaps they urged Lancelot's employment, although his association with Enville lacks direct evidence.

The Duke of Newcastle, who controlled patronage, was no fan of Lancelot's, and the 1758 petition did not succeed. It was no doubt mired in greater matters, for 1759 was the 'ever-warm and victorious' year – the year of victory at Minden, of General Wolfe's capture of Quebec, and of the destruction of the French fleet in Quiberon Bay: the *annus mirabilis* when 'in every quarter of the globe [Pitt] had young men after his own heart gaily carrying out his projects'. The weather colluded: 'Can one easily leave the remains of such a year as this?' wrote Walpole in late October:

> It is still all gold. I have not dined or gone to bed by a fire till the day before yesterday . . . we have not had more conquest than fine weather: one would think we had plundered East and West Indies of sunshine. Our bells are worn threadbare with ringing of victories. I believe it will require ten votes of the House of Commons before people will believe that it is the Duke of Newcastle that has done this, and not Mr Pitt.

Restraint at Wrest

'Even the great Mr Pitt himself visited Wrest,' the Marchioness Grey had noted in her diary in 1758, and Lancelot was there the following year. Jemima, Marchioness Grey (her own title), was married to Philip Yorke, Lord Chancellor Hardwicke's heir, and they had first met Lancelot at Stowe, probably in 1748. The Marchioness, portrayed by Allan Ramsay with her perfectly oval head, fair complexion and huge brown eyes, was slight but sturdy in her constitution and level-headed in her outlook; she had two daughters, Amabel and Mary Jemima, and believed in a woman's right of inheritance. She had inherited Wrest Park in Bedfordshire from her grandfather, the Duke of Kent, a rambling house of medieval origins and the garden that he had made between 1702 (when he inherited) and his death in 1740. The Duke had summoned many familiar names – William Kent, James Gibbs, Giacomo Leoni, Thomas Archer, Batty Langley and Thomas Ackres (who was George London's executor and heir at the

Brompton nursery). His grace had equally rejected most of their proposals: Wrest was famed for its long canal, the Great Water, culminating in Thomas Archer's domed pavilion, a tea house with bedrooms, and a kitchen and two-seater privy attached. Each side of the canal were blocks of woodland, cut with paths, groves and *cabinets de verdure,* as illustrated by Switzer and Batty Langley (who is thought to have worked at Wrest). The principle was very similar to Moor Park, where the canal and plant-ings were (fatally) raised on a terrace, but Wrest was more spacious, laid on level ground and very watery. The garden was completely surrounded by canals and streams, and Jemima, who had grown up there, was used to getting her feet wet.

Lancelot and the Marchioness were to be friends for a long time; twenty years later she recalled how he was in awe of the 'mystery' of Wrest's old garden. There was no shortage of money or faithful gardeners in this veritably old-school establishment, and the 'young mistress' respected her grandfather's ways. Wrest was the best garden of the old formality that Lancelot had seen. For him, it made sense of all the remnants of the works of London and Wise and Bridgeman that were 'beached' in the countryside, like so many crumbling hulks. Wrest resonated with the power of the Duke's controlling mind; it was a precise echo from a former age. On this and following visits, the Marchioness repeatedly asked for his suggestions as to improvements, and Lancelot steadfastly refused to make changes. He did agree to help the drainage by loosening the fringe canals into naturally flowing streams, as the Marchioness noted: 'the canals already joined are the circular canal, John Dewell's (named after the gardener that made it) and the mill pond; the stream which they make is to be lost, that in the end will be turned into and concealed by some plantation'.

Wrest Park made a deep impression upon Lancelot, fuelling growing pride in his profession. It further opened his eyes to the ways of water, fitting him all the more to understand Charlecote, Burghley and Chatsworth.

7

'THE ONE GREAT ARGUMENT OF THE LANDSCAPE GARDENER'

'And now for the Water, *the Element that I trade in. The water is the eldest daughter of the Creation, the Element upon which the Spirit of God did first move, the Element which God commanded to bring forth living creatures abundantly; and without which those that inhabit the Land, even all creatures that have breath in their nostrils must suddenly return to putrefaction.*
Piscator in Izaak Walton and Charles Cotton, *The Compleat Angler,* 1653

It would be mistaken to presume that Lancelot, either in the cause of jingoism or noble equilibrium, thought of himself as selling *privacy* to his patrons. Few were likely to suffer from an excess of celebrity (except for the tall and outstanding Mr Pitt in the years after 1759), and country living in the eighteenth century was a sociable form of existence. Running a farm or estate was outdoor business, with sport and conversation:

> Gravely inquiring how ewes are a score,
> How the hay harvest and the corn was got,
> And if or no there's like to be a rot.

Some seclusion – privacy on the large scale – may have been desirable, but mostly the need was for shelter: shelter from the elements that raged across the land threatening men and women, beasts and crops. To Lancelot, his boundary belts and plantations were providing such shelter in the short term, even if their returns from the sale of timber were very much in the long term, a legacy to unborn generations. He was, as he well knew, harnessing the age-old skills of farmland and estate management, but with characteristic verve, and he was perhaps slowly realising that in the process he was transforming ordinary land into landscape.

The word 'landscape' was then only just emerging from the Dutch *landskip*. (It has caused us trouble ever since; Nan Fairbrother coined the equation 'Landscape = habitat plus man' to explain it.) 'Landscape' is not a word that Lancelot uses, though he is soon assailed by poets and painters who do: interestingly, it is pride in the effects produced by his work that inspired patrons to commission paintings of the English landscape, as opposed to the Italian. Richard Wilson painted Lancelot's Croome in 1758, and three large studies of his Moor Park a few years afterwards, as well as Chatsworth. (Joseph Farington, Wilson's pupil, depicted 'Richard Wilson painting from *nature* in Moor Park – 1765'.)

As with shelter planting and painting, so it was with water; Lancelot's work was in tune with the spirits of his age. Dr Johnson had encouraged the reprints of Izaak Walton's and Charles Cotton's *Angler* (as it was simply known) in 1750 and 1759. It was, along with the Bible, the Book of Common Prayer, *The Pilgrim's Progress* and perhaps, in the Brown household, Sir Francis Bacon's *Of Gardens,* standard bookshelf fare. The *Angler* is not just a book about fishing, but 'a transcript of old English country life, a study of the folk-heart', wrote John Buchan. Because of its subtitle, 'The Contemplative Man's Recreation', it finds 'a place in the pastoral tradition', and it has strong connections with Derbyshire, for Charles Cotton was a Derbyshire man. It is also a book about water – water in ponds, pools, rivers and lakes – and, as such, it has a startling relevance to Lancelot's works. All of these themes coalesce at this time, with his grandest of flourishes, at Chatsworth.

The mild-mannered 4th Duke of Devonshire inherited Chatsworth at the end of 1755, when he was thirty-five; a reserved, 'amiable and straightforward man', he held the line between Pitt and Fox, and when neither would serve with each other, out of a sense of duty he formed the Pitt–Devonshire ministry of 1756–7, though 'the effort it cost him ruined his health and destroyed his peace of mind'. His wife, Lord Burlington's daughter Charlotte Boyle, had died in 1754, leaving him with a six-year-old heir, and her inheritance of Chiswick House, Burlington House in Piccadilly and Londesborough in Yorkshire, and with money to spend on Chatsworth. Money, but little time, for he was to die in 1764, aged forty-four. In his brief interim he summoned Lancelot and much was accomplished.

For Lancelot and his trusty steed, Chatsworth in the Derbyshire Peak District was miles from anywhere he knew, a long ride across the middle of England if he carried on from Burghley to Newark, then Mansfield and Chesterfield. Daniel Defoe had come from the east some thirty years earlier, and had been shocked as to how quickly the leafy valley roads gave way to 'a vast extended moor or waste, which for fifteen or sixteen miles together presents you with neither hedge, house or tree, but a waste and howling wilderness, over which when strangers travel they are obliged to take guides, or it would be next to impossible not to lose their way'. And what could be more wondrous, Defoe continued, when from that 'comfortless barren' the traveller looks down into 'the most pleasant garden, and the most beautiful palace in the world'.

The Chatsworth house that Lancelot found was in the process of being 'turned around'; not quite in the manner of a miniature palace on a musical box, for the house does not move, though almost everything else does. The Elizabethan house, built by Bess of Hardwick and her husband William Cavendish in the 1550s, faced east towards the old park hunting ground on the steep ridge that shelters the Chatsworth vale. The Cavendishes' hunting tower, known as the Stand Tower, gave its name to the Stand Wood, the 'wall of trees' that covered the ridge: Defoe thought

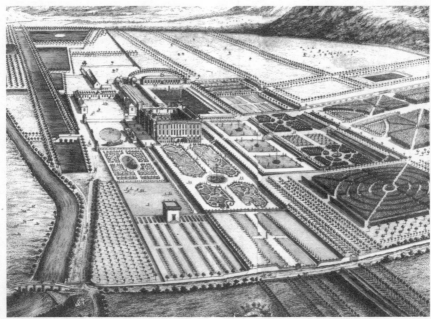

Chatsworth, Derbyshire, from *Britannia Illustrata 1707,* the house from the south, with the River Derwent and the numerous catchwater canals and pools, many removed after Lancelot had improved the drainage. He retained the formal gardens on the south front (they are there still) and also many of the evergreens, grown out after fifty years, on the east. These eastern slopes of Stand Hill were shown as much flatter than they are, giving greater status to what are merely regular plantings of clipped young evergreens: the insignificance of the stepped Cascade, hardly discernible (middle right) suggests the inaccuracy.

the 'very high mountain' wisely and beautifully planted, for mill-stones were dug at the top and the usual way of transporting them was to roll them down in pairs on a wooden axle, which would 'infallibly give a shock to the building'. The 1st Duke favoured the south front, which he had William Talman rebuild, facing out onto elaborate formal parterres planted by London and Wise. He 'found building so delightful that he could not stop' and so Talman rebuilt the east front, and then Thomas Archer was brought along to rebuild the west and north fronts. All was finished shortly before the 1st Duke's death in 1707, the year of Johannes Kip's engraving for *Britannia Illustrata*, which shows a deceptively flat array of segments and squares of clipped evergreens, very dull composi-tions, extending to the foot of the east ridge. Observers of the *Illustrata* in their town libraries would think that the Devonshires had tamed and flattened their whole valley, but Chatsworth in the flesh, so to speak, is sensuously undulating, which Lancelot would have discovered, much to his relief. Kip and Leonard Knyff are generally thought reliable amongst topographical artists, but Chatsworth's undulations disconcerted them: Grillet's Great Stepped Cascade, which was constructed in 1696 and is there still (albeit enlarged), is hardly visible as a puny runnel, having neither the force nor the fall to empower the Sea Horse Fountain, as was intended. Needless to say, other observers of the *Illustrata* have raised their hands in horror – did the 'destroyer' Brown really sweep all of that away?

The answer is 'Not guilty'. Fortunately a painting by Thomas Smith of Derby of 1743, a good dozen years before Lancelot's arrival, has come to light showing the 3rd Duke's gardening under the influence of William Kent. The lawns to the east are cleared, except for one flower bed, and the once-clipped and regimented yews and hollies are growing freely on the hillside, flanking the Cascade, much as they still do.

The 4th Duke now favoured the west front, where Archer's window frames were gilded to catch the setting sun. Kip had shown this as the entrance front, but with the coaches coming in from the south to a court with a gravel turning-sweep, and a double stone staircase for visitors to climb to the house level. The Duke knew exactly what he wanted with his new approach from the west: by a writ of the Court of Chancery of 1759 he was allowed to close a number of roads and build a new public road and a new bridge, James Paine's One Arch Bridge, at the south end of the park. This enabled his new entrance drive, contoured by Lancelot, to approach from the west, slowly dipping down to cross the Derwent, giving visitors a long view of the glittering west front, backed by the rising wall of trees of Stand Wood. This second new, private bridge was also

designed by James Paine, who worked at Chatsworth for ten years and
built the new stables, set away from the house to the north-east. Lancelot
and Paine between them created the landscape setting for Chatsworth as
painted by Richard Wilson: though perhaps Wilson was a little ungenerous
to both, painting Paine's bridge indistinctly (it might not have been finished),
and reducing the formal terraced gardens of the south and west fronts, so
carefully conserved by Lancelot, to hardly more than a painted line.

The works were quickly in hand; in August 1761 Walpole reported
that the Duke was 'making vast plantations . . . and levelling a great deal
of ground to show the river under the direction of Brown'. For the plantations of 1760–1 the accounts show 71,500 thorns, 15,000 rowan, birch
and spruce and 10,000 oaks. The 'vast plantations' that Walpole saw were
New Piece Wood and Calton Lees, a 'master-stroke' that closed the bowl
of the Chatsworth demesne on the west. Thus, 'crowning the long hill
with trees to define the distant rim of the park', Deborah, Duchess of
Devonshire wrote in 1990:

> gives the comfortable feeling of an enclosed space and, because you cannot
> see through it, seems to be far more heavily treed than it is. Brown planted
> the wood in wedge-shaped compartments, so when one section is mature
> and ready to be felled another is growing on and the line remains unbroken.
> All was planned to delight the eye from the house, making the best use
> of the contours in the wide expanse across the river.

Having set the planting in motion, Lancelot, his instincts now primed
from experience, explored the water systems. All that Walpole called
'foolish waterworks' – the pools and basins of the formal gardens, and
the apparently huge formal canal shown by Kip (1707) and by Thomas
Smith (1743) on the west of the house, almost parallel to the river –
were holding tanks for the copious storm-waters that poured off of the
eastern ridge and, unless stayed in their rushing, would bring the Derwent
into flood. Walpole had noticed how 'the river runs before the door, and
serpentises more than you can conceive'. At Chatsworth they have a
certain sangfroid about the vast labours involved – 'After the operation
it serpentised not at all, and the danger of floods was over,' wrote the
Duchess; 'the course of the river was straightened, so that the ugly ponds
could be dispensed with,' adds Charles H. Wood's guide.

'I am ever thankful,' wrote the Duchess, 'that Brown did not play his
usual trick of damming the river to make a soggy lake in full view of
the house.' Instead he conducted a serious exercise in drainage, secretly
controlling the water and playing his part in an eternal campaign to keep

the water moving, so that it does not have time to seep or sour. Drains – 'a regular topic of conversation' at Chatsworth – run for untold miles across the park and gardens, the very ancient stone soughs and modern clay-pipe drains, with Lancelot's somewhere in between. He does not appear to have built brick culverts and channels as at Croome (where bricks were plentiful and cheap), but used stone, or terracotta 'horse-shoes' about a foot long, laid on flat tiles or puddled clay. His drainage lines joined older ones, and nineteenth- and twentieth-century campaigns have added more still. The word is watchfulness, now as then: 'in the spring of 1989,' writes the Duchess, 'a patch of rushes near the bottom of the cascade' indicated a blockage; 'when they opened the place they found a drain filled with a dense mass of roots 36 feet long from a nearby yew tree. Fine and shining like a mermaid's hair, they stopped the flow of water as efficiently as a plug in a bath.'

Lancelot can only have visited Chatsworth once or twice a year at the most, when he would have discussed and pegged out the markers for the drives and plantations, making adjustments on his return visit. There is no record of his fee at Chatsworth, so it is assumed that the Duke paid him out of his own pocket. His role was as consultant, a private arrangement between themselves (rather as with Lord Exeter at Burghley), but the accounts do reveal some of the amounts paid to Lancelot's appointed foreman on the job, Michael Milliken (Melican), a Scottish gardener who was at Chatsworth from 1760 until 1765. Milliken had to tactfully lead his workforce to do *his* master's bidding without crossing swords with the estate managers: Chatsworth was the single, corporate employer, with its estate village at Edensor, but also drawing craftsmen and labourers from the surrounding villages (Curbar, Baslow and Beeley) as well as from Bakewell. Lancelot knew that his foremen in general (but especially Milliken) had to have likeable qualities so as to earn the cooperation of the men and women whose families had served Chatsworth for generations, and who had a fierce pride in belonging: this is why Lancelot was the Duke's man, something of a visiting celebrity, his bearing and the biblical authority of his dictates coming from on high, word being disseminated that *Mr Brown* was to be obeyed.

Some of the estate accounts have survived, and vivid pictures arise: of Mrs Travis and her team of women leading pony carts full of stone for the mill and new weir, being paid £52 for two years of patiently plod-ding; John Woodson and 'partners' were, under Milliken's instructions, 'draining, stubbing out old hedges and levelling the New Parke area west of the house', and were paid £25 for the year to Christmas Eve 1760.

The clearing and levelling continued: John Hayworth was paid £5. 10s. 'for twenty quarter Hayseeds delivered at Chatsworth in May 1762 to sow the New laid down grounds'. Finally, in 1764, William Vickers and his team of oxen appeared, 'to roll on ye Parke' – another patiently plodding task, for which he was paid £6. 15s., a substantial sum. Ongoing maintenance was assured with the arrival – first recorded in 1762 – of a flock of Jacob sheep. (Swaledales, Mashams and Jacobs still being the mainstay of farming here).

These long-ago labours are the foundation of Chatsworth's luminous greenness, the way the light is reflected from the uniformly green ground in this almost perfectly oriented north–south valley. For Lancelot, the green ground was simply that: the essential base for his trees, which added the textures and ever-changing colours. The thousands of thorns, rowans and birches in the enclosing plantations would have been planted as whips; well-grown trees – beech, plane, birch and oak – would have been picked out, personally marked by Lancelot, and moved to more prominent stations in the park. To these he added the signature cedars, their planting places staked out; they most likely came from Sheffield or London and still grace the valley. Scots pine, beloved for their burnt-sienna cones in May, spruce and other 'firrs' also had to be sourced; 'His Grace's waggon' was sent to 'Ashburn' (Ashbourne) to collect 'firrs' for the plantations below Beeley Moor. For acorns they had to go farther; a man was paid 10s. 6d. for a journey to Yorkshire for 'Acrons', but Dutch oaks were most highly prized – 'To the Revd Mr Barker for 8 Quart[ers] of Holland oaks £10; To 17 Q[uarters] Oates [sic] bought a[t] [King's] Lynn . . . £25'.

Michael Milliken's personality must have suited well, for in 1764 he married Mary 'Polly' Lees at Edensor; she came from an estate family, her aunt or perhaps her grandmother being the Widow Lees who figures as part of Mrs Travis's team of redoubtable stone-carters. More is revealed when, after the Duke's early death when work came to a standstill, Lancelot wrote to Milliken on 2nd January 1765.

I intend employing you in his Majesty's work at Richmond. I have spoken to the Lords of my intention and they approve as it will be doing you a service: I would therefore have you aprize Mr Barker of my intention with my compliments to him and I would have you give every information you can to Mr Travis and [tell] him about the finishing of the work that is to be done this season viz the finishing near the porters Lodge and Stables etc . . . I presume there can be but little carting done this winter time, but in everything consider the good of the work and the most prudent way of putting it in execution. Bring with you an exact acct. of the money you have recd. of Mr Barker from the beginning to the time you leave the work. I again repeat, do all the good you can whilst you remain at Chatsworth, because for the sake of the great good man that is you and on all other accts. I wish it as well my own self. My best compliments to the Family. If you are up in a fortnight from this time it will do very well, but if it will be of any use to the work stay longer. Let me hear from you and believe me your Friend.

In the middle of the Chatsworth works, in August of 1762, Thomas Gray visited his friend the Rev. William Mason in York, and then rambled on to Derbyshire. The weather was 'perverse', but the sun's rays occasionally managed to pierce the lowering skies. He found the Peak District 'beyond comparison uglier than any other I have seen in England, black, tedious, barren, and not mountainous enough to please one with its horrors' – and yet, Chatsworth:

> has the air of a Palace, the hills rising on three of its sides to shut out the view of its dreary neighbourhood, & are cover'd with wood to their tops; the front opens to the Derwent winding thro' the valley, which by the art of Mr Brown is now always visible & full to its brim, for heretofore it could not well be seen [but in the rainy season] from the windows; a handsome bridge is lately thrown over it, & the stables taken away, which stood full in view between the house & the river, the prospect opens here to a wider track of country terminated by more distant hills; this scene is yet in its infancy, the objects are thinly scatter'd, & the clumps and plantations lately made: but it promises well in time.*

There is a small footnote, in that Lancelot worked at another Cavendish house, at Latimer in Buckinghamshire, in the romantic and steep-sided valley of the River Chess, shrouded in Chiltern beech woods. The Latimer Court that Lancelot found was Jacobean, 'a fayre house, builded with brick' set in a 'little paradise' of orchards and gardens, with a dovecote, barns, stables, a coney warren and a church at the Court Gate – and a river running through the grounds. He widened the river (perhaps converting fishponds) into the Great Water, and Lower Water, with a series of cascades that still survive. He also did some planting, in the

---

* Lancelot did not work for the 5th Duke of Devonshire, portrayed as taciturn, silent and cold to his lovely wife Georgiana Spencer, whom he married in June 1774. Chatsworth is rather reduced to a stageset in their tumultuous lives, crowded with relations and visitors, neighbours (and voters), who streamed across Paine's bridge on summer days, dazzled by the great palace and its glittering windows, and by the prospects of the famed concerts and gambling parties. The gardens came into their own again with the 6th Duke and Joseph Paxton some fifty years later.

Chatsworth manner on the ridge behind the house and to screen the public road, and he apparently 'procured' the view to the west of Chenies church 'to Latimer', as there was a close connection through the Burroughs – William, rector of Latimer and Chenies, and his son Benjamin, rector of Latimer. In the cross-threading of history, Biddy Brown's kinsman, the architect Sir George Gilbert Scott, saw Latimer as a boy while staying with his uncle, rector in 1826 when the house was still owned by the Cavendish family; he found a 'little paradise':

> the village, which was in two parts – one on the hill and the other below – was very picturesque with old timbered houses, and a glorious old elm tree of towering height on the village green. The hills, valley, river, trees, flowers, fruits, fossils etc all seem to be encircled in a kind of imaginary halo. I fancy I never saw such wild flowers, or ate such cherries or such trout as there.

Lancelot must have enjoyed this Latimer, and the young Scott is witness that he did not remove the village on the hill beside the Court, although it was later moved.*

Return to Charlecote

On his ride scouting for work in the summer of 1750 Lancelot had come away from Charlecote, near Stratford on Avon, with great hopes, but progress had been slow because of George Lucy's frequent absences. That there was progress at all was undoubtedly due to Lucy's sprightly friend, the Dowager Countess of Coventry, and his housekeeper, Mrs Hayes, who both championed Lancelot's cause. To give him his due, George Lucy had gone to great trouble, including being taken to Chancery by Parson Venour of Wellesbourne, to move the road to Warwick away from his gatehouse. He had commissioned David Hiorn from Warwick to build the new (present) road bridge over the River Dene, and Hiorn demonstrates his sympathy with Lancelot's way of thinking: the bridge is to be 'a little decorated' on the side towards the park, 'the Balisters are only ½ round, and the wall at the back of them solid to the roadside, we have kept it as low as I believe in a flood it will admit of. If the Lake is opened and the banks sloaped as the line shows, I think it will have an agreeable Effect from the park side.' The bridge had been completed in the autumn of 1757 and Mrs Hayes noted in her Memorandum Book

---

* The Court was almost completely destroyed by fire in 1836 and rebuilt in the present Victorian Gothic. It had a distinguished (though often secret) service record from 1939 until 1987 and is now a conference centre. The beech woods, the Chess and the waterfalls remain.

that 'Mr Brown began to make alterations upon Wellsborn Brook', meaning that the brook – or the Dene, as it is now called – was 'opened' to flow leisurely into the Avon (perhaps via a sluice gate, as the cascade was not yet made).

Then it seems Lancelot left and George Lucy went on his travels, and so it was almost three years before a contract was signed, in May 1760, for the rest of the work. The redoubtable Mrs Philippa Hayes – in charge of Charlecote, receiver of packages of the finest green teas, pistachios, Jordan almonds, 'granulated' loaf sugar, damask linen and 'smooth flaxen sheets' from Lucy's shopping expeditions abroad and at home – struggled to maintain the lifestyle to match these luxuries, despite the cursed mud (which George Lucy went away to escape). Her ally, the Dowager Countess of Coventry, from Snitterfield (though much at Charlecote), now reinstated in the affections of Lord Coventry at Croome and witness to Lancelot's success there, took the initiative, and Lancelot returned.

Charlecote, he now appreciated, was the epitome of an older England; it needed tender care, but not modernising. His agreement was made up of five simple articles:

> Article 1: to widen the river Avon [on the west side of the house], and lay its banks properly, giving them a natural and easy level corresponding to the ground on each side of the river.
>
> Article 2: To sink the fosse [i.e. ha-ha] quite round the meadow, of a proper width, to make sufficient fence against the deer. [Here the phraseology is back to front, 'quite round the meadow' meaning around the old formal garden north of the house, though dug in the surrounding meadow or park.]
>
> Article 3: to fill up all the ponds on the north of the house, to alter the slope and give the whole a natural, easy and corresponding level with the house. [That is, dismantling the remnants of the old canals and levelling all the old beds, borders and paths to create the present lawn, 'shaped like the prow of a ship riding high above the green wash of the park'.]
>
> Article 4: the 'opening' of the banks of the Dene and making the cascade into the Avon.
>
> Article 5: to find all necessary trees, to replace any that might die, and sow all the altered ground with clean hayseed and Dutch clover. [Note the replacement of dead plants, not a modern concept.]

Charlecote was a commission of unalloyed good humour on all sides, displaying the gentlest side of Lancelot's art. His foreman here was the long-serving John Midgeley, and they returned together a little later on to alleviate the flooding of the stable-yard, and regraded the whole area to the south to make the house seem as though it was set on rising ground: more illusion than reality, but comforting all the same.

In April 1761, when Lancelot took a short break in Bath after another asthmatic attack, he called upon George Lucy, 'not upon business as he said, but to enquire after my health'. Lucy continued bemusedly:

> he told me he should not be at Charlecote till May, which I suppose will be June at the soonest. I did not well know how to construe this visit, I told him the time was elapsed for a second payment which he said was no matter as he did not want for money, but upon my offering him £100 note he pulled out his pocket book and carried it off with him

There was another stream-fed pool in Charlecote's park that Lancelot was forbidden to touch, for it housed Mrs Hayes's carp and tench, and possibly eels, destined for the table. This pool dated from the previous century, and the making of such pools for fish was a time-honoured skill. The *Angler* quotes numerous Ancient Greek and medieval authorities, declaring that fish 'of a much sweeter and more pleasant taste' came from such a pool 'refresht with a little rill'. The *Angler's* fishing advocate Piscator went further:

> to which end it is observed; that such Pools as be large and have most gravel, and shallows where fish may sport themselves, do afford Fish of the purest taste. And note, that in all Pools it is best for fish to have some retiring place, as namely hollow banks, or shelves, or roots of trees, to keep them from danger; and, when they think fit from the extream heat of Summer; as also, from the extremity of cold in Winter.

Piscator's use of the word 'Pools' is symptomatic for the times, when lowland England was a land without *lakes*: ponds, meres, broads, dells, pits, kettleholes, pingos and lagoons, but hardly 'lakes', which were seen by travellers on the Continent, but not at home. The 'lakes' of Cumbria were called 'meres' or 'waters', and like those high in the Welsh mountains and the Highland lochs, they were known to very few people.[*]

---

[*] The aesthetic virtues of the 'Lakes' were first praised in 1753 by Thomas Gray's friend, Dr John Brown of St John's College, Cambridge, who made an annual pilgrimage to Keswick. It was not until October 1769 that Gray wrote of the 'blew mirror' of Derwentwater, and 'the shining purity of the Lake just ruffled by breeze enough to shew it is alive, reflecting rocks, woods, fields & inverted tops of mountains'. The Rev. William Gilpin, connoisseur of the Picturesque, had not yet travelled at this time; and William Wordsworth, 'discoverer' of the Lake District, was not born until 7th April 1770.

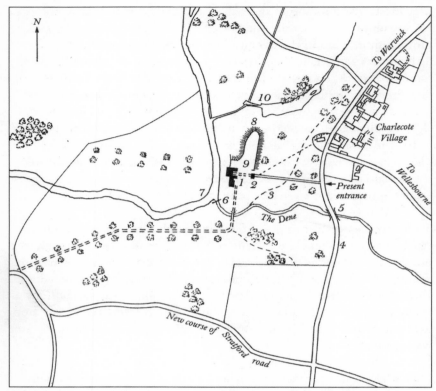

Charlecote Park, Lancelot's work for George Lucy *c.*1753–63. As there is no evident payment for this work, was it in return for Lancelot's tenancy of the house in Hammersmith Mall?

1. Charlecote house.
2. Entrance court with gatehouse.
3. Probable course of old road (surviving rights of way).
4. Line of new road.
5. New bridge built by David Hiorn, completed 1757.
6. Dene brook 'opened' to flow elegantly into river Avon, with sluice and later cascade (Article 4 of contract).
7. Avon widened and banks re-laid (Article 1).
8. Ha-ha or fosse around the raised gardens (Article 2).
9. Site of formal canals, filled and ground re-made (Article 3).
10. Old fish ponds retained for domestic use, but Lancelot engineered water flows throughout the park.

Lancelot's lake-making had begun in good stewardship, for the drainage of boggy land: at home in Kirkharle the Loraines' park had a prominent marshy stretch, which he had not had the chance to exploit, this memory of frustration adding to the satisfaction of draining the marsh at Croome. Then came the technical challenges of dam-building and controlling water levels, and when these were accomplished, the aesthetic delights of a stretch of water – as at Kiddington – took over. Along the way a fourth reason for lake-making was emerging, for no sooner was the lake filled and stocked, than the fishermen (and sometimes women) arrived. Fishing, with rod and line and usually only from the bank, was customarily allowed to local people, as well as those who worked on the estate (boating was only for the privileged). The new editions of *The Compleat Angler* highlighted the reality that if there was a truly national sport in the British Isles, it was fishing.

Lancelot would never have thought of himself as the inventor of the ornamental lake – the term indicating a lake made with skill and forethought – but, at a conservative estimate, he left 150 of them scattered across English counties from Yorkshire to Dorset, and from the Welsh borders to East Anglia. None of his professional successors (until the corporate water undertakings of the twentieth century) can claim a fraction of this number. He did have a royal predecessor: it was Queen Caroline whose wish it was to join the fish ponds in Kensington Gardens and Hyde Park into 'a long serpentine'. The *London Journal* of 26th September 1730 announced that 'next Monday they begin the Serpentine River and Royal Mansion in Hyde Park'; 200 men with barrows started digging, uncovering the elm baulks with which the Benedictine monks of Hyde Abbey had edged their fishponds. Four years later the waters of the West Bourn were let into the new lake, and soon, with much celebration, two yachts containing the royal family set sail. The royal mansion was never built, and after the Queen's death in 1737 her Serpentine Lake was opened to the public and has been called 'The Serpentine' ever since.

Following the Queen's example, pools and ponds were loosened into lakes in fashionable gardens like Stowe and Claremont. At Henry Hoare's Stourhead in Wiltshire, where the Temple of Flora had overlooked a formal basin, there was soon the lake. Even so, lakes did not come easily; the Duke of Devonshire did not want one at Chatsworth, and Lancelot had to be patient with the dithering Lord Dacre at Belhus in Essex for ten years: in 1761 Dacre was still protesting to San Miller, 'I have a number of Expences on me this year and yet I doubt whether I shall have prudence enough to abstain from meddling with my water in the lower part of the Park; the truth is that I never ride that way without longing to do something.' He knew only too well that 'Brown is of the same opinion', and eventually they did make the Long Pond out of the Running Water River, but his lordship must have doubted again, for Lancelot finally lost heart, or just became too busy elsewhere. The lake was finished by Richard Woods in 1770–1, but has now been cut through by the M25. Lancelot's successful plantations for Lord Dacre now screen part of Aveley from the motorway. The northern part of his park is now Belhus Woods Country Park, part of Thames Chase, a community forest that embraces Thorndon (now a country park) where Lancelot had also worked, and his lake survives.

George and Elizabeth Grenville's Wotton Underwood in north Buckinghamshire, which Lancelot knew well from its family connections with Stowe and Petworth, was low-lying in the meadows crossed by streams that eventually found their ways into the Rivers Thame and Thames: 'most people think that we are as much in the mud as you can be,' George Grenville wrote to San Miller in 1758. He was thanking Miller for his design for a five-arched bridge, as well as his 'ability to foresee improvements on unpromising land'. At the same time (1757–8) Grenville also gave Lancelot three payments of £100 (those £100 banknotes again, as there is no formal account?), suggesting that the mud was the result of the lake-making. Lancelot would have needed all his water-divining skills to search the meadows for the wandering tributaries of the River Ray, to capture the water into Wotton's lake system and retain it with two dams. The water forms a lake west of the house, with an island called The Warrells. From here an artificial river winds north-wards to a greater lake, which overflows into a natural stream and even-tually returns to the Ray. This was an enormously complicated piece of water engineering, but then Wotton was worth it: with a handsome house modelled on the Duke of Buckingham's house at the head of the St James's Park mall, with (then) a fine formal garden of terraces and radi-ating avenues, the Grenvilles' home was soon greatly admired for its 'deep shades of oak, softening lawns and tranquil waters'. Hester Pitt liked to bring her husband and small children back for summer holidays at her old home.

A Wiltshire Trio: Longleat, Bowood and Corsham

Lancelot's lakes had soon become an intrinsic part of his improvements, much in evidence in his new stamping ground of Wiltshire. For the work at Longleat he was paid an estimated £4,500 in five years, 1757–62, a vivid demonstration of the impact of a young heir on his decrepit inher-itance.

Frances Hertford, the patroness of the flowery Church Walk Wilderness at Syon, had grown up at Longleat, the home of her 'most affectionate grandfather', the 1st Viscount Weymouth, who was a passionate grower of fruit and planter of *Pinus strobus* (the Weymouth or white pine), the seeds being imported from New England. 'I hope we shall see you here very soon,' he had written to Frances in the summer of 1710, 'though Longleat had never less fruit; but the gardens are pleasant, and there is room enough for you and your sister to show off your good dancing.' Lord Weymouth had had George London lay out his gardens some twenty years earlier: a spectacular Great Parterre, with a central canal and fountain, divided into four-square lawns edged with clipped yews and flower-filled borders. Ranged on each side of the Parterre were whole sequences of walled gardens, their walls crowded with flowers and fruit; hardly a Longleat wall was without pears, apples, quince, cherries or apricots, and Longleat was famed for its fruit. Lord Weymouth had died four years later, in 1714, leaving an estate of 50,000 acres with an annual income of £12,000, 'a little paradise [run] on a basis of mutual service and benefit between landlord and community'. Confusion and sadness are the marks of the following decades, for the 2nd Viscount went to live in Horningsham after the death of his wife in 1736, and Longleat was emptied and shuttered, 'plunged heavily into debt and disrepair'.

In 1754 the 3rd Viscount came of age and returned: the splendours of forty years earlier were hardly evident, tastes had changed, and it was logical that Lord Weymouth should instruct Lancelot to set his house in a natural park, which the contours dictated as a bowl of greensward. Lancelot installed John Sanderson as foreman for this tremendous task; apart from the unceasing labours of dismantling, digging and barrowing away to make the smooth lawns around the house, there were the views across the 1,100-acre park to be manipulated with land-moulding and tree-planting; the ancient 'lete' from which the house took its name flowed down from the hill beyond Horningsham to the south, and it was engineered into an apparently natural series of lakes, 1 mile long; finally, a new walled kitchen garden, of immense proportions, was built at Horningsham and, apart from the drive to be constructed between the two, there were walks, adorned with shrubs and flowers, to be made from the house door to a hill called High Wood, and on from High Wood to Horningsham.

Unfortunately, these glorious achievements at Longleat were over-shadowed by the much-quoted verdict of the celebrated and well-connected Mrs Delany; as Mary Granville, she was married at Longleat in 1718. On returning in 1760, she noted 'not much alteration in the house, *but the gardens are no more*! They are succeeded by a fine lawn, a serpentine river, wooded hills, gravel paths meandering round a shrubbery *all modernised* by the ingenious Mr Brown!' Mrs Delany, a figure of some respect, has been frequently turned into an accuser, a witness to Lancelot's supposed crime of destroying old gardens. Her words should

perhaps be read in the context of her experience. She was lively, intelligent, poor and not quite eighteen at her marriage – 'sacrifice' is perhaps
the better word – to the ungainly, morose and crimson-countenanced,
but rich Alexander Pendarves, who was sixty. Some six miserable years
later she woke up one morning to find him dead beside her. She had
other reasons for expressions of loss on returning to Longleat, which
were probably nothing to do with the gardens. Nor was she necessarily
being critical of what Lancelot had done.

Some of the details of Lancelot's works have been changed in the
intervening 250 years, but overall Longleat remains glorious and truly
Brownian. What would he say if he could stand at Heaven's Gate and
watch the daily summer procession of cars winding their way down into
his park, bringing the visitors to enjoy Longleat's attractions and support
its upkeep. His great silver-trunked beeches at Heaven's Gate are gone,
lost in the storms of twenty years ago, but the guardians of British woodlands, the 'Men of the Trees' have replaced them and carved his name
with theirs.

Shortly after seeing George Lucy in Bath, in April 1761, Lancelot presented
himself at Bowood, just south of the London road at Calne, where he
had hopes of a lake. John Fitzmaurice, created Earl of Shelburne in 1753,
had bought the estate the following year, both his title and his fortune
being inherited from his mother Anne Petty, heiress of the polymath Sir
William Petty, physician, surveyor, political economist, colleague of Wren,
Pepys and Samuel Hartlib, and inventor of the 'catamaran' and the artificial harbour. His father, Thomas Fitzmaurice, 1st Earl of Kerry, was the
direct descendant of a twelfth-century baron of Kerry who had sired
swashbuckling generations loyal to their sea-misted mountain country,
and rather less so to the English Crown.

Landlocked Bowood was a passport to English society and politics.
The Earl had bought an unfinished house, which the architect Henry
Keene and the builders Holland's had completed for him, with a park
parcelled out of an old royal hunting forest (and, one fears, the grudges
held by the displaced locals to go with it). Lord Shelburne had been
recommended to consult Lancelot, but had not troubled to ask why:
'What wou'd you give to know the consequences of the visit of the
famous Mr Brown and the fruit of the 30 guineas which I gave him?'
he had written to his son and heir. 'He passed two days with me . . .
and twenty times assured me that he does not know a finer place in
England than Bowood park, and he is sure no Prince in Europe has so
fine a fruit garden.' Not knowing any European princes, Lancelot crossed

his fingers over the fruit garden, which was expensive and newly made; but the Earl, wistfully sighing over his Kerry mountains, perhaps did not appreciate how Lancelot *loved England,* and how it was all beautiful to him – especially if he had the improving of the plot in question. The Earl continued, 'I am persuaded that the man means to present me at some future time with a well-digested plan for this place, and perhaps to come to me to explain it.'

It was not a good beginning, the 'well-digested' implying facile repetition. The Earl received his plan, and was now (April 1761) – apparently happily – parting with £500 for the start of the contract. In May he died. William, 2nd Earl of Shelburne and Pitt's close colleague, was to be a much more understanding client, but a decent interval had to be observed.

The lull in proceedings at Bowood was no bad thing, for Lancelot was struggling with asthmatic attacks through the summer of 1761 and, besides checking on progress at Longleat, needed to make a start at Corsham Court, 5 miles west of Bowood in the Bath direction. He had already submitted a very cursory estimate for the park at Corsham to the owner, Paul Methuen, in December 1760, its ambiguities revealing the pressure he was under:

Making the great Walks and sunke Fence between the House and the Chippenham Road. [The only direction for the park to extend was to the north of the Elizabethan house, to the road, and it was to be divided for deer park and grazing land by the sunk fence, with a ha-ha in front of the house; the Great Walk, 1 mile long, was made.]

The Draining [of] the ground between the Sunke Fence and the line of the garden. To making the Water in the Parks, as also the levelling round it. [An oval lake was intended for Corsham, east of the house, but this unusual design was not explained or supervised, nor was the source of water identified; what transpired was a pear-shaped lake and was soon changed.]

The levelling round the House, as also on Front the New Building.

[The new building, a picture gallery on the east side of the house, made the commission appealing, providing the chance to relate the house to the setting.]

The Sunke Fence on the Front of the Church-yard. All the Planting included Mr Methuen to find trees ... the above Articles come to one Thousand and twenty Pounds.

In September 1761 Lancelot had to apologise for 'My health which

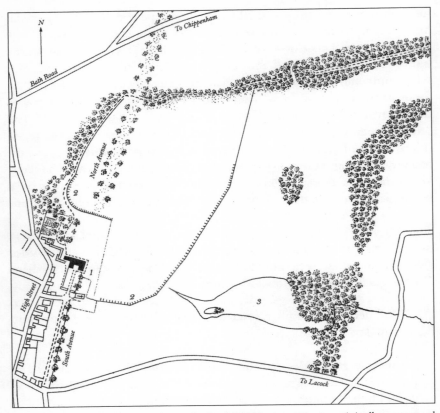

Corsham Court, Works carried out for Paul Methuen c.1761–64, originally concerned with the addition of a rectangular Picture Gallery to the east end of the house. Lancelot then persuaded his client that having built the gallery with east-facing windows, he had to contrive the views.

1. Corsham Court with St Bartholomew's Church.
2. Lancelot's ha-ha made to divide the park.
3. Lancelot's lake was more delicately shaped (pear-shaped) but this was modified after his time.
4. Gardens, shrubberies and wilderness walks to Lancelot's Gothic Bath House (also subsequently modified). The North Avenue and the South Avenue were conserved as part of the 'wilderness' walks.

has been extreamly bad [but] is now on the mend and I hope soon to be quite stout'. He intended to send John Sanderson from Longleat to Corsham to get the work started. In Paul Methuen he had found an enlightened client, who appreciated that a building needed to be carefully related to its setting, especially concerning the views from the windows. The picture gallery was to be added to the Methuens' mellow Elizabethan house, to make ready for a promised inheritance of paintings collected by Methuen's cousin and godfather, the well-travelled diplomat Sir Paul Methuen. However, it was not easy, for the church and the quaint streets of Corsham village clung close on the south and west sides of the Court – the juxtaposition of these buildings contributing to a stunning townscape. Only the east side of the house was unimpeded, so here the picture gallery – reminiscent of Lancelot's 1747 layout for Stowe's 'Long Room' (75 x 25 x 20 feet high) – was duly built.

The picture gallery is a plain block, with alterations to key it into the existing house; it has a fine coffered ceiling of 'Palmyra' design origins, the work of the stuccoist Thomas Stocking of Bristol. Despite the considerable attentions of both Repton and Nash to almost everything that Lancelot planned here, there is still the deep satisfaction of his coolly logical layout, especially in the line of the ha-ha which defines the garden; some of the trees are splendid and are certainly his, and the double-storey bath house (though Gothicised by Nash) nods to its parent, Sanderson Miller's pavilion at Farnborough Hall.

'An exceeding great tumble'

Corsham Court had its problems, for the lines of communication were so long and Lancelot's health suffered from the travelling, but there were other reasons for difficulties. These seemed to mount and almost overwhelm Lancelot in the early 1760s, the prelude to a frantic decade. In his letter to Paul Methuen of September 1761 he offered a tantalising grumble: 'but the Queen's not coming has made an exceeding great tumble in my business'. George II had collapsed and died while dressing for his morning walk the previous 24th October (1760), and the country was now ruled by his twenty-two-year-old grandson George III. George, inclined to melancholia and to falling in love with unsuitable girls, was also thought to be too much influenced by his 'dearest friend' John Stuart, the 3rd Earl of Bute. A Scot of such a clan and from a western isle, however much the elegant courtier, was clearly thought by many to be a retrograde influence, and the priority was a royal marriage to a good German princess. These things, however, are not arranged overnight – and even when they are arranged, and the princess, Charlotte Sophia of Mecklenburg-Strelitz, has been found – there are courtesies to be observed, and prayers to be offered that the weather in the Channel would be kind. Rumours were rife, facts were few, and through long summer days everyone waited. From Lancelot's point of view, several of his would-be clients dared not be missing in the depths of the countryside when the new Queen's household was appointed, nor would they commit to expensive works before their royal remuneration was assured. To Lancelot's lordly patrons, the court was a major employer:'the Queen's not coming' kept everyone in suspense.

The Princess arrived, after a stormy crossing, and was bundled into a coach at Harwich and then jolted on to London; matters were so delicate that no one had told her that she was to marry the first man she met. It was a day of intense heat, 8th September, and the young King and the seventeen-year-old Charlotte, weighed down in a dress of gold and silver, were married immediately after their first meeting, in the Chapel Royal at St James's, at ten o'clock that evening. Their coronation was celebrated on 22nd September.

St James's Palace was the accepted royal residence, but George III hated it, for it was ancient and he considered it filthy and affording little privacy. The garden – that is, St James's Park – had been open to Londoners for many years, and although it was the accepted haunt of the beau monde at the perambulating hours in the Mall, it was a played-out formal landscape dating from Charles II's time. There was a long and mouldering canal (the haunt of flocks of geese and ducks), an ancient pond (Rosamund's Pond, which stank) and ancient elms shaded the cow pastures where milkmaids sold beakers of warm and frothy milk. Londoners loved the park, but it was hardly a suitable royal garden.

Soon after the royal marriage a combination of immediacy, William Pitt and Lord Bute, resulted in Lancelot being asked to improve the park. His plan was to retain the Mall and Birdcage Walk avenues of limes, and in the space between them he proposed to replace the formal canal with a serpentine lake, as the young King favoured the natural style. Perhaps Lord Bute and his fellow courtiers had imagined that a refurbished palace and a redesigned and private park would do? Until, that is, they consulted the wiseacres with their memories of the King's grandmother, Queen Caroline, who had asked Prime Minister Robert Walpole what the cost would be of regaining St James's Park as a private garden. Walpole's sonorous reply, 'Only three CROWNS, madame', put an end to the idea.

A better solution was found when it was revealed that the Duke of Buckingham's heir, Sir Charles Sheffield, was disposed to sell his house at the head of the Mall; the beavering lawyers had discovered that part of the property was held on a ninety-nine-year Crown lease, which was about to expire. Buckingham House had long been coveted by the royal family for its large and private garden and its wilderness where nightingales sang; indeed, the young King had been taken as a boy by his father to hear them. The new plan was for the court to remain at St James's, while the beau monde and the milkmaids stayed in the park, and George III – or rather his trustees, Lord Bute and Philip Carteret Webb, acting on his behalf – paid £28,000 for what was to be called the Queen's House. The Queen's House was to be a triumph, the symbol of George and Charlotte's successful marriage, where their large family were reared in both privacy and apparent happiness.

The Duke of Buckingham's once-fine formal garden had been neglected since the Duchess died in 1742. Soon after the royal purchase, and in 1762 or 1763, Lancelot was asked to improve the garden. The survey made for the conveyance shows that he found a crooked hexagon of pasture crossed by a straggling double avenue of limes, which formerly flanked a long canal that had been filled in. With some extra acres acquired from what is now Green Park, he proposed alternative schemes: the more elaborate scheme used sculpted drifts of trees to create two large groves, the largest of these centred on the garden front of the house, containing a sublimely egg-shaped, oval lake. Sadly, this was not made (Queen Charlotte, a doting mother, perhaps feared for the safety of her young family?). Lancelot's generous 'ambits' or surrounds of trees gave just the desired privacy, and it seems that much of this shelter belt was planted. But there the elegance faded, for the 'garden' became paddocks for the animals that the Queen collected, particularly her Kashmiri goats, but most famously the elephant and zebra (the latter painted by George Stubbs), which could sometimes be seen through the railings and became a great attraction.*

There is no obvious evidence that Lancelot was paid for the St James's Park or Queen's House designs, and they do not appear in his surviving account book, which dates from 1762. Were they simply credited to him, royal appointment pending? Was he expected to become a polished courtier, as Henry Wise had been? Lancelot was far too busy to either wait around for patronage or become clubbable, though he did make one attempt at joining a fashionable society. This was the Society for the Encouragement of Arts, Manufactures & Commerce, founded in 1754 as a forum for discussions and publishing papers on a wide range of social and economic policies. It was based

---

* In 1766 Thomas Wright purloined the design idea for an oval lake for St James's Park but that was not carried out; John Nash eventually re-made the Park, largely based on Lancelot's scheme, which is basically the park we have today. Buckingham Palace garden has the successors to the belts of trees planted around the boundary, with a gravel drive meandering through them, which has survived from Lancelot's 1762–3 layout.

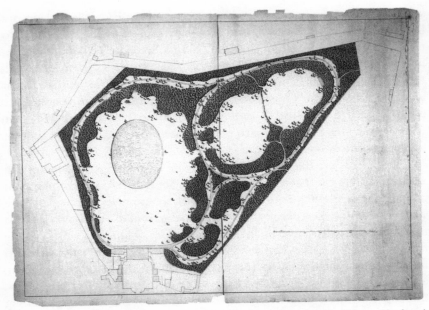

The Queen's House, now Buckingham Palace, Lancelot's proposals for Queen Charlotte's grounds, c.1762.

in the Strand, and one imagines Lancelot hurrying to or from Drummonds Bank or Northumberland House on a sunny morning, when he met Sir Thomas Robinson, a great proposer of members, in line with a drive to reach 1,200. Lancelot was proposed at a meeting on 6th August 1760, and elected on 20th August – 'Lancelot Brown Esq, Hammersmith' being entered in the register – and he paid his two-guinea subscription. He found his fellow members to be attorneys, cabinet-makers, soldiers, merchants, clothiers and booksellers, and there were also a great number of his clients and supporters, as well as Robert Adam, David Garrick and William Chambers. Most importantly for Lancelot, and elected at the same meeting, were the brothers Clive: Robert and Richard and George.

Robert Clive was the hero of the hour, newly returned to England, as Lady Northumberland had recorded in her diary just a month earlier, on 15th July 1760: 'Colonel Clive arrived from India dined in public at the White Hart in Guildford [with] all the doors and windows thrown open, that everybody's curiosity might be satisfied.' On his way to London, Clive had passed close to Claremont at Esher, and had perhaps been fêted there by the Duke of Newcastle – had he fallen in love with it then? Lancelot's fame would have been new to him, but their encounter was significant, for Colonel Clive was a fine judge of beautiful places and had a fortune to spend.

The new Society talked much of *landscape* – a word frequently noted in the minutes, though this emerged as the offer of premiums or awards 'for mezzotints, etchings, and engravings of woods, pastures or landscape'. A large sub-committee was set up for the promotion of these images, without Lancelot, but including the painters Joshua Reynolds and Richard Wilson and the architect William Chambers. Tree-planting was another favoured topic, frequently mentioned in the minutes as 'logging', because it transpired that the interest of many landowning members was in commercial forestry and the production of 'props' for the burgeoning mining industry. Lancelot's subscription was not recorded after that first year.

In these earliest years of George III's reign, Lancelot's innocent lake-making and planting activities were caught up in great matters, and many of his patrons and clients were currently mired in ministerial instability. He had two royal commissions, but still no royal appointment. He had well-founded hopes of Lord Bute as a client, but it was disconcerting that the amiable Lord Holderness of Sion Hill had been ousted to make way for Bute, the King's favourite, as Secretary of State for the Northern Department. This meant that Pitt and Lord Bute were in uneasy harness, with Pitt, the 'great hawk-nosed tyrant', scheming ever more expensively to win the war. Suddenly, just days after the coronation on 22nd September, Pitt announced his resignation. He lost his temper in disgust at the crit-icism of his policies, which were essentially to fight more wars to end the war, his patience and pride foundering on the rejection of his plan to capture a Spanish treasure fleet sailing from the River Plate in order to escalate Spanish aggression. He resigned on 5th October 1761, and this was the prelude to five years in the wilderness. He accepted a title for Hester, who became Countess of Chatham, and a pension of £3,000 a year.

In the ensuing Cabinet reshuffle, and much to Pitt's fury, his brother-in-law George Grenville defected to Lord Bute, causing a rift between Pitts and Grenvilles, which meant that the new Countess could no longer take her children to Wotton Underwood. When Lord Bute, hounded by gossip and lampoons – his 'erections' at Kew doubling for his develop-ments of Kew Gardens and his supposed affair with Princess Augusta – and disowned by the King, resigned in April 1763, it was George Grenville who rose to the top of the pile as First Lord of the Treasury. Grenville was apparently dull and domineering ('an unimaginative schoolmaster') and the King would soon tire of him, but he was in the highest office, and in charge of patronage, at the moment when Lancelot needed him.

'Will the Thames ever forgive me?'

After eleven years of sociable widowhood Lady Cobham had died in March 1760; Stoke Park was to be sold. She left her riches to her companion, Miss Henrietta Jane Speed, and it seems likely that to Lancelot she did a last good deed, in mentioning his name to her new young neighbour, the 4th Duke of Marlborough at Langley Park. Lancelot was duly summoned to Langley and presented his scheme, with a large lake, which the Duke liked 'very well'; but, he added in his letter of 29th June 1763, 'as I cannot begin to make alterations (at least *expensive* ones) at this place and [Langley] at the same time, I have a notion I shall begin here immediately so that the sooner you come the better'. 'This place' was Blenheim.

Ever since his small and successful lake on the River Glyme at Kiddington, Lancelot must have dreamed of Blenheim, hovering like Olympus on the near horizon. The Glyme also flowed through Blenheim's park, where it met the Evenlode, and thus the Thames. In the *Angler* Piscator asserted that of the 325 rivers in England:

> the chief is Thamisis, compounded of two Rivers, Thame and Isis; whereof the former rising somewhat beyond Thame in Buckinghamshire, and the latter in Cyrencester in Glocestershire meet together about Dorcester in Oxfordshire, the issue of what happy conjunction is the Thameisis or Thames. Hence it flyether betwixt Berks, Buckinghamshire, Middlesex, Surrey, Kent and Essex, and so weddeth himself to the Kentish Medway in the very jaws of the Ocean.

Neither Piscator nor Lancelot had our graphic ways of seeing river systems, but Lancelot knew well enough that the upper tributaries of 'this glorious River' were beautiful and challenging, and also that for his purposes the Thames itself could rarely be captured below Oxford – Syon being the exception.

He could easily reach Blenheim in that midsummer, for he was working not 10 miles away to the north at Aynho, which is an interesting essay in the ways of water. Aynho belonged to William Cartwright, a Northamptonshire Member of Parliament, fairly recently married to his second wife, Elizabeth Dormer from Rousham. Rousham was William Kent's romantic 'Elysian Fields' garden in the Cherwell valley to the south, and so Elizabeth Cartwright may well have been the spur to improving

Aynho, for it was a place of deep country ways and traditions: 'A Map of the Garden, Park & Some Landscape at Aynho taken by W' (the name has been torn off, but may be William Collison, who made a later survey) is dated 1758, about four years before Lancelot's arrival. It shows an old-fashioned place, the house and a cluster of courts and stables, the church close on the east side, with a southward view to a 'terras' and lawn and a long, long double avenue stretching out across the fields. On the higher land to the east is an L-shaped pool surrounded by trees, and Puck Well is a feature. This map tells all, for anyone standing on the terrace after a good deal of rain would see rivulets flowing across the middle of the park, which surveyor Collison (if it was he) has marked with Ys to indicate the wet areas.

The Aynho accounts of Francis Burton, the agent, detail the Cartwrights' complex affairs; they have property all over England, and in London, and are closely connected with their neighbours at Astrop (where Lancelot has been) and with the Knightleys at Fawsley (where he will soon go). William Cartwright habitually drew £50 pocket money, but then '£200 for Mr Brown' is entered on 29th August 1761, for his visit, staking out the 'lake', the line of a ha-ha to separate the lawn from the park, and the positions for six clumps of trees. From March 1762 to July 1763 his Drummonds account shows that Lancelot was paid a total of £480, indicating that these works were done. William Cartwright died in 1768 and was succeeded by his son Thomas; a good ten years afterwards it was decided to record those changes to the park landscape; by the time this was done even Lancelot was dead, but the map survives, beautifully cartouched and framed, showing the terrace flanked by wilderness plantations or 'shrubberies' of evergreens and deciduous trees, the ha-ha in place at the end of the lawn, and the whole park crossed by an elegant linear lake. The six tree clumps were in place, rather reminiscent of Kent's style at Rousham and elsewhere.*

There was a dramatic change of scale from Aynho to Blenheim, the latter huge in all senses and especially challenging. For Lancelot, Blenheim was mainly about a bridge, Vanbrugh's Grand Bridge over the River Glyme. The bridge, 'a truly monumental structure' with a main arch spanning 101 feet and flanking subsidiary arches, had been designed with towers and an arcade rising to 80 feet, and contained more than two dozen rooms, some with fireplaces and chimneys, and one 'plastered and fitted

---

* Less than a decade later the lake was gone: the Coventry–Oxford Canal was completed in early 1790, and presumably the need for water lowered the water table, sucking the local springs dry, including the sources of the Aynho lake, and of the healing Astrop Wells not far away, which also dwindled into memory.

with an elliptical arch as though for a theatre'. The main arch had been completed in 1710, and two more years finished the bridging structure, but then progress was halted and the towers were never topped, nor was the covering arcade built. 'I made Mr Vanbrugh my enemy,' wrote Sarah, Duchess of Marlborough, 'by the constant disputes I had with him to prevent his extravagance.'

'That bridge in the air' as she called it, was the cause of a major dispute, and another was Vanbrugh's campaign to preserve the ruins of the old royal manor of Woodstock close by: there was a strange irony in that the bridge only became usable when Woodstock Manor had been demolished, its walls quarried for rubble filling, and 'the very hill upon which it stood was reduced to provide material to fill those gaps at the valley side and to create a high causeway'. Vanbrugh's disputes with the Duchess ended in her sending written orders out to the lodge-keepers to prevent him entering the park, and the final ignominy came when he arrived one day with a coachload of friends, who were allowed to enter, while he and his wife had to spend the day in a Woodstock inn.

Such tales, frequently told, made Lancelot wary, and so to have things clear from the start he sent Jonathan Spyers to make a detailed survey of the 'Park and Gardens with some Land adjoining containing 2,314 acres'.* The surveyed area stretched from the Woodstock town boundary to the house, the course of the Grand Avenue (two double rows of English elms, 686 elms at 2s. 6d. each, their lines supported by battlemented blocks of four and eight trees) planted by Henry Wise in 1716. The Great Duke of Marlborough had asked Wise 'to consider he was an old man and could not expect to live till the trees were grown', so the elms were planted fully grown with the baskets that encased their rootballs. It is always said that Wise was a master at moving large trees, and certainly Spyers has drawn the avenue as if complete, even after more than forty-five years.

The Grand Avenue is on the axis that runs across the Grand Bridge, extending through the centre of the house to become the main axis of the Duke's military tribute garden, the state garden or Woodwork. This was the apotheosis of military gardens, and there was never anything like it at Stowe: a 'colossal polygon' with eight bastions and stone curtain walls, a walk along the walls giving a commander's view over Wise's 'ranks of rifle green', an immaculate planting of yews, hollies, bay trees

---

* Spyers was paid £57. 17s. The survey in pen and ink and watercolour over graphite (pencil) measures 20½ x 28½ inches and is clearly annotated in the top left-hand corner 'A Survey of Blenheim Park before Mr Brown's works'.

and laurels (measured for conformity of height before they left the Brompton nursery). The Woodwork and the wilderness plantings to the east and west of it, and Vanbrugh's gigantic walled kitchen garden, as well as the flower parterres on the east front of the house for the duchess, had constituted Brompton nursery's finest hour, a tour de force in growing, delivering and planting thousands of differing plants. It was clearly also a maintenance burden, work for an army of clippers and scythers, and it was ever a sore point with the Marlboroughs that the Grateful Nation may well have given them Blenheim, but there was no allowance for maintaining it.

At the time of the 1st Duke's death in 1722 a final military tribute scheme was in progress, the work of the Duke's former engineer officer, Colonel John Armstrong, who rejoiced in the title Chief Engineer of England: the Colonel devised the canalisation of the Glyme, which entered the park from the Woodstock direction, and was contained in a Pool, like a giant cistern, dug deeply into the side of the promontory upon which Blenheim house stands. The Pool has a long dam intended for a cascade and controlling the outflow into a narrow, militarily straight canal beneath the Grand Bridge. In 1723 the Duchess Sarah told the Duke of Somerset (the widower 6th 'Proud' Duke at Petworth, who had had the effrontery to propose marriage to her) that Vanbrugh had 'never thought of this cascade . . . which will be the finest & largest that ever was made'. She also mentioned her plan for a lake 'on the other side [of the bridge] . . . and I will have swans & all such sort of things . . .' But her lake did not appear, for she allowed

Blenheim, Oxfordshire, Boydell's engraving of Colonel Armstrong's scheme for the military canal for Sarah, Duchess of Marlborough.

Colonel Armstrong's sappers to continue their work, extending the canal on the west side of the bridge to a circular basin that enabled a ninety-degree turn southwards, the canal continuing to a dam, which controlled the flow through three large fishponds, and so back to the natural river. The antiquarian William Stukeley sketched Blenheim from above Rosamund's Well in 1724 and shows the bridge, the canal and the circular pool. On the other hand, *Vitruvius Britannicus* of 1725 showed Blenheim supposedly complete, but with a canal beneath the Grand Bridge and the lake looking 'natural', which has prompted questions as to exactly what Lancelot found.

He is supposed to have found the Grand Bridge looking ridiculous, the subject of Pope's wit:

> The minnows, as under this vast arch they pass,
> Murmur, 'How like whales we look, thanks to your Grace'.

Clearly this much-quoted quip displeased the young George, 4th Duke, who had adored Blenheim from his childhood and was now the proud owner. He must have asked Lancelot to restore some grandeur to his Bridge, but until fairly recently there was a deal of scepticism that the Colonel's canal had continued beyond the bridge to the circular pool, and beyond that; the discovery of an aerial-survey photograph from 1961 clearly shows the line of the canal, the circular pool and right-angled turn as ghostly shadows in the waters of Blenheim's lake. A plan and contract for building the canal *c*.1722 have also been found, the work of masons William Townsend and Bartholomew Peisley junior. (Peisley's father and Townsend had built the Grand Bridge.) In retrospect, what could have been more fitting in the 1720s than a military canal to complement the military garden?

Spyers' survey is therefore proved accurate on all points: he shows the artificial nature of the eastern pool with much of the cascade looking redundant, and the complete canal. He also shows the rather ragged state of the Woodwork, the military garden and accompanying wildernesses. Lancelot's 1765 plan of his proposals is hurried and unfinished – that is, it does not show the Woodwork on the south side of the house, the space being taken up by the annotation: 'A Plan for the intended alterations to the Water at Blenheim for His Grace the duke of Marlborough'. Even the house is only lightly indicated: 'To the Water' clearly indicates his intentions, but the omission of the details of the military gardens has encouraged leaping to the wrong conclusion that he demolished them, when he clearly did nothing of the sort. The evidence supporting Lancelot comes from Thomas Pride's 1789 survey plan, which shows the contentious areas much as Spyers' did in 1763.

So what did Lancelot do at Blenheim? He worked there for ten years and the Duke evidently paid him £15,450, an enormous sum implying that a permanent workforce was kept in his employ under the foreman, for much of the time John Midgeley.*

To begin with, as was his way, Lancelot had used his eyes and experience; he walked the land on horseback or on foot; coming from the Woodstock Arch entrance (as is most rewarding today), he would have been repelled by the slovenly and marshy course of the Glyme, and the steep and mostly bare banks of the 'cistern' pool. The foreground to the house had the appearance of a bare cliff, gashed out of the land: the area below and around the canal as it passed under the Grand Bridge was reed-ridden and marshy, indicating inadequate control of the water; beyond the bridge and around the curving valley sides, the ground was boggy and marshlike, indicating that the Glyme was intent on returning to the areas where it had naturally flowed. It was rather like a vast, over-grown moat surrounding the house on two sides.

For Lancelot, an elaborate drawing was unnecessary; it was all in his head, and in his mind's eye he could see the natural forms of the land and the flow of the water. Most of all, he could see how the Grand Bridge could be restored to dignity, and the minnows would no longer laugh. Beginning at the Woodstock entrance, with the Glyme and an additional stream flowing down from the park, he made careful 'openings' of the banks to softened profiles, grading the soil back considerable distances on either side, and making the level drives from the Woodstock Gate, and across the Grand Bridge. This great labour extended along the river's course, reshaping the valley until he reached the dam, where the water cascaded back into the 'natural' river. The work must have been done in stages, scouring and clay-lining the deepest course, waiting for the water to fill, then opening the banks further, and repeating the laborious adjustments to the banks and curves, and the dam, until the water reached the desired level, at the springing point of the main arch of the Grand Bridge. It was a stately ritual, with men, earth and water moving in tune to the rainfall and the seasons.

---

* The account book begins in 1764 with £1,900; 1765, £1,400; 1766, £1,800; 1767, £1,000; 1768, £3,600; 1769, £1,200; 1770, £1,000, and 1771 'a balance of All Accounts to October 27th 1770,' £2,550; Drummonds accounts show £1,000 paid in 1773. These sums included Langley Park, which began as a contract sum of £2,810, but probably escalated.

With the ground modelled to his satisfaction, the course of the lake was dressed with trees, a Lebanon cedar or two on a low bank, small clumps of shrubs and trees masking the bridge's ends, hanging woods where the banks were steepest. It was designed to be seen from horseback, or from a phaeton or curricle, the vistas opening and closing as a moving picture – the faster the trotting, the faster the picture changed. Even today on foot the slower magic can be made to work. At several points, but especially from either end of the Grand Bridge, looking south to where the lake appears beyond the planted promontory, Blenheim's lake makes a very fair imitation of a tree-girt reach of the Thames.

So, did Lancelot really say in his moment of triumph, 'Will the Thames ever forgive me?' He had tampered with two of the Thames's tributaries, for the Glyme flows into the Evenlode as it leaves Blenheim's park. But Lancelot and the River Thames had a very special relationship, and he could say what he liked; who could blame him, for he had wrought a patient and painstaking miracle, glorified in Turner's magnificent painting and evident to this day.

'Mimic desolation covers all'

The Duke's promised thousands for Blenheim were on a scale in excess of even Burghley and Croome, but at times when the Grand Bridge presided over an expanse of mud and ravaged earth and stones, not unlike a battlefield, Lancelot must have spent some nervous nights – if not weeks of them. Not everyone was on his side, his critics were ready to pounce, and his parks (or the people that owned them) were embroiled in political extremes of hatreds and favouritisms. His 'landscapes' were vulnerable, and so was he, with as yet no royal patronage as shelter. A nasty reminder now came in a footnote to his dealings with Henry Fox at Holland Park, far back in 1755.

Fox had succeeded William Pitt as Paymaster-General, reputedly making a profit of £400,000; after the Peace of Paris of 1763 he retired with his title, 1st Baron Holland of Foxley, to the extreme point of Kent, the North Foreland, where he built a mock-Roman villa, called Holland House. The bay, where legend had it Charles II had found refuge from a storm, was called Kingsgate; the villa was surrounded with follies, a miniature parade with cannon, a ruined castle (the stables), the Countess's fort (an ice house), a crumbling cloister and the 'gate' itself, a Gothic arch spanning a break in the chalk cliff. Horace Walpole lambasted the collection of 'ruins' as 'in no style of architecture that ever appeared before or has since', and Thomas Gray dubbed them the expression 'of a broken character and constitution'. Gray's lines 'On Lord Holland's Seat

near Margate, Kent' (published without his consent in 1769) find the
isolation of the place and the nearness of the treacherous Goodwin Sands
ominously disturbing:

> Yet nature cannot furnish out the feast,
> Art he invokes new horrors still to bring.
> Now mouldering fanes and battlements arise,
> Arches and turrets nodding to their fall,
> Unpeopled palaces delude his eyes,
> And mimic desolation covers all.

Gray's indictment goes further: that where Lord Holland creates horror
and desolation in his miniature landscape, he would have destroyed Britain
herself with his 'egotistical dreams of destruction and control':

> 'Ah,' said the sighing Peer, 'had Bute been true
> Nor Shelburne, Rigby's, Calcraft's friendship vain,
> Far other scenes than these had bless'd our view
> And realis'd the ruins that we feign.
> Purg'd by the sword and beautify'd by fire,
> Then we had seen proud London's hated walls,
> Owls might have hooted in St Peter's quire
> And foxes stunk and litter'd in St Paul's.'

8

THE KING'S
MASTER GARDENER AT
HAMPTON COURT

But your Great Artist, like the source of light,
Gilds every Scene with beauty and delight;
At Blenheim, Croome and Caversham we trace
Salvator's wildness, Claude's enlivening grace,
Cascades and Lakes fine as Risdale drew,
While Nature's vary'd in each charming view.

—Anon. to Lord Irwin, 1767

WHETHER BY ACCIDENT OR DESIGN, Lancelot met George Grenville in June 1764 at Shortgrove, in Essex. Grenville was halfway through his two-year term as First Lord of the Treasury, and he and his wife Elizabeth were visiting her kinsman, Percy Wyndham O'Brien. Though Lancelot knew Shortgrove, in the Cam valley south of Saffron Walden, as belonging to Sir John Hynde Cotton of Madingley, it was either recently sold or let to O'Brien (later Earl of Thomond), for whom Lancelot was 'dressing up' the Cam and the small park. In conversation with George Grenville, he took his chance to mention his hopes for a royal appointment.

When he moved on to Redgrave, near Bury St Edmunds, he sat down to pen a difficult letter to Grenville, dated 22nd June: 'You, I am sure [are] not un[a]quainted that those people you do the greatest favours' – here he stumbles over saying that they invariably ask for more, ploughing on, 'My case is that at this time, which liberty I hope you will excuse, I would have made the request when I had the honour of seeing you . . . but my courage failed me.' He finally reaches his point:

I should be very happy to have the garden at Windsor Castle included in the Warrant . . . I know it is a very small thing but if ever the King should like to do anything there I think it would give me a better [protection] my having the place to be employed; I understand that there are about eight acres of ground which is to be kept, but this I do not know but by hearing: I know you will do it if you think it is proper but, if it is not, I do not desire it.

George Grenville was swift to action, for *The Gentleman's Magazine* of July 1764 carried the news of Lancelot's appointment as Master Gardener at Hampton Court, though mistakenly it called him 'Surveyor', which was a courtier's sinecure and quite another matter. The Royal Warrant, dated 16th July, gives the curious amount of £1,107. 6s. a year, plus £100 for 'raising pineapples' and another £100 for 'parcel fruits', but Lancelot's account book shows that he received the expected £2,000 a year, paid in four quarterly instalments of £500, without fail. The warrant also mentions the garden at Richmond, the King's and Queen's favoured retreat beside the Thames opposite Syon, adjoining the garden of the King's mother, Princess Augusta, at Kew. Later in 1764 Lancelot was additionally appointed gardener at St James's, which included the Queen's House. Another £40 worth of responsibility was added for the care of the Treasury garden, part of which survives as the garden of No. 10 Downing Street.

The history of royal gardeners was chequered: sixty years earlier in 1704 Queen Anne had appointed her trusty Henry Wise as deputy Ranger of St James's Park, a high honour that allowed him the privilege of riding in the park. The mystique of the royal parks was already established in that the Rangerships were a prime gift of the sovereign, usually confined to members of the royal family: a deputy Rangership was the highest that a commoner could hope for, though deputies were usually courtiers. With the arrival of George I, the workaholic Wise assumed responsibility for everything, he and Charles Bridgeman being appointed 'Chief Gardiners' for the 'ordering and keeping' of Hampton Court, Kensington Palace gardens, Hyde Park, the King's palace at Newmarket, Windsor Castle and St James's. At George I's death in 1727 Wise had retired to his house in Warwick, and Bridgeman was left with an inventory of niggling duties for George II: 'supplying Horse Dung & all other sorts', carrying the King's summer fruit (much of this grown in the walled gardens at Hampton Court) and other 'eatables' to wherever the King was resident, 'daily by relays of men', along with the onerous pruning and tying tasks that were more usually the lot of apprentices.

With Bridgeman's death in 1738, the empire had fragmented into little kingdoms, and the name of Greening became prominent. Thomas Greening, a nurseryman at Brentford (Brayneforde), was gardener to the Duke of Newcastle at Claremont, but he also held responsibilities for Richmond, Kensington and St James's – all these posts becoming available with his death in 1757, which gave the opportunity for Lancelot's 1758 petition. Of Thomas Greening's three sons, Robert was gardener to Princess Augusta at Kew; John quietly succeeded his father at Kensington and Richmond, and may have taken over from George Lowe at Hampton Court; the third, Henry, was a royal gardener for a time, but inherited a fortune, changed his name to Gott, was knighted and became a country squire.

With the accession of George III, the merry-go-round started spinning once more, and John Greening apparently retired, leaving Richmond vacant for Lord Bute's choice of John Haverfield; meanwhile Bute's botanical colleague, the unfrocked apothecary John Hill, was given Kensington Gardens, and a modestly quiet man, John Kent, was at Windsor Castle. This was the rigmarole that preceded Lancelot getting Hampton Court and St James's; at Richmond, which the King asked him to redesign, he worked in reasonable harmony with John Haverfield.

Lancelot's nervous plea to George Grenville for Windsor to be added to his charges stemmed from his disappointment at the fate of his schemes for the Queen's House and St James's Park, where his lack of official status meant that they were implemented (or not) by other hands. His 'hearing' – gardeners' gossip – had been accurate about Windsor, for the 8 acres included a walled garden on the south of the castle giving onto the Long Walk, comprising a kitchen garden and the Garden House garden, soon to be enlarged by adding the garden of Burford House, originally built for Nell Gwyn. Apparently John Kent, the gardener in charge, was ailing, and Lancelot wished him to keep 'the whole project . . . so long as he lives'. If Lancelot imagined, as he seemed to do, that the King and Queen would use Windsor, he was right, even though 'every contiguous spot is open to public resort', which was the main drawback; Queen Charlotte soon made the Garden House into Queen's Lodge – a home for the family when the King hunted at Windsor – but the garden was not a priority and it was not added to Lancelot's warrant. (The garden and Queen's Lodge are the backdrop to Benjamin West's portrait of the Queen, and her children, of 1779, but the garden appears to comprise just lawn.)

Why did Lancelot want Windsor? Did he imagine that the King and Queen would require some private grounds, which would enable him to 'improve' part of the Great Park? After all, it was only at Windsor that the royal family made any semblance of living in the country, with a residence and attendant acres such as most of their courtiers enjoyed on their own estates. Unfortunately for Lancelot, since the King's uncle – William Augustus, Duke of Cumberland, Ranger of the Park and Keeper of Windsor Forest – had employed his soldiers returned from Culloden in earth-moving and planting in the southern part of the park (at Virginia Water), the Great Park was jealously guarded as a royal prerogative. At William Augustus's death in 1765, the posts of Ranger and Keeper were divided between two of the King's brothers, and Henry Frederick, Duke of Cumberland, became the Ranger. The Sandby brothers, Thomas and Paul, who served William Augustus in Scotland, also came south to work at Windsor; Thomas was made deputy Ranger of the Great Park in 1765 and, with his brother as artist and draughtsman, they were firmly in control of improvements.

Not for the first time, the one thing at which Lancelot excelled was the jealously guarded perquisite of a member of the family – it was becoming a hazard of his lonely profession. Lancelot was a phenomenon that the King and Queen did not really wish to understand: George III preferred architecture to gardens, and Queen Charlotte, when her child-bearing allowed, was an avowed miniaturist, loving her botany and flower paintings, and eventually her private garden at Frogmore, where only her friends were allowed. The royal establishment seemed happiest with old-fashioned, string-around-the-trousers gardeners, bred to tending pineapple pits, like 'old James' who lived in a shed at Hampton Court. Lancelot could see little scope for his particular talents, and the implication was that he would continue his private practice, and that his royal recognition would give him added status amongst his clients. He assumed his honour with a characteristic appearance of amusement.

Wilderness House at Hampton Court

The Brown family's move from Hammersmith Mall followed soon after the confirmation of Lancelot's royal appointment, probably in the autumn of 1764. It was to make great changes in all their lives.

The family had been completed with the birth of Margaret, known as Peggy, baptised on 2nd November 1758, and Thomas (an infant Thomas had been born and died in 1757), the baby of the family, baptised on 24th July 1761. That year their eldest son, Lance, had started at Eton College, boarding with Mrs Yonge, and Jack followed a year later. Had Lancelot not heard of William Pitt's opinion, based upon his own miserable experience, that he 'scarce observed a boy who was not cowed for life at Eton; that a publick school might suit a boy of turbulent forward disposition but would not do where there was any gentleness'. Pitt determinedly educated his children at home, as was to be the happy fate of young Thomas Brown. Presumably, from Lancelot's point of view, he wanted the best for his older sons and could pay for it; after all, the Pitt children lived in a society of influential relatives, but Lance and Jack Brown's playmates in Hammersmith were much less likely to be the kind of friends who could help them through life; hence their dutiful, if naïve father assumed that Eton would be the making of them. It is said that Lance's Eton nickname was 'Capey', in allusion to 'Capability', thus revealing (out of the mouth of some noble babe) that a clique of Lancelot's clients called him this – but between themselves and never to his face. (The Eton College archives give no source for the 'Capey' story, which could have been imaginative hindsight, as no contemporary mention of 'Capability' has been found so far.)

The Browns' new home, Wilderness House, was named for its position close to the huge Maze or Wilderness (in fact between the Wilderness and the walled gardens) on the north side of Hampton Court Palace, and inside the wall. The house was built in William III's time, of dark-red Hampton bricks, and is shown clearly on Leonard Knyff's spectacular bird's-eye view of the palace and the Thames of 1702. Two years earlier it had been identified as the 'Master Gardener's House & Court' in a plan by Wren, when the scheme (originally drawn by Hawksmoor in 1689) for a magnificent north entrance to the palace aligned on the Bushy Park avenue (and demolishing the Wilderness and the house) was still a possibility.

Wilderness House was secluded from garden activity, with a private court, stables and a coach house; the Browns may have had a coach in their last years at Hammersmith, and certainly acquired one with their move. The ground floor of Wilderness House had small but elegant panelled rooms, with bedrooms above, and an attic storey. Lancelot complained of the condition as he found it: 'the Offices are very bad, the Kitchen very offensive and the rooms very small and uncomfortable for one who at times am afflicted with an Asthma'. The house was refurbished, both at this time and later in his tenancy.

One of the panelled rooms became his workroom, and there was a breakfast room as well as a parlour, or perhaps they called it the drawing room; remembering that Biddy Brown had come from a fine Georgian town house in Boston to a Vanbrugh pavilion 'fit for a gentleman' at Stowe, and latterly to a riverside terraced house in Hammersmith, she knew how to furnish Wilderness House in comfort and style. In his later letters Lancelot mentions the paintings he has seen in other people's houses, and he is soon part of a circle of collectors in Hampton. They had family books – other than his architectural and gardening books in his study – and Bridget prided herself on her fine linen and china; Lancelot surely brought her some treasure from his travels, especially his visit to Staffordshire when he saw Josiah Wedgwood's wares – perhaps a piece of early green glazeware or even creamware, 'a species of earthenware for the table quite new in its appearance, covered with a rich and brilliant glaze', which was available at the time. They owned for certainty one special silver-branched candlestick, requiring perhaps four expensive (one penny each) wax candles for an evening's light for Lancelot to work by; his eldest daughter Bridget so loved this candlestick that he promised to leave it to her in his Will.

In true fashion, the Browns were an extended family: Biddy's niece, Philippa ('Philly') Cooke from Boston, lived with them, soon occupying a firm place in their affections. Their domestic staff, the cook and the young maids, were surely fortunate in their employers, though we know nothing about them, but mention is made of manservants, the brothers William and George Davis, who were with the Browns for the rest of Lancelot's life. Either William or George may have been an outdoorsman, in charge of the stables, horses and stable boys. As Wilderness House was inside the palace wall, its surroundings were looked after by the Hampton Court gardeners. Lancelot did acquire a separate yard – apparently Henry Wise's old garden yard – which he used for holding plant consignments and as a store.

It was an enchanting, if otherworldly place to live in during the 1760s. While for Lancelot it was merely a different base for his travels up and down the country, Biddy Brown noticed the changes, and perhaps saw a repeating pattern in her life – her move from lively Boston to Stowe now paralleled in their move from busy Hammersmith to Hampton Court. Hampton Court had always been a community in the service of a potentate who loved a garden, from Cardinal Wolsey and Henry VIII to William III and Queen Mary, but since Queen Anne's time it had seen only occasional use, and now George III had declared that he would never live there. Paintings, furniture and tapestries were gradually moved from Wren's splendid court apartments, spirited away to other royal residences. The palace was now in the charge of a well-born resident housekeeper, Mrs Elizabeth Mostyn, who was paid £250 a year salary, but was allowed to pocket one shilling a head from visitors whom she conducted around, sometimes bringing her £800 in annual income. There was still a regiment of Foot Guards at the palace barracks, but the military presence was lessening and the Master General of Ordnance had little to command; and the courts of the Tudor palace were rapidly emptying of such luminaries as the Pastry Officer, the Scullery Sergeant and the Keeper of the Fish Larder, all of whom had had their proud titles on their doors since the time of Henry VIII. The armies of footmen and cooks, seam-stresses and starchers, and the dairymaids, had all wandered away.

Soon the process of converting the Base and Clock Courts and the Master Carpenter's Court into sheltered housing of the 'grace and favour' kind would begin, and to this end the masons, carpenters and plumbers were continuously employed under the control of the Clerk of Works, William Rice, who was there all through Lancelot's time. 'Grace and favour' was a popular idea; it was well known that Dr Johnson had applied for an apartment, but none was available; William Brummell, private secre-tary to Lord North and father of the famous Beau, was luckier and moved in during the early 1770s, becoming one of many strollers in the gardens who regularly raised his hat to the Master Gardener, and whom Lancelot acknowledged in return.

The gardens were a great attraction; every morning Lancelot would pass a knot of visitors waiting by the Lion Gates for admittance, which was granted to everyone of respectable appearance. It made a refreshing change to meet with more ordinary opinions and manners in one of 'his' gardens, where he had been used to lordly families and labourers, with few of 'the middling sort' in between. His neighbours' and visitors' appreciations of the gardens perhaps weighed with him when the King invited him (or so the story goes) to 'improve' the Great Fountain Garden, which he declined, 'out of respect to himself and his profession'.

From Lancelot's point of view, Hampton Court was irredeemably flat; but he did his homework, discovering the pride of his profession here, of all places, and so perhaps nostalgia did stay his hand. As he and Biddy took their walks down to the river on summer evenings, the tranquil-lity of the almost deserted palace brought out the ghosts; the red-robed Cardinal Wolsey arriving by water, as did Henry VIII and Elizabeth, thereby dictating the orientation of the river palace; King Henry and his love of games, his tilt yard and tennis court and his King's Beasts, and Charles I's commission to Francesco Fanelli for *Arethusa*, supported by four boys and dolphins. This statue, also called *Diana* (and probably meant to be Venus), was for the Privy Garden. Charles II had brought to Hampton Court the French gardeners André and Gabriel Mollet, who 'drafted' (designed) the *patte d'oie* (goose foot), the great splay of avenues east-wards out into the Home Park, so that John Evelyn noted in June 1662 'The Park, formerly a naked piece of ground, now planted with sweet rows of lime trees; and the canal water now near perfected.' William and Mary had loved Hampton Court most of all, King William setting his heart on the Great Fountain garden – thirteen fountains in their pools interspersed with beds of scrollwork, to match Wren's new east front, and with Wren's south front gazing out on their splendid Privy Garden, which was enclosed by Tijou's gilded screen and river gates. That most persistent of ghosts, Henry Wise, had started work here in 1699 and managed to spend nearly £7,000 in just over three years, until the day when William III's horse White Sorel (which Lancelot knew came from Sir John Fenwick at Wallington) stumbled on a molehill in Home Park, and England belonged to Queen Anne.

Four of the £7,000 was for 'The Charges of planting all ye trees in Bushey Parke, Gravelling ye great Avenue of sixty foot wide, digging and making ye Bason and other workes', for William's great northern approach, a mile-long avenue from Teddington. Queen Anne cancelled the north entrance (diverting the money to build Blenheim), but encouraged Wise with his subsidiary lime avenues (10 miles of them) and his 'Grate Avenew' of chestnuts: 274 horse-chestnut trees planted 42 feet apart, which he had begun planting on his forty-sixth birthday, 2nd August 1699. 'Though forever it should lead nowhere,' David Green wrote in his biography of Wise, 'nothing could dim the glory of the trees themselves on Chestnut Sunday or indeed throughout all those many years.' Bushy, largely a deer park, was hardly less flat than the Home Park; Wise had moved *Arethusa* or *Diana* to her place in the great pool that he had dug for her, and the chestnut avenues were complete in themselves. Apart from guarding all this, there was very little that Lancelot could do. If the King had insisted, he might have thought of some project, but the King did not. At Hampton Court it must sometimes have seemed that Lancelot and Biddy had joined 'the quality rest home' it was becoming. The only thing for Lancelot to do was to energetically return to his work.

Business Matters and the Account Book

A rare and tangible connection with Lancelot at this time, offering a vignette of his work and finances, is his thick, vellum-bound account book, the only one known to survive. Accounts did not amuse him, for he was too large-hearted and active a man to have patience with details (and quite happy to deal in round £100 notes) and he must have managed this far by carrying figures and dates in his head or on papers folded into bulging pocket books. Any notebook was so battered at the end of each year that all he could do was extract the vital information and throw the rest into the fire. With his new status, in his new study, he intended a fresh start, and with a sharpened quill and a flourish he made the first entry, for the Earl of Bute: 'December 1764, Received of his Lordship

£200'. This was the first payment on a contract of £1,780 for the work at Luton Hoo in Bedfordshire.

The book is hand-ruled in left-and right-hand columns for the date, description of business and the amount; it is hand-stitched, but there is no maker's or stationer's mark; the left-hand column records amounts received, while the right-hand has details of the contract sums and other outgoings; the headings are uniform, giving name and place, (for example, Rowland Holt Esq. at Redgrave, Suffolk). Allowing for differing qualities of quills and inks, the handwriting is probably all Lancelot's, though sometimes his heavy scrawl might indicate the end of a tiring day or an overly indulged supper. It was not in his character to allow his wife or children to know the details of his income; his daughter Bridget, who was eighteen in 1764, may have been allowed to rule the book, but little else. His sons never apparently showed any interest at all. The book is about half-full; it almost certainly never left his study at Wilderness House until it was taken by his executors at his death; all the 'live' accounts were followed up, settled and ruled off by them. It subsequently remained with the family and is on permanent loan to the Lindley Library of the Royal Horticultural Society.

The first tranche of accounts entered alphabetically, from the above mentioned B for Bute to W for Sir Armine Wodehouse, has sixteen names representing his portfolio of contracts active in these early 1760s. Briefly, in addition to that referring to the Earl of Bute the entries can be paraphrased thus:

- The Duke of Bridgewater at Ashridge in the Chilterns, payments 1762–8 totalling £2,946. 11s. 7d. (mostly passed to Hollands for building the house, say £500 for Brown).
- Sir William Codrington at Dodington in Gloucestershire, south-west of Chipping Sodbury. ('lakes and fine contouring in a narrow Cotswold valley', two contracts, 1761–4 (£738) and 1765–8 (£630);
- Sir George Colebrooke, Gatton, near Reigate in Surrey; Gatton was one of the most infamous of rotten boroughs, a tiny clutch of estate houses where the 'election' of two MPs was announced from a classical pavilion, 'the Town Hall', possibly Lancelot's. May 1762 to March 1768, total £3,055, for lake system and serpentine woodland walks.
- The Earl of Coventry at Croome, an ongoing commission, 1755–1763, but no contracts; £1,080 paid to Drummonds a/c + £1,300 paid by the Earl's brother, J. B. Coventry, to Drummonds, 1756–8, this for Spring Hill House at Broadway, where Lancelot organised the building, and where John Bulkeley Coventry was living.

- Ambrose Dickens, Branches, near Bury St Edmunds, Suffolk, contract Lady Day 1763, for two years, £1,500. A note is added: 'extras were charged at £58. 1/8d in 1765 which Mr Brown could not get'.
- Granville, 2nd Earl Gower, Trentham, Staffordshire, second account opened September 1762 (the lake ongoing), but work resumes in the 1770s (see page 190).
- Sir John Griffin Griffin, Audley End, Saffron Walden, Essex, first contract £660, 22nd April 1763–66; second contract disputed (see page 170–2).
- Rowland Holt, Redgrave, in Suffolk, 4 miles west of Diss (Norfolk), £2,280 contract, 1763, mostly for conversion of the seventeenth-century house to Palladian style by Hollands (since demolished). 'Lovely remote park with a lake, and boat house and orangery by Lancelot with Master Carpenter John Hobcroft'.
- General Howard, Stoke Place, Stoke Green, Buckinghamshire. The General was related to Sir John Griffin Griffin of Audley End, and Lancelot worked here in 1765–7 making a lake with islands; £800 paid.
- His Majesty the King – this is a record of the quarterly payment of £500 from March 1765 until January 1777 ('when carried to page 132 of this book').
- Duke of Marlborough, Blenheim, Oxfordshire and Langley Park, Bucks, ongoing commission (payment details as on page. 150).
- Lord Milton, Milton Abbey, Dorset, contract dated 14th October 1761, £1,400 paid, completed October 1763 (see page 176).
- Lord Northampton, Castle Ashby, Northamptonshire, new contract dated 1761, but complicated by the purchase of the manor of Fenstanton in 1767 (see page 196 ff.).
- 3rd Earl of Shelburne, Bowood, Calne, Wiltshire, and at Wycombe Abbey (then called Loaches), High Wycombe, Bucks, new contract 1762–6, totalling £4,105.
- Sir Armine Wodehouse, Kimberley, Wymondham, Norfolk, first payment £200, 22nd January 1763, then £200–300 a year until 1767. 1777–8 new plans 'for alteration of the water', and a kitchen garden near the house and a greenhouse. (Three journeys to Kimberley were charged at Christmas 1782.)

On the basis of these entries, Lancelot's gross income for 1764 can be conservatively calculated at £6,000 (excluding his royal pension, charmingly entered under K for King, which started in April 1765). That would equate to the stipend of the Bishop of Durham of the day, while a seat in Parliament could be had for £2,000, and a year at Oxford or Cambridge

Lancelot's account for the Duke of Ancaster, Grimsthorpe Castle.

cost £90, a curate might have to manage on £50 a year and a school-teacher on a lot less. Twenty years earlier Lancelot had been earning £25 a year at Stowe.

However, there are pitfalls in reading his accounts. He was working harder than these entries reveal, for Burghley, Petworth and Temple Newsam in Yorkshire (to name but three) were active at the time, but do not appear in the accounting window. The accounts in the book have to be read in conjunction with Drummonds Bank's ledger accounts, and there is no sure way of knowing if Lancelot's bank credits duplicate the account-book receipts or are additional. That £6,000 gross figure was more than halved by payments to his foremen and other craftsmen, for which he used his own bank account; the known payments to his foremen average £300 a year – with perhaps twelve foreman to pay in 1764 (one foreman supervising two sites where the distance was small) that would be £3,600. However, it seems that his housekeeping expenses were covered by the money he collected directly from clients, the surplus being paid into Drummonds, and that his bank balance was kept high enough to cover his wage bills; in 1760 he had just over £10,000 in the account, with recorded payments to eighteen men, including William Donn and Thomas White the surveyors/draughtsmen, John Hobcroft the master carpenter, Henry Holland the builder (£540), and foremen including Mickle (Dodington), Milliken (Chatsworth), Midgeley (Charlecote), Ireland (Luton Hoo) and Sanderson (Longleat). These foremen received £300–500; Nathaniel Richmond at Moor Park and Syon liked to charge one guinea a day.

In 1768 the credit in the account reached £32,000, but there were thirty foremen to be paid fairly large payments (more like £500 each) and possibly £3,000–4,000 or so due to be paid to Holland's for building work. Lancelot's 'nest-egg' was still substantial, and accruing – a far cry from his modest beginnings, though little enough when set against the majority of his clients, who were in the top bracket of income as landowners (the top '400'), with an income of £10,000–15,000 each year. Lancelot's bank balance was his family's future security, and the late 1760s were its peak. His earnings were the result of his self-sacrificial work rate, which the account book also reveals: he was travelling over half of England, riding out to Staffordshire and Worcestershire in the west, and back to Suffolk in the east; then to Luton, Oxford and Northampton, north to Leeds for Temple Newsam, and south to Dorset. He drove himself to limits that perhaps he felt he must exploit, but knew he could not sustain.

The foremen paid their own labourers, the rate of one shilling a day, six days a week, equalling £15. 12s. a year for senior men, although the rate was ninepence or even sixpence a day for old men, women and boys. These were the rates recorded at Wakefield Lawn in 1751, paid to the estate labourers, who would have had lodging and fuel in addition. The rates were about the same in 1779 at Wimpole, where the wages for six men in the gardens were estimated at £113. 16s. for a year, also with lodging and produce. At Wakefield Lawn there were about twenty-five labourers at a peak time when the Duke of Grafton and his friends were in residence, but these figures suggest that twelve to twenty workers were the usual number employed on improvement works, and certainly nowhere near the 100 or even 500 that worked for William Holbech at Farnborough Hall.

It is worth looking briefly at the pattern of Lancelot's working. His preference was for contracts to be neatly packaged, or at least staged, into two-year periods, so that he could see the return on his costs. However, his personal involvement was inevitably longer: his first visit inspired the vision that might suit both the place and his client, though more prosaically he requested a detailed survey of the site, as at Croome and Burghley; a second visit might be necessary to fix his proposals, which were drawn on an overlay of the survey. William Donn and Thomas White, both accomplished draughtsman and surveyors who worked on Lancelot's schemes in the 1750s and 1760s, seem to have drifted away to their own practices, to be replaced by Jonathan Spyers as Lancelot's regular draughtsman (and sometimes as travelling surveyor), from 1764. Six months often elapsed between Lancelot's first visit and the production of the plan of proposals (outlined by Lancelot in his flamboyant style, with the details drawn by Spyers), and then a visit was necessary to explain it and begin the setting out. Then came the contract, with another visit for signature and collection of his preliminary payment, if there was one, and intro- duction of the job foreman; the end of the first year required a visit, and collection of payment, and another a year later for the second payment. There might well be a clearing-up visit to deal with any problems or extra works, and at another year's interval a final visit to check on tree and shrub plantings. Lancelot makes few mentions of planting orders in his accounts, and he preferred to use stock from the estate nurseries or – if ordering from Lee & Kennedy or John Williamson, or from James Wood at Huntingdon – expected the nurseryman to deal directly with the client.

Soon after the move to Hampton Court the name of Samuel Lapidge is mentioned; he was a foreman, but also the nearest to an assistant that Lancelot employed, for he acted as a clerk and courier and eventually became familiar with Lancelot's accounts. John Midgeley, the foreman at Charlecote, Castle Ashby, Wynnstay and Ashburnham, stayed loyal to Lancelot all his life, as did William Ireland (Lancelot's foreman at Burghley, Trentham, Cliveden and Luton); Lancelot wrote to Lord Bute, 'I am very glad your Lordship has taken William Ireland. My order to him was to submit himself to your Lordship's terms. Your Lordship, I do believe, will find him sober, industrious and honest.' Michael Milliken, who had run the work at Chatsworth for five years, was moved to royal Richmond, reporting Lancelot verbatim to his wife (still at Edensor), 'Milliken I sent for you here as I saide before to do you a service. This will be a great and lasting worke and where you will be known to his Majesty and other Great Men.' The Millikens settled at Kew, where they lived happily till the end of their days.

Most loyal of all was Benjamin Read, who worked at Croome and Blenheim; in August 1767 Lord Cadogan sent his thanks to Lancelot for permission to take a party of friends around Blenheim, mentioning Mr Read 'by whose attention and civility we saw it to the greatest perfection & indeed it *beggars* all description'. 'The water is by much the finest artificial thing I ever saw,' Cadogan continued, 'meaning the banks and the advantageous manner in which you have set it off. I don't like the bridge but think it might be altered by expense to answer well', although he thought the park under-planted. Lord Cadogan owned Caversham Park at Reading, and he concluded his letter, 'I had the mortification to find on my return that I had miss'd you here. I flatter myself you found Justice done to your works in the manner of keeping them.'

Lord Cadogan's note prompts the suspicion that the account book has tip-of-the-iceberg tendencies and may not tell all; there is no account for Caversham. Charles, 2nd Baron Cadogan, had been a young soldier in Marlborough's army and had married Elizabeth, daughter of Sir Hans Sloane; he was an MP and a grandee and could well have met Lancelot at Stowe. Moreover his son, Charles Sloane Cadogan, the MP for Cambridge, was in April 1764 appointed Surveyor of Hampton Court and Bushy and therefore Lancelot's immediate overlord.*

Lord Bute, Luton Hoo and Richmond Park

It was typical of Lord Bute to be at the forefront with the services of the new royal appointee: Bute was a serious plantsman, having been taught to plant trees on his holidays from Eton by his uncle, the Duke of Argyll, at Whitton, and had gone on to study botany at the University

* Turner, p. 178, suggests that Lancelot also worked at Downham House, Santon Downham, Suffolk, on the Little Ouse in sandy Breckland – a shooting lodge – for the latter, again with no charge.

of Leiden. He was apparently happily married to Mary Wortley Montagu. But perhaps he had the volatility of the rich, for he vacillated between botany and politics, between retreating to his island home, Mount Stuart, and strutting the great stage in London; he was the perfect courtier, as painted by Reynolds in his Garter robes, in a short embroidered surcoat that displays his silk-stockinged and fabulous legs, with a lean and handsome face, deep-set eyes and wide, sensual mouth. Botany and gardening had brought him the friendship of Frederick, Prince of Wales, and the Prince's death left him chief supporter (and reputed lover) of the widowed Augusta. He ruled the roost at Augusta's Kew, where he had a house on Kew Green, having sold his mansion of Kenwood (Caen Wood as it was then) to Lord Mansfield. Catapulted into power and influence with the accession of George III, he found himself Prime Minister for a time, but soon resigned and bought Luton Hoo for his return to botany and gardening.*

At the death of his uncle, the Duke of Argyll, in 1761, Bute had moved some of the rarest trees from Whitton to Kew for safety (a sophora, zelkova, oriental plane and *Gingko biloba* survived into our time) and now the doting Augusta allowed him to help himself to others for Luton: 'We have got as many trees as we wanted this season from the Princess of Wales's garden,' wrote Lancelot on 11th March 1767, 'on which acct I desired Mr Haverfield to forward the trees for your Lordship as fast as possible. I have sent by the bearer another plan for the walls of the kitchen garden without a green house. The walls are the aspect I think best.'

Luton had a priority in the mid-1760s, and the park gave itself gracefully to Lancelot's treatments. The agricultural observer Arthur Young travelled at the end of this decade (*A Six Months' Tour through the North of England*, 1770) and, though ostensibly looking for Lord Bute's advanced agricultural methods, he found a park of well over 1,000 acres (reports vary from 1,200 to 1,500), 'very fine beeches' and the 'finest water I have ever seen' with a 'sloop with ornamental sails and flying colours' and two other boats at anchor. The immensely long water was made by damming the River Lea; Young noted a wooden bridge concealing the dam and the unfinished cascade, 'but a *capability*; when a little improved, and catched from a proper point of view, it will add to the variety of the scene'. Is this the first use of 'capability' in print, and was it Young who coined the nickname?

---

* Bute bought the Hoo from Francis Herne, MP for Bedford, who acquired Flambards, or Flamberts, at Harrow-on-the-Hill, where Lancelot worked; this park was spectacular, flowing down the steep hill to the east, into the spacious and empty meadows crossed by tributaries of the River Brent, with 'Wembly' in the distance. Lancelot tamed the soggy meadows and made a lake, which survives amidst the green-striped games-pitches of Harrow School.

The kitchen garden, a huge octagon of dark-red, heat-retaining bricks, is sited well south of the house, adjacent to the ornamental Flower Garden Wood, and both were designed to be visited from the house. A design similar to the Luton octagon is illustrated by Switzer in his *Practical Fruit Garden* of 1727, with entrances on the east and west walls, the whole having an orientation a little to the east of south, for full sun an hour before noon. The 'morning air is purer' was the accepted lore, as Switzer wrote, and the heat of the afternoon sun 'generally languid and unhealthy'. Where space permitted, as at Luton, orientation and free airs were critical to the siting of the kitchen gardens, more so than soils that could be mollified by labours. Luton's walled garden – the building supervised by William Ireland – was completed by 1770. Lancelot's design without the greenhouse suggests that Robert Adam, who was altering the house and designing the stables for Lord Bute, was also to design a conservatory.

Unhappily no records of the planting have been found, for the warm red walls would have had space, inside and outside, for hundreds of pears, apricots, cherries, peaches, figs, quince and all manner of wall fruit, with espaliers for apples and pears inside the garden, and frames and pits for melons and pineapples and hothouses for vines still leaving room for swathes of vegetables and salad greens. Lancelot never forgot that he was apprenticed in the garden at Kirkharle, where fruit was greatly prized.

In 1761 Lord Bute had been appointed as Ranger of Richmond deer park, the vast 'new park' of something like 2,500 acres of 'unspoiled old English land' that Charles I had enclosed as a hunting preserve. The park – not to be confused with the Old Deer Park by the Thames, which was then part of George III's favoured retreat next door to Kew – stretched from Richmond town in the west to Roehampton on the eastern boundary, and from Sheen in the north to Kingston Hill in the south; it had been kept and carefully guarded as a vast royal game larder, once home to flocks of turkeys, although these had mostly been eaten and replaced by red deer from Hanover. George III intended to turn the park over to corn, but the soil proved too poor and the deer too rampageous. Lancelot is thought to have organised the planting of belts of trees on the north, between the Richmond and Roehampton gates, and on the south along the Kingston Hill boundary between Robin Hood and Kingston gates. Elms on the ridge in the north-east corner near Bog Lodge were felled in the 1970s and reputedly planted by him. Any additional landscaping was undesirable because the park remained a 'game larder', the 'Kew Cart' making regular deliveries of venison, pheasant, partridge and hares to the royal kitchens at Kew and Windsor. Perquisites of venison and game also found their ways to Wilderness House.

Audley End

When work began in earnest at Luton Hoo in Bedfordshire in the autumn of 1764, Lancelot was already involved at Audley End in Essex, where events reveal the pressure that he was under. If he included them in the same expedition they were about 34 miles apart, a cross-country ride along the road from Luton to Hitchin and Royston, then across a forgotten patch of old England, through Barley and Wendens Ambo to Saffron Walden. Audley End was in the still-enchanting valley of the River Granta (or Cam), a river in no hurry, winding its leisurely and willow-shaded way through small communities of ochre-walled cottages and huge barns, these being indicative of its well-being. It is still a countryside of delightful architectural miniatures, which abound in the villages of Newport to the south and in Littlebury, Audley End's community to the north; the road between them runs parallel to the river, along the Shortgrove boundary to present a grandstand view of the fabled Audley End. The house sits – rather like a dowager who no longer paints and powders, but retains her beautiful bone structure – as one of the most exquisite of park ornaments, and the Brownian miniature park suits her to perfection.

By that summer of 1764, Lancelot had learned that new heirs could be difficult, especially those that had waited patiently for their inheritance, and Sir John Griffin Griffin at Audley End had waited for more than forty years. He was born John Griffin Whitwell in Northamptonshire in 1719 and, as any inheritance seemed remote, he opted for the army as a twenty-year-old ensign in a Hanoverian regiment, where he fought at the Battle of Dettingen in 1743 and rose rapidly in rank. He knew that his uncle, the 3rd Lord Griffin, had dissipated the Griffin fortune and estate, and so his hopes rested on his mother and his aunt, Anne Whitwell and Elizabeth, Countess of Portsmouth, as granddaughters of the 3rd Earl of Suffolk. For the Earls of Suffolk, Audley End had proved an extravagant beauty since they had started building in 1603, breaking both their fortunes and their hearts; once palatial, with two courtyards and numerous garden courts, admired by Cosimo de Medici and coveted by Charles II, who acquired it for his Newmarket house-parties (though his successor and less merry monarch William III quickly returned it to the Suffolks), it was by now a fragment of its former self. When the 10th Earl died in 1745 with no direct heir, there was a family scramble for the estates, in which the proud and feisty Elizabeth (née Griffin), Countess of Portsmouth, successfully acquired half the lands, some 3,500 acres, continuing her campaign until she also acquired the neglected house at a bargain price. The Countess Elizabeth, using the funds amassed from her two marriages, was determined to regain the Griffin pride for the benefit of her favourite nephew, who was directed to change his name from Whitwell to Griffin, hence the strange doubling of the Griffin, on which he was insistent.

The Countess Elizabeth died in 1762, leaving a restored Audley End and having instigated (with her friend Colonel William Vachell, in league with the estate steward Thomas Pennystone) a military-style campaign for the buying-in or enclosing of dozens of fields and strip-tenancies to the east and south of the house. At the moment of his inheritance Sir John Griffin Griffin was Lieutenant-Colonel of the 33rd Regiment of Foot Guards, based in Hanover, MP for Andover in Hampshire (in the gift of his kinsmen, by his aunt's marriage into the Wallop family, Earls of Portsmouth), mildly Pittian in his politics, and honoured by the King, who had ceremoniously installed him as a Knight of the Bath in May 1761. Sir John was a tough-looking and imposing figure, muscular from his hard military living, portrayed in his ceremonial robes by Biagio Rebecca, and in his regimentals by Benjamin West, fulfilling perfectly George III's ideal of a commander in his beloved army. His first wife died in the summer of 1764 and he soon remarried. His new wife was Katherine Clayton of Harleyford, a house by the Thames at Marlow (where Lancelot would soon go).

On 29th October 1762 'the common brick bridge' over the Cam carrying the public road into Saffron Walden was badly damaged by flood waters, and Sir John took the opportunity to ask Robert Adam, who was already designing interiors for the house, to design the new bridge, prominently in view from the house. In March or April of 1763, with the bridge under construction, Lancelot had been summoned, and he hastily entered into a contract with Sir John for works to be completed in thirteen months. The contract had seven clauses, beginning with his agreements: (1) to widen the Cam into a linear lake as it crossed the park lawn; (2) to make the drives that enclosed this ellipse of lawn connecting the house to the Littlebury–Newport road; (3) to make good the surface for the sowing of this lawn, using grass seed and Dutch clover or turf as thought best; and (4) to plant the dozen clumps of trees and the copses that connected the views from the park into the surrounding landscape, including the construction of a ha-ha on the east side of the house to protect the

flower gardens. Other clauses covered the making of a grove, a sheltered lawn and tree garden on the south side of the house, where
some Lebanon cedars survive, screening the house from the Saffron
Walden road, and finally the making of the new road on both sides
of the Adam bridge. The work was to be done 'between the date
hereof and May 1764', for the sum of £660, with Sir John to find the
trees and shrubs, tools and wheelbarrows.

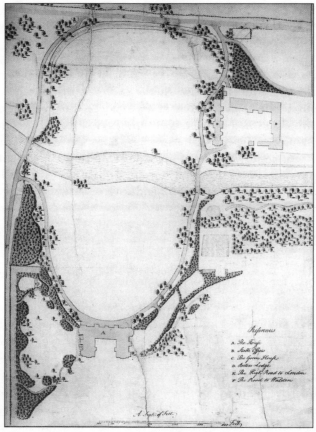

Audley End layout: north is to the right, the house (A) at the foot and the Newport to
Littlebury road at the top; Adam's bridge is on the left.

    This was clearly a rash agreement, with so much weather-sensitive
work on the river (and a misunderstanding about which way it was to
be made to bend) and the risk that Sir John's supplies of trees might
not suit Lancelot's planting intentions (1,300 larches, with limes, silver
firs, Portuguese laurels, poplars, birches and 3,000 Dutch alders from
Rotterdam – Sir John clearly had his continental sources – and great

numbers of Scots-pine seedlings were planted). Unsurprisingly, May 1764 came and passed, and Audley End was not finished: Sir John wrote that work 'was very backward at the latter end of 1764 – when I was neither satisfied with the delay, nor with the manner in which some of its parts were finishing'. The contract was cancelled 'by a gentleman's agreement', Sir John having paid the £660; and work continued, possibly with a second contract (though this is uncertain), with amounts being paid as necessary.

Things seem finally to have been settled in May 1767, and Sir John very reasonably gave Lancelot £150 'for his trouble'. But in October that year Lancelot wrote to say that there was a sum outstanding, as it had been for a year, and so an amount of interest was charged, about £90. He had looked into his accounts and found that he had had to sell some 3 per cent stocks to fund work continuing at Audley End, and so felt justified in reclaiming the interest. Sir John was adamant that he had paid everything and everybody – meaning the workmen at Audley End – on time and that the interest was not due. A long silence ensued, and in February 1768, addressing each other stiffly in the third person, each held their ground, with Lancelot finishing, 'Mr Brown will never labour more to convince Sir John as he knows that there is none so blind as him that will not see.'

Much has been made of this infamous wrangle, Sir John being slated as Lancelot's most unpleasant client; Thomas Hinde writes that 'the whole incident is a strange one' because the subject of interest arises nowhere else in Lancelot's accounting, so why was it charged on this occasion? The answer surely lies in Lancelot's frantic efforts to keep up with his workload, in his employment of Samuel Lapidge ('Mr Lepidge [sic] knows my accounts' appears in his draft Will, 1769) and in Lapidge's new-broom tendencies in trying to unravel Lancelot's undoubtedly chaotic affairs. The whole process, and the very idea of interest – and certainly the stiff 'Mr Brown informes Sir John Griffen', with the spelling mistakes and leaving out the essential second 'Griffin' – are completely uncharacter-istic of Lancelot himself. But having appointed his accounts assistant, he had to support his actions, and the only way out was to let time pass so that the faux pas was forgotten.*

The plan for Audley End is a beautiful drawing in a different style of detailing, and is perhaps by Lapidge instead of Spyers. On the ground the plan, with its hesitantly oval framework of drives, comes to life on

---

* Sir John was to outlive Lancelot by fourteen years, becoming a noted supporter of Pitt the Younger and rising in ranks and titles to the House of Lords, and though additions and alter-ations were his lifelong passion, he remained faithful to the essentials of Lancelot's scheme.

two levels: it is a theatrical landscape, with the house on the stage, the entrance drive sweeping in from the road, over Adam's bridge, with deceptive undulations (which are hardly there) and, at least in the nineteenth century, judiciously grouped trees along the drive allowing the views to open and close. Today, and on foot, walking around the house to the Grove and the formal garden, and then across the lawn to the River Cam, the views from 'the stalls' – the lower tier – evolve and dissolve. As well as the cedars, some marvellous plane trees (also Lancelot's favourites) remain. Lift your eyes then to the 'grand tier' – to the west, beyond the road, is Ring Hill with the Temple of Victory, on the north the feisty Countess's memorial column is backed by the spring wood clothing its own hill, and southwards is the Temple of Concord on its green hill; these immutable hills, which embrace 'the quiet splendour' of Audley End, are so perfect that they seem to have been cast by a giant's hands. Or painted as scenery? In reality they are the canny wooing of Mother Nature by Mr Brown!

'My western expedition', late 1764

It was the nature of Lancelot's virtually one-man profession that the jobs sprang up like proverbial mushrooms over which he had no control. He did try to 'cluster' or 'group' them to save his horse-miles – perhaps for good business reasons put forward by Samuel Lapidge, though more likely for the sake of his health, prompted by his wife's concerns. We can never know how many requests he rejected, but his journeyings of the fourteen years since his epic ride from Stowe to Croome had fallen into a kind of pattern: he only ever had a sprinkling of jobs in Kent, Sussex or Surrey; he had more in Wiltshire, Dorset and Somerset, and even more from Croome in Worcestershire northwards into Staffordshire. The 'fallout' from Stowe in Buckinghamshire and Oxfordshire was lessening, but the requests for him to return to the North, northwards from Burghley up the Great North Road into Yorkshire and Northumberland, were multiplying. His small-scale stamping ground of Essex and Suffolk had spread into spacious Norfolk, with Melton Constable in the far north near Holt. His adored Thames valley still kept him sallying forth, but usually in the happy knowledge that he could be home for supper.

Sometimes he wanted to see his client and wrote ahead to make the appointment; sometimes he preferred to study progress or problems quietly with his foreman or the head gardener. His 'expeditions', extended trips, were carefully planned: encouraged by the fine and fair autumn that lingered, he set out in early December 1764 'on my western expedition', and the 8th of the month found him at Testwood near Southampton.

He was writing a letter and typically excusing himself to Lord Northampton, who wanted him at Castle Ashby in far-away Northamptonshire, but was also asking where he could find the cough lozenges that Lady Northampton had given him on his previous visit, as they suited him so well.

At Testwood he stayed with the hospitable Serles: 'Mrs Serle flatters herself Mr Brown will not for ever pass by Testwood without taking any notice of his friends there whose best comp[liment]s. and good wishes always attend him.' These friends possessed some of the best salmon- and trout-fishing in England, if he had time to spare, for their old house over-looked the lush meadows and streams of the sprawling Test estuary, with a famous salmon-leap nearby.*

The Serles' house was more than convenient for Broadlands, about 5 miles to the north beside the Test at Romsey, and the first goal of this expedition. Celia Fiennes had given a copious, if chaotic description of her relatives the St Barbes' fine old house, full of tapestry-hung closets and painted staircases, with an outside Bathing House as well as a generous collection of stills, barns, dairies and stables. Most intriguing of all, 'there is a water house that by a Wheele casts up the water out of the River just by and fills the pipes to serve all the house and to fill the bason designed in the middle of the Garden with a Spout'. The house supply was stored in three golden balls, each holding several gallons, placed conveniently on the roofs. When Fiennes visited, seventy years before Lancelot, the gardens were being made ('the Mold and Soyle is black and such as they cut up for peate'), with walled courts, a railed bowling green and massed clipped evergreens.

Henry Temple, a relative of Lord Cobham at Stowe, had bought Broadlands in the 1730s and, after living with the massed evergreens for twenty years, had resorted to 'giving away all the fine pyramid greens to those that will fetch them, of which many cartloads are gone already', as he wrote in a letter to his son. The son, also Henry Temple, 2nd Viscount Palmerston, had inherited in 1757 at the age of eighteen. Now returned from the first of three trips to Italy, he had summoned Lancelot, and as a result of this first visit Lancelot was commissioned to tidy up the old place by encasing the house in a classical façade and evoking a Claudian setting beside the beautiful river. Celia Fiennes had noted that the old stables were brick, but said nothing about the house materials, which could have been clunch or chalkstone (by now difficult to acquire and expensive), so it was decided that Broadlands should be of whitish

---

* The Serles' house, Great Testwood, has now gone, but the river landscape remains wonderful, and the salmon-leap survives.

bricks, made not far away at Exbury. Lord Palmerston had admired the
pale bricks of Holkham Hall in Norfolk and it was well known that
Lancelot had an aversion to red houses, or at least new red houses, in
his settings. The King's Master Gardener on progress in his coach, and
with his assistant Mr Lapidge, clearly inspired confidence, for his young
lordship was soon writing that he had 'only settled the plans with Brown
and have left everything in the execution of them to him'.

After another night at Testwood, they set out in stormy weather to
cross the bleak heathland of the northern New Forest, continuing through
Ringwood and Wimborne Minster, and then on the Dorchester turnpike for a dozen miles or so until they turned north for the town then
called Middleton. Milton Abbas or Middleton was a community of more
than a hundred families, a wool town where a cottage industry of spinning thrived. Their approach from the south revealed two streets, Broad
Street and Newport Street, lined with cottages and gardens, and the High
Street, equally lined with shops and small houses, breasting the rise to
the monumental Market Cross in the square. There were inns, the Red
Lyon, the King's Arms and the George with its own brewery, but whether
it was advisable for the coach party to stay at any of them was doubtful,
for Lancelot was headed for a meeting with Lord Milton, an already
unpopular landlord. Middleton had grown alongside the Benedictine
abbey founded by King Athelstan in about AD 938. At the Dissolution it
had been bought by the Tregonwells, who had remained until 1752, when
the estate had been sold to Joseph Damer, the eldest son of John Damer
of Winterbourne Came House, near Dorchester. Joseph Damer, now
Lord Milton, was very soon at loggerheads with the Middleton worthies
when he complained of the grammar-school boys who stole his fruit
and frightened his pheasants; it was a running feud, and boys were expelled
for dropping stones down his chimneys, stealing eggs and cucumbers and
appropriating the housekeeper's cockerels for fighting. He was resorting
to an Act of Parliament to move the school into Dorchester, and eventually succeeded.

Lancelot had been to Milton Abbey before, in the summer of 1763,
but he had arrived from the north-west through Hilton, following Lord
Milton's instructions, and came on horseback. If he was lucky enough
to arrive with the setting sun, this view is breathtaking, the long low
house washed pale gold against its green backdrop and dwarfed by the
huge and pinnacled bulk of Abbot Middleton's church. From this direction there was no inkling of the town's existence at all. The reverse view,
back from the west front, or from the west door of the church, is stupendous: the buildings are marvellously sited on a col, or ridge, between

two valleys that sidle off, giving alternate views. A dry valley called Delcombe Bottom widens into Broadfield, then narrows and stretches for 2 miles north-north-west to high ground east of Bulbarrow (at 902 feet, the second-highest hill in Dorset). Delcombe Manor at the head of the valley was used as an eye-catcher. West of Broadfield was a combe, where a ride was made around the edge of the woodland, to the menagerie. Farther west the Hilton valley ended at the village, with the church tower as an eye-catcher.

Lancelot's first plan for Milton Abbey was to level the great lawn that afforded these views, to make thick plantations on the hills and sculpt their outlines to enhance the valley forms, and make the drives that enabled this landscape to be enjoyed. It was purely a landscape project and a fine one – it was more than a park, it was the capture of a substantial stretch of Dorset downland for the eye's delectation.

Independently of these marvellous views, Milton Abbey – in ways similar to Petworth House and Corsham Court – was pressed on one side by town buildings; Middleton's streets and houses were to the south and did not impede this first landscape scheme. Lord Milton had paid Lancelot £200 for his plan and initial visit, the contract for the works had been drawn up and agreed in November 1764 and now it was time to set things in motion. Lancelot had ordered the purchase of 1,120 pounds of Dutch clover seed for the great lawn.

On his earlier visit the Abbey House was being encased 'in a beautiful modern manner', in the opinion of Bishop Pococke, to the plans of John Vardy. Lord Milton now found the Gothic effect too 'theatrical' and was looking for another architect. Would Lancelot take over? In the ensuing discussion Lord Milton also raised the question of a lake; the only water supply came from the Hilton-valley 'rivulet' and the only possible fall for the water, and hence the lake, was to the south – the way Lancelot's coach had just travelled, through the Middleton streets. Maybe the schoolboys did their worst at that moment, or maybe Lancelot was flippant (for he certainly could be), and the dreadful words were spoken either in anger or in jest: in order to have a lake, you will have to *move the village!* It was not an unusual thing to do, for Lancelot had come fresh from Audley End where Sir John Griffin Griffin was carefully and fairly (it must be said) moving aside a street of cottages for his park; and back in Northumberland, at Kirkharle, the village where Lancelot had been born was swept away. However, Middleton was more than a hamlet or village, it was a medieval town on the scale of Petworth or Corsham, which no one had dreamed of demolishing. Surely it was a joke? On that note, the King's Master Gardener took to his coach and sped away.

They returned to the Dorchester turnpike and travelled on through the town, westwards, making for Exeter – an industrial town, full of woollen manufactories and mills and numerous smiths making spades, nails, horseshoes and gun-barrels – and on south towards Newton Abbot. After about 10 miles they came to the Starcross turning and, shortly, the entrance for Mamhead. Here was more than a whisper of Drake's glorious Devon, a seventeenth-century house of greater antiquity, set on the eastern slope of Great Haldon ridge with views to the Exe estuary and the sea. The estate had come to Wilmot Vaughan on his marriage to a Miss Nightingale, and they were considering rebuilding as well as improving the grounds. It would be nice to think that Lancelot bridled at the idea of demolishing the romantic old house, but he liked the Vaughans and promised to supply new plans.

Back on the Newton Abbot road at Ideford they passed through the demesne of Ugbrooke, an eleventh-century retreat for the Bishops of Exeter, but since 1604 home of the Cliffords of Chudleigh. At Ugbrooke there was almost an architectural competition for rebuilding, as the 4th Lord Clifford had asked for designs from Robert Adam, John Carr and James Paine, and Lancelot clearly thought he had a chance. It was a brief look, then back on the road, through Newton Abbot and on to Totnes – another town busy with mills, weavers and smiths – where the coach continued southwards, taking the rather obscure turning for Ashprington, and in the village the rough track up to Sharpham House. Even today this countryside of the South Hams seems a world away from the rest of England; how remote must it have felt on a misty December afternoon in 1764? Something out of the ordinary must have brought Lancelot this far – unless, of course, he had not imagined that the long, winding and rutted roads of the south-west could seem so interminable.

Gossip as well as invitations had brought him this far, for all three projects – Mamhead, Ugbrooke and Sharpham – promised new houses to be built as well as parks to be improved. Sharpham was an old and mainly Elizabethan house on a bluff overlooking the River Dart, with views inland to Totnes and, on the other hand, down the winding estuary towards Dartmouth and the sea. It was, and is, one of the most covetable settings of the Devon (if not the entire English) coastline. The new owner was one Captain Philemon Pownoll, rich with prize money from his capture of the Spanish treasure ship *Ermiona* in the war. As it turned out Sir Robert Taylor built the new Sharpham as a Palladian villa, and if Lancelot was left with the landscape – tradition and field evidence (the line of the drive, groups of trees and other features) suggest that he was – then even he would have despaired of outshining the Dart estuary.

It transpired that south Devon was just too far, and he had overreached himself. No payments are recorded for Sharpham. At Ugbrooke the house eventually built – a square house with castellated corner towers – is credited to Robert Adam, as his earliest castellated design for a country house. Lancelot's plan for the park was carried out in the early 1770s: the drive approaches, the planting of evergreen oaks, chestnuts and cedars that loved the marine microclimate and the damming of the Ugbrooke to form two irregular lakes, separated by a picturesque rocky cascade. However, not unusually, these lovely effects were attributed to the owner, Lord Clifford, by Father Joseph Reeve, family chaplain and tutor to the Clifford children, who sought to emulate Alexander Pope:

> 'Tis yours, My Lord, with unaffected ease,
> To draw from Nature's stores and make them please:
> With taste refined to dress the rural seat,
> And add new honours to your own retreat.
> To shade the hill, to scoop or swell the green
> To break with wild diversities the scene,
> To model with the Genius of the place
> Each artless feature, each spontaneous grace.

Lancelot was understandably attracted to south Devon, the landscape being already so lovely as to be a joy to improve. But his volatile health and the great distances involved defeated him also at Mamhead – where again Robert Adam worked on the house – at least for the time being.

Turning homewards through Exeter, the December days darkening, their road was the more northerly turnpike through Honiton to Ilminster. Lancelot knew well, as did most of the nation, that a Somerset squire Sir William Pynsent was leaving his estate in gratitude to the saviour of the nation, Lord Chatham; Lancelot was to take a look, but with discretion, for Sir William was not yet dead (he died the following month, January 1765). Burton Pynsent, valued at £4,000 a year in rentals, was superbly sited on the narrow ridge that runs south-west from Langport through Curry Rivel to Fivehead. The house, at almost 250 feet, had spectacular views, and on the north side the ridge dropped dramatically down into West Sedge Moor, only about 20 feet above sea level. Lancelot was probably not the only 'spy' that Lord Chatham sent to see if Burton Pynsent was worth having, but he at least could give an expert's report.

From Langport the old road eastwards eventually rejoined the turnpike heading for Wincanton, where inns were plentiful. A diversion to Longleat would have been possible, but hardly inviting in the December gloom; by now it was nearing the 20th of the month, and it was still a long haul home through Amesbury, Basingstoke and Staines. The Thames must have been a welcome sight, the pinnacles and chimneys of Hampton Court even more so, with the relief of being home for Christmas. Can there be any doubt that, at the end of this landmark year, the festival was well celebrated with family and friends at Wilderness House – the dark-panelled rooms coming alive in the dancing lights from log fires and candles and wine glasses, the celebrated arrivals of roast sirloin and the newly fashionable turkey (for which Mrs Martha Bradley's *The British Housewife* of 1756 gave instructions for stuffing and roasting) to be followed by plum puddings, syllabubs and unnumbered delicacies, orange flower cakes, and sugared peaches and raspberry wines (these last made from Biddy Brown's perquisites from the palace fruit gardens)?

Lord Spencer's Wimbledon

However, the workaholic Lancelot had one more task for the year, a short journey across to Wimbledon, where a new phase of work was to start on the park.

It was curious to have been discussing William Pitt's windfall of Burton Pynsent, for twenty years earlier when Sarah, Duchess of Marlborough died, only her rather frail ten-year-old grandson John Spencer stood in the way of Pitt as her nominated heir to Wimbledon and Althorp. Pitt lost out (though he had £10,000), for the boy had survived to become a very rich, but timid and retiring man, tall, with 'russet-coloured' hair; his friend Lord Palmerston bemoaned, 'the bright side of his character appears in private and the dark side in public . . . it is only those who live in intimacy with him who know that he has an understanding and a heart that might do credit to any man'. This was evident in John Spencer's marriage, famously made in 1755 at the moment he came of age, in an upstairs room at Althorp house while the party was in full swing downstairs, because he and his bride, nineteen-year-old Margaret Georgiana Poyntz, were deeply in love and need wait no longer. Elizabeth Montagu thought her 'a natural good young woman, no airs, no affectations, but seemed to enjoy her good fortune by making others partakers and happy with herself.'

Lancelot's Drummonds account shows that Lord Spencer, created Earl Spencer in 1765, who tended to pay on drafts on Hoare's Bank, paid £800 in 1759 and £1,000 a year in 1760–3, with a final £1,000 in the autumn of 1766; this is also shown in the account book. (Payment as early as 1759 suggests that Lancelot may have done something at Spencer House, overlooking Green Park.) In 1779 the rail fences at Wimbledon were renewed and painted white; the final account sum of £750 paid in 1781 was apparently for Althorp House in Northamptonshire. Now, in late 1764, the new contract was agreed (£1,760) and work was to start immediately in January (1765).

Even when Lancelot saw it, Wimbledon House (now the All England Lawn Tennis & Croquet Club, the golf course and the park) spoke of the ephemerality of gardens. Wimbledon had belonged to the Cecils, then Charles I acquired it for Henrietta Maria; the gardens were a cavalcade of baroque fashions – lime walks, orchards, vineyards (Vineyard Hill Road remains), fountains, knots, embroidered parterres, a green-painted circular banqueting house and a maze were just a few of the lost delights. Sarah, Duchess of Marlborough had bought the mouldering estate from a bankrupt South Sea company director, Theodore Janssen, in the 1720s and had 'designed' her own house, with a little help from Lord Burlington, Henry Herbert, the 9th 'Architect' Earl of Pembroke, and architect Roger Morris, and from Charles Bridgeman for the garden. The park was enormous, at 1,200 acres, stretching from the edge of Wimbledon Common (Parkside) on the west to the Durnsford road (almost to the River Wandle) on the east. The house, and Wimbledon village and church, were all on the high land at the south end of the park (the present Ridgeway and Wimbledon Hill); according to Dorothy Stroud, the house 'stood close to what is now the upper end of Home Park Road [junction with Arthur Road] from where there is still a fine view towards inner London'. Even so, the Duchess Sarah's house was apparently damp, and on old maps springs are marked on the slopes of the park, which must have been the prompting for Lancelot's lake in the valley. Some of his cedars and pines survive in gardens around the remnant park that remains.

Lancelot's work at Wimbledon was completed in two years; in 1768 Thomas Richardson (shortly to survey the Kew and Richmond gardens) made a survey of Wimbledon as Lancelot had improved it, but the survey also shows the approach of residential development in this desirable area. Lancelot made a garden in 1767 for Sir Ellis Cunliffe off what is now Parkside Gardens, where a remnant lake survives. Nearby on Putney Heath, for 'Baron Tracey', the 6th Viscount Tracey, he recorded 'waiting on the Baron three times and a plan', for about twenty-five guineas in 1774, but the exact site of this garden is unknown.

This Wimbledon park landscape, the mecca for hundreds of thousands of tennis fans – and the eyes of the world – each summer, must be the most complex of Lancelot's places, a green palimpsest of fabulous history, where he joins a glorious cavalcade of heroes, heroines and villains.

9

BROWNIFICATIONS!
(HAMPTON COURT 1765–7)

While from the Thames the balmy zephyrs spring,
And fan the air with odif'ruous wing;
While every grove resounds with warbling notes
From soaring lark the trembling music flotes.
There Sion lifts her venerable pile
Where hospitality still wears a smile,
Where taste and elegance and grandeur shine,
And every virtue decks brave Piercy's line!

Sidney Swinney, verse epistle to Lord Irwin, 1767

THE TAG OF HIS ROYAL APPOINTMENT boosted Lancelot's business (which was attracting a poetic form of its very own) and the pattern of frenetic travelling set in 1764 continued through the next year, into his fiftieth year (1766) and beyond. The coldest months were no break, for there was so much essential winter work: the pruning and moving of trees, laying of hedges and planting in open weather, and the crucial structural work of fencing and staking out to be organised. In February 1765 he took the long journey to northernmost Norfolk, to Sir Edward Astley's Melton Constable Hall, where he collected £200 for the first stage of work. It promised well, but the land was flat and a lake was made 'with uncommon difficulty'; Sir Edward paid out £200–300 for the next four years for planting and plans for a number of ornamental buildings, but the schemes faltered and Lancelot's work was overlaid by other hands.

The Norfolk prize would have been the Cokes' Holkham, but little came from a visit to its chatelaine, the widowed Margaret, Countess of Leicester, for whom Lancelot is supposed to have enlarged and 'softened' the park. He may have felt that merely continuing Kent's work was not enough (and what little he did was overlaid by Thomas William Coke, with William Emes and Humphry Repton). Remote and lovely Kimberley, north-west of Wymondham, was progressing, as also was Redgrave, near Diss; and Bedingfield family tradition has it that he worked at Ditchingham, just north of Bungay, as well as 5 miles to the north at Langley near Loddon, where he did visit in 1765.

The pace did not lessen. Catching his clients for critical decisions was always difficult, as Tottenham Park, in Savernake Forest near Marlborough, illustrates. Lancelot's March expedition was carefully planned, to begin with Lord Bruce at Tottenham and continue to Blenheim, then across to Croome and back via Dodington. Lady Bruce at Tottenham was Susanna Hoare, the sister of Henry Hoare of Stourhead, who had already made sketch suggestions for Tottenham, and Jonathan Spyers had spent three weeks surveying the ground, so that Lancelot was armed with *his* preliminary ideas. In the first week of March, Lord Bruce cancelled – he was a great favourite of the King and Queen and so subject to peremptory commands. Lancelot did not hesitate to express his 'real mortification' that he would not see the Bruces, for they 'were the objects of my western expedition' – but he would come anyway, dismiss the unsatisfactory foreman (who is unnamed), and make one Winckles, the bailiff, 'Master of the work'. And so Sunday 17th March found him at Tottenham, arriving in time to make an afternoon tour 'in a storm of snow'.

Tottenham, as Lancelot knew it, was an enticing proposition; Lord Burlington had designed it for his sister Juliana – who was married to the Lord Bruce of the day (the uncle of Thomas, 2nd Baron Bruce, Lancelot's client) – as a neo-Palladian forest lodge, hardly more than a picnic house, square with a Venetian-windowed room in each corner, and flanked by free-standing pavilions that were the kitchens on one side and stables on the other. After about ten years Lord Burlington had added corner wings, making 'a miniature Holkham', as John Harris called it, entered by a straight drive out of the woods of Savernake Forest, through huge rusticated gate piers that guarded the walled courts. After dinner and a night stop with the agent Charles Bill, on the Monday morning (18th Mar 1765), with the weather 'tolerably favourable' (his temper hardly so), Lancelot 'allowed lining out and finally settled the serpentine walk all round the garden, marked such trees as were proposed to be taken away and gave general directions to Winckles upon everything that occurr'd'. 'In general,' reported Charles Bill to Lord Bruce, 'he approves of what has been done except the taking away [of] a few large trees in one or two places. If the high bank and trees had been taken down, great would have been the fall indeed. Brown would have excommunicated us all . . .'

Lord Bruce did not escape lightly, either. Lancelot wrote of his being obliged to keep his dates at Blenheim, Croome and Dodington:

> which will take me up at least eight or ten Days. I wish your Lordship could stay a few days longer in the country . . . I have been calculating my time entirely for your Lordship and it will be an extreme mortifica- tion to me not to meet your Lordship. I beg your Lordship will contrive as much about this matter as possible because I have been contriving to make everybody meet me at their respective places which puts it out of my power to alter my rout[e].

Feathers ruffled, he arrived at Blenheim, not to fritter his frustrations away, but to get down to serious engineering, as the landscape architect Hal Moggridge appreciates and explains: 'Brown was [therefore] faced with and managed to overcome a very difficult technical problem, the critical fixing of the finished height of the dam with its sluice and cascade that governs the level of the lake, including the preservation of part of the medieval causeway which crossed the valley . . . in the form of a long island.' In addition, Lancelot was making the artificial river below the cascade, 1½ miles long and curling back towards the Evenlode: 'a long side cut and embankment borrowed from canal technology was employed – a quite difficult operation . . . and all the more impressive given that this was made at the very start of the Canal Age'.

Away from the serious water engineering, Lancelot, rather unac- countably, wished Blenheim to have a legacy of his favourite castella- tions: he transformed the rather elegant Georgian High Lodge into a castellated Gothic folly, and designed an enormously long screen 'with pointed windows, battlements and turrets to conceal the granary, carthorse stables, cart sheds and carter's house at Park Farm'. He later assured the Duke of Marlborough that he had taken account of the practical needs of grain storage, as well as that 'the Effect of the Building would be very proper for the situation'. Most audaciously of all, he proposed that a long stretch of park wall on the Woodstock boundary should be castellated, along with the tops of prominent buildings in the town. Neither the Park Farm nor Woodstock screens were ever built.

The second alphabetical tranche of entries in Lancelot's account book confirms the business of 1765, and that his efforts were often unrewarded: Sir Edward Astley at Melton Constable appears, but nothing was appar- ently forthcoming from Holkham, Ditchingham or Langley near Loddon. The Knightleys of Fawsley in Northamptonshire – the account opened with £150 paid in July 1765 – were great hunting and sheep-farming neighbours of the Spencers. Lord Spencer's Wimbledon account is entered, followed by Lord Palmerston's Broadlands at Romsey, where the rebuilding work sends the figures soaring into many thousands, the money passing through Lancelot's account before he paid it on to Hollands. Two 'jobbing' contracts of small payments, for General Keppel at Derham (Dyrham) near Enfield and Lord Waldegrave at Navestock, show that he was keeping his friends on the Essex/Hertfordshire borders warm. Then he 'flies' across country to Sir Henry Bridgeman's contract for £765 for Weston Park in Staffordshire; it is impossible to keep up with him.

Early August found him at Bowood, where there was a happier working atmosphere with William, 2nd Earl Shelburne, than with his father; Lord Shelburne (later 1st marquess of Lansdowne) was close in politics and friendship to Lord Chatham, and his new wife, Sophia Carteret, was very interested in landscape gardening: 'Mr Brown the gardener came to dinner,' she noted in her diary for 5th August, 'and spent the evening giving directions to his men.' These directions concerned the lake, for on 16th June of the following summer she noted, 'As soon as breakfast was over we took a walk and were vastly pleased with the effect of the water which flows into a magnificent river and only wants now to rise to its proper height, which it comes nearer to every day.'

Later in that August (1765) Lord Bruce was discovered making amends – 'I am very obliged to your Lordship for the venison,' wrote Lancelot on the 26th, 'which arrived in perfect order and very good.' Lord Bruce wanted to settle his account, and not for the first time the question of money spurred Lancelot's temper, for he hated to be thought disorganised:

> I have been hurried beyond measure of late . . . Mr Bill has twice hinted to me that your Lordship wishes to have my account. All I can say on that matter is that I should be extremely sorry to make any demand that is not very agreeable to your Lordship; for my journeys and plan, the admeasurement of the ground I suppose one hundred and ten pounds, but I shall be very happy if your Lordship will satisfy yourself.

Lord Bruce was soon appointed tutor to the princes George and Frederick, and subsequently Comptroller of the Queen's household, so Tottenham came into the embrace of royal obligations.

From Tottenham and Bowood it was logical to continue into Bath, where Lancelot found some amusement on his brief visits. This time he went to see the King's Sergeant-Surgeon, Sir Caesar Hawkins, who had bought Kelston Park overlooking the Avon valley (the Hawkins' had sixteen children, all being portrayed by Thomas Gainsborough at the time). Lancelot earned £500 for work at Kelston in 1767–8.

A great deal of intrigue surrounds a payment of £100 that Ralph Allen of Prior Park made into Lancelot's Drummonds account at Christmas 1760; the sum would appear to be for a consultation and a plan, but no connection between Lancelot and Prior Park has been found. At that time Ralph Allen, known for his good humour and generosity, and Sir John Sebright of Beechwood (where Lancelot worked) were controlling Bath politically in William Pitt's favour, presenting him with the Freedom and a gold casket, as well as the parliamentary seat. The £100 might belong to any of these connections.

And there was still Lord Chatham's business: Sir William Pynsent having died in the January of 1765, the Pitt family had come into their country estate, despite a challenge to the Will from the family. Needless to say, his lordship was in seventh heaven, exclaiming 'how the passion of dirty acres grows upon a West Saxon of yesterday, and that I meditate laying rapacious hands on a considerable part of the county of Somerset'. He planned a new children's wing for the house, a library for himself and a 'bird room' for Lady Chatham; he intended to farm, and experimentally at that, to improve the roads of the area and plant hundreds of trees. He was obsessive about the privacy for which Burton Pynsent was so well sited, but this was to be enhanced with evergreens, especially cedars and cypresses, many sent from Lancelot's friends in Hammersmith – for all the nurseries in Somerset 'would not furnish a hundredth part of his demands' – and with pines and maples from Nova Scotia via Plymouth. Of course Pitt wanted to do all the interesting designing and laying out himself, but Lancelot was only too happy to help.

'I called [at] your Builder's in Bath but found he was set out for your house the same day I arrived at that place,' Lancelot wrote on 10th September. 'I shall have some other opportunity of talking and giving him best advice in my power concerning the construction of pillars, scaffolding etc., as Agreeable to my promise.' His experience of Lord Cobham's column at Stowe had perhaps inspired the idea for the memorial that Lord Chatham wished to erect to Sir William Pynsent. Lancelot sent the design:

> which I hope will merit yr approbation . . . the figure I have put on the
> pedestal is Gratitude conveying to posterity the name of Pinsent; which
> indeed he himself has distinguished & without flattery done in the most

The Burton Pynsent column, Somerset, designed and constructed by Lancelot for the Earl of Chatham, drawn by Barbara Jones.

effectual manner by making you his heir. On this topic I could say more but may my silence convey my respect, and that your King and your country may be long, very long, very long blessed with yr unparalleled abilities, is the constant wish of *Lancelot Brown*.[*]

Late September found Lancelot in Staffordshire, but still wrestling with his conscience over Lord Bruce and Tottenham. Unsurprisingly he was ill: 'I have been so much out of order that I have not been able to write nor do anything else,' he wrote on 21st September, presumably from Weston or perhaps Trentham. He had sent his assistant Samuel Lapidge to assess the work done at Tottenham, but it was clearly still worrying him:

he writes me word that the surveying and map[p]ing bill with the man's [Spyers'] expenses at 6d per acre comes to near twenty-five pounds and as to my journeys and plans I have no fixed rule about it nor is it possible to do it but to charge less or more according to the size and trouble. All

[*] Burton Steeple, as the tower is known locally, still stands on the ridge overlooking West Sedge Moor; park in Curry Rivel and walk along the A378 to a road signed Heale and Stathe: the path to the tower is 300 yards up the road on the left in Moortown Lane.

I can say upon it is that I should be very sorry to diminish my friends, and very sorry to increase my business, for I have so much to do that it neither answers for profit nor pleasure, for when I am galloping in one part of the world my men are making blunders and neglects which [make] it very unpleasant.

Tottenham was a place where prides clashed – Lancelot's against the steward Charles Bill and bailiff Winckles, who felt it necessary to protect their own positions; but all the angst eventually illustrates a subtlety of Lancelot's working, as steward Bill continues describing the view from the large study window:

> Mr Brown complained of its being a straight line thro' a perfect avenue – he directed the cure of it by rounding off the plantation of laurels at the entrance of it on the left hand. There is a fine Beech there, and he directed the scrub trees to be cleared away a little from behind it which would also enlarge the entrance to the narrow avenue.

This was a subtle trick, saving the fine beech and masking the blatant opening of the avenue, leaving it as a surprise when one had gone round behind the laurels.

Lancelot was attentive to Tottenham through 1766 and beyond, his visits gradually lessening as work was completed in 1773. He is so often accused of destroying avenues, but here he incorporated the Savernake rides, including an avenue 2½ miles long, into his scheme. The house was released from its walled court to stand upon a forest lawn; a rose garden, pleasure grounds and a new kitchen garden were made, but no lake. Much of Tottenham's charm was in the fairytale juxtaposition of a house surrounded by sunshine and flowers, but in the heart of a deep, dark wood – all lost today because of private enclosure against the public access to much of Savernake Forest.

Staffordshire's 'lake district'

In March 1766 *The Gentleman's Magazine* printed the words of a popular song celebrating canal promotion.

> In Lancashire view what a laudable plan,
> And brought into fine execution
> By Bridgewater's duke; let us copy the man,
> And stand to a good resolution:
> If the waters of Trent with the Mersey have vent,

What mortal can have an objection!
So they do not proceed, to cut into the Tweed,
With the Scots to have greater connection.

The 'long side-cut and embankment' from early canal technology used at Blenheim did indeed come from canal country, and the connections are intriguing. Croome and the Coventrys were Lancelot's most likely introduction to the young Francis Egerton, 3rd Duke of Bridgewater, who in 1758 became engaged to the widowed Duchess of Hamilton, the former Elizabeth Gunning, sister to Maria, Countess of Coventry. Lancelot was summoned to Ashridge, the Duke's vast estate of high commons and beech woods in the Chilterns above Berkhamsted, which included the villages of Little Gaddesden, Ringshall and Aldbury.

Ashridge was a monastery of the Bonhommes, willed by Henry VIII to his daughter Elizabeth 1st, and the home of the Egertons since 1604; as living quarters it was rather chaotic, with a medieval great hall rising above a gaggle of Tudor outbuildings, the most manageable and prettiest part being the three-storey north gate-house. Adjoining this gate-house Hollands built a house of Totternhoe stone, of seven bays with a hipped roof, looking like any comfortable village manor house of that time. This house is shown on George Grey's estate map of 1762, casting its modest gaze out onto Ashridge park, the deer-grazed lawns dividing around an oval clump of trees, all seeming like Lancelot's softened setting for the house, before the old straight rides stream off in all directions through limitless acres of undulating woods.

All became lost in disappointment and diversion, for the young 3rd Duke proved strait-laced and forbade his fiancée to see her sister, Maria Coventry, who was behaving badly. Sisterly affections stood firm and Elizabeth and the Duke parted (she married the Marquess of Lorne) and he turned his attentions to his passion for canals, conceived on his Grand Tour when he had seen the Canal du Midi at Carcassonne. Lancelot continued extensive plantings at Ashridge, especially in the Golden Valley north of the house, but it is now difficult to identify his work. Ashridge was to be completely rebuilt in nineteenth-century Gothic glory by the Wyatts father and son, using the fortune from the Bridgewater canal ventures, and Humphry Repton made faux-monastic gardens: seeing all this, John Claudius Loudon felt that the park lacked a lake, and that the required water could be steam-pumped up from the Gade valley to these Chiltern heights.

The Duke of Bridgewater's first canal, to carry coal from his mines at Worsley to Salford, was started in 1759 and opened in 1761. The Duke had met and taken to 'the careful, solid millwright' from Derbyshire named James Brindley, and Brindley was soon employed surveying the line for the Trent & Mersey Canal to link the potteries with Manchester and Liverpool, being promoted by the Duke in a partnership that included Lord Gower from Trentham and Thomas Anson of Shugborough; the Trent flowed through both of their parks. Lancelot was familiar with these places, and it might be said that he had a *tendresse* for south Staffordshire, Izaak Walton's watery country. The Pitt connection had introduced him to Lord Gower, and the affable Admiral Anson at Moor Park had sent him to his family home at Shugborough, where his brother was spending a good deal of the Admiral's prize money on improvements. Did Lancelot work at Shugborough? There they do not think so, but then the records are admittedly poor. There was a lake, with an island and two bridges, all lost after serious flooding in 1795, with a pagoda (also lost) and the Chinese House, built from a drawing brought home by the Admiral, but similar to the one at Stowe and of the same date, about 1747. There are other Stowe-like monuments, to a cat and an enigmatic shepherd, both by Thomas Wright. An explanation may lie with the huge Triumphal Arch set on high in the park, which was turned into a monument to the Admiral, who died, aged sixty-five, in 1762, and his much younger wife, Elizabeth Yorke (sister to Philip Yorke and his wife, Marchioness Grey of Wrest), who died just before her husband. This double bereavement brought a stultifying sadness to Shugborough. It has to be said that Shugborough lacks the graceful cohesion that Lancelot would have brought to the layout, but then, with its wreathing rivers, the Trent and the Sow, it is a place he must have longed to 'beautify'.

Just to be tantalising, there is at Shugborough a huge landscape painting showing the house in its well-watered plain, bathed in summer sunlight, with the Triumphal Arch, and with neighbouring Tixall Hall and its gatehouse, and – the third of this trio – Ingestre Hall, and even the diminutive Ingestre pavilion on the skyline; Lancelot worked at both Tixall and Ingestre. Ingestre is an understated masterpiece, where he made sense of the fragmented efforts of the Chetwynd family, and it has a Wren church in which it is easy to see another pattern for his churches at Croome and Compton Verney. He did not touch the surroundings of the Jacobean hall, but the balustraded terrace became a viewing platform for his 'intended lawn', with views to the north and west rising gradually to the edge of a bowl. The skyline was already ornamented with eye-catchers: Sanderson Miller's tower (similar to his own at Edge Hill and those at Hagley and Wimpole) and the classical Pavilion, dated 1752 (possibly also Miller's). This Pavilion, Lancelot cursed, sat at an awkwardly oblique angle as seen from the Hall, staring eastwards and closing the vista of an old drive that forged its way across the valley and river towards Hixon and eventually Uttoxeter, but belonging to an earlier age. Lancelot's solution was to surround both tower and Pavilion in a wilderness/plantation of walks, a miniature park-within-a-park, with an oval pond, all enclosed by a ha-ha and intended as a destination for picnic teas. The Pavilion was used for these Arcadian adventures for many years; the tower, tainted by a murder, was demolished in the mid-nineteenth century. The larger park was defined with a sweep of planting that echoed the line of the ha-ha, and beyond this the old axials of the seventeenth-century avenues to Weston and Hopton were retained.

Lancelot's work at Tixall came in the early 1770s, when Thomas Clifford paid twenty-five guineas for a plan for widening the River Sow in the park, with a bridge, the 'lake' being known locally as 'Tixall Wide'. He was working for Clifford's brother at Ugbrooke in Devon at the same time.

So, as Lancelot was mixing with the canal promoters at the turn of the 1760s, when his own prospects were looking dim, there comes the inevitable question: was he tempted to join the canal boom? His undoubted affection for Staffordshire, the many commissions he found there, and Lord Gower's generous and long-standing patronage all suggest attachments. On the other hand, there were vast differences between a utilitarian canal and an ornamental lake – and equally fascinating contrasts between the characters of James Brindley and Lancelot Brown.

Brindley was the same age as Lancelot; he came from a comfortably-off yeoman family in the Peak District, and was apprenticed to a millwright, which gave him a much-respected trade. As Lancelot was settling in Hammersmith, Brindley was moving to Burslem, renting a millwright's shop from the Wedgwoods. Likenesses of Brindley make him appear good-humoured, but he had a habit of worrying at a problem and was nicknamed 'the Schemer'. He brooked no nonsense. As Jenny Uglow writes of him: 'we can still hear his forthright voice in his spelling, as he makes an "occhilor survey or a ricconitoring" for the duke'. (Lancelot may have kept his Geordie lilt, but he was never indecipherable). Whereas Lancelot loved the very greenness of his hills and lawns, and the froth of tumbling waters and roughness of barks, Brindley was obsessed with all things mechanical and, frankly, oily – though something written of Brindley in a newspaper of 1771 can be applied to both: 'He knew Water, its Weight and Strength, Turn'd Brooks, made Soughs to a great Length.' Brindley also 'made Tunnels for Barges, Boats and Air-vessels; he erected several Banks, Mills, Pumps, Machines, with Wheels and Cranks', and though Lancelot could do tunnels and bankings, he would never have called himself an engineer, though others did. Both men were happy with the techniques of clay puddling, and Lancelot used it before it became accepted canal practice. But in ways of 'design' they were chalk and cheese, and surely Lancelot recoiled at the straight-line canal philosophy. Brindley followed contours to save on earth-moving, and wherever possible sent his canals in straight lines; curves were anathema to him, and nothing could change this rule: in 1767, when Josiah Wedgwood bought the Ridgehouse estate for his new home and pottery works, he did so because it was on the confirmed canal route, which he needed for transporting his raw materials and pots. But Wedgwood, who commissioned the Derby architect Joseph Pickford for his elegantly pedimented Etruria Hall and pottery-works buildings, hoped for a little fashion in his landscape; after long arguments with Brindley's assistant Hugh Henshall, Wedgwood reported glumly, 'I could not prevail upon the inflexible Vandal to give me *one line of Grace* – he must go the nearest & best way, or Mr Brindley would go mad.' (William Emes, who worked frequently with Pickford, landscaped Wedgewood's Etruria Park.)

Lancelot did not engineer canals, for the lines of grace were in his bones and he would go no other way, as he demonstrated with Lord Gower's lake at Trentham, just south of the pottery town of Longton. At Trentham he had the Trent itself to play with; nothing argues so well for Lord Gower's power in the locality as the fact that he could purloin the waters of Piscator's third river of England – 'Trent, so called for thirty kind of Fishes that are found in it, or for that it receiveth thirty lesser Rivers' – and Michael Drayton's 'Chrystal Trent for fords and fish renown'd'. The lake is spectacular, three-quarters of a mile long, subtly weaving with the contours of the tree-covered hill on the west bank, with space enough for serpentine walks, sometimes open to, and sometimes hidden from, the water. The east bank is lawn, open and sunny, home to some magnificent cedars: Trentham's lake must rank as one of the finest examples of Lancelot's intuition, his ability to endow a landscape with strength to withstand future times. Despite the nineteenth-century onslaught of Charles Barry's Italianate palace and William Nesfield's vast formal gardens, the lake has held its own; and it still does, a calming presence, amid Trentham's regenerated and 'active' landscape.

A few miles south of Trentham, the Fitzherberts' Swynnerton, a lovely park of deep undulations, has a 'Brownian' lake and boundary plantations. Farther south between Shifnal and Wolverhampton there is a cluster of four more certain commissions, for Weston Park, Tong, Chillington and Patshull. Weston is close to Watling Street, and in the mid-1760s Lancelot fulfilled two contracts for Sir Henry Bridgeman, for evident modernising, with earth-modelling, 'lowering the Hill in the manner agreed to by Sr Henry', a sunk fence and screening plantations, drives and sloping lawns; two pools are also thought to be his. At the same time he was working at Tong Castle for George Durant, a site cut by the M54, although the lake survives. Just to the east of Tong at the Giffards' Chillington, approached by a 3-mile avenue from near Brewood, Lancelot's pool is still the largest in the county, except for the modern Belvide Reservoir. The water source came in from the north and he widened it into a river, more than half a mile long, gradually widening further into The Pool. James Paine designed a bridge for the north end of the river, and he wrote of it all as:

> confessedly one of the finest pieces of water, within an inclosure, that this Kingdom produces; the verges of which are bounded by fine plantations, intermixed with groves of venerable stately oaks . . . at another neck of this beautiful water is erected another bridge, concealing the other extreme of the water, built by Lancelot Brown Esq., who designed and conducted the execution of the improvements of this justly admired park.

Finally, in 1765, Patshull Hall and Old Park, near Pattingham, were bought by George Pigot, the recently returned Governor of Madras, where Robert Clive had been his deputy. Patshull cost Pigot £80,000; he paid Lancelot £52. 10s. for a plan that resulted in a spectacular J-shaped lake, which is today a mecca for carp and pike fishermen.

'Brownifications' at Temple Newsam

'We have had a long continuance of fine weather,' wrote Frances Irwin from Temple Newsam in Yorkshire in early October 1765, 'but at length the rain is come which I am very sorry for as my Lord has just begun with Mr Brown & wet weather is very unfavourable for their operations.'

Trentham and Temple Newsam were very closely connected, though a good 100 miles apart, and so once again in this frantic year Lancelot had had another long journey, to what was then countryside just east of Leeds.

Temple Newsam was another of his petticoat places, in the 'good-looking, shapely, assured, intelligent' personage of Viscountess Irwin, who sweetly let the world think that her husband was in charge. She was born Frances Gibson, the natural daughter of the Tory fortune-maker Sam

Shepheard (who had challenged Sir John Hynde Cotton's right to Madingley and lost); he left her a great heiress (£60,000) as long as she did not marry an Irishman, a Scot or the son of a peer. She chose the eligible Charles Ingram, whose uncle then died, making him the 9th Viscount Irwin, and after two years of legal wrangling Frances won permission to marry him, in 1758; he was thirty-one, she was three years younger. They were happy enough, and had five daughters whom they adored, but Frances was most 'deeply smitten' by Temple Newsam itself, the tall red-brick Tudor-Jacobean mansion with huge windows, almost 'more glass than wall', set in white-railed courts in a park well watered by a tributary of the River Aire. From the start she urged her husband to send for Lancelot; they had met in Whitehall in 1758, and Lancelot promised to be in Yorkshire the following year, but it was not until January 1763 that Lord Irwin was pleased to hear the plans were ready – would Lancelot send them by the flyer, the Leeds Machine, 'the most expeditious way'? The impression is that Lord Irwin was lukewarm about the whole business, but occasionally stirred himself to please his wife; she had by this time produced three daughters, Isabella, Frances and Elizabeth, and undoubtedly many lace-edged handkerchiefs, for she was a fine and determined needlewoman.

The Temple, as they called it, was a lovely place, as Sidney Swinney's verse implies, addressing Lord Irwin:

> But you, my Lord, at Temple Newsam find,
> The Charms of Nature gracefully combin'd
> Sweet waving hills, with wood and verdure crown'd
> And winding vales, where murmuring streams resound:
> Slopes fring'd with Oaks which gradual die away,
> And all around romantic scenes display.

The plan was for two lakes, a lawn and ha-ha, and numerous delights: a dairy, menagerie, thatched cottage, grotto, rotunda and bridges in variety. Frances, however, treasured an existing and undoubtedly straight gravel walk for her exercise, and in April 1766, the weather 'quite like summer', she wrote, 'I am out of doors all day long, Mr Brown has put us in a wo[e]ful dirty pickle, but my gravel walk is always a resource and very much made use of.' On 26th July, just after the birth of her youngest daughter Louisa, she wrote, 'Mr Brown left this morning and indeed we are prodigiously busy in his way as a deal has been done.' Six months later in the February 1767 fog, she was not out much, but 'stood still while Col Pitt & my husband have been Brownifying my dear gravel walk, his little wife carried stakes for them to mark out places for shrubs & I stood by to give my approbation'. Clearly the walk had been serpentised and planted; sometimes she called the works 'Brownifications'.

Once a year in the summer the Irwins went south to Sussex, to what Frances called 'my little Horsham business', Hills Place, and the business was to keep the local parliamentary seats in the right hands. Lancelot went to Hills twice, but perhaps just to discuss the Temple. Otherwise Frances was at home in the north, 'an old fashioned country gentlewoman in an old worn out house with my girls'. She became a hands-on gardener with itchy fingers to plant in the spring, defying the cold. Lancelot continued his visits well into the 1770s, but it is hard to know what he did, for the park is much altered. Some clues may be in the continuation of Swinney's verse:

> Delighted still along the park we rove,
> Vary'd with Hill and Dale, with Wood and Grove:
> Oe'er velvet Lawns what noble Prospects rise,
> Fair as the Scenes, that Reuben's hand supplies.
> But when the Lake shall these sweet Grounds adorn,
> And bright expanding like the eye of Morn,
> Reflect whate'er above its surface rise,
> The Hills, the Rocks, the Woods and varying Skies,
> Then will the wild and beautiful combine,
> And Taste in Beauty grace your whole Design.

Lord Irwin and Lancelot were both shy about the publication of these verses, and Thomas Hinde suggests they wanted to wait for the lake to be finished. Little more can be learned from Frances's own description, except that she was content:

I apply myself to my beauteous Claude where the scene always enchants me; the trees are green, the waters placid & serene & the air has a warmth very comfortable. Altogether it is just as one's mind should be; no boundless passions or turbulent ambition to perturb one's breast but the stream of life to flow peacefully & unruffled, sometimes through flowery meads & sometimes through brake till at length it reaches the ocean of eternity.

Lord Irwin died in 1778 and Frances lived on at the Temple until her death in 1807. In her Horsham political 'business' she supported the younger Pitt. The Temple Newsam landscape clings on as a 'green lung' for ever-encroaching Leeds.

'My power is but small'

The hot gossip of early July 1766 was that the King 'sent to Mr Pitt with carte blanche to form a ministry' and Pitt agreed 'to extricate the country out of a faction'. Lancelot was amazed, for Pitt's health was appalling, his temper 'fire and brimstone', and while Lady Chatham and the children were on holiday in Weymouth, Pitt was dashing to and from Bath, believing in any cure that would fend off his black dog. As he was now Earl of Chatham and Viscount Pitt of Burton Pynsent, he intended to govern from the House of Lords. Lancelot was caught in a maelstrom of gossip because so many of his clients were sent revolving like planets about the sun – or cast into oblivion, for the King had broken with Lord Bute and was never to speak to him again, and Lord Chatham was treating his brothers-in-law George Grenville at Wotton and Earl Temple at Stowe in the same way. The Duke of Northumberland had spent three years in Ireland 'without any mark of favour' and so he asked for his dukedom, which he got on condition that he stayed out of the way, but it gave a fillip to his plans for Alnwick. The Duke of Grafton's Euston and Lord Shelburne's Bowood were both 'rested', as they became ministers. Lady Chatham appealed to Lancelot for help to find a spacious and airy London house (for the St James's Square house and Hayes Place had both been sold in favour of Burton Pynsent) and they were reduced to borrowing.

Lord Gower, Granville, 2nd earl, at Trentham was briefly out of office, and Lancelot was on his way there, calling at Castle Ashby in Northamptonshire on the way, where he missed Lord Northampton, but saw his agent, Mr Foulerton. Lancelot's was a familiar face at Castle Ashby, where he had inspected the old-fashioned gardens and grounds and started work on a first contract, on 14th October 1761, for the young 7th Earl of Northampton, 'of advanced taste and great potential as a patron', who died abroad in 1763. For Spencer Compton, 8th Earl, Lancelot was now expanding the fishponds into lakes, and building an ice house in 'expensive manner', for £68, which was set into one end of the dam between the lakes. A ha-ha, ditch and wall were built to protect the kitchen gardens (now the Italian gardens) for £53, and sundry temples, a dairy, a bridge and a domed menagerie (designed by Robert Adam) were all part of the ongoing works.

However, quite another matter was raised in his conversation with agent Foulerton, as we learn from Lancelot's letter from Trentham, dated 30th July 1766 to Lord Northampton, saying he understood 'that you and Mr Drummond had not agreed about the Huntingdon estate. If no other person is in treaty with your Lordship I shall be glad to have the refusal of it, your Lordship shall have very little trouble with me upon it – I shall give an immediate answer as soon as I know the conditions and have looked it over.'

The Mr Drummond was Henry Drummond, old Andrew Drummond's nephew and recently married to Elizabeth Compton, the Earl's sister; he was clearly trying to help the Earl's known financial difficulties by selling outlying properties. Whether Drummonds were holding the 'Huntingdon estate' as surety is not known. Nor do we know if Lancelot had scouted around Huntingdon, though he had surely found out that Fenstanton Manor, with Hilton, was the estate in question. He seems to have decided that, with money in the bank, it was time for some security and investment in a property of his own.

He was busy, as ever, and looking within a 10-mile radius of Westminster for the Chathams, growing ever more concerned at the conflicting rumours:

> I had the pleasure yesterday to hear at Richmond that his lordship was much better – it gives one hope that [he] will soon be able to stand forth for himself and convince the world that singularity (which they complain of) is laudable when in Contradiction to a multitude [and] it adheres to the dictates of conscient morality and honour. My power is but small but my good wishes for Lord Chatham are unbounded, not new nor altered.

Lancelot added the wish 'to see (but am doubtful I hope too much) yr ladyship's family once more in perfect union', knowing that she was banned from Wotton Underwood and Stowe.

On 25th May 1767 he reminded Lord Northampton, from whom he had heard nothing about 'Huntingdon': 'I shall be much obliged to your Lordship for an answer as I am kept in suspense and have other things on offer, but I was determined to have nothing to do with anybody 'till your Lordship had given me your answer.' For the Chathams he had found a villa with 100 acres near Barnet, or possibly a new house at Wimbledon with 150 acres. Was he thinking of himself as well – his 'other things on offer?' On 28th May he wrote to Lord Northampton:

> I have this moment received a letter from Midgley [the foreman at Castle Ashby] in which he informs me your Lordship desires to know when I shall be at Castle Ashby. My intention was to have been there soon after the King's birthday [4th June] but he informs me your Lordship means to set out for Derbyshire on Sunday next [so] I will defer my journey.

'Huntingdonshire' was distressing him and he hoped for an answer.

Lancelot was at Castle Ashby on the Sunday, 7th June, but the Earl

must have been on the point of leaving, for they discussed minor alterations to the Dairy, but 'Huntingdon' was not mentioned; Lancelot did
not feel he could visit his wished-for estate without Lord Northampton's
express permission, and left a letter politely telling him so. Then he went
off on an extended visit to Blenheim, Croome and Staffordshire. At home
a letter from Lady Chatham, of 7th June, awaited him, full of apologies
for not having written before, but they had settled on North End House
at Hampstead, ending, 'I am extremely sorry not to be able to give you
the pleasure of knowing that my Lord is better, but as yet there is no
amendment in his health to mention.'

As the summer days passed, the news went from bad to worse. Lord
Chatham 'was physically and mentally shipwrecked', in a deep melancholia, with little appetite, 'no strength, recurrent fever, no ability to
concentrate, no power of will or command of himself' – Horace Walpole
saw 'too clearly, the gout flown up into his head'. His fledgling administration was in chaos, no one was able to placate the American colonists
into 'duties' that they did not regard as 'taxes' and lift their boycott of
British goods, let alone deal with domestic disloyalties. The King wanted
to visit Lord Chatham, who begged him not to come, for 'the honour
and weight' of such a visit 'would crush him in his enfeebled state'. All
prayed for a lucid hour, but it did not come; tearful, insisting on a darkened room, Pitt became delusive, making plans for extending North End
House (which belonged to Charles Dingley) or for demolishing the
buildings that cluttered his views. Anyway, he blustered, he did *not like*
North End; he wanted Hayes – so Hester wrote pleading letters to the
new owner, Thomas Walpole, who agreed to sell it back again, fearful of
causing a national disaster if he did not.

Lancelot, distraught, wrote to Lady Chatham on 7th August, 'I have
very near as many anxious hours as yr ladyship can have for his Lordship's
health because I love my King and my country and am most faithfully
devoted to Lord Chatham.' This is such an extreme outburst that it
suggests he must have been closely involved: Lady Chatham had power
of attorney and she had to sell some of the land at Burton Pynsent in
order to raise enough money for Hayes Place; Thomas Walpole had paid
them £11,780 for it, and now demanded £17,400 to cover the repairs
and improvements that he claimed were necessary. Lord Chatham was
aware of these negotiations, though 'more than once bewildered', and
surely Lancelot must have seen him in this state to have become so upset.
He would also have found it inexpressibly sad to go down to Burton
Pynsent to identify the land that could be sold without detriment to the
house or its views.

Unsurprisingly he was 'much out of order for the last five or six days' of the first week in September. On the 7th he wrote to Lord Northampton:

My intention is to have the estate at the price your Lordship had agreed with Mr Drummond which was I think thirteen thousand pounds. Your lordship will be so good as to signify your pleasure in regard to the time of payment, and a final answer shall be sent when I have seen the estate, at which time an article may be drawn up binding both sides to the conditions that shall be thought necessary.

Lancelot hoped for an immediate answer, and that the family were all well.

Three days later he wrote to Hester Chatham, having heard that the doctors had recommended a change of air and they were leaving North End for Pynsent – 'I hope in God that his lordship mended every day & that you all had a good journey. Pardon my Zeal, Pardon my Vanity, but I wish above all things to know [how] my lord does.' Lancelot's last words revealed that he had been down to Pynsent and inspected the steeple, newly completed to his design: he hoped to hear 'how the Pillar pleases his lordship'. After a few weeks the Chathams moved to Bath, and then back to Hayes Place, where Lord Chatham's health inexplicably improved, though he was persuaded to resign his office.

Lancelot's deal with Lord Northampton was closing too; he promised to pay £6,000 or £7,000 at Christmas, and the remainder at Lady Day in 1767. In his account book he wrote off £1,556. 8s., the amount to cover the extra works at Castle Ashby, which he deducted from the settlement. The conveyance was completed with all the historic rights and details of tolls and taxes, and Lord Northampton wrote eccentrically on his copy of the transfer deed, 'I take the Manor of Fen Stanton to belong to Lawrence [sic] Brown Taste Esq., who gave Lord Northampton Taste in exchange for it.' To be fair, the Earl appreciated 'the taste' he had bought, and taught his son to do so by severely telling him off for attempting to jump over the newly planted cedar of Lebanon by the Menagerie, for fear of damaging it, a story that was handed down in the family.

However, Castle Ashby is chiefly notable as the park that enabled Lancelot Brown to become a country gentleman. What had he bought? The estate was the manor of Stanton cum Hilton, two ancient villages, Fenny Stanton and Hilton, 1½ miles apart on the edge of the Great Ouse valley in Huntingdonshire. Fenny Stanton (now Fenstanton) lies

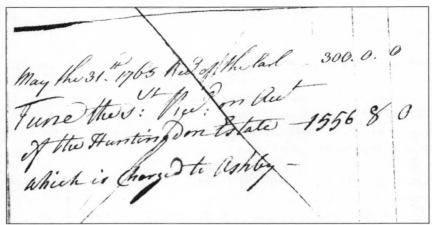

Note in Castle Ashby account – 'May the 31st 1765 Rec'd of the Earl £300. June the
1st [1767] Rec'd on Acct of the Huntingdon Estate £1556. 8s. 0d which is Charged to
Ashby'.

9 miles north-west of Cambridge on a road that the Romans made;
Hilton is to the west, close to the Old Great North Road on its course
from Royston to Caxton and Huntingdon (A1198). These were remote
places in a watery and gentle countryside in a small and quiet county:
there were no large houses, no dramatic inequalities of landscape that
Lancelot might feel he had to improve, and there was plenty of good
fishing in the quiet meadows beside the Ouse. The Stanton manor
house was a good seventeenth-century brick house with little distinc-
tion except for its double-height porch; Grove House nearby had once
belonged to Joan, Queen of Scotland, who had planted twenty oaks
there in 1235. Across the silvery streams of the Ouse was St Ives, the
destination of the Man with Seven Wives (with seven hats and seven
cats), named for Ivo, a seventh-century Persian holy man whose bones
were found there. Along the river was Hemingford Grey, where the
beautiful Gunning sisters had grown up; was it dabbling in the dew-
washed meadows that made their milkmaid complexions? Whatever the
stories, it was a lovely place.

    Why Lancelot bought Fenstanton is a much more difficult question
to answer. He certainly made the decision when he was under great
stresses and arguably not at the best time. Did he simply want to invest
in land? Jonathan Spyers did not complete his survey for ten years, so
for the time being it was estimated at about 1,000 acres. More likely
Lancelot wished to make provision for his family in the event of his
death, as the news of his brother John's sudden death in March 1766 had
shaken him. He had his Will drafted (eventually dated 1769), which in

the midst of all this heady activity makes poignant reading, but allows an insight into his thoughts.

His foreman Benjamin Read was to be employed 'to go from Place to Place' to clear up all the contracted work, 'and I hope such employment will prove of use to him'. Samuel Lapidge, who 'knows my accounts,' was to be an executor, along with 'my dear wife', friend John Drummond (old Andrew's son), John Edison of Cooper's Hall, London (gentleman and lawyer) and Henry Holland (senior). The Fenstanton estate was to provide annuities for Biddy, Lance, Jack ('whom God preserve in his hazardous employment' in the navy) and his eldest daughter Bridget, who was of age and was to have the silver candlestick, as he had always promised. The 'liberal education' of Thomas was in his mother's care, as was their youngest daughter Peggy (their daughter Anne had died).

The remainder of the Fenstanton estate was put in trust for Lance, and Biddy's dowry land in Lincolnshire was similarly left to Jack. There were legacies to his surviving sister Mary Hudson, to his nephew Richard Brown, to Biddy's brother and married sister and their niece Phyllis 'Philly' Cooke, who lived with them. The housemen William and George Davis were not forgotten, nor were the livery men and boys, nor the housemaids, for all were to have a year's wages.

It was wise and thoughtful planning, but Lancelot was not finished yet.

Indeed, he was dancing, or nearly so; as the crises had cleared in the September of 1767, he had explored Fenstanton and Hilton and his patch of Huntingdonshire. He intended no hasty decisions and the well-tenanted holdings and houses were left in peace, hardly knowing that their landlord had changed. But for Lancelot, a new northwards pattern was introduced into his travelling life; hardly 10 miles from Fenstanton, he made his first visit to Wimpole in Cambridgeshire, now Jemima, Marchioness Grey's home with her husband, Lord Hardwicke. 'Break off. Break off, we tread Enchanted Ground,' she wrote, 'Mr Brown has been leading me such a Fairy Circle & his Magic Wand has raised such landscapes to the Eye – not visionary for they were all there but his Touch has brought them out with the same Effect as a Painter's Pencil upon Canvass.' Though she knew every inch of her own Wrest, the farther reaches of Wimpole's vast park were unfamiliar, and 'after having hobbled over rough ground' for two hours she returned 'half Tired & half Foot sore'. Lancelot was to concentrate upon the dramatic chalk scarp in the north of the park: Lord Hardwicke was his only client who was apparently interested in forward planning, for he wanted gross costs for three years' work: 'perhaps it is absurd to look so far forward but however the sketch of the whole may be of use in every event. If it were not too old-fashioned I wd make you the Complimts of the season,' he wrote on Christmas Eve. He hoped Lancelot would work through the holidays to complete the plan of operations for the next year.

10

RETURN TO THE NORTH

When You bid Me farewell, I was mute & was dull,
A little too Selfish, my heart was too full . . .
I left thee with CECIL, *our right noble Host*
O Cambridge, the Worth of such Men thou well knowest:
With Patoun too I left thee, & left thee w'th West,★
Who in painting will tell thee & do what is best,
With the great planner Brown, who's himself ye best Plan,
I envy his Genius, yet doat on ye Man;
Then be not Surpriz'd I was Silent & Surly,
I left Thee with these & I left thee at Burghley.
           David Garrick to Richard Owen Cambridge, 8th August 1770

ROYAL CLERK OF WORKS, Joshua Kirby noted that 'great alterations and improvements' were started 'by Mr Launcelot Browne'
at the King's garden by the river at Richmond in the autumn
of 1765. Work lasted for five years, the ground was very flat and Lancelot
endeavoured to create dells and private groves as the setting for George
III's desired new palace: the palace was not built, and the grounds were
amalgamated into Kew Gardens, where the Rhododendron Dell is the
surviving fragment of Lancelot's work.

A single plant, the Great Vine at Hampton Court, is the more famous
survivor of the King's Master Gardener's work of the late 1760s. The vine
was planted in 1768, as a cutting taken from a prolific Black Hamburg
variety growing at the home of a retired East India Company seafarer,
Sir Charles Raymond, at Valentines at Ilford in Essex. The connection
was in the relationship through marriage of the Raymond and Burrell
families, Peter Burrell being the King's Surveyor-General of Crown Lands,
another of Lancelot's overlords and much concerned with the gardens.

★ William Patoun was one of a circle of clever amateur painters living at Richmond, d. 1783;
Benjamin West (1738–1820), born in Pennsylvania, settled in London in 1763 and became George
III's favourite painter.

The vine was planted in open ground, but trained to grow inside the south-facing Vine House, one of the then-revolutionary new stove houses 'based on the Amsterdam design', built in 1689 to hold William and Mary's collection of exotic plants. The house had underfloor heating, fireplaces fed by little wheeled furnaces, with vents and flues, and the back and side walls were boarded and painted white, so as to show any contaminations that threatened the precious plant. The venerable vine, now with its own keeper, and as prolific as ever, is one of the most wondrous sights for visitors to Hampton Court, but in Lancelot's time it was an almost experimental addition to the fruit gardens. Inasmuch as Richmond Park was the official 'game larder', the Hampton Court gardens were the 'fruit basket', supplying soft summer fruits and wall fruits (apricots, peaches, quinces, medlars, pears) to the royal family and others of importance. A note survives from Lord North, as Prime Minister, to Lancelot requesting that fruit be sent to Downing Street, where he was entertaining a deputation from Oxford University.

Now that the Brown family had settled, Hampton Court was proving a very pleasant place to live, all Lancelot's 'lordships' could be confined to the accounts, and they had found their level amongst friends. Upon closer acquaintance, Hampton Court proved more than a palace, for an incipient privatisation was moving in on the royal demesne as the copyhold leases that had been granted to court officials were inherited by their grandsons with independent careers, or even sold to complete newcomers. Henry Wise's descendants still occupied his house 'Between the Walls', as did George Lowe's; Lowe's daughter married Samuel Lapidge, and Lancelot stood godfather to their baby son, who grew up to become the architect Edward Lapidge. On the green, Sir Christopher Wren's Old Court House had been sold by the Wren family about twenty years before, and was now the home of Thomas Nobbs, about whom little is known except that he too was one of Lancelot's circle. Hampton had the advantage of a bridge over the Thames to Molesey, a seven-arched construction of wooden lattice with two pairs of Chinese-style guard pavilions – it looked rather as though it had been copied from a blue-and-white Willow-pattern plate. At the Hampton end the bridge was flanked by The Mitre, a coaching inn, and the much less sedate drinking house, the Toy Inn, where royal hangers-on and sometimes minor royals let their hair down. On a rare day when there was nothing in particular to do, Lancelot strolled across Hampton Green of a fine morning to be saluted by the Foot Guards on patrol and chat briefly to the old gate-keeper at the Hampton road. Biddy Brown was shy of 'society' and content with her family and household of young people, but Lancelot enjoyed a little celebrity amongst his friends, and he was on his way to visit one of the most celebrated.

David Garrick and Lancelot had much in common, even if the actorly excesses of the former made the gardener blush. Garrick was a year younger with a better education, famously taught by the young Samuel Johnson, with whom he had left their home town of Lichfield, with one horse between them and pennies in their pockets. In London they had fallen in with fellow searchers for fame and fortune; it was said that 'if Johnson had taught Garrick ways of reading, Hogarth taught him ways of seeing'.

Garrick had had a ready-made profession to fall into – two in fact, though he had failed at the wine trade; in the company of William Hogarth, Peg Woffington, Aaron Hill and Colley Cibber, Garrick had discovered his vocation on the stage. Lancelot rarely had time to see a play, though Garrick was forever plying him with tickets, but he knew – as all the world did – that Garrick's chamaeleon persona assumed a character as he put on the costume, or even at will without any special dress, as with his famous 'Cushion' demonstration as reported by Diderot:

> Garrick picked up a cushion, saying 'Gentlemen, I am this child's father'.
> Thereupon he opened a window, took his cushion, tossed it in the air,
> kissed it, caressed it, and imitated all the fooleries of a father . . . but then
> came a moment when the cushion, or rather, the child slipped from his
> hand and fell through the window. Then Garrick began to mime the
> father's despair . . . his audience were seized with such consternation and
> horror that most of them could not bear it and had to leave the room.

As with the cushion, so with his Shakespearean roles – Garrick 'quit his own mind' and put himself into character, so that 'he becomes so different from his own self that his face and body change, and we can scarce believe it is the same man'. His Richard III was famous beyond even the performances for Hogarth's portrayal of the King rising from his nightmare on Bosworth's morning, 'frozen by terror, reaching for his sword and fending off the ghosts with his raised hand'. He had first played Richard III in 1741, the year Lancelot settled at Stowe, and in a sense both their futures were made. In 1749, five years after Lancelot's marriage, to the respectable and demure Miss Wayet, Garrick had wooed and won the mysterious Eva Maria Veigel, a dancer from Vienna who was the Burlingtons' ward; Garrick's fans hated his marriage, but soon forgave him. He did not have an easy victory, for Lady Burlington had intended Eva Maria for none other than George William Coventry.

The Garricks had a blissfully happy marriage, and the Burlington connection made them more than comfortable; they lived almost 'on the job' at 27 Southampton Street, close to Drury Lane Theatre, but had holidays at Chatsworth or at Londesborough, and stayed at Chiswick House whenever they wanted. The Burlingtons' son-in-law Lord Hartington (who became the 4th Duke of Devonshire, Lancelot's Duke at Chatsworth) and Lord Holderness at Sion Hill were Garrick's particular friends.

With success, Garrick wanted a country house: after false choices in Derbyshire and Hertfordshire, 'I shall content Myself with ye Bank of ye Thames,' he had told his friend the Rev. Joseph Smith, rector of Stanmore – the Rev. Smith being the first and most likely link with Lancelot, who was at Stanmore with Andrew Drummond at this time. Garrick had rented Fuller House in Hampton and in August 1754 decided to buy it, changing the name to Hampton House.

Hampton House was not right on the Thames – the point that had made Garrick think twice – but on the north side of the Hampton Court road, on the edge of Hampton village and just under a mile from Hampton Court's gate. Garrick knew that Alexander Pope's villa at Twickenham was similarly sited, and that Pope had had a tunnel dug beneath the road to link with a lawn on the river's bank. Garrick acquired his lawn, and it is generally believed that Lancelot supervised the building of the tunnel for him. Dr Johnson quipped, 'David, David, what can't be over-done, may be under-done.' There is a lovely story cited in Dorothy Stroud's book, that when Garrick asked Robert Adam to build a new front onto Hampton House, and the Orangery, the architect arrived with his brother James and two other friends, with their golf clubs: '[John] Home, seeing the tunnel, offered to drive his ball through it in three strokes, a feat which he accomplished. The ball, however, came to rest in the shallows of the river from where it was retrieved by Garrick and kept as a memento.' Lancelot bending his stolid frame to a golf club – now there's a thought!

The tunnel was not long, as the road was narrow and the technique used was an extension of the passages into an ice house, of which Lancelot had plenty of experience: his ice house at Syon is at the corner of the walled garden, and the one at Ashridge has a long entrance tunnel. Ice houses at Tong Castle (now at Avoncroft Museum at Bromsgrove), Petworth, Stowe, Wakefield Lawn (beneath the lake), Milton Abbas and Hampton Court (at Kingston Bridge) were all part of his experience so far.

The tunnel entrance in the main garden is shown in Zoffany's *A View* *of Hampton House with Garrick Writing* of 1762; in the companion picture, *A View of Hampton Garden with Mr and Mrs Garrick Taking Tea*, Mark Laird has identified two newly planted *Salix babylonica*, weeping willows on the river bank, early associations of the willow with water and another inspiration from Pope's garden at Twickenham. Although Garrick vehemently claimed his garden as his own work, it was probably Lancelot who obliged by finding trees and shrubs – including the willows, cedars, sweet chestnuts and a tulip-tree – from his friends' nurseries at Fulham and Kensington.*

Naturally Garrick had fun with Lancelot's profession. In 1757 he had revived his first play, *Lethe, or Aesop in the Shades* – a sharp commentary on the tribulations of marriage and on 'the difficulties playwrights, actors and public have to endure from aristocratic patrons'. Aesop invites ordinary mortals to drink the waters of Lethe, the river of oblivion, and then return to normal lives, freed of their troubles. The new character in the revival was Lord Chalkstone:

> I came merely for a little conversation with you, to see your Elysian fields here – [looking about thro' his glass] which, by the bye, Mr Aesop, are laid out most detestably – No taste, no fancy in the whole world!

His lordship asks the name of the river – Styx:

> . . . why, 'tis as strait as Fleet-ditch – you should have given it a serpentine sweep, and slope the banks of it – The place, indeed, has very fine capabilities; but you should clear the wood to the left, and clump the trees to the right: in short, the whole wants variety, extent, contrast, and inequality – (going towards the orchestra he looks into the pit) – Upon my word, here's a very fine hah-hah! And a most curious collection of evergreens.

20th February 1766 had seen the first performance of *The Clandestine Marriage,* in which Garrick had included a garden, half-seen in the dusk:

> Lord Ogleby: What steeple's that we see yonder? The parish church I suppose.
>
> Mr Sterling, the nouveau garden owner: Ha! Ha! Ha! That's admirable. It is no church at all my lord! It is a spire that I have built against a tree, a field or two off, to terminate the prospect. One must always have a

---

* Garrick died in 1779, but Eva Garrick lived to be ninety-eight and maintained her garden until 1822. Hampton House was badly damaged by fire in 2008, but the tunnel is still there, as is the Temple and the lawn by the river, the latter slightly diminished by road-widening.

church, or an obelisk, or a something to terminate the prospect, you know. That's a rule of taste, my lord.

The gregarious Garricks were at the centre of Lancelot's Hampton friendships, and he may even have come face to face with Horace Walpole there, for though Walpole comments so frequently upon Lancelot's doings, he never actually mentions speaking to him. Lancelot's circle included Richard Owen Cambridge, who lived on the river at a house upstream from Richmond ferry and was the source of the oft-repeated quip that he hoped to die before Lancelot, as he wished to see Heaven before it was improved. And Edward Lovibond, the leisured son of a director of the East India Company, poet and rural economist, spent most of his life in Hampton, living at Elm Lodge; he reputedly left one-third share of his estate to Lancelot.*

One imagines the two of them, Lancelot and Garrick – the one tall and perhaps ponderous if his breathing was bad, the other shorter but infinitely livelier, his fire damped down, but sparkling with good humour – doffing and bowing to everyone they met, as they progressed across Hampton Court Green in pursuit of the latest local gossip. Another of Lancelot's overlords, the Ranger of Bushy Park – George Montagu Dunk, 2nd Earl of Halifax (he had married Miss Dunk for her money, and her uncle had insisted that he take the name and 'be of some trade', which meant entering a City livery company) – had acquired a lease of some of Bushy's acres and built Hampton Court House for his mistress, the former chanteuse, Mrs Anna Maria Donaldson. Now the garden was being made; it was not large, but had a heart-shaped lake and a most remarkable grotto. Seeing this, Garrick broke into verse, as he so often did:

> A Grotto this, by Mortal hand!
> O no – we tread on fairy-land,
> 'Tis rais'd by Mab's inchanted Wand!
> So rare, so elegant, so bright;
> It dazzles, while It charms the sight;
> In all you see her Magic Skill,
> The velvet green, the tinkling Rill,
> The crystal Lake, the little Isle,
> The various flow'rs that round it smile . . .

---

* The Lovibond sale of 1776 was where Horace Walpole bought Sir Peter Lely's *A Boy as a Shepherd*, now in Dulwich Picture Gallery. It seems that conversations with Garrick and Lovibond inspired Lancelot's interest in paintings – portraits especially – which began at about this time.

In the garden they met presumably not the Queen of the Fairies, but her amanuensis, Thomas Wright, a well-set-up and rather sprightly gentleman a little older than themselves, who had already built a series of decorative garden buildings, including a menagerie, for Lord Halifax at Horton House in Northamptonshire. Wright hailed from County Durham – Westerton outside Bishop Auckland – and he and Lancelot had been travelling their parallel courses for years. Wright was a serious astronomer and a mathematician, but he had earned his crust being a country-house tutor in star-gazing, and in designing flower gardens for the ladies, such as the Duchess of Beaufort at Badminton House, and he had also worked at Shugborough. The survival of a number of his sketches and drawings has intrigued garden historians, but it is not clear how seriously Wright himself took his garden works – he clearly owed a great deal to Switzer and Kent, but his iconoclastic attitude to architectural disciplines made him whimsical, an 'Artinatural', and he was never Lancelot's rival.

'Till a lawn looks like a ten of spades'

Augustus Henry Fitzroy, 3rd Duke of Grafton, was well known to Lancelot: the Duke had acted the assiduous go-between for George III and the ailing Lord Chatham, and as a result now found himself Prime Minister, though 'not really up to the job'. The Duke (who was probably too nice to last more than three years) had been a boy when Lancelot worked for his father – a jowly grandee, very like Charles II, his grandfather – at Wakefield Lawn, and so it was for old times' sake that Grafton summoned Lancelot to Euston Hall in Suffolk. Lancelot had followed William Kent at Wakefield Lawn, and now followed him at Euston, where Kent worked in the last year of his life, 1748. One of Kent's deceptively simple sketches perfectly captures the great eastern arc of Euston's park as seen from the hall, the green slope 'propped up' as on an easel; the green slope that Kent sprinkled with clumps of trees, so that Walpole said that it looked like the ten of spades. Euston was a much-loved family home, and the Graftons (who evoked Lancelot's Stuart loyalties, with their greater right to the throne of England than the present incumbent) were disdainful of the designer's 'flim-flam' and Kent was remembered as absolutist in his demands, which did not suit; his temple was moved to where it was more convenient for watching the racehorses being exercised. The Duke was passionate about horse-breeding and racing; he commissioned George Stubbs to paint his *Mares and Foals* on the river bank at Euston. This is the Black Bourne, which flows in meandering fashion from ancient

Euston Mill to Fakenham, and which bears the marks of Lancelot's widening and planting for about a mile to the south of the hall. Some magnificent cedars of Lebanon also speak of his presence. The 3rd Duke was portrayed in sober brown country dress by Nathaniel Dance, probably in about 1770, at the same time as Dance portrayed Lancelot in sober green for his portrait at Burghley.

It would be nice to think that Lancelot met George Stubbs (at Euston?), for they had much in common, including patrons and their journeyings. Lancelot had a permanent, practical interest in horseflesh, for a good saddle-horse had made his early career possible, and at Wilderness House, besides his 'chaise cattle', he kept a riding hack for a quick response to a summons from the King, or simply for the pleasure of riding across Hampton Green on a fine morning. Stubbs was the younger by eight years, but also a northerner with (stronger) Jacobite loyalties and openly Catholic. Like Lancelot, he had to work his way from his northern obscurity, teaching himself the skills of his unusual profession. Stubbs had been to Italy, which of course Lancelot had not, but now the country-house rounds governed both their lives.

According to his biographer, Robin Blake, Stubbs's silent protest against the cruelties of horse-racing was to portray his thoroughbreds in elegant landscapes: the Duke of Grafton's *Antinous* appears against the background of Euston's park, as also *Mares and Foals*. Stubbs painted Robert Pigot's *Sharke* walking towards his trainer, beneath trees beside a lake, and he also portrayed Pigot's father, Lord Pigot, on horseback in Lancelot's park at Patshull. *A Hound Coursing a Stag* was painted for Lord Midleton of Peper Harow in Surrey in a parkland setting 'exceptionally fine and surely not imaginary', according to Blake, and Lancelot had worked at Peper Harow. The Grosvenor Hunt at meet in the flat landscape of Cheshire, painted by Stubbs in or around 1762, shows a view of the country as seen from the saloon of Eaton Hall, the view Lancelot had just 'dressed' (or may still have been working on), and for which Lord Grosvenor paid him £800.

'I left Thee at Burghley'

As Garrick's verses to Richard Owen Cambridge suggest, visits to Burghley could become very sociable affairs, and Lancelot was at his happiest there, knowing he was appreciated. One of Lord Exeter's familiar short notes in his modest rounded handwriting arrived at Wilderness House early in December 1767, giving precise measurements for the statue of Bacchus for a new pedestal so that he could stand in the new entrance hall. The Earl was planning to go to Italy in 1768 with his new wife Anne Cheatham, and would be gone for almost two years, and the attention to Bacchus marks the culmination of many of Lancelot's tasks supervising alterations, buildings and decorations in and around Burghley House; at last he could attend to the work he had anticipated a dozen years earlier, the managing of the park drainage and making of the lake.

This was not one of his quick assessments in an afternoon's ride, for he had had seasons wet and dry to observe the habits of the water, which filled so many ornamental canals and ponds, which now were – as at Chatsworth – regarded as both unpleasant and ineffectual. Burghley was a more subtle problem than Croome, but just as difficult. (The drainage problems of houses so far apart geographically suggests that they were built in drier times.) Springs from the limestone ridge west of Burghley's park were the source of the house water supply, but instead of running freely across the south front of the house on a 'fault line' that Haynes's 1755 survey had marked out, the supply had to be captured and diverted to a pump house, and the surplus channelled elsewhere. Additionally the platform on which the house stood had to be drained, to stop the flower beds filling with water.

The solution is one of Lancelot's fanfare effects: from a viewpoint in the park north-west of the house, the whole sweep of his ha-ha is seen curving round from the north entrance court, passing the west front at a distance, ending on the south-west at the lake's edge. From the house it is a traditional ha-ha, invisible in a carpet of green that is eventually closed by trees, but effectively preventing even the deer – the ditch is so wide – from leaping into the gardens. From the park, stand back and the line of the wall sinks into the contours; close up again and the 'seep holes' in the wall reveal an efficient drainage device, leaving the house on its green stage. Setting the house dry allowed the water to be channelled into the long lake, somewhat in the 'river stile' that crossed the park from west to east, ending in the Great Pond, with altered outline, to the south-east of the house. This was the work of several years and must have been starting – with the ha-ha – when David Garrick wrote his ditty about the jovial house-party at Burghley in August 1770.

Future 'landmarks' included Lord Exeter's choice of the three-arched bridge design in a letter of 4th January 1773. From August onwards, supplies of regular stone, finishing ashlar, lime from the Wothorpe kilns and masons' cramps and pegs were steadily acquired. The Stamford mason Thomas Manton was finally paid £538 for his handiwork in January 1778 (the total cost of the bridge was about £1,000). In May 1778 Eleanor Coade supplied four terracotta lions for £114 (though these were replaced in 1844). The digging of the lake moved steadily eastwards, and the Great Pond had to be excavated to the correct level;

Burghley House. Plan showing Lancelot's works for Lord Exeter 1754–1779:

1. Burghley House and north entrance court.
2. Site of north-west wing, removed by Lancelot to improve views.
3. East courtyard and stable court.
4. Orangery.
5. Boat-house and spillover sluice for the lake.
6. Site of former Great Pond filled with spoil from new lake.
7. Three-arched bridge, design sent by Lancelot but constructed after his death.
8. 'Capability's Leap', the cutting in the south drive used in the Burghley Horse Trials.
9. Dairy buildings, probably designed by Lancelot.

wheelbarrows and carts were constantly being repaired or supplied. It is clear from the accounts that the bridge was built before the dam at the eastern head, as it was the critical feature in the water level; the lake is shown fairly well filled in an etching by Paul Sandby in 1780; the stock-fish were bought two years after Lancelot's death, so the patient, careful process was completed, but he never saw it. Queen Anne's Avenue still marked the central vista from the south front of the house, but now with the bridge a new drive to the south was made; the amount of earth-moving involved for the lake and the grading of the surrounding land is evident in the deep cutting of this drive, and is recalled to this day in the names 'Capability's Leap' or 'Capability's Classic', as obstacles in the annual Burghley Horse Trials.

Alnwick, Rothley and Kirkharle

Lancelot was regularly at Burghley and even in Yorkshire, but he could rarely have made those long extra miles to his native Northumberland. There is no record of him returning until July 1769, when after breaking his journey at Burghley, he headed on northwards for Alnwick. His head sent him because the Duke of Northumberland wanted him to work at Alnwick Castle, and he liked the Duke, and the Duchess Elizabeth even more. But his heart had a say too, prompted especially by his brother John's sudden death in March 1766, for he had owed John so much in the way of his early training and had never had the opportunity to thank him, or even raise a glass to John's own success. Lancelot was swimming in the larger pond (or lake), but John's reputation in the North was quite as considerable: 'he will be missed in this part of the country very much,' wrote the Wallington agent William Robson to Sir Walter Blackett with the news of John's death. John had long overcome Dame Anne Loraine's disdain at his marriage to her daughter Jane, and it had been a good marriage, with their fine son, Richard. John's progress from farm manager to agent at Kirkharle, then as a surveyor to the turnpike trust, had landed him the plum position of agent to the Duke of Portland's northern estates (thought to equal the holdings of the Duke of Northumberland) in the early 1760s.

The Duke of Portland was largely an absentee landlord and so John's monthly reports tell more of his working life than Lancelot knew: he worked from his home, Whitridge on the Kirkharle estate, and dealt directly with the Duke on matters concerning his tenancies, rents, boundary disputes and coal-prospecting, often working with the distinguished mining engineer William Brown of Throckley. John was both fair and kind; typically he asks for a 'charitable benefaction' on behalf of farmer Richard Embleton, who has looked for limestone on his land without success 'and has now lost his eyesight'; the Duke liked his land dressed with lime, and sent five guineas. Like Lancelot, John also rode miles in the foulest weathers, high up into the Cumbrian fells – where the Duke was having an infamous dispute with Sir James Lowther – and deep into the Coquet valley, as well as into Yorkshire (to visit Lord Holderness at Hornby or Aston) and down into Nottinghamshire on mining business and to see the Duke at Welbeck Abbey. In October 1763 he noted work starting at the new Welbeck colliery. Just over a year later he was organising for '4 Isle of Skye cows and one bull' purchased at Crieff Fair, to be driven down to Welbeck for the Duchess, although he feared they would not be the right colour. His letters are full of his good humour, and he appeared to love his work.

In February 1765 John was laid up with 'a severe cold', but appeared to return to normal work: a year later he suffered from 'a pleuratick feaver' that the doctor could not relieve, and he died on 11th March. He was fifty-eight years old. George Brown, much the shyest of the three brothers, wrote to Lancelot the next day, asking him to tell the Duke, which he did immediately. From Blenheim on 20th March he wrote to the Duke a second time to arrange a visit, putting forward the hope of Jane Brown and William Robson (the Wallington agent who was Richard's godfather) that Richard could take his father's place, with all the guidance that Robson could give him. Lancelot was a persuasive ambassador and the Duke agreed.

Then a year later, in March 1767, William Robson died, leaving Richard 'a pretty good fortune which I hope he will deserve,' said Lancelot, once again giving the Duke of Portland bad news. Richard had enlisted the help of George Robson, possibly William's brother and Sir Ralph Milbanke's agent, as his mentor, and promised 'unwearied diligence' in the Duke's service. He grew in confidence, as his letters show, and his relationship with the Duke prospered; in February 1768 Richard came south and stayed at Wilderness House (Lancelot had probably not seen him as a grown man) and they went to Blenheim together. Richard probably came again in the spring of 1769, spurring Lancelot's conscience for his trip to Northumberland.

Lancelot was at Alnwick Castle in the first week of July 1769, for he was given £300 on the 10th, as recorded in the castle accounts; the same amount received on the same day appears in his own account book, and though he lumps payments for Syon and Alnwick together, he could not have been in those two places at once. July 1769 is a certain start for work at Alnwick – indeed, £300 would have been his customary first payment on a contract, to cover his expenses for a long journey.

From Fenstanton it was about 34 miles to Burghley, or The George at Stamford, but with so far to go it is likely that the coachman pounded on up the Great North Road to one of the traditional intermediary stops, the Ram Jam at Stretton (or Colsterworth if they could not make

Grantham). From Grantham, it was the long haul to Newark and crossing the Trent, then Retford and Doncaster; from Doncaster, it would be just under 40 miles to York via Selby, although as he had a sprinkling of commissions to the west – at Byram near Ferrybridge, at Temple Newsam on the road to Leeds, at Harewood on the Leeds–Harrogate road, at Allerton Mauleverer near Knaresborough and at Ripley Castle – there would be some diversions. There was then nothing to delay him through the long stretch of North Yorkshire until Aske Hall near Richmond, where he worked for Sir Lawrence Dundas; and then it was the Roman road to Piercebridge, Bishop Auckland and Durham, before the penultimate stretch to Newcastle. From the centre of Newcastle it was a slow 30 miles to the north-west to Cambo and Kirkharle, or a rather faster 40 miles to Alnwick via Morpeth.

It meant a great deal to be returning to the countryside of his birth. Northumberland is a large county, but not so large that the Percys of Alnwick did not pervade its cultural memory. In Lancelot's youth these had been rather faded memories, for the Percys were at low ebb, their estates broken and rented out, their woods shorn of ancient trees; all this had changed with the coming of the new Earl and Countess in 1750. The Countess Elizabeth, with her Percy blood inherited from her grandmother, Elizabeth Percy, Duchess of Somerset, was especially determined to restore the family's legendary pride. Her husband, born Hugh Smithson (in 1715), but changed to Percy, was the son of a royalist baronet of Stanwick Park near Catterick in North Yorkshire – a capable, dynamic and handsome man, excellently ducal material, though they did not know it at the time they married, in 1740. With the death of Elizabeth's only brother, Lord Beauchamp, on his Grand Tour in 1744, then of her grandparents, the Duke and Duchess of Somerset, followed only too swiftly by that of her father in 1750, they found themselves Earl and Countess of Northumberland and, as we know, owning Syon and Alnwick. Thanks to Lord Northumberland's vigorously interfering politics, and Lord Chatham and George III, they were now Duke and Duchess of Northumberland (and, thankfully, do not change their names again).

In Northumberland the Duke's role was as improving landlord and a gardener on the grand scale, having earned Philip Miller's dedication of his *Gardener's Dictionary* of 1752 for his 'knowledge and skill in every part of this subject'. The Duchess was a gem, undoubtedly Lancelot's most spirited duchess; she was no beauty, and the genesis of her childhood name of 'Poke' is only too easily gathered from her portrait by Reynolds. But she was the product of an idyllic childhood, an only child for ten years, loved wisely and well by her parents; her mother Frances Thynne was married 'out of the schoolroom' and was just sixteen when Poke was born; as Countess of Hertford she had onerous court duties, and hated them, but managed always to put her daughter's welfare first. The Hertfords had a touchingly restrained marriage, and they were both passionate gardeners, making their Virgilian groves at Marlborough Castle, filling them with poetic shepherdesses and hermits; the Duchess's mother had a wildlife garden for partridges and butterflies and a love for all wild creatures – Thomson cast her for ever as 'the gentle Hertford'. When not at Marlborough and necessarily in London, their taste was for romantic hideaways: their tumbledown house on St Leonard's Hill in Windsor Forest, followed by Lord Bathurst's beautiful garden at Richings, near Iver in Buckinghamshire, which they named Percy Lodge.

The Duchess was the product of all this, and of her habitual travels all over Britain, as well as to Germany, Switzerland and France; she had sought out Voltaire and visited Versailles, but was equally interested in a wider spectrum of people and buildings, in whatever caught her lively interest – her peers dubbed her 'vulgar'. At Alnwick, in the summers, she had taken 'upon herself the role of the Percy heiress in her homeland with great seriousness' and with gusto and determination that everyone should enjoy the presence of 'our duke and duchess' in their lives. The castle was opened to visitors, she revived the local theatre and July fairs, and was particularly keen on the traditions of Northumberland pipers.

In all this she was aided and abetted by Thomas Percy, a brilliant cleric of modest Bridgnorth background who became the Northumberlands' chaplain and tutor to their younger son, Algernon, in 1765; 'For Percy,' wrote his biographers, 'made to feel at home from the start' in Alnwick, 'his new position must have been nothing less than enchantment: the scholar whose favourite subject was ancient English poetry had been magically transported to the very heart of the country where much of the poetry he liked best had its origin.' Percy, who had the living of Easton Maudit in Northamptonshire from his Oxford college, Christ Church, owed his exceptional fortunes to his discovery of an old book of forgotten poems and ballads being used to light a fire in a friend's house in Shifnal; rescued and researched, edited and polished, the ballads and heroic poems of the North Country were published – encouraged by Dr Johnson – as *Percy's Reliques of Ancient English Poetry* in three-volume sets (of which 1,100 sets were sold) in 1765. He began exploring immediately upon his arrival at Alnwick, pouring forth lyrical descriptions – of how he rode down from the castle into 'a deep sequestered Valley' passing under a high cliff, with overhanging trees 'watered at the foot by a clear running Brook, which after a shower affords one or two very fine Waterfalls', then up over 'wide swelling slopes' from where he could see the sea, and up more onto heathland, with 'the vast swellings of Chiviot' appearing to the west; he found a 'hermit's cave' and crossed over 'the Flowery Head of Carmel' – called by the country people Brisley (Brizlee) Hill – and down again to ford the Aln, 'meandering in the most beautiful and whimsical irregularities', until he reached his goal, the ruin of Hulne Priory, where – protected by the Percys in the twelfth century – Carmelite friars had lived peaceably gathering honey.

The Duchess was delighted with Percy's outpourings, had his description printed and given to visitors, so prompting a taste for the picturesque at Alnwick.*

All this explains the atmosphere of conscious enchantment – his first real encounter with an early enthusiasm for the picturesque – that awaited Lancelot at Alnwick; he was also somewhat compromised by his status as a visiting celebrity, with the emphasis on the 'visiting'. The established incumbent was Thomas Call, whom the Duke had brought from Stanwick, as 'principal estate servant' responsible for the landscaping of Hulne demesne and especially the extensive tree-planting. Call had the 'ear of his master', wrote the Duke long letters full of his ideas and advice, and 'his readiness to act without consulting others' on the estate caused great ruffling of feathers; when the Duke and Duchess were away, Call was virtually in charge. What was there left for Lancelot to do?

Canaletto had painted the castle in 1752 showing it in a rocky, boulder-strewn and wild setting; now that there was exquisite wildness in plenty in Hulne demesne to the north-west, the castle – magnificent in itself – required a contrasting softness. Daniel Garrett and James Paine had made alterations in the castle, and Robert Adam was to decorate the state rooms. Lancelot planned a new causeway approach (the present approach) and a general smoothing of the castle mound. The extensively rolling contours down to the meadows beside the Aln that make for such a beautiful setting today have a definite Brownian look. The workmen rolling the causeway were depicted in a drawing by J. Vilet, and Thomas Call records payments to Cornelius Griffin's men (Griffin was Lancelot's foreman) in September 1770.

The extent of Lancelot's softening of the landscape and planting of shelter belts and clumps extended beyond the Aln to the meadows and gently sloping fields of the North Demesne, effectively the castle's park. Having made the immediate setting for the castle, he would naturally have regarded all the views out from the approach and from the castle ramparts – and the responding views back to the castle – as part of his

---

* The Duchess immediately placed a statue of a hermit in the cave, called the 'Nine Year Hole' because of thieves' treasure buried there for nine years, and it soon became a great attraction, and featured in an illustration for Josiah Wedgwood's 'Green Frog Dinner Service,' made for Catherine the Great.

scheme; the dramatic possibilities of the Hulne park would also surely have tempted him? Lancelot certainly knew Thomas Percy – it was rarely that he met a person who so nearly shared his own perceptions of land-scape – and Percy treasured some of Lancelot's sketches of Syon's park, still in the possession of his descendants. Would Lancelot have done far more at Alnwick, but for the possessiveness of Thomas Call, and his own recurrently failing health? He was expected to provide Alnwick's lake; in his 'Letter' Thomas Percy had noted how the Aln, as seen from Brizlee Hill, was to be received into a huge lake of 20 acres. In 1770 the Duke's surveyor Thomas Wilkin, at Lancelot's request, had shown the lake covering the whole of the marshy area known as Palmstrother. In the summer of 1771 Thomas Call and Cornelius Griffin accompanied the canal engi-neer, James Brindley (who was paid £450), on a site inspection to plan for the dam and cascades. Lancelot must have nominated Brindley because he was unable to be there, but Brindley too was ailing, and died later in the year. In the November a great flood came – the Tyne bridge at Newcastle was swept away, as was Alnwick's town bridge, and the Aln swept through the valley below the castle, taking away the bridge (and the idea of a lake) in its wake. The bridge was rebuilt by James Adam, with the Northumberland lion on the parapet, but the lake was forgotten. The Duke's pleasure boat, delivered in anticipation, was moored at the Lion Bridge.

Cornelius Griffin, still working for Lancelot, was taken ill in the summer of 1772 and died in early September at Alnwick. Urgent messages were sent to Lancelot, who was himself unwell at home at the time, and he arranged for a replacement; in 1773 Thomas Beisley, who had worked at Syon, moved to Alnwick – the Duchess noted that he had a team of seventy-eight men planting and creating pleasure grounds around the castle, which must have given Lancelot some satisfaction that his vision for the castle in its landscape was being fulfilled. Beisley was to stay for forty years, becoming Keeper of the parks and pleasure grounds. But it is unlikely that Lancelot was there himself, for his account with the Duke stutters to a close with £100 paid in full for 1771, and in February 1773, in a rather emotional scrawl, he notes £100 paid – the completion of the balance and 'for my trouble'. The Duchess died in 1776 and the Duke placed memorials at several of her favourite places, most spectacularly the Gothic tower designed by Robert Adam on the top of Brizlee Hill. It is inscribed by the Duke: 'Look about you I have measured all these things; they are my orders; it is my planning; many of these trees have been planted by my own hand.' Such is the privilege of dukedoms.

On leaving Alnwick in 1769, Lancelot went to see his brother George at Cambo. His round of visits included seeing Sir Walter Blackett at Wallington and Lady Loraine and her son, the young Sir William, at Kirkharle – the grandson of the Sir William of his childhood. He discussed schemes for both places; in October, Ralph Forster, the agent at Wallington who had succeeded William Robson, was writing that 'Lady Loraine is so very pressing for the loan of [the Wallington] Theodolite', urging Thomas Duffield, the Wallington head gardener, to finish his job as best he could 'and so let the Lady have the instrument for the present'. The following 3 March (1770) Forster was receiving instructions from Sir Walter in London, for Thomas Duffield and George Brown, 'that he would have all the old and new plantations properly fenced, the roads and hedges taken care of, the head of the Low Lake at Rothley to be proceeded on in the Summer according to a plan which will be sent to them drawn by Mr Lancelot Brown'.

The plans duly arrived (and are still at Wallington). They are delicately drawn, but have a peculiarity in that they are isolated details: half a lake, an end of a lake, a five-arched rustic bridge, and alternate ideas for a Gothic, castellated fishing and picnic house. They present ideals of design, and are a great tribute to Lancelot's visual memory, for the half a lake – Rothley lower lake – is fitted into the actual landscape and appears exactly as the drawing, but apparently with no contextual survey. (The detail for the head of the lake is marked with pricked survey lines; they are all in the same hand, most likely that of Samuel Lapidge or Jonathan Spyers.)

Lancelot was back in September the following year, staying with the Loraines at Kirkharle Hall; it was 3 miles to Cambo, the Wallington estate village, from where his brother George conducted him along the straight, well-made roads that were Sir Walter Blackett's (and George Brown's) pride, northwards from Scot's Gap to Rothley Park. Rothley Crags form the most dramatic outcrop, upon which Sir Walter had built his most ambitious folly, 'a vast ruin'd Castle built of Black Moor Stone' designed by Daniel Garrett, the beginning of his detached and Picturesque park, rather in the manner of Hulne park at Alnwick. Beyond the Crags was a smaller outcrop, Codger Crag, for which Thomas Wright designed a miniature fortress (the walls survive), overlooking the valley where Lancelot's lower lake was being dug. The spoil, piled on the northern bank, made the site for a planned fishing house, with a miniature enclosed garden. The eastern head of the lake, given a characteristic Brownian serpent's-head curve, was to be made 25 feet wide – as a note instructs – 'the earth to be taken away from the banks to give it this form'. And it was. Arthur Young saw 'a very fine newly-made lake of Sir Walter

Blackett's surrounded by young plantations, which is a noble water; the bends and curves of the bank are bold and natural, and when the trees get up, the whole spot will be remarkably beautiful'.

The road to Rothbury was carried on the five-arched bridge, which dammed the water flowing in from the Donkinrigg and Hardwood burns to the west into a long Upper Lake, which appears to have filled to the natural contours (at least there is no word from Lancelot on this lake). Subsequently the Upper Lake was enclosed in woodland; Lancelot's Lower Lake has remained open, for fishing, its beautifully graded banks roughened by time and grazing animals, but with relics of the softening waterside planting that he decreed.*

Back at Kirkharle in September 1770, Lady Loraine's need for the theodolite is explained in a detailed survey that she had prepared for the surroundings of the hall. The survey, presuming that it showed the landscape in 1770, was of the park dominated by the old west–east avenues and straight lines of the formal gardens that Lancelot had known in his childhood; the Kirkharle burn ran through the park, passing close to the hall; the site of the old village, where Lancelot was born, was marked, but the little street of cottages was gone, rebuilt in the modern manner as substantial two-storeyed houses higher up the hill. Armstrong's map of 1769 shows the chief of these houses as belonging to 'Mr Brown', which would have been Richard, still a bachelor and newly established as agent for the Duke of Portland, working from Kirkharle; his widowed mother Jane Brown had probably returned to live in the hall with her sister-in-law, Lady Loraine. (Richard Brown was shortly to move to Newcastle, where he wrote from a house in Big Market, and where he married and lived for the rest of his life.)

Quite what Lancelot did at Kirkharle in 1770 or thereabouts is the subject of much controversy. In 1983, on the 200th anniversary of his death, an exhibition in Newcastle revealed the recent discovery by John Anderson, the present owner of Kirkharle, of a design drawing showing the transformation of the Kirkharle burn into an S-curving linear lake. The field, or park, boundaries are softened with shelter planting, but

---

* Stroud, pp. 136–7, implies that Lancelot worked on Wallington Hall's gardens, damming the Wansbeck into a long lake, and adding ornamental buildings including a 'Chinese Temple' and a Sanderson Miller-style Gothic tower. Nick Owen, regretfully, finds no evidence that Lancelot ever worked at Wallington (George Brown, as master mason, worked on garden walls and buildings and on James Paine's 'whoops-a-daisy' bridge: the view of this bridge from the walled garden is very cleverly devised). The surviving plan for these works could have been the work of the head gardener Thomas Duffield, whom we know had been busy with the theodolite; if Duffield was as competent as the plan implies, it was no wonder he was jealous of Lancelot. Duffield was pessimistic about the Rothley Lower Lake plan, which he thought 'cannot be executed under £2,000 which is a large and difficult sum to be raised'. He asked Sir Walter to consider postponement.

there are no 'circuits' of serpentine drives through these plantations. One might argue that the climate in Northumberland was not conducive to pleasure drives. Another significant feature is a grand semicircular entrance drive sweeping in and out via two lodge entrances; also shown is a walled kitchen garden north-west of the house, on the south-facing slope, a pool in the garden being filled by the passage of the Kirkharle burn. The plan is unsigned, and has a tentative air about its drawing style, but upon closer examination it is limited by the straight field boundaries that dominate the 'park' and were clearly not to be relinquished.

Uncertainties about the location of the hall buildings, and the general lack of sophistication in the plan drawing, have encouraged many people to believe this is Lancelot's first work, his apprentice graduation piece, dating from when he left Kirkharle in 1739, when indeed he longed to make a lake, and spent hours looking at the boggy nature of the burn's course through Kirkharle park, which would have indicated certain success. However, it is clear the the Kirkharle plan for the linear lake is in the same hand as the plans for Rothley lake so recently delivered to Sir Walter Blackett. The landscape architect Nick Owen, having patiently examined the evidence, suggests that the scheme was drawn up at Wilderness House as a result of Lancelot's 1769 visit, and as a present for the young Sir William Loraine, Lancelot's nephew by marriage, for his coming of age. Sir William was born on 1st June 1749.*

Unfortunately, despite what must have been a very warm and welcoming visit to Kirkharle Hall in 1770, his stay ended on a sour note. He had asked Sir Walter Blackett for some shooting, but on 18th September came a note from Sir Walter's secretary in Newcastle (Sir Walter had been abroad for much of the summer and was now in Paris) 'desiring me to acquaint you that such leave from him will be a very bad precedent, as it must open a gate to any gentleman that will ask him, and that the gentlemen of the county have been so obliged as not to shoot upon those moors but when he was at Wallington and they go out with him.' It sounded ungrateful, but was in fact wise; the new Game Laws (and a new Act was passed that very year) made it illegal to shoot over another landowner's land even with permission, if the owner was not present. Or rather, if the owner's gamekeepers were not exactly sure who was in the party or who might be poaching. The matter was of great controversy, which Lancelot, had he been closely connected with shooting circles,

---

* The former farm buildings of Kirkharle Hall are now converted into the shops and workshops of Kirkharle Courtyard, where there is an exhibition telling the story of Lancelot's life. John and Kitty Anderson have initiated the brave project for the making of the lake that Lancelot designed for Kirkharle's park. At adjacent Wallington Hall, owned by the National Trust, the Rothley drawings are on display.

would have known; George Stubbs had at that time, and equally inno-cently, produced a sequence of four 'shooting pictures' of two friends with their dogs and guns spending a day out on the Duke of Portland's land at Creswell Crags near Welbeck; no matter how respectable these solid citizens were, how innocent their desire for a day in the fresh air, theirs was an illegal activity. The paintings as popular prints were much about, causing consternation that an innocent citizen could be so easily turned into a criminal, and liable to extreme punishment, simply by being in the wrong place at the wrong time.

Lancelot, as he left, was further informed by Sir Walter's Newcastle amanuensis, whom he had never met, that work was stopped at Wallington and Rothley until Sir Walter's return, 'and gives me some direction, in respect of the trouble he has already given you, which I hope I may have an opportunity of communicating to you before you leave this part of the country'. Lancelot had the last word, leaving a message for Sir Walter that he readily understood 'the impropriety' of his request for the shooting, but 'he would not take any payment . . . and any trouble he had been at was entirely at your service'.

'A Miniature Picture from a Raphael'

By now it has become clear that the King's Master Gardener was at least watchful of his duties, and his stately figure clad in Lincoln green, with his ruddy, outdoors face and amused grey eyes, topped by his frizzled grey periwig and beaver hat (soon raised), had become a familiar figure in the royal gardens. The guards all knew him well, and the youngest dairymaids dropped their curtseys; if he encountered the Queen and her ladies, Lancelot smartly removed his hat, bowed and stopped to chat. His assumed right of passage into any or all of his gardens, which might have seemed pomposity to lesser mortals, was simply part of his job.

At Queen Charlotte's house at the head of the Mall the evidence on the ground is that he did supervise the layout of the serpentine drive all around the garden, and the original planting of the boundaries. Proof that he was a familiar figure there comes in a letter from Frederick Nicolay, Queen Charlotte's music librarian and violinist in her orchestra, whose main duties were at the Queen's House, although he lived in Hill Street in Richmond. 'If you have five Minutes to spare when you come to Richmond,' Nicolay wrote:

> I should take it as a great favour if you would give Yourself the Trouble to call at my House. I am in very great Distress and Trouble, which one Coup d'Oeil of yours into a large piece of Ground of mine (almost half

an Acre) would soon relieve me from: I hope it is no Offence to wish for a Miniature Picture from a Raphael!

Nicolay could only have watched the planting materialising at the Queen's House, as well as perhaps work at Richmond Lodge, to appreciate the master in action.

On the other hand, Lancelot suspected that any aggravations he suffered originated in the bureaucratic Office of Works, in charge of all the royal buildings and their budgets, though most definitely not of the King's Master Gardener, who was the King's servant and his own man. Lancelot's quarterly imbursements came directly from the Chief Clerk at the Treasury in Downing Street. The two chief Architects of the Office of Works had been installed at Hampton Court when Lancelot arrived, Robert Adam and William Chambers. With Adam – who worked at Croome, Syon, Luton Hoo and Alnwick, to name but four of the places where they met – his working relationship was good: their styles were very different, each recognised the other's worth, and Adam was known for his charm and ease of manner. William Chambers was the favourite of Princess Augusta, for whom he had laid out Kew Garden, a mixture of scientifically bedded garden, *ferme ornée*-style pastures for sheep and a lake, all embraced by a tangle of walks with no fewer than twenty-three ornamental buildings: temples, a mosque, the Orangery, the Ruined Arch and of course the Pagoda, this last being gloriously decorated with gilded dragons. Chambers was jealous of his royal territory; he had been the young George III's drawing master and had moved easily into feeling himself to be royal architect. He worked at the Queen's House, had built the King an observatory at Richmond for the royal observance of the transit of Venus in 1769 (for which Captain Cook had been despatched to the South Seas for a better view), and now the King was minded to commission Chambers for a palace at Richmond.

Chambers also had a high opinion of his own talents, and little of anyone else's (even Robert Adam was wary of him), and so when Lancelot strode into Richmond Lodge intent on transforming the flat riverside gardens, Chambers was perturbed. The foundations of the new palace were being dug, and the King was eager for progress on his gardens, having ordered a complete change from his mother's very flat Kew – an emphasis on natural groves and glades, with undulations that were dug by under-employed royal guardsmen, and a ha-ha to protect the walks from paddocks for his rare breeds of cattle, sheep and goats. In this process the King banished the mouldering remains of his grandmother Queen Caroline's follies, the Hermitage and Merlin's Cave – the last-named with an elf-cap roof of thatch (much nibbled) built forty years earlier, and where the poet Stephen Duck had played the wizard. Much more fuss was made of the demolition of Merlin's Cave than of the King's clearance of the hamlet of West Sheen, which, in anticipation of Highland history, had to make way for sheep.

Lancelot relied upon Michael Milliken, now happily installed as the gardener, to keep him informed. 'Their Majestys came into the works on Saturday after you were gone,' wrote Milliken:

> I told the King you stayed till two o'clock and that I had said to you that their Majestys seldom ever came after that time. He said He had been detained but should see you next Saturday. The King did not bid me inform you so. But I do it in case you should be engaged you can possibly put it off for that Day and I think he rather wishes to see you. He was much pleased with the Levels and asked if you was not so too. I told him you found no faults.

The loss of Merlin's Cave and the appearance of a new naturalness in the King's garden was too much for Lancelot's enemies; if there was no opportunity for attack at Richmond, they would try elsewhere. In late October of 1770 he opened a letter complaining of the state of Hampton Court gardens, 'not in so good a condition as they ought to be . . . none of the Walkes being fit for use, and most of the other parts of the Gardens much neglected'. Lancelot was furious: 'I believe I am the first King's Gardiner that the Board of Works ever interfered with,' he spluttered. He knew from experience these warnings, 'under the Colour of Friendship', and clearly believed that this letter, signed by William Robinson, Clerk Itinerant to the Board of Works, had quite a different source and an ulterior motive, 'because I know both the Author's meaning, & his Conduct on that Subject'. He answered:

> I know the Gardens are in exceeding good order, & I can assure you that I lay out an hundred Pounds a Year more than my Predecessor did, my wish & my intention is to keep them better & put them in better order than ever I saw them in, & have stopp'd at no Expense in procuring Trees & Plants, nor grudged any number of Hands that were necessary.

He had been through the gardens 'this day' (5th November 1770) 'and my Foreman told me that they had more hands than they knew how to employ'. The walks, he admitted, were in winter dress, for the gravel had had to be dug over three times, 'otherwise it would have been as Green as Grass'. He ended with a flourish: 'You will be so good as to inform the Gentlemen of the Board of Works that Pique I pity, that Ideal Power I laugh at, that the Insolence of Office I despise, & that real Power I will ever disarm by doing my Duty.'

The following year, 1771, Thomas Richardson's survey of the royal properties at Kew and Richmond was published, and the juxtaposition of Chambers's Kew and Brown's Richmond revealed a glaring truth — that Kew was a clumsy and ugly layout, and was completely outshone by Lancelot's elegant riverside groves. The King's bid for more land for his proposed new palace had fallen foul of local interests, notably the Selwyn family, who, having been ousted from West Sheen, had bought considerable properties along what is now the Kew road, and were certainly not inclined to be pushed out again to allow an extension of royal territory. Then fate took a hand, when Princess Augusta died in February 1772 and the King realised he could unite his Kew and Richmond properties. There was now adequate accommodation for the royal family, and so Chambers's new palace was cancelled. All unwittingly, Lancelot had acquired an enemy in William Chambers, who now plotted his revenge.

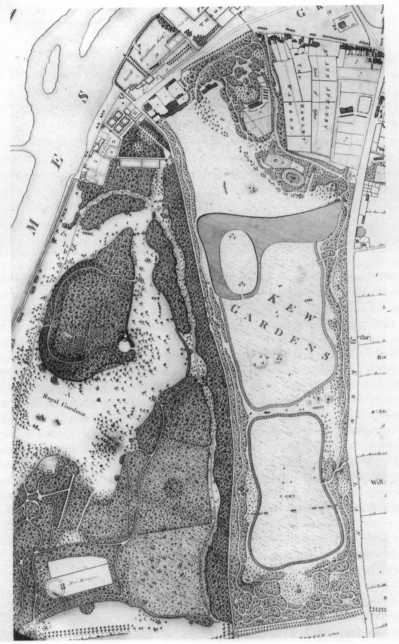

Richmond and Kew Gardens, survey 1771 by Peter Burrell and Thomas Richardson
revealing the pedestrian layout of Kew Gardens by Sir William Chambers, and the elegance
of Lancelot's riverside groves for George III.

11

'ALL OVER ESTATES AND DIAMONDS'

No man that I ever met with understood so well what was necessary for all ranks and degrees of society; no one disposed his offices so well, set his buildings on such good levels, designed such good rooms, or so well provided for the approach, for the drainage, and for the comfort and convenience of every part he was concerned in. This he did without ever having had one single difference or dispute with any of his employers. He left them pleased, and they remained so as long as he lived.

Henry Holland on his father-in-law, 1788

L ANCELOT'S INNOCENT INVESTMENT IN the Fenstanton estate turned rapidly into a poisoned chalice, for he had hardly drawn breath before he found himself 'pricked' or nominated to serve as High Sheriff from February 1770. The workings of the political machinery were slowly revealed; he had been at Trentham at least twice during the negotiations and had discussed them with Lord Gower; Gower was a government colleague of the Earl of Sandwich, whose home was at Hinchingbrooke outside Huntingdon, from where he ran the political life of the county as a very tight ship, as befitted his famously colourful role as First Lord of the Admiralty. For administrative purposes, the counties of Cambridgeshire and Huntingdonshire were conjoined twins and provided sheriffs in alternate years (with the Isle of Ely), but they were sparsely populated, especially little Huntingdonshire, and candidates were hard to find. 'The nomination of the Sheriff is absolutely in my hands,' Lord Sandwich had explained to Lancelot's client, Sir John Hynde Cotton of Madingley a few years earlier, 'have you no friend that will undertake that office for you, it will be a great stroke in your favour, & more for the appearance of it than the reality, as a pocket sheriff of your nomination will sufficiently show the support you have from above.' (Sir John seems to have found his pocket sheriff in the prosperous farmer Edward Martin the younger of Fenstanton.)

Officially, in the eighteenth century, the Sheriff's position in 'county dignity' came third, behind the Lord Lieutenant (George Montagu, 4th Duke of Manchester) and his deputy (his cousin, John Montagu, 4th Earl of Sandwich), but in practice the Sheriff was below the 'social grade' of a Justice of the Peace, 'hence a sort of tacit conspiracy to let the office fall either on the minor gentry, or on a young man who had come early to his father's estate, or else a commercial gentleman recently settled in the county', who in this way 'paid his footing'. Clearly for Lancelot, with a more than full-time profession, and not even living in the county as far as we know, the onerous task of administering the courts and prisons, entertaining the assize judges and 'answering for the behaviour of a host of minions over whom he had no control' was out of the question; and yet his name does appear in the list of High Sheriffs, serving from 9th February 1770 until 6th February 1771. How did he do it? Part of the answer comes in correspondence between Lords Sandwich and Gower, who concocted a plan whereby 'Brown should be relieved of the burden,' and that the relief should come as a favour from Lord Sandwich. 'It might not be amiss,' Sandwich concluded in his letter of 19th November 1769, 'if you was to send Mr Brown to apply to me, as it might occasion the beginning of a Huntingdonshire connection between us.'

No official records or accounts for the shrievalty in that year can be found, but there is evidence from a surprising source, Uvedale Price, who was diverted during his *Essay on the Picturesque, etc.,* to write: 'I remember hearing, that when Mr Brown was high sheriff, some facetious person observing his attendants straggling, called out to him "Clump your javelin-men" – a piece of ridicule that might have served as a lesson that such figures should be confined to men drilled for formal parade *not* to "loose and airy shapes of vegetation".' So, Lancelot did appear in the Assize procession, and the witty observer indicates that it was in Cambridge. (The *Cambridge Chronicle,* 19th February 1770, reports that Lord Chief Justice Wilmot on the Norfolk circuit was at Huntingdon on 10th March, and in Cambridge on Tuesday 13th.) Otherwise Lancelot's solution was disarmingly simple, and shows the wisdom of naming your eldest son after yourself. Lance Brown was fortunately of age, *just* (twenty-two in early January 1770), and completing his law studies at Lincoln's Inn (he was called to the Bar in 1772), and was the perfect 'pocket sheriff' of his father's nomination. Lance was apparently on Lord Sandwich's staff at Hinchingbrooke – the locals did not know one Lancelot Brown from the other – and this is how things were managed, and how Lance found his taste for politics. Lance lived in Elsworth (perhaps as a tenant of Sandwich), an airy village on the downs south of Fenstanton, where his sisters Bridget and Peggy were soon visiting, and before long his name appeared in the county list of Justices of the Peace.

'By Lincoln I lie in the Road'

Burton Constable in the East Riding of Yorkshire has a unique claim to fame, in that Lancelot turned up there with clockwork regularity in September (once in August) for six or seven years during the 1770s. One explanation is that he left Biddy at Boston for a family holiday, and then returned for her; otherwise his punctuality is a wonder. The jovial and corpulent William Constable ranks as one of his most interesting clients: Lancelot proposed his first visit in the late summer of 1772, 'if possible', to which Constable replied, 'Permit me to hope that the If is merely possible. Was I young and provident I would not press, but feeble and keen in my wants a year seems to me an age. Mr Lascelles flatters himself with seeing you in September. By Lincoln I lie in the Road and most sincerely hope and wish you may think so.'

Lancelot would be a fool, had he thought the journey that easy. For as Yorkshire gossip clearly flew across the 60 miles from Edwin Lascelles at Harewood, west of York, to Burton Constable, within sight of the North (German) Sea, so it appeared that Lancelot was expected to fly over the wide Humber estuary. The road from Lincoln ceased at the water's edge, and his coach and its contents had to be surrendered to the New Holland ferry crossing to Hull; it was a journey he grew to hate, more than once 'a most shocking passage', as he later reported to Biddy. The Humber, if not storm-tossed and murky, was crowded with shipping, for Hull was the busy transit port for the Russian and Baltic trade, and for the coastal carriers and barges that freighted inland up the Humber to the Ouse and York, then via the Trent and Aire to Leeds. Through the crowded wharfways his coach would be jostled by heavy loads of Swedish steel; the air of the town was thick with pungent smells, from maltings, oil and cake mills, brickworks and limekilns; but the merchants' houses, where fortunes were made in the names of Kirkby, Sykes, Thornton and Wilberforce, were worthy of Lancelot's notice, for he was bound for the countryside where those fortunes were spent.

As Lancelot discovered, the River Humber guards the East Riding, and particularly the seigneury of Holderness like a moat, from lesser mortals of the south. As his coach hauled out of the town for some 10 miles along the Holderness road, he could breathe the salty tang of the sea, mixed with the airs of a low-lying countryside, with windmills and hayfields; the stacks were new made, some rounded and peaked, others gabled like barns. Beyond Sproatley, Burton Constable Hall was suddenly in full view, not shyly peeping from the trees, but proclaiming itself a magnificently tall and winged Elizabethan mansion of brick (reminiscent of Temple Newsam at first glance) standing proud in a flat countryside. It was the home of an ancient Catholic family who had weathered persecutions and wars. William Constable, who had inherited his house in 1747 when he was twenty-six, remembered what he found as his 'park', low-lying (60 feet above sea level), '400 or 500 acres of Wilderness of Old Thorns, old decayed forest trees, whins or gorse higher than a man on horseback, rushes, hillocks, deep ridge and furrow, rivers and swamps'. In the midst of this wildness there were consolations: 'plenty of red and fallow deer' and some 'wild' white cattle, similar to those at Chillingham in Northumberland.

William Constable listed his 'amusements' as 'the Management of my affairs, Agriculture, Gardening, Botany, Embellishing my place with taste and propriety and Magnificence. In which I Employ the best Artists of the Kingdom.' It is said that the embellishing was prompted by his engagement to a distant cousin, Ann Fairfax of Gilling, but this was broken off in about 1755 and for a time William lost interest.

The great head gardener, Thomas Knowlton of Londesborough, well into his sixties and 'freelancing', had made a kitchen garden out of old formal gardens, and in 1760 he was paid for a design for the menagerie, soon built in the park, at one end of a swampy area that William Constable had turned into a long lake. Knowlton was proud of '2 stoves with a Little Green house in the middle of them 206 feet long' – the 'greatest' he knew. Constable employed a collector, Thomas Kyle, to travel around England collecting exotic fruits and rare plants, and to pick up ideas: Kyle reported on the 'gardenesque' notion where 'hollies and laurels are planted round the Higher trees which Hides their Stems', as practised most notably at Painshill in Surrey. Constable also, as he had said, collected 'Artists': the architect Timothy Lightoler had submitted designs for the kitchen garden, possibly the park, and the stable block. This last, a handsome four-square range, survives to Lightoler's credit, completed in 1771, the year before Lancelot arrived.

Thomas White, a Shropshire farmer's son with a fine feeling for trees, a surveyor and draughtsman (who worked for Lancelot at Temple Newsam and Harewood and in Staffordshire), was paid ten guineas in January 1769 for a watercoloured plan, which survives at Burton Constable, entitled *A Plan of Alterations Designed for Burton Constable the seat of Will[iam] Constable Esq by Thomas White 1768*. This shows the hall and surrounding buildings and gardens nestling in a foetal manner, protected by a semi-circular ha-ha, in the centre of a very large park, lightly sprinkled with

trees, hesitantly clumped. Lightoler's new stables are included, south of
the hall; to the west is a new, outlying kitchen garden beside the road
to Old Ellerby, and the lake has become exceedingly long and serpentine. The roads around the park are planted with belts and clumps of
trees. It is a perfectly respectable layout with Brownian themes, but lacking
verve. (Lancelot thought well of Thomas White and his keenness to get
on, and he may have sent him to make this preliminary plan and survey,
as was his habit, but White saw an opportunity on his own account.)

At this point William Constable and his sister Winifred had become
consumed in plans for a grand tour, and they left in late November 1769.
William comes vividly to life in a pastel portrait of the following year
by Jean-Étienne Liotard – his sensual and intelligent face sandwiched
between the fur hat and fur collar of a costume 'after the manner of
Rousseau' – whom they met in Lyons. They returned home in July 1771,
having spent £7,000 on their trip and books, paintings, antiquities and
sculptures: William, in his own estimation, had become 'a Collector, a bit
of a Vertu', and his interests were extended to archaeology, anthropology,
the sciences of electricity and astronomy. Having sorted his treasures, his
energies were renewed for making his home fit for a virtuoso. Lancelot's
reputation had clearly gone before him, and William listed his expectations:

How to Clump my Avenues. Whether the Pales may stand in E Front &
opposite to N Wood – to make my Gallery into a Library & Philosophical
Room – High Roads from the Stables to the Kitchen Garden – How to
Fence the Kitchen Garden, south Border etc., Whether the Road to the
House would not be better Higher Up – Whether more Clumps would
be proper in the East Front – consult about Water in the park, mention
springs – Stake out Everything in W Front Single trees as well as clumps,
which kind of Evergreens for the W Front?

When Lancelot arrived, some things became immediately clear to him:
that William Constable had great difficulty in walking (and, like Henry
VIII, would require a hoist to get him onto a horse), and that he could
not accompany Lancelot farther from the hall than his wheeled chair
would take him (he wore out a succession of specially made wheeled
chairs, and one remains at the hall). His Steward, Raines, was to take
notes, as verbatim as possible, which were faithfully written up, and thus
we have a detailed record, almost *A Manual of Brownifications*, not too
distantly removed from one that Lancelot might have written himself.

He did not arrive at Burton Constable with pre-conceived notions, but addressed William Constable's requests with meticulous care: 'how to Clump my Avenues?' The task was how best to restore an outdated land-scape. It was sixty years since Kip and Knyff's *Britannia Illustrata* had first presented their fantastical picture of the great houses of England, each surrounded by a starburst of avenues, whether real or imaginary, whose fingers touched across whole counties into a Pythagorean landscape. A well-grown and maintained elm or beech avenue was a truly wonderful thing, and Lancelot had restored and repaired Queen Anne's avenue at Burghley and the great avenue to Yardley Chase at Castle Ashby, planted at William III's suggestion, amongst others. But many avenues were too far gone, gap-teethed and broken by wind and weather, and William Constable was understandably ashamed of his relics. Lancelot *never* destroyed a healthy and well-shaped tree without heart-searching, nor did he like lopping or heavy pruning, but he did move large trees if he thought this possible. A fine tree could be left as a single specimen. Even less good, or 'bad' and spindly trees, elms and ash, might be cut to 6 inches and allowed to shoot, growing on the strongest shoot. The best way with broken avenues was to remove the rubbish and incorporate the survivors into uneven numbered clumps using oak, elm and beech, and ash and larch as 'nurse' plants: the clump thus became a utilitarian as well as a decorative device, and a refuge for wild animals and birds, as well as game.

Steward Raines wrote Lancelot's words down seemingly verbatim, so that his instructions are clear:

Trench the ground before you plant;
Three things must be attended to, space, clean-ness and shelter;
Small clumps are nothing, pimples on the face of Nature, make
    your Clumps large and massy!

They needed fencing if they were outside the ha-ha. On return visits Lancelot stressed, 'Clumps must be weeded and thinned', especially by taking a useful crop of ash and larch poles from the 'nurse' trees.

Obviously the siting of the clumps – both new ones and judiciously using existing trees – was his art, perfected by the endless walking and staking, and integrated with choosing the path and drive-lines that governed the views. The walks were of gravel, domed in the centres for good drainage, and 6 feet wide; drives were to be 8 feet wide, and the road across the park in a south-westerly direction towards Ellerby, crossing the lake by a bridge, was to be 12 or 15 feet wide. Steward Raines, with a garden boy carrying stakes in tow, followed the striding Master Gardener.

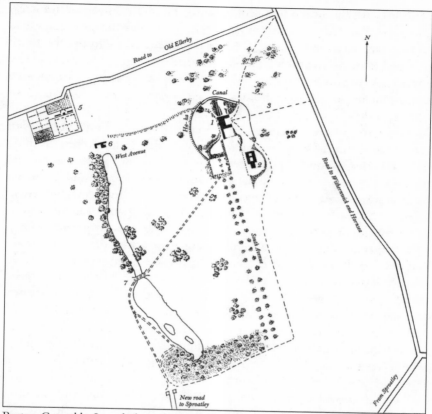

Burton Constable. Lancelot's works for William Constable during the 1770s:
1. House, with gardens including Knowlton's stoves etc. enclosed by ha-ha.
2. Lightoler's new stable block with shelter belt.
3. Old, and present drive approach, apparently not changed to
4. Lancelot's preferred new entrance.
5. New walled kitchen gardens beside road to Old Ellerby.
6. The Menagerie.
7. Bridge and dam where Lancelot extended the lake.

The path lines were always purposeful: Lancelot suggested a tea pavilion or an ornamental arch (but William Constable grew parsimonious before these were built); views were opened (by cutting) and closed (by planting); and occasionally came that eureka moment as Raines's pencil flew, 'by breaking the side of the hill to the R and the top of the hill to the L from the place where Mr B stood will make some opening of Light which may be pleasing'; followed by 'Tom' (for the boy surely had a name), 'an extra large stake to mark where Mr Brown is standing'.

On the east entrance front where William Constable queried 'Clumps'

Lancelot gave the house wings of planting. He did move the drive back, if that is what Constable meant by 'higher up', and the pale fence was replaced by a sweeping fosse, a ha-ha, around the east front (the fence returned later) and entirely around the north and west sides as well. The copied instruction was 'the lawn before the house was to be eaten with sheep which must be kept from the shrubberies' – that is, the wings of planting.

As for the water, Lancelot did indeed consult: 'lower the surface of the water in the lake by 6 or 8 inches in order to keep the adjoining grounds drier, round off the edge of the lake, not so sharp as at present' (this was the lake that Constable had made himself). It was to be extended southwards so doubling its length, and was to be considerably widened: 'make a clay wall along the east side (of this extension) and the opposite, west side if necessary, by making a trench 1½ feet wide and so deep until you come to the clay, then make a dam across the (outlet) drain and pen up all the water you can get this winter'. This was in 1775; the next year two islands were to be made from the spoil: 'the islands to be about 2½ or 3 ft above the level of the water, the islands to be planted up'; and two years later he changed his mind, ordering one island removed and the other enlarged. Raines recorded, 'Mr Brown will send the design' for the bridge that masked the controlling dam between the two lakes, which 'would cost £3–400, the plinth and cornice of stone, the rest of brick'. This fine five-arched bridge survives.

Lancelot provided the sparkle to the Burton Constable landscape (he also made the south entrance court with his favourite crenellated walls); he seemed to be practising his new approach, that of the visiting consultant who criticised or praised on a regular basis, and so eased his ideas into reality. This depended upon good men on the ground, and William Constable was fortunate in Steward Raines, and one James Clarke, who rejoiced in the title Director of Groundwork: 'in levelling and uniting grounds, forming swells . . . [and] plantations and the whole executive part of beautifying and finishing a place with the most accurate neatness Mr Clarke excels'. Thomas White, whose proposals had by no means been disgraced, continued profitably to supply trees and other plants.

After his first visit to Burton Constable in the autumn of 1772, Lancelot was still travelling far and fast. A note from Croome in November told him that 'since the water has been let into the River it has been found that the Head (dam) is faulty, in many places'. Repairs were beyond the skill of the home workforce, so could Benjamin Read come to help? Lord Coventry also mentioned the hoped-for plan for the model farmhouse, ending cheerfully that he heartily gave the invitation 'to a Christmas gambol'. Whether Lancelot gambolled we do not know, but he visited Fisherwick, near Lichfield, where the young Arthur Chichester, 5th Earl of Donegall, had ambitious rebuilding plans; and he inspected Oakly, on the edge of Ludlow, on behalf of Lord Clive. He also appears to have made his first visit to the Earl of Derby's Knowsley Park in Lancashire, for he definitely stayed with his friends the Jodrells in Manchester, taking them a gift of venison. A warm letter from 'your much oblig'd friend' James Jodrell, on 21st December, mentions the 'fortunate swain' – meaning Henry Holland, who was newly engaged to Lancelot's daughter, Bridget: 'we drank your health as the Founder of our feast, nor did not forget the rest of your family, who always share in our best wishes'.

After more ill rumours about Lord Chatham's health, Lancelot had exchanged anguished letters with Hester; the anguish was mostly on his side, for he saw some 'sinister purpose' in the gossip. Hester, ever sympathetic, and dancing in her phrases, assured him 'that my Lord has enjoyed quite a good state of health' at Burton Pynsent, though she understood only too well 'there are ever restless and intriguing spirits, who employ themselves in framing dark schemes'. They were thankfully far removed 'from the scenes of Public Action' and spending times of greatest cheerfulness with their friends and neighbours in the country. Her only ailments were the results of attending too many country dances with her 'Young People'.

Lord Chatham's health was to continue improving, but not so Lancelot's. The New Year of 1773 opened with Lord Exeter's little note choosing the three-arched bridge for Burghley, and ending with the wish 'that many happy New Years attend the family at Hampton'. Two days later another came from Lord Brooke at Warwick, wanting a character reference for a gardener, and with 'the compliments of the Season to his old friend Mr Brown'. Lancelot was too poorly to reply and a message was sent to the Duke of Northumberland, who knew the gardener in question and provided the reference; the Duke was sorry to hear Lancelot was unwell, and hoped to see him at Syon before too long.

He was not to be at Syon for many weeks, for as the letters piled up unanswered and his world went on without him, fifty-seven-year-old Lancelot was seriously ill. Whether it was his usual pleurisy and pneumonia, or something else entirely, we cannot know, but he was laid low well into the spring, if not the early summer. It was an agonising lowness for all concerned, for he was hardly an easy patient; out of his feverish wanderings came more lucid moments when he was obsessed with fears that he could not, would not, be strong enough to work and travel and collect his fees, that he could not keep his royal appointment, let alone the tied house they all depended upon. In such stark dawns the demons rose, cackling at the insubstantiality of his profession.

A letter from George Brown, unaware of Lancelot's illness, told of his concerns that their sister Mary was in debt to a woman who was making threatening demands; George seemed to have the matter in hand and understood that Lancelot could do little from so far away; he promised a gift of 'a piece of hung beef'. Kindly Lord St Quentin at Scampston sent Yorkshire hams, and his best wishes, and so it was with gifts that Bridget's wedding was celebrated, observed by her father through the opiate haze of his illness.

Henry Holland and Bridget were married by special licence in the fashionable select vestry church of St George's in Hanover Square on 11th February 1773. This seems to have been managed by the Holland family, for though Mary and Henry Holland still regarded Fulham as their home, they were now living at 31 Half Moon Street off of Piccadilly, while the firm was building whole streets in Mayfair. It does indicate that Lancelot was too ill to take much part, and that even if he had wished for some royal blessing on his eldest child – marriage at Hampton Court or at St Anne's at Kew – he did not have the strength to arrange this. Henry Holland was twenty-seven, Bridget six months younger: as they had grown up together since they were five, it seems both fathers made them wait until Henry was confident in his architectural skills. Lancelot's weakness added an urgency for a younger man's help, and an heir to take advantage of all his good contacts, and so his 'partnership' with the young Henry Holland was forged with the marriage (there never had been any formal partnership with Holland senior). Lancelot settled his investment share on property in Carrington Street, Mayfair, on Henry and Bridget, who soon moved into a house that Holland's had built, no. 17 in adjacent Hertford Street. On 5th March 1773, a note from Drummonds confirmed the transfer of £5,000 worth of 3% Consolidated Stock to his son-in-law, whether as part of the marriage contract or a partnership agreement, or even payment for work at Claremont, is not clear.

More than a dozen letters survive from the six months of December 1772 to early June 1773. They were put aside for Lancelot's recovery, and then perhaps forgotten, remaining with his descendants for years, until Mr G. R. M. Pakenham lent them to Dorothy Stroud, who in turn gave them to the British Museum Library. This cache allows us to glimpse the minutiae of the King's Master Gardener's life: Lord North, now Prime

Minister and living at Bushy Park House (by courtesy of Lady North being appointed Ranger of Bushy Park) has already been noted requesting fruit from Hampton Court gardens. Lord St Quentin, at the very flat Scampston in North Yorkshire, wrote to say that he was conscientiously following instructions: 'I have made the sunk fence on both sides of the gateway to the most charming effect' and 'filled in the angle of the water at the west end, made an island where the water was too broad, widened it north of the bridge, according to your plan . . . which answers prodigiously well'. He promised to call.

Edward Hussey Montagu of moated Ditton Park in Buckinghamshire also promised to call on his way to Clandon in Surrey at Easter; Ditton was a small job, and Clandon materialised in 1780. On 12th April Lord Donegall of Fisherwick wanted a reference for a gardener named Turner from Ickworth, and sent his 'regards to Mrs Brown'. The next day, Lord Clanricarde, for whom Spyers was surveying Warnford Park in Hampshire, wanted special permission for his family to visit Kew whilst the King and Queen were away.

Undoubtedly Lancelot had worried about their son Jack, whose commission on the sloop HMS *Savage* had been confirmed to them by Lord Sandwich the previous August. Eventually Biddy persuaded Lancelot to write for news: the reply came in Sandwich's big, assertive scrawl, on 21st April 1773, saying that Jack was at New Providence in the Bahamas and 'going on very properly'. Their letter to him had been passed on, and he thought the enclosed £150 a 'very handsome' allowance.

On 8th June the Earl of Craven importuned from Benham, near Newbury, hoping 'you can possibly spare a day next week'. Lord Craven was under the thumb of his beautiful wife, Elizabeth Berkeley, and continued, 'Lady Craven wishes to make some alterations here and to begin immediately.' Lancelot was already working for the Earl on the park at Coombe Abbey near Coventry, but it seems likely that he took the job of the new house at Benham for the sake of his new partner, the architect Henry Holland: they jointly submitted drawings in September 1773 for a handsome house with a portico, with the River Kennet winding through Lancelot's park and crossed by a Chinese bridge. Craven was a sporting sort of a fellow, and finished his letter with mention of his horse-racing friend Jenison Shafto, who 'is here and desires his compliments and will be glad to pledge you in the Wooden Vessel'. This was one of the Northumberland Shaftos, probably from Benwell outside Newcastle, where he knew both John and Lancelot Brown as young men. Their meeting is celebrated in a sketch by Richard Cosway, which does no favours to Lancelot, who appears an overweight and bemused convalescent.

'Walls so thick as to keep out the devil'

All the time Lancelot was ill, Claremont was progressing; this house and comparatively small park should rank as one of his most glittering prizes. Robert Clive had returned in triumph in the summer of 1760, the hero of Plassey, with skin burnt 'the colour of mahogany' and rumours of a fabulous diamond 'worth upwards of £100,000', and he had seen Claremont. When he returned from his third tour of duty in July 1767, even richer, he had found the Duke of Newcastle ailing, and when the Duke died the following year, Clive had been quick to help the Duchess with a mortgage. He soon bought Claremont for £25,000.

Clive was a native of Shropshire, and had left there in an idle sort of way when he was coming up to twenty, to work as an East India Company clerk, but found a talent for soldiering, donned the Company uniform and made his name defending Arcot. At the end of this first tour he had married the musical and cat-loving Margaret Maskeleyne; they came home in 1753, and their son Edward was born the following year. Margaret's brother Edmund Maskeleyne was the astronomer, with whom she stayed at Greenwich during Clive's subsequent absences. His second tour began as Deputy Governor to George Pigot at Madras, but they soon diverted to the defence of Calcutta and victory at Plassey followed. In gratitude, Mir Jafir, the Nawab of Bengal, 'followed tradition' and gave Clive a fortune in diamonds, jewels and gold, whose value it was impossible to calculate. So on that second return he had bought 45 Berkeley Square as a London home, and rented Condover Hall near Shrewsbury whilst he looked around; he is revealed as having a touching affection for his native countryside. He also paid a reputed £90,000 for Walcot, an estate in the beautiful Welsh border country about 5 miles north-east of Clun.

In the traditions of Lancelot's profession, Claremont was a very special place, a coup: it was not out in the wilds, but a civilized distance just across the Thames from Hampton Court and through Esher village. Named by the Duke of Newcastle for his preliminary title, Earl of Clare, the 'mont' was a sandy outcrop above the valley of the River Mole, spotted by Sir John Vanbrugh for himself when it was simply known as Chargate Farm. Vanbrugh built a 'small box', which he loved dearly, but being permanently short of money could not afford to refuse the offer to buy it made by the then-Earl, Thomas Pelham, the rising man who became Duke of Newcastle in 1715. The small box was enlarged with spreading wings; the park was arrayed with double – nay, quadruple – avenues, and a massively walled garden similar to the kitchen garden at

Richard Cosway's sketch of himself (left), Lord Craven, Jenison Shafto and Lancelot (right), probably made shortly after Lancelot's serious illness in 1773.

Blenheim, with a 'Van' miniature White Cottage, or 'Mr Greening's house' (as it is still known), for the head gardener. Vanbrugh's towering Belvedere, equipped with a Butler's Pantry and Hazard Table, topped the outcrop behind the house, from where St Paul's dome and Windsor Castle could be seen. The Duke had Charles Bridgeman make the pleasure garden, a fantastic tiered amphitheatre covering 3 acres and dug to perch improbably on the west-facing slope of the Belvedere's ridge, above a round, spring-fed pond. In the manner of Blenheim and Stowe, Claremont had a decidedly military character, the pleasure gardens being 'defended' with brick and earthwork ramparts and ornamental bastions. Vanbrugh's walled kitchen garden, again like Blenheim's, was (and is) a fortification in itself, with rugged walls and arches.

After Vanbrugh's death in 1726 William Kent had loosened the pond into a lake, with an island and latticed bridge, a cascade and a fishing house: the Newcastles were fond of water fowl and kept swans, geese, turkeys and Chinese pheasants, and pea-fowl, as the peacock was the Pelham family crest. The surrounding ramparts were softened into a ha-ha. Most people would have forgotten, though Lancelot remembered, that Claremont was as famous as Stowe in the 1740s and 1750s, but as the Duke declined, so did his house and park. For Lancelot, to get his hands on Claremont was still momentous, and he found reminders of Stowe as he had first seen it, which reignited his pride in his professional traditions. Was it his informed reading of the landscape that won Lord Clive over? Or even Lancelot's appreciation of Clive's native Shropshire? Or Holland's Mayfair connections? Clive had had William Chambers work on his Berkeley Square house (and on his family's Shropshire home, Styche Manor, as well as Walcot Hall) and yet Chambers was rejected for Claremont, much to his fury. Henry Holland may have had something to do with it, for his father's Pall Mall houses were the first homes of those pinnacles of fashion, Boodle's club and Almack's Assembly Rooms, and Henry was in line for the newest clubland venture, Mr Brooks's in St James's Street:

> Liberal Brooks, whose speculative skill
> Is hasty credit, and a distant bill.

Lord Clive, though far from a macaroni, loved being well dressed in rather flamboyant clothes, and the haunts of the gentlemen of St James's were the shrines of aspiration.

It was decided that the rambling and crumbling house at Claremont was too low and damp, and it would be demolished, to build again higher up. The new house was positioned, with genius, by Lancelot; from the south it appears to be on top of a hill, but it is in fact built into the end of the Belvedere's ridge, and the 'offices' are cut into the hillside and connected to the house via a sunken court, screened with planting. Lord Clive particularly wanted the effect of an unbroken sweep of lawn all around and below his windows, for clear views. None other than Macaulay reported the local whisperings, 'that the great wicked Lord had ordered the walls to be made so thick in order to keep out the devil, who would one day carry him away bodily'.

Lancelot's Claremont account was opened in January 1771 with a handsome £4,000, and another £3,000 in the August. Bricks and slates were recycled from the old house, but additional thousands of bricks were made from clay deposits in the park, the ground carefully made good afterwards. When the interiors were started in 1772, it seems that Lancelot had time to study the park and give his instructions before he succumbed to his lowness at the New Year. He treated Claremont with sensitivity and gentleness: Vanbrugh's avenues had been dismantled by Kent, so the remaining trees were formed into clumps, with a great deal of thick shelter planting around the boundaries of the small park. He modified the ha-ha and the park roads into elegant curves. In the pleasure garden he attended to the overgrowth of Bridgeman's and Kent's planting by rationalising the walks, and it appears, though it is difficult to know for certain, that he found the amphitheatre so overgrown with self-seeded trees and shrubs that he left it so. It was an outdated curiosity (and was virtually lost, until it was restored by the National Trust in 1975–9).

Claremont was the perfection of Lancelot's house and garden ensemble ideal. His name and celebrity had won the commission, along with his honed skills for positioning the new house in its landscape, for setting the orientation of the rooms and for the convenience of the service quarters (especially for the servants) and efficiency of the drainage. The contracts were in his name, and he managed the money and signed off agreements and drawings. His control is evident in a letter from Sir John Lambert, the agent for the Parisian suppliers of the pier glasses for the grandest rooms, when after confirming the measurements Sir John ended with: 'always ye Greatest Veneration for yr Universally Known Talents'.

Henry Holland's modesty about his own role at Claremont has led to the misunderstanding that Lancelot was the *architect*, in our meaning of the role, and this has burnished misunderstandings about Lancelot's role in earlier buildings. In his tribute to his father-in-law at the head of this chapter, Holland has explained, as Lancelot never did, that the levels, the proportions of the rooms and their outlooks, the approaches, the drainage as well as his estimations of each client's standards of comfort were all his contributions to a building – except that he could not present them in a stylised drawing, conforming to theories plucked from architectural treatises. Lancelot worked these things out on the ground, and often utilised pattern-book drawings to enlighten his clients. The triumph of Claremont, which lies behind Henry Holland's words, is that Lancelot poured out his abundance of knowledge and experience to inform Holland's drawings, at least as far as these 'outside' matters were concerned. With the interiors Holland was on his own, and confident of his studies in France and his love of French style.

The total paid into the Claremont account by June of 1774 was £27,612. 16s. 11d. It seems, and is to be hoped, that the Clive family moved into their new house later that summer. 'Local legend' has it that Lord Clive had a large and comfortable bedroom on the top floor, and that when he was woken by the wind rattling the windows, he wedged them tightly with golden guineas. The chambermaids were only too happy to liberate the guineas! Lancelot apparently told Dr Johnson that Lord Clive 'had shewed him at the door of his bed-chamber a large chest,which he said he had once had full of gold'. Lancelot was apparently unnerved that he could bear it so close to his

Claremont, Surrey, Princess Charlotte and Prince Leopold of Saxe-Coburg made their home here after their marriage in 1816, and they are shown here in Lancelot's maturing park, with a handsome young cedar.

bedroom. It is worth adding Johnson's related comment, 'a man had better have ten thousand pounds at the end of ten years passed in England, than twenty thousand pounds at the end of ten years passed in India, because you must compute what you *give* for the money'.

Claremont had hardly started before Lord Clive discovered that the 1st Earl of Powis was being forced to sell his favourite Oakly Park at Ludlow, in order to concentrate his resources on Powis Castle. Lancelot visited Oakly twice, finding a fertile and undulating park hemmed in by the River Teme, just west of Ludlow town, and full of possibilities, and Lord Clive bought it in 1771 or early in 1772. Shropshire society being small, and its denizens unlikely to miss the momentary doings of a native son returned, a letter was soon wending Lancelot's way: 'Two of Lord Clive's sisters are now at my house and my Lord himself did me the honor to call on me two days ago, but I was so unlucky as to be from home.' This came not from a breathless matron, but from the distinguished fellow of St John's College, Cambridge, and biographer of Handel, John Mainwaring. Dr Mainwaring lived at Caer Caradoc at Church Stretton (where he was rector), at the apex of a small triangle between Oakly and Walcot, and in matters of taste felt all Shropshire belonged to him: he was glad, he continued in his letter of 21st August 1772, that Lancelot thought so highly of Oakly, 'rude and savage though it now is', for he was certain that Lancelot could make it 'the glory of the County if not of England itself', and he was confident Lord Clive would agree.

Oakly sounded a wonderful opportunity, but it was to be lost in over-work and illness: if Lancelot did have the chance to return in the summer of 1774 (and Oakly does show signs of eighteenth-century features, though of an uninspired kind), all was soon completely lost. On 24th November, at the age of forty-nine, Lord Clive was found dead at his house in Berkeley Square. It was apparently from an overdose of his usual medicinal drugs, but whether intentional or accidental we cannot know. The Claremont account was closed with an additional £3,000 paid by his executors, and the account for Oakly was settled, giving no details. (Lady Clive chose to live at Walcot; she sold Claremont in 1786, and it eventually became the home of Princess Charlotte and then of her widower, Leopold of the Belgians, and a favourite royal retreat.)

A good half of 1773 was lost to his illness, but Lancelot was out and about in July and August, and back to quartering the countryside in September, going to Burton Constable and then heading for Dorset and Devon. On the way west he called at Wardour Castle in Wiltshire, in response to Lord Arundell's letter of 16th August, introducing himself and his idea of improvements. He had seen, he said, 'several specimens' of Lancelot's fine taste and flattered himself that Wardour 'will be worthy of your attention'. Flattery was the order of the day, and perhaps measured to match the miles, for Lord Lisburne, a Lord of the Admiralty, had written from Mamhead in distant Devon, 'I should be glad to make what Improvements the scene is capable of under the Direction of a Genius whose Taste is so superior, & unrivalled'. Lancelot spent two days at Mamhead (where he had been on his 1764 expedition) in September, taking in the sea airs and spectacular views over the Exe estuary. He was warmly received by the Lisburnes, who still wished to build a new house, and in fine weather they planned drives and rides, woods and water in the up-hill and down-dale parkland, already rich in Spanish chestnuts, American oaks, acacias and cedars collected by the previous owners, the Balle family.

Returned home, Lancelot sent his plan and proposals to Lord Lisburne; he had over exerted himself and was ill again. Lord Dacre of long acquaintance, in a shaky hand, wrote on 7th November: 'sorry to find you have been and are so ill' and was disappointed not to see him at Belhus, where he 'dare not move a step without your advice'. He hoped they would meet in London during the winter. Lord Lisburne's reply came on the same day: Lancelot had made an error in the siting of the proposed new house, 'which may be material & occasion you more Trouble & difficulty than I could wish'. Was this his kindly way of saying that the lines of communication were just too long for Lancelot to work in Devon? (Robert Adam, twelve years Lancelot's junior, rebuilt Mamhead in 1777–8.) Work at Wardour Castle had to be deferred.

In December 1773 the prospect of an interesting client materialised in a letter (dated the 18th) in a tall, thin, clear hand with imperious and commanding tone but gentle manner, expressing the hope 'that the amendment in your state of health' would enable 're-establishment', for 'it is my ambition to benefit by your lights [though] upon a matter of so little importance'. This was 'Black Dick', the sailors' friend, Admiral Richard, Lord Howe, writing of his home at Porter's Park at Shenley in Hertfordshire (which had once been Nicholas Hawksmoor's home). He supposed Lancelot must avoid the severest weather, and he would be guided by 'your own convenience'. The Howe brothers, William and Richard, were popularly imagined to be the offspring of George I, so this was practically a royal commission, and Lancelot would have liked the idea. Did he and Black Dick walk through Porter's Park together? Little more is known and even less survives; the Boston Tea Party took place on 16th December 1773 and, once the news reached England, Admiral Howe's 'matter of little importance' faded before events, as he was despatched across the Atlantic.

As Lancelot resumed his routine of travelling in 1774, it became immediately clear that Biddy had made him promise to write home regularly so that at least they knew where he was; she sweetened the pill by suggesting that their youngest daughter Margaret – Peggy as she was always known – would love to hear of his progresses. Indeed, it is Peggy, aged fifteen, who now emerges as her father's devoted message-carrier and helper, the one child who seems really interested in his work and who treasured his letters. While Samuel Lapidge was close at hand to carry out the serious business instructions, Peggy often ran the short distance from Wilderness House to Lapidge's Hampton lodging, to get answers to her father's concerns about lost or delayed drawings. In return her 'affectionate Friend and Father', as he signs himself in a letter from Lord Bute's of 20th March 1774, was seeking out exotic birds on her behalf, for Peggy was a fowl-fancier, a popular female interest of the day (as it was for Philippa Hayes at Charlecote). A pea-hen is due to come from the Duke of Northumberland, writes Lancelot, and though at Lord Bute's he is told this is 'an improper time' for chicks, he adds, 'I shall find some for you before I am much older.'

Visiting Lord Bute at Luton Hoo was a sad business. Lancelot's magnificent park was blithely maturing and growing, innocent of the wiles of man, but the handsome courtier, dropped from all contact with his once-adoring George III and hated by the anti-Scottish faction in government, had succumbed to a certain paranoia: 'I have now lived with my door locked these 8 years past,' he wrote in 1774, 'broken and at an end I see no body, I no longer know those I was once intimate with nor they me . . . but spend the poor remains in my own way, & the greater part of it, in the inexhaustible researches into the works of nature.' Luton Hoo had been damaged by fire three years before and, though Robert Adam was restoring it (Mrs Delany visited that year and admired Adam's sensational library), his plans were never completed. It might be imagined that Lord Bute would have retreated to his Scottish island, but his interest had taken him in the opposite direction, and was now centred upon a patch of Hampshire cliff – Highcliffe near Christchurch, which was rich in chalkland flora, perfect for his 'inexhaustible researches'. He planned to build at Highcliffe, the matter he was discussing with Lancelot on this visit. The only account sum for Highcliffe is £140 for a site visit and plan, paid in 1777, but the house appeared in William Watts's *Views of Seats* (1784): 'a little box' with a long façade to the sea view, proving that Brown & Holland did build it. Rev. William Gilpin did not like it, and thought it 'a pompous pile', and soon after Bute's death in 1792 (from the lingering injuries after a fall from the cliff whilst botanising) it was pulled down.

Lord Bute's misfortunes were threefold: he had lost his place amongst the capricious society that so largely made up Lancelot's patrons (a salutary warning?); he had failed to find recognition for his tremendous labours upon a system of plant classification that rivalled Linnaeus's sexual system, set out in *Species Plantarum* of 1753 (but by no means completely accepted); and third, he was at loggerheads with the new favourite and

Director of Kew gardens, Sir Joseph Banks. Jealousy and hurt were evident in the facetious manner in which Bute replied to a request from Sir Joseph and Dr Carl Solander to visit Luton:

> [Lord Bute] is sorry Mr Banks thinks it necessary to ask a permission to see Luton Garden. Can there be a spot dedicated to vegetables & shut up from the first Patron of Botany. The truth is Ld Bute has long wished for the pleasure of seeing Mr Banks & Doctor Solander at the place, when he might profit by their superior knowledge in his favourite Science.

Lancelot was determinedly loyal to Bute – whose son, Lord Mount Stuart, did pay Henry Holland a substantial sum for alterations to Cardiff Castle – and this may have counted against him, especially with Banks. Many years later, Lancelot's youngest son, Thomas, claimed that Banks and his father were 'old friends', but there is no evidence for this.

Of Peasants in Periwigs and Melon Grounds

In the cold spring of May 1772, Horace Walpole wrote from Strawberry Hill to William Mason, complaining that 'the dreaded East is all the wind that blows', and adding, 'the newspapers tell me that Mr Chambers has Sir-Williamized himself', by the desire of the Knights of the Polar Star (a Swedish honour), 'and is going to publish a treatise on ornamental gardening'. Clearly thinking of Kew, Walpole supposed that Chambers would think a garden 'as a subject to be built in – in truth our climate is so bad that instead of filling one's garden with buildings, we might rather fill our buildings with gardens, as the only way of enjoying the latter!' Later in the month, on 25th May, Walpole wrote again, 'I have read Chambers's book ... it is more extravagant than the worst Chinese [wall]paper, and is written in wild revenge against Brown, the only surprising consequence is that it is laughed at, and is not likely to be adopted.'

'Written in wild revenge against Brown?' Was this really the case, or just the waspish Walpole's dramatisation? Chambers's infamous book, *A Dissertation on Oriental Gardening by Sir William Chambers Kt, Comptroller of his Majesty's Works,* was printed in 1772 by W. Griffin, printer to the Royal Academy, then in Russell Street, Covent Garden, and sold widely in London. An actual reading soon discovers his aims: to praise the Italian Renaissance villa gardens and Versailles-like French formalism, for their straight lines, temples, banqueting houses, topiary pyramids and spouting waters (without any recognition that such things had been in high fashion in England a century earlier). Chambers rages, 'In England, where this antient style is held in detestation', a new manner has been adopted whereby 'our gardens differ very little from common fields, so closely is common nature copied in most of them'; he imagines the discomforts of some putative stranger, who 'is often at a loss to know whether he be walking in a meadow, or in a pleasure ground', who has nothing to amuse him or excite his curiosity and is lost in a large space, 'doomed to walk one unvarying path, to find a hard seat which comforts him little', so that he must either drag on to the end or 'return back by the tedious way he came'.

Chambers had spent much of his life abroad, but it seems he had not opened his eyes to England – nor his ears to English sensibilities. The 'antient' gardens were the fashions of monarchs who ruled by divine right, and those days were banished. The English loved their green acres, the simple freedom of being out of doors, a virtue that Sir William Temple had liked to quote regarding Charles II on his return from exile in France, saying he 'liked that Country best, which might be enjoy'd the most Hours of the Day, and the most Days in the Year, which he was sure was to be done in England more than in any country whatso-ever'.

Chambers might just as well have blamed the new taste on the Hanoverian regime, but he chose instead to point out the lack of 'regular professors', or rather too many 'peasants [who] emerge from the melon grounds to commence professors'. In abandoning gardens to 'kitchen gardeners, well skilled in the culture of salads, but little acquainted with the principles of ornamental gardening', he might well have meant his nearest target, the Scots gardener William Aiton, raised in the kitchen-garden apprentice system and now in charge of Kew Gardens. The good-natured Aiton was portrayed by Nathaniel Dance in his 'uneasy' periwig. Lancelot's newly made Sion Hill and Syon House gardens could be read as 'a large green field, scattered over with a few straggling trees, and verged to a confused border of little shrubs and flowers' by an ignorant eye – ignorant of nature, trees and flowers. But Chambers goes farther: 'whole woods have been swept away to make room for a little grass and a few American weeds' – and this is surely directed at Charles Hamilton's theatrical plantings of American shrubs at Painshill, and at the works of Joseph Spence and Thomas Wright? He does not name 'our virtuosi', but accuses them of not leaving 'an acre of shade, not three trees growing in a line, from Land's End to the Tweed', and if their 'humour for devas-tation' continues, there will not be a forest-tree left standing in the whole kingdom'. If Lancelot had not risen in wrath at this last accusation, he would have spluttered in fury at Chambers's opening on the virtues of the Chinese: 'the Chinese Gardeners take nature for their pattern – their first consideration is the nature of the ground – to which circumstances they carefully attend' as to 'the wealth and temper of their clients'. So much for Pope's dictum of thirty years before on consulting 'the Genius of the Place'.

In the name of Chinese gardeners, Chambers proceeds to reinvent well-practised themes, vistas – as taken from a seat or pavilion – the ha-ha, a winter garden, 'waters for sailing, rowing, fishing' (China has lakes of several miles in circumference) and 'in the centres of plantations large tracts of land laid out for secret and voluptuous engagements' – close walks and hedges that sound much like a maze. He goes off to flights of fancy on 'gloomy woods with distorted trees, where tiger and jackal howl'; on instruments of torture used as ornaments (gibbets and crosses); and on dark passages ending in steep precipices. His chaotic fantasies offended Walpole's sense of due restraint and historical accuracy, which he had so deftly managed in his Gothic novel, *The Castle of Otranto* published in 1764.

Chambers's *Dissertation* foreshadowed the taste for the Picturesque in garden styles, and the standard he raised for the betterment of professional gardeners was not in vain. He ended with a plea: 'Gardeners must be men of genius, experience and judgement; quick in perception, rich in expedients, fertile in imagination and thoroughly versed in all the affections of the human mind.'

It was not an attack on Lancelot, but it was written in complete ignorance of what he and others had been doing for half a century.

We only have it from other people that Lancelot was offended; probably all would have been soon forgotten, had not his old ally, Rev. William Mason, decided to have a little fun with the contretemps, striking out with *An Heroic Epistle to Sir William Chambers, Knight,* which appeared in January of 1773, when Lancelot was far too ill to read it, and was more concerned with his daughter's wedding:

> Come then, prolific Art, and with thee bring
> The charms that rise from thy exhaustless spring;
> To Richmond come, for see untutor'd Brown
> Destroys those wonders which were once thy own.
> Lo, from his melon-ground the peasant slave
> Has rudely rush'd and levelle'd Merlin's cave;
> Knock'd down the waxen wizard, seiz'd his wand,
> And marr'd, with impious hand, each sweet design
> Of Stephen Duck and good Queen Caroline.

It might be pertinent that Mason had come from spending dark weeks in Cambridge, sorting and collecting the papers of his friend Thomas Gray. However, it was to Pope's idiom that he then turned:

Haste, bid yon livelong terrace re-ascend,
Replace each vista, straighten every bend;
Shut out the Thames; shall that ignoble thing
Approach the presence of great Ocean's king?
No, let barbaric glories feast his eyes,
August pagodas round his palace rise,
And finish'd Richmond open to his view,
A work to wonder at, perhaps – a Kew.

The *Heroic Epistle* was very popular and much laughed at. Lancelot, even when well enough, would not have regarded satire as his rightful field, though he might just have totted up the numbers – the hundreds of thousands of trees he had planted in the previous decades.

'Let Vanity take a look at Ambition'

Lord Clive leading Lancelot to the border counties had a happy legacy. The Harleys were the ancestral lords of the country flowing south via Knighton and Presteigne, living at Eywood at Titley, tucked into the steep hills that divided the valleys of the Hindwell brook, a tributary of the Lugg, and the River Arrow. Eywood must have seemed extremely remote in the eighteenth century, but the Harleys, in the person of the 4th Earl of Oxford, were not to be ignored, and so Lancelot made his way there in the August of 1775, presumably as a result of the gentry grapevine. (He noted his visit, but nothing else, and today Eywood is a broken and much-maligned landscape, where it is impossible to be certain of his civilising hand.) At Eywood he met Lord Oxford's younger brother, Thomas Harley, who, in his middle forties and with his City fortune, was returning 'home' and had bought Berrington just north of Leominster.

It seems they drove the 20 winding miles eastwards into England, for Lancelot to have a look at Berrington, where Thomas Harley immediately asked him to design the park. Indeed, he may have asked Lancelot to design him a new house as well, but Lancelot was pleased enough to fall back on a Claremont-style working partnership with Henry Holland. How fortunate this was, for Berrington is an exquisite smaller cousin to Claremont, though red rather than creamy-white, encased in red sandstone quarried from Shuttocks Hill a mile away, and brought by horse-drawn carriages on a tramway constructed across the park. For us in retrospect, Holland's interiors, with their swirls and swags and ice-cream colours suffused in dramatic lights, reveal an enchanting interlude between the styles of Robert Adam and John Soane.

Unmistakeably Lancelot had the siting of Berrington. Perhaps, in his famed way of speedy grasp and judgement, he paced around with Harley, and told him, 'There, just there, that is the place for your house.' That it was a matter of *finding* the right spot rather than *making* it is borne out by the Foreman's notes for the shell of the building, taken from Holland's drawings, with their implicit economy of labours: 'dig out for the Basement story four feet deep (except in Stewards room 7 feet) dig for the foundations of the walls 18" deeper, dig for a dry area round the House 6" lower than the floor, dig for the drains to the outside of the Building, dispose the Ground round the House, Make the drains in Brickworks.' The walls were of brick faced with stone and roofed in Westmorland slates. The foundations for the portico and steps were added to the south entrance front, setting the perfect stage for the view, which is typically 'Brownian' and equally typically economical with effects. Nature had done most of the work, providing a wide valley crossed by a tributary stream; Lancelot provided a silvery pool, a 14-acre lake with a large island (made of the spoil), the wooded island bestowing on generations of happy children the stuff of their dreams.

Berrington Hall, Herefordshire, built for Thomas Harley by Lancelot in partnership with his son-in-law Henry Holland as the architect. Lord Clive's Claremont in Surrey and the now vanished Cadland house by Southampton Water were built by the same partnership methods.

We can almost hear the Harleys' talk of the extravagant panorama that can be taken in with so little effort from the portico: to the south, beyond Lugg and Arrow, to steep-sided Westhope Hill and the Roman Watling Street; farther south across the Wye to the distant ridge of the Black Mountains; swinging westwards, the view brushes over Eywood, backed by the old Radnor Forest, and then northwards to the family's Brampton Bryan beside the Teme, coming homewards across the watery ways of Leintwardine and the thickly wooded ridges of Leinthall, where the Iron Age fort of Croft Ambrey sits on the skyline. Berrington is a fine example of how Lancelot gave his client more than a house in a park, but a home set in the mists of time. His house cost Harley about £15,000, paid to Henry Holland; Lancelot earned £1,600.

In early December of 1775 Lancelot set out for the Midlands, with Biddy's last words ringing in his ears, 'Don't forget to write.' His intentions were good, but he had a little leeway, as he was headed for Luton Hoo and the safe harbour of Lord Bute's. Or was it so safe? He stayed two nights and they drank a bottle of sweet, rich Tokay each evening, as he confessed to Biddy, 'which was rather too much for me as my cough has been very troublesome'. His confession was preambled with some of his mischief, written on 11th December, from Coombe Abbey at Coventry, which he had reached by way of Fawsley in Northamptonshire:

> I came by Mr Knightley's where I stay'd one night and met a cheerful domestic wife that never wishes to stir from home – she looks after her Birds and makes her husband's pleasures her own – she had all the wifely virtues, but no child, and I am sorry for [that, for] perhaps she would have had more pleasure and better appetite for it if she had a few.

The cheerful wife was Catherine Dashwood, married to Lucy Knightley (named for a connection to the Lucys and Charlecote, although he is known to have disliked his name), who left the matter of progeny to his youngest brother John Knightley and his wife Mary Baines, who had six children: their daughter Elizabeth was married to John Fleming, and earlier in the summer Lancelot had visited the Flemings at North Stoneham near Southampton, conveniently close to Broadlands.

The Knightleys had been at Fawsley, which was about 10 miles west of Northampton in surprisingly remote countryside, for long centuries. Their monuments crowd the ancient church, and hall and church are situated in a watery vale. Fawsley was a noted lost village, though cleared for sheep-grazing a good two centuries before Lancelot's arrival. He had been making the lake and plantations in the valley for several years, and the Knightleys' home, as so many other houses of his clients, had become his convenient overnight halt. Most of the hall was Elizabethan, and Lancelot found himself sharing his dark bedroom with the portraits of martyrs, Charles I, Bishop Laud and Lord Strafford, which led him 'very much upon the Phylosophick strain' and the contemplation of vanity, ambition and the wages thereof. 'A Day so spent is not one of the worst we spend,' he wrote to Biddy, 'and just to conclude it, I have entered into a conversation with you which has every charm except your company which will ever be the sincere and the principal delight, my dear Biddy, of your affectionate h[usband].'

Lord Craven's Coombe Abbey at Coventry, hardly less haunted than Fawsley, was the very fictional Gothic image of a Cistercian abbey, its ghostly grey stones sprawling around the cloisters – these enclosed and furnished with the horned heads of dead cattle and a stuffed wild cat – and around cavernous halls. The Great Hall had welcoming log fires, and the newer rooms were richly furnished, but for Lancelot, in his philo-sophic mood, there was no escape from the doleful dark eyes that gazed down from the many portraits of the 1st Lord Craven's beloved Stuarts: the murdered King Charles I, his sister, Elizabeth of Bohemia, her sons Rupert and Maurice, and generations of the warrior Cravens. Was it only his tired imagination, or were they accusing him of destroying their old gardens, even the image of the garden that was Stuart England?

Coombe had a large and nondescript deer park; it was more suited to ranges of sweet chestnut or lime avenues as in the olden days, but Lancelot had found these broken and moth-eaten, full of dead trees, through lack of care. If John Byng – that noted 'observer' and nosey parker, who called him 'my friend Capability Brown' (a more general than personal bonhomie, and made in 1786 after Lancelot's death) – thought he had 'ruined old avenues' and not planted enough in their places, it was fair comment, for his plantations had not had time to grow. Byng's other jibes concerning Coombe Abbey, that the water stagnated and there was no 'inequality' of ground, revealed Lancelot's difficulties: the park was a feebly contoured desert and it was job enough to persuade the streams to fill the lake at all; the water lolled about in a great hook-ended pond, which at least would serve for boating and fishing (150 years later the lake had become the oldest and largest heronry in the country). Had Lancelot overreached himself at Coombe? Were there some places that just did not respond to his persuasion? Faced with a December morning and cold hours to spend inspecting the great drab park, the gruelling necessities of his profession perhaps weighed heavily.

Coombe was not a happy commission (today it is a spacious 'green lung' and country park). Lord Craven was more interested in his racing, having airily told Lancelot, 'I shall leave everything else to you' – meaning the park. Lady Craven, the former Elizabeth Berkeley, was hostile, writing in her later *Memoirs* (1826) that they had been 'plundered' over the costs by 'the famous man called Capability Brown'. She noted that £12,000 was laid out, whereas Lancelot's account shows just over £7,000, and added that she felt herself perfectly capable of 'adding to Nature'. The Cravens' marriage was foundering, perhaps an underlying cause.

His next port of call, Lord Donegall's Fisherwick, near Lichfield, also appeared to slip beyond Lancelot's complete control. Lord Donegall was kind and prompt in his payments of £500 or £300 (and sometimes more), which had arrived regularly for six years and now amounted to more than £6,000 (with £1,000 paid to Drummonds, which may, or may not, have been additional). The house, rebuilt on old foundations and somewhat in the manner of Croome, appeared huge and bulky, though Lord Donegall was very happy with Henry Holland's silk-hung rooms. Outdoors, Lancelot's wizardry conjured lawns and curving waters, joined by a cascade, but there was a sense of impermanence about Fisherwick, and it was not destined for long life. The Marquess, as he became, died in 1799 and the estate faced an uncertain future; sale particulars of 1808 describe flourishing plantations, 'with the finest trees and shrubs of all descriptions and ornamented in various parts with greenhouses, temples and seats, and the canals and rivers with Bridges and Cascades'. The park was 'abundantly stocked with deer and game and richly ornamented with groups of fine forest trees'. But the gloss failed to find it all a secure future, the house was demolished, the park broken into lots and eventually used for gravel extraction. For the *Staffordshire* volume (2009) of his *Historic Gardens of England,* Timothy Mowl explored the remains of Fisherwick, finding:

> the approach road to the site is flanked by a dramatic ha-ha of squared and coursed red sandstone, stubby gatepiers with the Earl's coronets survive near the site of the house, and there are still discoveries to be made . . . amongst the thick undergrowth is a silted-up winding stream and stretches of water that are now little more than pools, but Brown's Cascade just clings on, as do the Kitchen Garden walls.*

---

* Mowl thinks that Lancelot may have worked at Byrkley Lodge north of Fisherwick, where a cascade also survives. Himley Park, the last of Lancelot's Staffordshire commissions, is now a public park, just west of Tipton and Dudley.

One Last Diamond, Milton and Sherborne

In the New Year, of 1776, Lancelot was on the road again, making calls as he headed for Dorset. Lord Chatham's glee at rediscovering himself as a West Saxon with dirty acres at Burton Pynsent referred to his family's roots in Dorset, and they might have remained in country obscurity, were it not for the exploits of his grandfather, Governor Thomas Pitt, who had done well in India and bought himself a fine diamond. (The gem, so the story goes, was brought home in the heel of Robert Pitt's shoe, Robert being the Governor's eldest son and Lord Chatham's father. The diamond was bought for £24,000 and the wily Governor managed to sell it to the French for five times that sum. It was set in the crown for Louis XIV's coronation in 1722, then adorned Napoleon's sword of state; it was restored to Louis XVIII, but has since disappeared.)

With his diamond money, Governor Pitt bought Boconnoc in Cornwall, property in Okehampton including control of the parliamentary seat, and Swallowfield Park in Berkshire (close to George Pitt's Stratfield Saye, and Lancelot could well have worked at both places). He also added to the Blandford St Mary estate where he had been born. This last is the Down estate, just over the hill from Milton Abbas; work mentioned in the accounts for Down seems to tally with Lancelot's visits to Milton. In the 1770s Down was the home of Thomas Pitt, Lord Chatham's nephew, in whom he had taken a considerable interest, and an Orangery was being built, the work done by Stephen Carpenter of Blandford, who also worked at Milton. The house has gone, but Down remains a sequestered vale of green, with Lebanon cedars and a fugitive elegance that suggests an abandoned Brown landscape. Needless to say, Down does not appear in Lancelot's accounts; is it just one more strand in the skein of mutual obligations that ties Lancelot and Lord Chatham?

At Milton he found an unhappy place. Lady Milton had recently died and her husband was absorbed in her memorialising; their son John Damer, less than ten years after his brilliant match with Anne Seymour Conway, was estranged from the beautiful and talented sculptress, and was drinking and gambling himself to perdition. Lord Milton, refusing to pay his son's debts, was branded cruel and unheeding; Lancelot probably knew more than most, but said less, for he had worked at the Conway home, Park Place at Henley, a heavenly spot overlooking the Thames valley. Lord Milton had also quarrelled with William Chambers and brought in James Wyatt to finish his abbey house, but there were still small building jobs that fell to the good-natured Lancelot.

When, almost a dozen years earlier, his lordship had expressed the

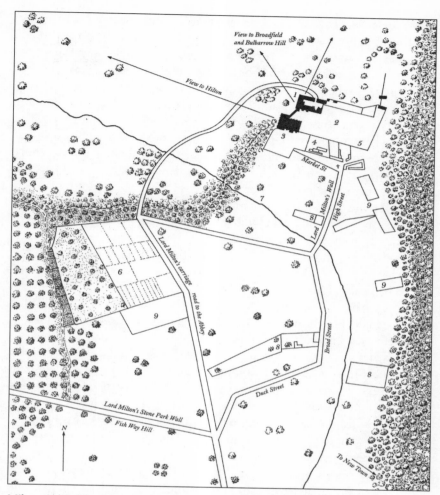

Milton Abbas. The lawyer's plan *c.*1770 showing Lord Milton's clearance of the houses of Middleton town, from Duck, Broad, the High and Market Streets, with the exception of the properties of Mr Harrison, who refused to sell, but was eventually flooded out. The Rivulet was dammed to the south, the valley flooded but the lake was never satisfactory.

1. Milton Abbey.
2. Abbey garden.
3. Abbey church and churchyard.
4. School – later moved to Dorchester.
5. Lord Milton's wall.
6. Lord Milton's kitchen garden and orchard.
7. Rivulet running across Lord Milton's estate.
8. Harrison plots.
9. Other plots.

desire for a lake, Lancelot had replied that the only source for the water was the Hilton stream, and the only way for the water to go was down the valley to the south, where it flowed through Middleton village. Lord Milton had taken him at his word, and in the intervening years he had been buying in the plots, in line with a plan commissioned from Surveyor Woodward; this is a large plan of childlike clarity, every building coloured red, every plot outlined and measured, with the name of the tenant. The dullest villager could not fail to see the logic of the system: vacant plots were taken in hand, and life tenancies all too frequently proved short, for instance: 'Plot 120 *late* John Heron, in hand; Plot 29 John Hallet an orchard [worth little]; Next door on lower Henbury lane plot 66 Francis Vacher for life, died 1773, in hand; Plot 42 Barn meadow *late* William Muckles, in hand', but Muckles's fifteenth-century cottage on Mount Pleasant survived, and is there still; was it thought ornamental?

Woodward's survey moved relentlessly through the plots – often the tenancies were Lord Milton's own, or there were only absentee execu-tors to be dealt with – and soon it becomes clear that Lord Milton would eventually have control. Only one man is known to have stood firm, a lawyer named Harrison, who was eventually deliberately flooded out.

Where was Lancelot in this nefarious dealing? He had already seen such a scheme of surpassing ingenuity at Audley End, where Sir John Griffin Griffin had acquired swathes of land in just this way, following the example of his revered aunt, the Countess of Portsmouth. He had seen the earliest 'model' villages, the new rows of housing at Harewood designed by John Carr of York, and at Lowther by the Adam brothers; he had spoken to gardeners who were delighted with their modern houses, as any sensible person would be. He recalled the stone cottage where he was born, and contrasted it with his nephew Richard Brown's fine modern house at Kirkharle. All over the land – at least the land he knew – owners were removing scattered dwellings and replacing them on better sites; this was just one of the lesser despotisms of the role of a landowner. But Middleton was different; it was a thriving township, and it was (as has been mentioned) as though the Egremonts had decided to demolish Petworth, or the Methuens had removed Corsham.

Prior to their falling-out over expenses, and Chambers calling Lord Milton an 'unmannerly, imperious Lord' who treated everybody ill, William Chambers had supplied 'a plan of a part of the intended Village' with a description, in a letter of 3rd April 1773. This plan has not been found, but John Harris notes that 'from Chambers' description . . . the layout of the village was his'. On the other hand, Dorothy Stroud asserts that in November 1774 Lancelot noted that he 'had given plans for the village

The new village of Milton Abbas, 1770.

for which he was paid' 100 guineas, and on this evidence she seems certain that the village was his, though Lancelot's plans have not been found, either. Posterity has largely taken the Stroud view: that the outrageously pictur-esque street of toy-like thatched cottages was designed by Lancelot, another stroke of his surprising genius, for which he is applauded – and vilified.

In Lancelot's defence, it seems only pertinent to suggest that such prodigy picturesqueness – only to be matched by Nash and Repton's Blaise Hamlet almost thirty years later – was unlikely to have come from the ponderous hand of the practical and overworked Lancelot Brown. He simply did not have the *architectural* imagination to take so many years' leap in philanthropic design. Nor would he have had the heart to place the village in such a deep valley, orientated almost east–west, so that half the houses spend half their days in chill and mouldering shade, the chimneys hardly draw and the gardens are so steep and shaded as to be almost useless. The final insult was that each cottage, though they were originally pairs of cottages (that is, two rooms down and two up, with a communal staircase), was separated by a horse-chestnut tree (suppos-edly to deter pests). These naturally grew so large, shading each cottage even more, raining inedible 'conkers' and leathery, useless leaves, that they were eventually felled in 1953. Lancelot would never have allowed such a use for the huge trees he planted in avenues or on great lawns – or even as 'beneath the spreading chestnut tree' on village greens.

The clearance of the old town was completed in about 1779, the year that the Tregonwell almshouses in the old town were dismantled and re-erected in the new village street. It was to be another eight years before the estate accounts mention payments for levelling the west lawn of the abbey house, and grubbing out the hedges to open the view to the new lake. Clearly, the greater villainy at Milton would be to have made the lake that flooded the former orchards and gardens of Middleton, but here Lancelot is innocent. Though he was paid a final 100 guineas, which might have been for a plan and a visit (but could equally easily have been one of his 'for my trouble' clearing-up payments), there is no plan. Several years later in Lord Milton's ongoing dispute (with the immov-able Harrison), the lawyers had to make their own plan, showing an ungainly stretch of water with indications of dams ending in the main dam that carries the road to Cheselbourne. Subsequent maps, and the present appearance, show the lake to have been a poor thing, impossible to have been Lancelot's, on either technical or artistic counts. It simply did not work, and after a dispute over water rights to Milton Mill, it was abandoned.

To return to the winter of 1776, Lancelot was snowed up at Milton and so anxious to get away that he abandoned his chaise and took to horse-back for a ride to Sherborne on 15th January; it was 10 rough miles through country lanes before he reached the Dorchester–Sherborne turn-pike, and with 6 or so miles more to go, it was no wonder he arrived 'with great difficulty'. His welcome was warm, for he got on well with the Digbys at Sherborne Castle and they with him, and despite the weather the prospect was sunny. Sherborne Castle has the happiest of situations, and there were no troubles with the neighbours here, even though it was close to the town. There might have been, for the old castle built by Roger, Bishop of Salisbury, in the twelfth century was on the hill at the east end of the town, but this had been abandoned by Sir Walter Raleigh (who found it too expensive to alter) and he had built a new house farther to the south, on a secondary hill. The valley between was crossed by the River Yeo, and here Raleigh's half-brother, Adrian Gilbert, who was some-thing of a plantsman, made a garden with canals and cascades, using the unusual plants that Raleigh brought home from his voyages. A spot called 'Raleigh's Seat' survives, and with it goes an old story with new meaning – he was enjoying a quiet smoke one evening when an anxious servant doused him with ale, thinking he was on fire.

With Raleigh's sad fall from grace and execution in 1618, James I sold Sherborne Castle estate to the Digbys, who enlarged Raleigh's house

Syon House, a conversation sketch by Robert Adam and Lancelot Brown, standing at the door of Syon House and looking north to where the siting of the obelisk conflicted with the site of the new bridge over Lancelot's 'river stile' lake. The bridge was offset. This drawing, with others, was saved by Thomas Percy.

Thomas Percy, later Bishop of Dromore (1729–1811), by William Dickinson, after Sir Joshua Reynolds, 1775. Percy was chaplain and tutor at Alnwick Castle, myth–master to the Northumberlands in their restoration of Hulne's romantic landscape and a good friend to Lancelot.

Hampton Court from the south, by J. Kip and L. Knyff, 1702–14, showing the newly-built Wilderness House at the far corner of the Wilderness or Maze. This was the palace and garden as completed for William III and Queen Mary, with Henry Wise's new avenues in Bushy park (top right), and the extensive kitchen gardens. When Lancelot arrived in 1764 the gardens were intact, though considerably matured.

Hampton House and Garden with Garrick Writing, 1762, by Johann Zoffany,
showing the ground modelling and entrance to the tunnel beneath the Hampton road,
made by Lancelot to connect the garden to the riverside lawn. Lancelot was a
frequent visitor to Hampton House and the sociable Garricks.

Blenheim by J.M.W. Turner, 1830–31. Painted sixty-five years after Lancelot started work a Blenheim, this is the most powerful tribute to his skills in planting and making virtues ou of the difficulties with Vanbrugh's great 'bridge in the air'. Turner takes his view (though foreshortened) from the Woodstock entrance, showing that the townspeople were in the habit of enjoying the park, though this was perhaps not such a good idea on days when the hunt was out!

Labourers by George Stubbs, one of three pictures commissioned by Lord Torrington
of workers on his estate at Southill in Bedfordshire. Apart from the atmosphere of bucolic
well-being – the dozing dog, the interfering pensioner – there is the poignancy of the end
of an era, imminent through Torrington's bankruptcy, which he undoubtedly foresaw.
Lancelot worked at Southill in the late 1770s, immediately prior to the disaster,
so these men had almost definitely worked on his schemes.

Hannah More (1745-1833) by Frances Reynolds.
Frances was the same age as Lancelot's daughter Bridget,
and yet he spent a companionable two hours in the garden
at Hampton Court discussing his work with her, in the
last autumn of his life. What a pity he had not warmed to
such an inquiring mind before, and revealed his secrets?

The new lake at Kirkharle in Northumberland, imagined by the landscape architect
Nick Owen from the plan of 1770-1, and now being made.

Rev. William Mason and Mrs Elizabeth Montagu, caricatured as Abelard and Heloise, mezzotint, 1775. Whatever the social commentary, these two great personalities of the eighteenth century were Lancelot's loyal friends and lifelong supporters.

into a storybook construction of white towers, essentially unfortresslike, but still a 'castle'. Edward, 6th Lord Digby, is said to have made the lake between the old and new castles after he watched a flash-flood of the Yeo; Lancelot may have advised him on this, but any further works were halted when Edward died suddenly, aged twenty-seven, in 1757. Now, albeit nearly twenty years on, his younger brother Henry, 7th Lord Digby, was seriously embellishing his grounds. He and Lancelot spent two January days riding out and giving instructions; Lancelot had already installed Cornelius Dickinson as his foreman for the works. The same pattern followed the next year, in January 1777, when it was recorded in the Game Book that 'Mr Brown came from Lord Milton's while we were at dinner – and was very agreeable'; and after two days, 'Captain R[obert Digby] went with regret to Minterne before breakfast sorry to loose any of Mr Brown's company.'

Lancelot's pleasing relationship with the Digbys resulted in a serene and understated, typically 'Brownian' setting for Sherborne Castle, as if the mood of its making imparted some blithe spirit. The view (reminiscent of the same aspect at Corsham Court) from the Georgian windows of the east front is across an apron of swelling lawn, which falls (the fall unseen) into a curtain of majestic trees, mostly beech, which Lancelot would have underplanted with holly. A break in the trees allows a glimpse of water, which fades into the distance, where the land begins to rise on either side and the lake begins, transforming the Yeo stream. Turn to the south-east and, beyond the unseen ha-ha, the land is still rising, smoothly green punctuated by substantial park trees, which gather as the slope steepens until they clothe the top of the ridge. Turn to the north and the tree curtain breaks for a view across the lake, the water seen through the hovering branches of a huge cedar of Lebanon, one of Lancelot's favourite tricks. On the far side of the lake, the bank pleasingly open, is the 'Dry Ground', which was above the Yeo's flood, a wide green slope with an echoing cedar and more beech, the trees masking the boundary line of Pinford Lane.

These 'simple' views constitute a masterclass in the Brownian landscape style; the materials are merely earth, water and trees, but the way he has disposed these familiar elements launches them into a kaleidoscope of fugitive (the favourite eighteenth-century word) effects. The near lawn, painstakingly moulded and rolled into a swelling curve, cut smooth for summer dancing through the shadows, is at other times thickly flowered or sheep-grazed; the lake – comfortingly controlled within 'natural' contours, inviting fishing and boating picnics, and skimming swans and geese – is open to the sky and seasonal lights; in some places

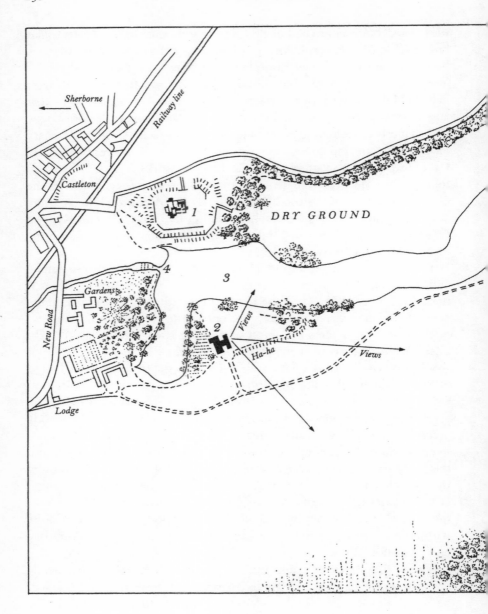

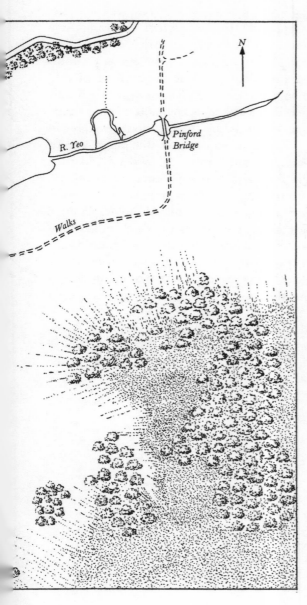

R. Yeo

N

Pinford
Bridge

Walks

Sherborne Park. Plan of works for the 7th Lord Digby 1776–79. The park has been sympathetically maintained with great respect for Lancelot's ideas. Especially good are the walks around the west of the lake to the old castle and the Dry Ground, and along Pinford Lane, and the views to be taken from the east lawn of the new Castle.

1. Old Castle.
2. New Castle.
3. Lake inspired by a flash flood of the river Yeo, as watched by the 6th Lord Digby.
4. Dam and outfall where river Yeo continues its journey.

it is shaded, dark, mysterious, appealing to the amorous or adventurous, and the long-resident pike. Beyond the ha-ha the park is lushly green and grazed, shadowed with browsing lines along the lip where the contours take a lurch and green changes to rough bracken, the preserve of wild animals and birds. The specimen trees, oaks and planes, can stand proudly alone; the more gregarious beech and chestnuts are gathered into sturdy fortresses, their seasonal colours enhanced by the occasional evergreens. The scene changes subtly and slowly, indeed is never still, just as 'nature' intended, through numberless lights and seasons. All is good and true. There are no falsities, no rigid avenues flatten the natural inequalities of land, no water from an improbable source spurts from a carved stone, no alien contortions or colours of tree or flower offend the eye. Though subject to twenty-first-century management, Sherborne Castle still exhibits a good plain example of what is now called the essential English Landscape Style: it is intriguing to discover that the Digbys owned an Italian pastoral landscape painting by Claude – a view across a lake, framed in trees – which gave them their inspiration and informed their agreeable talks with Lancelot.

Many of the walks and rides that Lancelot planned with Henry Digby can still be taken at Sherborne: to the old castle and along the top of the Dry Grounds to Pinford; the views they discussed, the breaks in the trees that suddenly open out glimpses of the old castle, or the new, are still cherished.

TREADING THE ENCHANTED GROUND

Now I must request you to inform Mama that a great Man has paid us a Visit, which Visit (as happens sometimes with great Men) has ended in very little. You will guess that I mean the illustrious Mr Brown, who walk'd unexpectedly in[to] the Garden on Tuesday Morning, & Din'd with us, in his Way to Hawnes. He did not pay much Attention, or open any Scheme relative to the middle of the Garden. He saw indeed that the Water might appear to come from one Wood & flow into the other, but he did not know whether a winding Water through a strait Avenue might not look inconsistent, as if the Avenue was destroy'd & part of the Wood clear'd away it might unravel the Mystery of the Garden.

Lady Amabel Polwarth at Wrest,
to her sister Lady Grantham, 19th November 1778

THE THOUGHT ARISES THAT Lancelot really enjoyed his times with people like the Digbys too much – they were his social life, the cause of his teasing of Biddy about the cheerful wife who never wished to leave home. Biddy Brown was certainly justified in wishing that her husband would stop for a while, for leisurely outings and pleasurable companionship. She would never have accompanied him to his grand clients' houses, for she would have been very awkwardly placed and at the mercies of pompous dowagers and unctuous servants, as she knew full well. In her own home she entertained with grace, any of Lancelot's clients from the Prime Minister Lord North, their neighbour at Bushy Park house (and perhaps even the King) downwards, and many lordly regards and compliments came her way. Lancelot, on the other hand, made a charmed progress, partly because of the freemasonry of gardening for whom the low green door in the garden wall led directly to the hub of any establishment, and partly because he was Lancelot. At Wrest, Lady Amabel (as quoted above) seemed to be caught mid-aperitif by his arrival, and quickly had to arrange for another place at the table. Lady Amabel had grown up with his sudden arrivals, and been well taught by her mother, Jemima, Marchioness Grey, but not everybody was so aware: Lord Chatham had to brief Lady Stanhope at Chevening:

> I will not fail to obey your Ladyship's commands by writing to Brown. I do so with particular pleasure, persuaded that you cannot take any other advice so intelligent or more honest. The chapter of my friend's dignity must not be omitted. He writes Lancelot Brown, Esquire *en titre d'office*: please to consider, he shares the private hours of [the King], dines familiarly with [the King's] neighbour of Sion [*sic*: Syon], and sits down at the tables of all the house of Lords, etc. To be serious, Madam, he is deserving of the regard shown to him; for I know him, upon very long acquaintance, to be an honest man, and of sentiments much above his birth.

When he was at home Lancelot had his comfortable cronies at Hampton and his strolls across the green to the Garricks' hospitable house, where he had continued to make suggestions for the garden. David Garrick was contemplating his retirement, but having acquired sole ownership of the Drury Lane Theatre, had set himself a final task of refurbishing the interior, then still as Christopher Wren had designed it in the seventeenth century. His masterstroke was to employ Robert Adam, who designed the classical entrance portico and raised the height of the auditorium, so that the entire house seemed bigger and brighter; when the public arrived at the opening of the 1775 season it seemed like a new theatre, and it had no rival. Garrick was now in profit, by the increased value of the patent to run the theatre, which he was selling to Richard Brinsley Sheridan and his partners, and his final performances were announced. This was the background for their conversation when Lancelot returned from his Sherborne visit at the end of January 1776, and Garrick promised him tickets for a gala night. But, after telling Biddy, Lancelot must have written to refuse. 'My dear Sir, You make Me and my Wife mad,' spluttered Garrick's reply of 5th February:

> you shall be prefer'd to the whole body of Nobility, if you will give me Notice but one day of your coming – I have kept places till 12 o'clock the two last times of my Playing, but you never sent – there is not a single place in the Whole house but what is Engag'd – Don't use me so again for I love & esteem you and am moreover oblig'd to you.

Was the obligation for the Hampton garden, or had Garrick needed reminding that Robert Adam would be the best architect for the theatre?

Garrick's many farewells, playing Hamlet and Lear, and *Richard III* expressly for the King and Queen, as well as lighter roles, had galvanised society. The writer Hannah More described one night:

> The eagerness of the people to see him is beyond anything . . . you will see half a dozen duchesses and countesses of a night, in the upper boxes: for the fear of not seeing him at all has humbled those who used to go not for the purpose of seeing but of being seen, and now they curtsy to the ground for the worst places in the house.

Garrick insisted upon Lancelot and Biddy coming to the theatre. He gave them more dates, and then a hasty postscript: 'My Wife is resol'vd to make room for You, as well as She can in her Box – Come to the Stage door & Enquire for her Box – Ye Ladies not in hats.'

'The People that surround us threaten an Attack'

The more serious matter of the day broke in upon Wilderness House with a letter from Jack. Lancelot had written more than six months earlier, in mid-July of 1775, after the news of British casualties at Bunker Hill reached London, and Jack had received that letter on 10th November when his ship HMS *Nautilus* took on supplies in Boston. His reply was written immediately, on the 14th, so it should have reached them in late January or early February. *Nautilus* had returned from chasing a rebel schooner that had gone aground near Marblehead, Massachusetts, only to be surprised by the crew manhandling their guns onto a nearby hill and firing on them, wounding two men (one of whom died) and damaging the sails and rigging. Jack found it 'beyond conception how well they are prepared all along the Coast', and though Boston seemed quiet, 'how long it will continue so I cannot tell, the People that surround us threaten an Attack, but I believe they know us to be too well prepared to receive them. It is natural to suppose the Congress (who have Hancock and Adams to urge them on) and their Generals would wish an attack'. He wondered that the rebel army would refuse to fight, as 'the deserters that come in dayly' were starving and unpaid: on the other hand, 'Our Troops are in general very healthy', though he feared for the wounded with the onset of a harsh winter, and 'the greatest inconvenience the immense price of provisions' – the beef and mutton very poor, and very little of it. He sent his affectionate respects and duty. Jack had surely found his niche, however hard it was, and they could be proud of him.

Lord Chatham, 'though in a wretched condition of body and mind,' dragged himself to Parliament in May 1776 for one last plea for the withdrawal of the 'oppressive' measures inflicted upon the colonists – America was 'the source of all our wealth and power', so what was the point of driving her into the arms of France? Lancelot would have supported his hero. In the small compass of the Browns' concerns were the nation's in miniature: too long and uncertain lines of communication, an under-estimation of – though sneaking regard for – the colonists' determin-ation for their cause, and poor and inadequate supplies to the army and navy in the field. Add one proud king, George III, and his intolerance of 'rebellious children', and so he 'in effect disowned the Americans as rebels and treated them accordingly'. On the following 4th July Congress's Declaration of Independence set out the charges against him at length.

One rather curious outcome of the King's break with America was that, at home, he started going out more, ostensibly to bolster morale in his army and navy by the staging of magnificent reviews, at Coxheath in Kent, Warley in Essex, or at Portsmouth or Weymouth. Once, in London, someone had sent a missile (which turned out to be an apple) into his carriage, which had unnerved him; but after a quite different progress at Godalming when returning from his first fleet review – the women throwing nosegays until he was knee-deep in flowers and everyone singing 'God Save the King' – he was encouraged to let the populace see that he was not the ogre that the Americans had painted him. After his visit to Portsmouth, Hans Stanley, Governor of the Isle of Wight, wrote: 'as he has lived so much in retirement, I thought he would have been embar-rassed and reserved in so large a company . . . but Charles II could not have been more affable'. Consequently there was a flurry of activity amongst the King's friends in the south with houses that he might choose to visit; more work for Lancelot.

Stanley, a Chatham loyalist and friend of David Garrick, was also 'Cofferer to the Household' or Treasurer, hence his place in the royal entourage. He was a grandson of the great Sir Hans Sloane, President of the Royal Society and owner of Chelsea Manor, and his aunt Elizabeth was married to Lord Cadogan, Lancelot's appreciative client at Caversham. Stanley was lively, a bachelor in his fifties, and gregarious, friendly with all Lancelot's Hampshire clients and others. His family home was at Paultons Park, about 6 miles south-west of Romsey; through the park flowed a beautiful stream, a tributary of the Blackwater and the Test, which rose on the heathery heights of the New Forest. Lancelot seems to have persuaded this stream into a U-shaped 'river-stile' lake around the house – which stood on a knoll – with a pretty white lattice bridge, for which he was paid £640 in all. His taste for these curving, if not semi-circular, lakes (as also at Fisherwick) and Chinese-style bridges and pavilions was seemingly softening. Stanley also owned South Stoneham near Southampton, whilst his friend John Fleming was at North Stoneham.*

Lancelot had worked around the fringes of the New Forest, and crossed its bleakest northern stretch of heathland on the road from Totton to Ringwood many times. He was paid £165 by Thomas Tancred at Cuffnells, outside Lyndhurst in 1780, but it is now difficult to see what was done; so it was at Cadland, where the Forest touched the shores of Southampton Water, that he really experienced the ancient forest. He was in awe of the abundant 'old timber' that made the New Forest 'the oldest new place' he knew in England. The forest oaks could be 500 years old, and certainly dated from the early sixteenth century; the oldest, usually pollards, could be 16–23 feet in girth at a man's breast-height. Huge silvery-skinned beeches were hardly younger.

Cadland was easily reached from Broadlands or his friends the Serles at Testwood, over Eling bridge and southwards through the park-like forest landscape at Dibden and Hythe, then it was a matter of 3 miles through sandy lanes to Mr Drummond's place. Lancelot's friend and executor John Drummond had died in 1774, and he was now working for his cousin, the Hon. Robert Drummond, who was coming up to fifty and a partner in the bank. Drummonds were thriving, 'enjoying the patronage of the Treasury and the contracts to pay the British troops fighting in America', arranged for them by Thomas Harley, who bolstered the bank with his own healthy deposit account of around £300,000. This was of course Thomas Harley of Berrington, so it comes as little surprise that Robert Drummond's house was the result of another masterly partnership in siting and building by Lancelot and Henry Holland. It was a pale house, as befitted its setting by the sea, built of bricks made at Exbury, the same as those used for Broadlands.†

Robert Drummond was a passionate fisherman, and in addition to his house by Southampton Water he built a fishing cottage facing the Solent shore a few miles to the south, at a place called Bournehill. The 'hill' was hardly more than a knoll but gave just enough elevation for the pretty octagonal cottage or picnic house to have fine views across to the Isle of Wight. Lancelot contrived both shelter and views

* All three places, Paultons and the Stonehams, had their real Brownian enchantments, though little is recognisable now. Paultons is a well-maintained, but greatly altered amusement park.
† The building of Berrington was delayed for some unclear reason, and so Cadland, was built first; Claremont, Cadland and Berrington were the triumph of the Holland/Brown oeuvre in understated elegance, but sadly Holland's Cadland house is no more, the site now covered by the Fawley Oil Refinery.

in his miniature park for Bournehill: the drive along the shoreline runs through belts of planting but these are judiciously broken to allow surprise views of the waves and gusts of salty air. The drive 'circles' the lawn in an irregular oval, with one large free-standing clump of trees, which undoubtedly utilised some of the ancient specimens. Lancelot noted in his accounts that the building of Cadland house and the fishing cottage amounted to £12,500, and that a balance for the outdoor work, presumably in both places, would be settled later. In July 1779 he was going through his account book, and promptly wrote to Robert Drummond, 'I find you added for my trouble on the Out of Doors work, two hundred pounds, which is more than I can possibly accept from you by one hundred pounds'. Accordingly he returned £100, a perfect example of his integrity, and much appreciated by most of his clients.

'Go you, and adorn England!'

This exhortation from Lord Chatham, and Lancelot's reply, 'Go you, and save her', are the much-quoted evidence of bystanders, illustrating their friendship. The exchanges took place variously on a stair at St James's or outside the Blue Anchor inn at Staines – this being plausible if Lord Chatham was returning from Burton Pynsent and Lancelot was on his way westwards, in the autumn of 1777. What is certain is that Lord Chatham was concentrating all his failing energies on saving England from herself, for it was his view that war with America would be like England falling upon her own sword.

Lancelot was playing the diplomat as he wrote to Hester Chatham in the second week of November, 'Today, and indeed many opportunities have occurred of late, in which I have had very favourable conversations' with the King; on an autumn afternoon at Kew he had met the King and dared to tread on tender ground:

> I then ventured to repeat [what Lady Chatham had already written to the King] that Lord Chatham was not changed in sentiment; that I was very sure what his Lordship had advanced was meant for the dignity of the crown, the happiness of his Majesty and the royal family, and the lustre of the whole empire; that I had always considered his Lordship in the light of being a friend to the whole, not parts of the empire; . . . because I knew, after forty years' experience, that no man loved his country more; indeed, nothing could be so strong a proof of it, as his Lordship standing alone, unconnected with party or faction.

The King, in sunny mood, heard him 'favorably' and responded, 'no acrimony, nor ill will appeared'. Hester Chatham replied, in a letter of 13th November, strong in ink, script and sentiment:

> It is impossible not to feel sensibly the Animation of your Conversations in support of the rectitude of my Lord's Principles, and of his Zeal for the Prosperity of the Whole Empire, and for the true, Solid Glory of His Majesty. You may be perswaded that your having been heard favourably and without Acrimony, affords real comfort and Happiness to my Lord, who is most undoubtedly actuated in all he does, or means to do, by the purest Motives of disinterested concern for the King, and the Country. You know that this is not Words, but an existing Truth, to which his conduct has been always consistent.

Meanwhile, in a field by the River Hudson on 19th September, General 'Gentleman Johnny' Burgoyne's troops were repulsed at Freeman's Farm; three weeks later they were checked at Bemis Heights and withdrew the 7 miles to Saratoga, where on the 17th October they were surrounded and forced to surrender. These were the 'three' battles of Saratoga, of which London remained in ignorance.

At home, Lady Chatham had told Lancelot:

> From the Stamp Act to this day, [my lord's] judgments, he says, concerning America, have never varied. In the present terrifying Crisis, to be silent the first day, wou'd be want of Duty to the King, and utter insensibility to the public Calamities. The Ardent Wish of my heart co-operates entirely with him, that the Past may be redeem'd by happier Councils! You join, I am sure, in the same honest hope.

On 20th November, Chatham told the House of Lords of 'a rugged and awful crisis' to come. News of the defeat at Saratoga arrived on the 5th December; Lord North tried to resign, but the King would not let him, and the government dissolved into factional dementure. Chatham persisted in his belief that the colonists did not really want independence, if only they were treated properly. He was proved right, in that now it was a very different war, against France in alliance with the colonists, supported by Spain: Chatham, his voice shrill with passion, reminded the House that the Spanish used bloodhounds to hunt the Native Americans and asked: are these 'hell-hounds' to be unleashed 'against our brethren and countrymen'? Once again, Lord Chatham was seen as the only possible saviour of the situation, and all through the dark months efforts were made to persuade him back into office. The road to Hayes was churned with coaches, including Lancelot's – Hester Chatham's words ringing in his ears: 'The sentiments of Esteem and Friendship which my Lord, and my self, have for you are of the most unfeyn'd sort, which I beg you to believe.' But he was on dangerous ground once more, for he went 'piping hot from Lord Bute' and the implication is that Bute was using Lancelot's loyalties to find favour – and office – with Chatham, who would have none of it.

Lancelot must have known and despaired of that fateful day, 7th April 1778, when Lord Chatham struggled to the House of Lords, on the arms of his son William and son-in-law Lord Mahon, to make his last plea against war with the colonists, saying that he would never consent 'to deprive the royal offspring of the House of Brunswick' of 'their fairest inheritance'. But if peace could not be made with France, then war it must be – 'and if we fall, let us fall like men'. When the Duke of Richmond rose to point out that even the name of Chatham could not bring victory against France, Spain and America 'without an army, without a navy and without money', Lord Chatham, incensed, rose – and collapsed into the arms of those around him. He was carried into the Prince's Chamber where he recovered, and two days later was well enough to be taken back to Hayes Place.

Perhaps thinking there was no more to be done, Lancelot was on the road once more. On 12th April he reached Compton Verney, where his new church had a strong resemblance to Henry Flitcroft's St Andrew's at Wimpole. He was much amused by the presence of an 'Old Woman', the daughter of a Staffordshire gentleman, who was staying in the house, and whose foibles he relayed to his daughter Peggy. Next day he reached Trentham, where he worked on plans for Lord Gower's new house with Henry Holland, and then they parted: Holland to Berrington, Lancelot back eastwards to Sandbeck in South Yorkshire, reached on 17th April and where he perhaps stayed for two days. At this point he is lost to us for a week, possibly at Byram near Castleford, or back at Temple Newsam, or at Harewood. Could he have been at Thoresby Hall? There are still many mysteries about the places where he worked. There is also a suggestion that he met Lance, who was looking for a parliamentary seat and was relying on his father's funding support. On the 25th he arrived at Brocklesby in north Lincolnshire, where he acquired plovers eggs, which were boiled and packed in bran and sent off to his daughter Bridget Holland, for 'she likes them, you know ones Children always likes what their Father likes'. He went into Boston and found the Wayet relations were all well, and presumably did not stay, for he made the short journey to the Rose &

Crown at Wisbech, from where he wrote to Peggy, glad 'that my Old Woman story was not unpleasing'. Peggy, aged nineteen, was confiding in her father about her friend Miss Secker's bid for her independent income and her parents' apparent refusal, to which Lancelot replied:

> I am sorry for Miss Secker and for the feeling of her Parents, but they are behaving properly. If you should turn Fool, which I think there is but little chance for, I believe I should do the same, with this precaution that I would take care that you should have the benefit of your Fortune your self, and not be a [beggar] in old age. Remember this is not Parental Pride, but it's Parental protection to a Daughter that I Love Dearly.

On 30th April he reached Kimberley in Norfolk, then came across to Hawnes in Bedfordshire, before spending a final night at Luton Hoo. Gossip greased his journeyings, especially the national speculation as to Lord Chatham's ability to save the hour, or not. Once back at Wilderness House, he wrote to Lady Chatham, 'I am just returned from a long northern expedition on which I have spent many anxious hours, on account of Lord Chatham's health, when however I had the comfort to find one universal Prayer, one wish that his Lordship's life may be preserved to save this Devoted Sinking Country, but alas, I am doubtful it is too far gone even for his Lordship to redeem us.' He asked her pardon for his passion – 'I feel too much for the situation' – and assured her of his being 'devoted in Heart and Wish'. The letter was dated 9th May. Lord Chatham died two days later.

The King's antagonisms and Cabinet controversies meant that the funeral was understated, if not meanly organised, except that for those in real grief these things would not have been noticed. The coffin lay in state in the Painted Chamber at Westminster and then, in pouring rain on the afternoon of Tuesday, 9th June, was taken the short distance across to Westminster Abbey. The crowd was huge and clamorous, but then the space for them to gather in was very small. The chief mourner, the tall slim figure walking behind the coffin, was nineteen-year-old William 'the Fourth', whom Lancelot had first known as a small boy at Hayes; Lancelot must have been reminded of the tall 'commanding' Mr Pitt , who talked a lot and loudly and expected to be listened to, whom he had first met all those years before, in the garden at Stowe.

To Grimsthorpe, Brocklesby and 'a Godforsaken place'

In the early August of 1778 came news of a tragedy at Grimsthorpe, of the drowning of Thomas Linley, the musical prodigy already spoken of as England's Mozart. Grimsthorpe was a musical house, and the Duke and Duchess of Ancaster had discovered Linley, aged seven, performing at Covent Garden. They had sent him to Florence to study the violin with Pietro Nardini, and there he met and became friends with Mozart – they were both fourteen. Returned to England, Linley was revealed as a prolific prodigy, composing oratorios, anthems, songs and scores – including the music for Sheridan's comic opera *The Duenna* (Linley's sister Elizabeth was to marry Sheridan) – and by his early twenties he seemed set fair to become – in Mozart's opinion – 'one of the greatest ornaments of the musical world'. However, on his annual visit to Grimsthrope that August, Linley and some friends set out for a sail on the lake, a squall blew up and capsized the boat; while the others clung to the rigging, Linley, in boots and greatcoat, jumped in to swim for help and sank after about 100 yards. No one could rescue him or, when rescued, revive him. The tragedy was widely reported; on 12th August, the day after Linley's funeral, the Duke himself died, aged sixty-five, his death, they said, hastened by the tragedy.

It was a cruel fate, and Lancelot was mortified. He had lost out to the Grundys at Grimsthorpe early in his career, it will be remembered, and only in the past six or seven years had he gone back, planning the planting around the castle, and for a causeway to carry the road between the two lakes. The work was being done by the Duke's own estate workers, and John Grundy's lake wasn't his responsibility, though he surely blamed himself for not checking the depth of the water and accumulation of mud for the dangers of which he was well aware. He called with his double condolences as he passed in late August, and then headed for the Pelhams' Brocklesby farther north in Lincolnshire, where he had been earlier in the year.

Apart from his regular visits during the 1770s, Brocklesby was familiar, forming a stately architectural trio with the Queen's House and Wotton Underwood. From a work point of view it was a moving target, Lancelot was never sure if he was working on the house or the grounds, and his coved-ceiling gallery, à la Stowe and Corsham, was 'a great deal of trouble', as he recorded in his account book. His plans for the park were ambitious: for a lake, seven-arched bridge, temples and an extensive ha-ha, an asymmetrical kitchen garden with melon ground and stoves, and a greenhouse facing onto a flower garden with bizarrely petal-shaped beds. The ruins of Newsome Abbey were to be brought into the views from the pleasure gardens. But Lancelot touched the heart of Brocklesby with his interest, on Peggy's behalf, in Sophia Pelham's fowls; she was the former Sophia Aufrere, whom Charles Pelham had met while she was travelling with her parents, marrying her in 1770 when she was seventeen and he was twenty. Sophia was painted by Reynolds feeding her chickens.

On 1st September (his letter to Biddy reporting 'a most shocking passage over the Humber') he arrived at Burton Constable. On their round, Steward Raines noted that 'Mr Brown's directions' included 'Make the lake 3½ or 4 feet deep at most – better so than deeper'.

Leaving Burton Constable, he turned west towards Beverley, across the flat wetlands – the carrs – of the River Hull valley, making for Great Driffield. Through the narrow streets of the little market town he continued north-westwards to Garton, and on top of Garton Hill turned sharply onto the Malton road. It is a surprising turn still, as if one has stepped onto the plane of some gigantic chequerboard, the regulation fields of gold, green or brown stretching out across the distances of the Wolds: in unpleasant weather it can seem 'a Godforsaken place'.

Lancelot must have questioned the prospect as he first saw it, a seeming wasteland of thin, stony soil, grass tracks and scrappy fields, given over mostly to sheep and huge rabbit warrens. As he progressed along the ridge (to the high point of some 500 feet above sea level, where Sir Tatton Sykes's 120-foot Gothic memorial now stands) the bareness softened into well-hedged fields, with young trees that thickened into belts and woods as he dropped down into the valley of Sledmere. He recognised an ancient countryside, strewn with the relics of peoples that passed long ago, the trackways, and the settlements of Kemp Howe and Cottam to the north and of Wharram Percy a few miles to the west.

His destination was Sledmere (sometimes spelt Sledmire), a church and a large mere ('Sledmere' meaning a pool in the valley), a small village and the Sykes's 'new house', which was about twenty years old. The house was cleverly sited north of the mere, looking across it towards the dramatic valley that would form a park. Sledmere exuded an empathetic air, for its late squire Richard Sykes, with his family's Hull-made fortune, had actually given his planting priority over his building: his consciousness that 'landscape' mattered dated from the time of William Kent's death in 1748, for Kent was a local Bridlington boy made good. As a kind of salutation, Sykes had attacked his treeless landscape, with the help of John Perfect, sometime twice-Mayor of Pontefract, doyen of five generations of famous nurserymen who had arisen from the fabled liquorice-growers of Pontefract. (Perfect had revealed the secret of liquorice-growing in a long letter, which Switzer published in *The Practical Husbandman* of 1733; he had supplied plants, but not liquorice, for Harewood, Studley Royal and Nostell Priory, and was happy at Sledmere, as Sykes recorded in

December 1749:'Mr Perfect likes this Air very well.') With Perfect, Richard Sykes had planted thousands of young trees, mainly beech, in a widely splayed 'avenue' southwards from the house, so enclosing a hundred acres of parkland. The mere, shaped into a regular oval, was the feature of a great lawn, protected from the farther parkland by a ha-ha wall 'with triangular, rectangular and semi-circular buttresses'. Richard Sykes and Perfect had established tree nurseries – 'my trees come forward and grow almost beyond all imaginary expectations and [give] great pleasure when I view them,' he recorded in his notebook – as well as a kitchen garden; and, using up old sash windows as frames, he grew and enjoyed 'upward of a hundred Pine Apples' and melons, and wall fruit, peaches, nectarines and plums.

All this Lancelot had learned on his first visit. Richard Sykes (a martyr to gout *and* a connoisseur of port) was long dead, and his heir was his brother, the Rev. Mark 'Parson' Sykes – not a gardener, for 'his primary interest was making money' and clerical politics. The Parson's son Christopher had married Elizabeth Tatton in 1770, a marriage of love and good fortune that was to ensure Sledmere's future: they lived in a house on the 5,000-acre estate, and Christopher Sykes, a keen, improving husbandman, had summoned Lancelot. 'The Great Brown came to Sledmere this morning early,' he had written in his notebook on 18th September 1777, and had stayed for most of the day. The year before, Thomas White had already submitted a 'General Plan for the Improvement of the Grounds at Sledmere', which proposed filling the mere, sweeping away Richard Sykes's young avenue and encasing the house in plantations, with vistas opened to three model farms built as eye-catchers, unifying beauty and usefulness. White had overstepped the mark, hence Lancelot's appearance, with his habitual reluctance to destroy good trees; and, as Christopher Sykes made clear, the mere was to remain a feature.

Lancelot's first visit had been a crash course in teaching Christopher Sykes a new understanding of his own home and land; they acknowledged that the sites of White's eye-catching farmhouses had been well chosen, but it was with Brownian verve that their attendant plantations were set streaming around the ridges of the new park, linking in with the splayed 'arms' of his uncle Richard's avenue to form spacious groves. Sykes's mind was now 'thoroughly concentrated on the great task ahead'.

The next week he started staking out his plantations, making notes on the 'small holes made in the turf . . . the holes are made in the autumn at three feet asunder, and eight or ten inches over, returning the soil into the hole at the time of making it with the turf downwards'. A month later he had several thousand holes prepared and was on the lookout for no fewer than '20,000 seedling Larches, 50,000 Scotch fir seedlings, 5,000 spruce [two years old], 10,000 one year old Spruce, 1500 Weymouth pine, 2,000 Silver fir, 10,000 Beech seedlings, 1,000 Sycamore and 10,000 seedlings of Birch'. Once they arrived, batches of seedlings were earthed into rows in the estate nurseries, until they found their proper places, sometimes several years later.

Now, for his second visit, Lancelot had been expected on 31st August, but arrived on 5th September, spending the day with Christopher Sykes riding over the estate, and dining at his house at Wetwang. Sykes had 'built fourteen dwelling houses with several Barns and Stables' that summer. These included the eye-catcher Castle Farm, a mile south-east of Sledmere House, designed by John Carr of York, and – proving himself an apt pupil – Sykes had designed the others himself: Life Hill to the south-west and Marramatte to the north-east; these were functional farm-houses, but with ornamented gable ends to fit them to the park scene. Lancelot's visit was essentially a fine-tuning exercise, for which he sent a revised plan. That autumn and winter, 1778–9, became 'a veritable orgy of planting', Sykes now 'dreaming of creating a Paradise amongst the bleak hills of the Wolds'. Lancelot had clearly not been a disappointment. Sykes later addressed the local agricultural society on his plantings: 'forty Wild Cherry, sixty Mountain Ash, 300 Yews, 358 Silver fir, 500 Weymouth pine, 600 Birch, 1,540 Oak, 6,400 Holly, 12,000 beech, 25,260 Spruce, 33,600 Ash, 42,122 Scotch fir and 54,430 Larch'. He was awarded the prize for the greatest quantity of larch planted: five guineas' worth of books of his own choosing.

The emphasis on the larch, with the Scotch fir and spruce, indicates the influence of Thomas White, who had become enthused about the challenge of commercial forestry, meaning the planting of softwoods to secure future supplies of pit props for the collieries of Yorkshire and Nottinghamshire. The Society of Arts 'logging' scheme, which Lancelot had rejected as of no interest to himself or his landowners, was now in widespread operation, with medals being awarded for the greatest numbers planted. White's career seems to have turned in this direction, for he was conifer consultant to a group of Midlands estates, and won eleven of the Society's medals for his plantings (though three of these were for hard-woods). The commercial-forestry 'bug' did not seem to attack Lancelot, and everywhere he remained true to the planting of mixed hardwoods, though he happily used larch as a 'nurse' tree, and spruce – as well as yews and hollies – for the dark understorey. The planting of oaks, for the future of the navy, was still a patriotic duty and was widely pursued. The native Scots pine (*Pinus sylvestris*), with its beauties of bark and outline, and lingering Stuart symbolism, was a favourite second only to the cedar of Lebanon. In the one known instance of planting on his own account, on the stream-fringed green at Hilton in his Fenstanton manor, Lancelot ordered '160 Elms at 6d each' from James Wood's nursery in Huntingdon.

'Wonders on a plain surface'

Cambridge, as Lancelot knew it, was a Gothic place, a town of crumbling medieval houses and unlit and unpaved muddy lanes, starkly contrasted with the colleges – walled as castles of privilege, their courts haunted by flocks of Fellows in their fluttering, raven-black gowns. Student numbers were low and academic standards even lower, and there was plenty of the licentiousness that the satirists came to love; but it has recently been shown that there were also rumblings of an innovatory kind, and though marked as 'minor' subjects, botany, geology and astronomy were paving the way for the later triumph of the natural sciences. The Duke of Grafton became Chancellor in 1768 and immediately offered £500 towards paving the streets, but being Cambridge, nothing could be done without reference to the House of Commons, or without appointing a committee of seventy worthies to see this through, and the paving and lighting took twenty years.

As things moved slowly, so memories lingered, and there was a corpus of appreciation for the old college gardens and gardening, which owed much to the Rev. Richard 'Frog' Walker, who had died in 1764, was a favourite memory as a fixture at Trinity College since Queen Anne's time, 'devoted to horticulture' and friend of Philip Miller, the long-serving Curator of Chelsea Physic Garden. Miller's son Charles was appointed to be the first Curator of the Cambridge Botanic Garden, founded on 5 acres in Free School Lane, the property bought by 'Frog' Walker. Walker had cultivated exotic pineapples, coffee, cereus and jasmines in his greenhouse and stoves, in the garden that had formerly been Sir Isaac Newton's, beside the Great Gate at Trinity. He had lived long enough to take part in the decision by Trinity to build a new bridge over the Cam, completed in 1765 to the design of James Essex (who was paid £50), whom Lancelot encountered at Wimpole. The bridge was part of a slow improvement spreading along the back entrances of the line of colleges: St John's, Trinity, Clare, King's and Queens' – all had gradually established their claim to territories on the west side of the Cam, their back entrances, hence known as 'the Backs'. Clearing and turfing of these 'pieces' of flood-plain land was carried out during the 1760s and early 1770s; it must be realised that this was more a competitive exercise than a co-operative one, with each college jealously guarding its independence.

In 1769 St John's college employed a surveyor to enclose its lands, the business being in the hands of the newly admitted Senior Bursar, Professor John Mainwaring. Lancelot's name appears in a College Order of 10th July 1772, when it was agreed that he should supervise the repair of the river bank. He had, of course, been prominent as High Sheriff in Cambridge just over two years earlier, his name was known even amongst the closeted dons, and Professor Mainwaring knew Lancelot was working for his fellow Salopian, Lord Clive. Six months later Lancelot was asked to do more and provide a scheme for the St John's college gardens, in conjunction with the facing of the First Court in stone, under the supervision of James Essex. Lancelot estimated £800 for his works, and with these two expensive undertakings, 'and no very great funds to support them' in view, the Master William Powell proposed opening a subscription appeal, to which he contributed £500. Lancelot's accounts have nothing concerning St John's, nor do the college records show anything amounting to £800, only that £44 was spent on trees in 1776–8 and £62 paid to a gardener and a 'workman'. By a College Order of March 1778 it was 'agreed that a piece of plate of the value of £50 be presented to Mr Brown for his services in improving the walks'. It seems that his intentions for St John's sank beneath his illness, which lost him the first half of 1773; when he tried to catch up he paid a visit, staking out the walks and plantations, which 'transformed an entirely formal fellows' garden' of the seventeenth century 'into a more natural one, along the lines of the present lawn and wilderness', as Dr Boys Smith concluded in his history of the college grounds. Knowing this was a far more cursory task than he intended, Lancelot would have waived his fee, protesting that it was his honour to have been of service. The silver cup actually cost £52. The St John's Wilderness, Brownian in character, remains enchanting.

The university, undoubtedly prompted by the Duke of Grafton, gave Lancelot a further commission for 'Some Alterations' in 1779. The resulting plan in the university library is now a dullish document (for long years it hung in the entrance to the old university library), buffed and grey with age, water-damaged at the lower right colophon corner. It shows the extent of the Backs from St John's Wilderness to Queens' college and Silver Street bridge. The formal courts are shadowy green shapes; Trinity's pride, its avenue of limes, is broken and thinned to a casual sprinkling of trees; the causeways built by Trinity, Clare and King's are private, gravelled walks, all formality discouraged and status transferred to the main 'drive', the public right of way along Garret Hostel Lane. The whole sweep of land is divided into four large paddocks, 'lawns to be fed with sheep and cattle', all sheltered from the west by a thick belt of trees. In Lancelot's hands the Backs had become a linear park. He also suggested shifting the river's course westwards outside Trinity college to lessen the sharpness of the bend at St John's, something that Sir Christopher Wren had suggested for improving the view of his Trinity library from his St John's bridge, and vice versa.

The only trouble – and the downfall of Lancelot's dreaming design, and his ability to 'do wonders on a plain surface' as they expected – was that in visualising the Backs as a serene and serpentine park, he had imagined King's Fellows' building, by his old friend Jemmy Gibbs, as the 'mansion' to which the park design made obeisance, thus relegating Trinity college to the stable block and Clare to the offices. There was a furore, with mutterings and oathings, and the design was rejected. Lancelot had been inadequately briefed, for he had completely underestimated the prides – the overweening prides – of the individual colleges and their determined independence. By way of apology the university presented him with a silver tray, embossed with its coat of arms. But there were those who regretted the loss of the 'general satisfaction and delight' of his scheme, for 'the eye would certainly have been pleased with walks more winding, with a greater variety of trees, with something more of a winter garden of ever-greens, and of light underwood near the banks of the river'.

Lancelot's commission for the Backs originated in 1770, the year of a disastrous flood in Cambridge and neighbouring counties. Thomas Gray was still at Pembroke college, where the Fellows burying their nonagenarian master, Dr Long, realised to their horror that he was being lowered into a watery grave. Gray and William Mason perhaps proposed Lancelot's skills at drainage as the solution to the Cam's habitual cascading into college cellars. In retrospect, the plan for 'Some Alterations' was not entirely wasted, the Brownian messages being subliminally absorbed by those who passed it in the old library lobby: in the nineteenth century when the Queen's Road was made (named for Queen Victoria), the Backs gained a western boundary and, with much reallotment of lands, the college territories expanded westwards again, into the next block between Queen's Road and Grange Road. The green 'pieces' alongside the Cam, too flood-meadowlike for development, were used for exercise and then, as organised sports took over, they were softened into lawns and paddocks – these for the ageless brown cows that seem to shuffle there eternally. In the 1970s, when the dominant Cambridge elms succumbed to Dutch elm disease, the estates Bursar of King's college, B. R. Arkwright, proposed a joint and long-term approach to the management and planting of the Backs, a combined approach that still survives. The Backs are now a World Heritage Site; though the back drives to Trinity, Clare and King's colleges are as straight as ever, there is a Brownian softening, which provides the setting for the architectural fireworks of the buildings.

It is unlikely that Lancelot was worried by his difficulties in Cambridge. He hurried westwards to Wimpole, where there was much to detain him, for he had been involved with Wrest and Wimpole – combined in the lively presence of the Marchioness Grey – for a decade, and there was clearing up to be done.

It was about 10 miles from Cambridge to Wimpole as the crow flew, but longer if the coach became entangled in the lanes around Haslingfield and Barrington, for this was not a country of direct roads. Wimpole was easily reached from London, or from the north, as it was right on Ermine Street, a few miles beyond Royston, or 15 miles south of Huntingdon – and a perfect example of how travel was stuck in a north–south, Roman rut, but it was so difficult going across the grain from east to west. Once reached, Wimpole seemed the abode of some benevolent giant, an agricultural giant who loved husbandry and blessed his fields with sleek, fat cattle and monstrous woolly sheep. It had been a Harley house, owned by Edward, 2nd Earl of Oxford, before Lord Chancellor Hardwicke bought it in 1740; the combined efforts of ambitious owners had resulted in the red-brick hulk of a house, settled into the centre of a huge park.

At Wimpole, Lancelot had inherited Charles Bridgeman's array of avenues and vistas, which seemed to stretch from horizon to horizon. Fortunately, Bridgeman's schemes had ceased to the north of the house, where a chalk escarpment, 250 feet high, made a dramatic effect. At the foot of the scarp, where it met the gault clay, was a line of springs that fed the Halden stream, a tributary of the Rhee and eventually the Cam. This was the 'enchanted ground' where the Marchioness had 'danced' with Lancelot, as they explored its possibilities on his visit in September 1767. Now the works were almost complete, with upper and lower lakes made along the course of the stream (where wet woods had existed) and the controlling sluices between them hidden by a seven-arched bridge. The sense of enclosure on the north had been created with The Belts, a series of wide plantations sheltering a serpentine drive. All that remained was the finishing of the round-towered Gothic castle that Sanderson Miller had sketched more than twenty years earlier as an eye-catcher for this north part of the park. This began as the 'Semblance of an old Castle', a ruin in the view, but Lord Hardwicke had changed his mind and asked

James Essex to adjust the design to make it habitable. Lancelot was left with the construction, necessarily more robust, and watertight, and the Marchioness Jemima was disappointed, complaining that 'Mr Brown has quite changed from our plan'. She added, 'that is, he had "Unpicturesqued" it by making it a continuous solid object, instead of a broken one'.

The Marchioness Grey had by no means relinquished control of her own Wrest Park, where her eldest daughter, Lady Amabel, lived with her husband Lord Polwarth. Jemima and Amabel both seemed amused and usually delighted at Lancelot's visits; after his sudden appearance at Wrest in November of 1778, described by Lady Amabel as the visit of 'a great Man', which 'as happens sometimes with great Men' ended in very little, and lunch, Lancelot was left conversing with Lord Polwarth. His lordship, rather sickly and ineffectual, happier hunting hares and planting his own trees, thought Lancelot 'a very odd mortal, but entertaining for a little while'. They might have talked of Southill, the Bedfordshire estate a few miles north of Wrest, where Lancelot worked briefly in 1777 for George Byng, Lord Torrington. Torrington's finances were very bad, he was shortly declared bankrupt and Lord Polwarth was renting Southill for £100 a year. Soon plants were in transit from Southill to Wrest (they were paid for), perhaps the very ones that Lancelot had originally planted. Lord Polwarth died in 1781, and Southill was eventually bought by the brewer Samuel Whitbread, in 1795, who employed Henry Holland to work on his house.

A last word on Wrest: all through that lunch, as Lady Amabel tried to tease Lancelot into activity, he made some interesting protestations. He could not be persuaded to make any sketch, 'a Pencil & Paper he thought would do more Harm than Good, the Trees should be mark'd upon the Spot', he favoured letting in the south-west sun, and even a view of the Old Park, and also felling 'the high Trees' near the house, to let in 'a free-er Current of Air to the old part of the House'. Detailed considerations such as these are always lost in the passing of the years, and with overlays from clumsy hands, but it is well to observe Lancelot's fine sense of when to act and when to stay the axe.

THE OMNIPOTENT
MAGICIAN

Lo! He comes,
The omnipotent magician, Brown appears.
. . . He speaks. The lake in front becomes a lawn,
Woods vanish, hills subside, and valleys rise,
And streams, as if created for his use,
Pursue the track of his directing wand.

William Cowper, *The Task*, Book III, 1785

LANCELOT WAS NOW WELL INTO his sixties (his sixtieth birthday had been in the summer of 1776) and there was no sign of him slowing down. His world was a duller place without Lord Chatham, and also David Garrick, who died in January 1779. Garrick was buried on 1st February, in Westminster Abbey and with great splendour; most of the noble pall-bearers were Lancelot's clients. He had been working for one of them, Lord Palmerston at Broadlands, for thirteen and a half years, and the summer was to see the clearing up; 1779 also saw a settling of the account at Burghley, where he had been working since 1754. With two such momentous jobs withdrawn from his schedule, he might at least have taken a holiday, but on the contrary, he was driving farther and faster. He seemed to relish new opportunities in areas of the country that were quite fresh to him; his affection for the sporting estate was as strong as ever, but he also ventured to the wilder shores of romantic settings that others called the 'picturesque'.

There was rejoicing at Wilderness House in the autumn of 1779 with the safe return of Captain Jack Brown from active service in the coastal waters off New England. The war had moved to the south, where General Cornwallis was still optimistic of victory. Not so the British admirals, for Lord Howe had come home, saying that it was impossible to hold on to the American colonies, and the enthusiasm for trying was rapidly

My Dear Peggy

Annexed to this you have a draft
for Mr Close for the payment of his mare
which you will give him as soon as you
receive this. If Jack is with you tell him
Lord Palmerston & my self were ten hours
between London and this Place I believe where we
stoped to Dine, it mite take three Quarters of an
hour. We came all the Way as hard as four
horses could lay feet to the ground, a Servant
Went on before to order Horses, and is comparing
the goodness of the Road not one third of the
way between London & Exeter, I will give
up the Sea to him, but the Land he had
best leave to me; It will not be very long before

he will be convinced how wrong he was, and how
improper his behavour was when, he maintained
an impossibility, My Love to him & those
that are with you I remain my Dear
Child your Affectionate
                              Father L. Brown

Broad Lands

My Dear Peggy
Annexed to this you have a draft
for Mr Cloase for the payment of his men
which you will give him as soon as you
receive this. If Jack is with you tell him
Lord Palmerston & myself were ten hours
between London and this Place – I believe where we
stop[p]ed to Dine, it mite [sic] take three Quarters of an
hour. We came all the way as hard as four
horses could lay feet to the ground, a Servant
went on before to order Horses, and is comparing
the goodness of the Road not one third of that
way between London & Exeter, I will give
up the Sea to him, but the Land he had
best leave to me.
  It will not be very long before
he will be convinced how wrong he was, and how
improper his behaviour was when he maintain'd
an impossibility. My Love to him & those
that are with you, I remain my Dear
Child your affectionate
Father
L. Brown.

Lancelot's letter, in full opposite, is transcribed above; the letter is undated but was written in the autumn of 1779 from Broadlands at Romsby in Hampshire.

receding. Jack could have come home with Admiral Howe, for his service at sea for more than seven years had merited his captaincy – listed in *The Commissioned Sea Officers of the Royal Navy* on 25th March 1779 (but there is no subsequent record of his name being attached to any ship, though he steadily rose in rank).

The advent of Jack, well built, weatherbeaten and twenty-eight years old, who had raced up from Devon upon landing, was wonderful – at least at first. But father and son had been apart for so long they had forgotten how to behave, and they were both considerably changed and both used to giving orders. Differences of opinion were inevitable, especially on the eternal subject of how fast a journey could be made. Lancelot wrote from Broadlands at Romsey in early November, to Peggy, 'If Jack is with you tell him Lord Palmerston & myself were ten hours between London and this Place.' They had taken three-quarters of an hour for a meal, otherwise 'we came all the way as hard as four horses could lay feet to the ground', with a servant sent forward to arrange the changes of horses. Had Jack challenged his father on his slowness, using colourful ship's language, for Lancelot was undoubtedly hurt: 'It will not be very long before he will be convinced how wrong he was, and how improper his behaviour was when he maintain'd an impossibility. My Love to him and those that are with you.' But Lancelot's love was preceded by his thunderous phrase, 'I will give up the Sea to him, but the Land he had best leave to me.'

His outburst left Lancelot mellowed, and at Broadlands he was docility personified, bringing a 'very sober and very honest', though 'old man' from another job, to finish the levelling of the hedges. Lord Palmerston had paid £21,150 for his new house and grounds, at least three-quarters of this amount for Henry Holland's building and decorating. In closing the account, Lancelot wrote on 17th November:

> There Remains due to workmen & myself under five hundred pounds which shall be delivered to your Lordship with the Papers and Accounts when your Lordship comes to Town and [I] shall then with an unfeigned Heart return your Lordship my Thanks for numberless Civilities, kind usage and pleasant imployment.

As a work of the Brown and Holland partnership, Broadlands had not the same restrained elegance of composition as the trio of Claremont, Cadland and Berrington, but it sat (and sits) splendidly enough (perhaps more of a stately matron as opposed to three exquisite brides) on its lawns beside the River Test.

At Burghley, Lord Exeter had paid over a total of £8,122. 16s. 3d. to Lancelot since 1769, as in the account book (though there were the lost amounts for 1754–68). Lancelot saw his lake was almost filled, and promised that he would submit plans for the new entrance hall and staircase at the south-east corner of the house, which would lead directly up to the first-floor sequence of painted George Rooms. The promise slipped his memory for his plans were not sent for two years, by which time Lord Exeter had made other arrangements; on the other hand, Lancelot's design for the Gothic banqueting house was not implemented until 1787, when it was built by the Stamford masons John and Robert Hames. Lord Exeter, outwardly still the cheerful potentate, had private worries in that the glamorous marriage between his heir, Henry Cecil, and Emma Vernon has disintegrated and was to end in divorce. (Henry Cecil retreated into the Shropshire countryside, calling himself John Jones, where he fell in love and married a country girl, Sally Hoggins. On Lord Exeter's death in 1793, 'John Jones' disappeared and Henry Cecil returned to Burghley, with Sally becoming known as 'the cottage countess'.

Harewood 'diligently overseen'

Lancelot's coach seemed to be on the Great North Road more frequently than ever. Having left Burghley, there was still activity at Harewood, to the north of Leeds. Lancelot had known Harewood, then called Gawthorpe, some twenty years earlier when Edwin Lascelles had rejected William Chambers's designs for his new house, briefly considering Lancelot's ideas, before settling on John Carr of York. Carr had been pushed aside when the charming Robert Adam came to restore the church, but Carr and Adam had 'boxed and coxed' over the house (the interiors remain some of Adam's most beautiful) and the gardener, Mr Sparrow, had started to naturalise the setting by damming a tributary of the River Wharfe to make a lake. Edwin Lascelles's second wife, the former Jane Colman (widow of Sir John Fleming, who insisted on being called Lady Fleming), was keenly interested in both interiors and gardens, so Lancelot returned in 1774 to enlarge and reshape the lake, add an island and do a great deal of planting. It was not always smooth running, Lascelles having refused to make a payment in 1778 because, as he wrote on 28th March, 'I have always said and did insist upon it that the ground was Scandalous Lay'd, and beggarly sown, and that several other parts were slovenly run over and badly finish'd, particularly by the Island.' Lancelot quickly repaired the damage to the grounds and his client's temper – the importance of the work can be judged by the size of the bill, over £6,000, finally settled in 1781.

While Lancelot was at Harewood he heard all about the wedding of Lady Fleming's elder daughter, seventeen-year-old Seymour Dorothy Fleming, married in 1775 to Sir Richard Worsley. This sent him, a few years later, journeying to the Isle of Wight, to the Worsleys' house, Appuldurcombe, set in an arcadian landscape on the south of the island near Ventnor. It was a single visit, charged at £52. 10s., and one of those instances of Lancelot's famed speedy assessment of the place, which left Sir Richard with the blueprint for a sweeping drive and the sites for his eye-catching monuments. By judiciously cutting back the surrounding woods, leaving clumps that either stopped or channelled the views, there was the illusion of magic, or at least sleight of hand. Sir Richard was an apt pupil, and was deeply interested in his home landscape and its historical connections – he was at the time compiling a pioneering topographical history of the island, which was published in 1781. However, his marriage ended in a sensational divorce the following year, and Sir Richard left on an extended expedition to the Mediterranean and farther east, buying up antiquities, paintings and jewels, which were found in Appuldurcombe House when he died in 1805. His heiress was Henrietta Pelham at (Lancelot's) Brocklesby, whose husband became the 1st Earl of Yarborough, a keen yachtsman and member of the Royal Yacht Squadron at Cowes. Appuldurcombe was used for sailing holidays until his death in 1846, after which it was sold, left uninhabited in the early twentieth century and eventually in ruins. It now belongs to English Heritage, and the tantalising ghost of Lancelot's landscape may still be seen.

At Harewood – where Reynolds's portrait of Lady Worsley, wearing the red riding-dress uniform of the Hampshire Militia, still hangs – the outcome could not have been more different. Lancelot's park has been 'diligently overseen' by generations of the Lascelles family, and it must rank as Lancelot's most painted park, apart from Petworth. The planting he did in the 1770s was sufficiently mature to show effectively when Girtin and Turner, friends who travelled and painted together, arrived in 1797. Thomas Girtin's *Harewood House from the South-east,* a large canvas view looking to the sunset – the house lit on its distant hill, the light catching the lake's surface, the dark massings of trees filling the vales, the clouds rolling across the crags and Wharefedale fading into the distance – illustrates J. M. W. Turner's remark, 'If Tom Girtin had lived, I should have starved.' Turner, taking the same view, stood back to include some deer and a group of spindly trees in the foreground. Thomas Malton and John Varley, as well as the Lascelles ladies, also painted the park; most endearing of all, George Richmond, who arrived in September 1855 to paint a portrait of Louisa, Lady Harewood, had 'a sudden re-action to Capability Brown's wonderful vista' and 'dashed down' the view from his bedroom 'while he was changing for dinner'. Richmond's view looks into the Turner and Girtin views, and the trees – like threading, interlocking, fingers of dark green – take their places below the sunlit heights. As all these paintings tell the same story, they must be telling of Lancelot's landscape rather than of their own painterly visions.

'With Poet's feeling and with Painter's eye'

Somewhat as a surprise, this phrase leaps out of the contract for work at Sandbeck Hall, on the border between Nottinghamshire and South Yorkshire, home (at least his second home, after Lumley Castle in Durham) of Richard Lumley, 4th Earl of Scarbrough, a member of the royal

household and deputy Earl Marshal of England. The first four articles of
the contract are conventional enough: to make a 'proper drain' at the
foot of the ha-ha wall (as at Burghley); to demolish all the old ponds (as
at Charlecote and Chatsworth as well as Burghley); draining, levelling
and planting the ground; and making good a pond for the use of the
stables.

> Those magic seeds of Fancy, which produce
> A Poet's feeling, and a Painter's eye

is a quotation from William Mason's epic poem *The English Garden*,
published in parts through the 1770s, which Lancelot surely perused,
though he would have needed unbounded leisure and patience to *read
through it*. The fifth and final article of his Sandbeck contract reads:

> To finish all the Valley of Roach Abbey in all its Parts, according to the
> Ideas fixed on with Lord Scarbrough (with Poet's feeling and with Painter's
> eye) beginning at the Head of the Hammer Pond, and continuing up the
> Valley towards [Laughton en le Morthen] as far as Lord Scarbrough's
> Ground goes, and to continue the Water and Dress the Valley up by the
> Present Farm House until it comes to the separation fixed for the Boundary
> of the New Farm. N.B. The Paths in the Wood are included in this
> Description and every thing but the Buildings.

Perhaps it was Lord Scarbrough who had read his Mason and realised
that he owned the ruins of the Cistercian abbey of Roche at the end
of his park, and that the ruin could be adapted as a fashionable feature.
Or did Lancelot persuade him? The contract was written in 1774, to be
completed in 1777: Lancelot was fresh from Wimpole, where great efforts
were being made to build Sanderson Miller's 'ruined' tower; in fact he
had been all too conscious of the value put on his friend's 'ruins' for all
of his career. The recognition of Roche Abbey seemed nothing new,
except for the context of the times – of a growing popularity for the
mysterious and faintly horrific as elements of picturesque beauty. Roche
seems to place Lancelot on the brink of the 'new' fashion: the 'roche' of
Roche (like the 'mont' of Claremont) being the outcrop, in this case of
magnesian limestone, that adds drama to the site. William Aislabie's Studley
Royal and Fountains Abbey (and rugged, rocky Hackfall) had been
recently discovered by tourists and were becoming all the rage. The Rev.
William Gilpin's *Essay on Prints* had been published in 1768, and was
much talked of, wherein he defined the 'picturesque' as 'that kind of

beauty which is agreeable in a picture' (though the word did not acquire a capital P for several years yet). Gilpin had taken his *Tour* to the Wye valley and south Wales, sketching and painting the ruined castles, and rocky outcrops cradled in ferns and the dark waters, in 1770. His views were hand-copied (the aquatints not published until 1782) and had a limited circulation, sending the painters and poets who saw them scuttling to gaze on Tintern Abbey and gasp at Coldwell Rocks: it seems likely that Lord Scarbrough – and possibly also Lancelot – had seen the King's copy.

At Sandbeck the achievement was in the spectacular contrast. James Paine's imposing block of a mansion gazed out upon rolling parkland, grazed by particularly fat and contented-looking deer, cattle and sheep. The open park was surrounded by trees – not merely trees, but those lush green cloudscapes of trees that are the legacy of Sherwood Forest to Nottinghamshire and of the 'Dukeries' a little to the south of Sandbeck. From such sybaritic comforts the visitors could walk or drive – it was a good 2 miles – through the woodland paths to the tree-shaded and ivy-draped ruins in their narrow sequestered vale. The steep-sided valley that Lancelot dressed extended for about another 2 miles to the southwest, the paths keeping company with the stream that the monks had harnessed for their fishponds, until the tired 'pilgrims' – 'we picturesque people', as Gilpin dubbed those who shared his tastes – reached the comforts of Laughton, and the waiting carriages. Even Gilpin admitted that Lancelot had done well, writing in his *Observations relating chiefly to Picturesque Beauty* of 1776, 'he has finished one of the valleys which looks towards Laughton spire, he has floated it with a lake and formed a very beautiful scene. But I fear it is too magnificent and too artificial an appendage to be in unison with the ruins of an abbey.' As the beauty of Cistercian sites is invariably that they are by water (naturally a practical priority), this was a fatuous remark; what he really objected to, it transpired, was that Laughton Pond, where it had been enlarged by Lancelot, showed spade-marks and bare edges, whereas a few osiers and bushes would make it suitable in time.*

Gilpin may have been codifying the Picturesque in the late 1770s, but the taste had been growing for fifty years. Lancelot was no novice, for he had worked through much of what Christopher Woodward has so nicely called 'the springtime of the Picturesque', meaning the first half

---

* Sandbeck Hall and Roche Abbey have been rent asunder by subsequent history, especially mine-workings, and the effective contrasts are now impossible to gauge. The once 'dressed valley' is virtually derelict, and the abbey, now managed by English Heritage, is rather too tidy for romantic effect; the archaeologists, with their changed priorities, now curse Lancelot for dismantling the cloister and levelling part of the footprint of the building in the Picturesque cause.

of the eighteenth century. 'It was as if the corpses of the abbeys and castles,' writes Woodward in *In Ruins*, 'had been given a second life by artists and "men of feeling".' John Aislabie had annexed Fountains Abbey into Studley Royal, and the terrace at Duncombe Park was built in 1758 to allow the ruins of Rievaulx into the views. Lancelot had said that he admired Sanderson Miller's passion for building Gothic ruins, his own Edge Hill and his designs for Hagley and Wimpole, but one wonders whether he ever took his eccentric mentor quite seriously. Lancelot had also seen plenty of examples of William Kent's rusticated exedras and rock-works, firstly in the Elysian Fields at Stowe, but he found these too fanciful for emulation; Brownian rocky cascades owe more to his native Northumberland's tumbling rivers. Horace Walpole's Gothic extravaganza at Strawberry Hill at Twickenham, which he began in the late 1740s, did not apparently attract Lancelot's attention. On the other hand, James Gibbs's Gothic Temple at Stowe (every detail of its construction noted by Lancelot) remained as an iconic image in his memory, inspiring his love of castellated effects, used at Blenheim and Burghley, and wherever else he thought the Gothic style fitted. The Picturesque – 'as agreeable in a picture', as Gilpin defined it – the lessons of Claude's dispositions of his buildings and groupings of trees had been frequently discussed ever since the time Lancelot was carving out the Grecian Valley at Stowe.

As for the Rev. William Gilpin, he was a familiar figure too: Gilpin had been a curate of some twenty-three summers when he visited Buckingham to preach, and so 'discovered' Stowe, when Lancelot was head gardener. Gilpin's *Dialogue upon the Gardens*, published in 1748, had been the beginning of his 'picturesque' career, though he did not actually use the word for another twenty years, until his *Essay on Prints*. Gilpin's real career was schoolmastering, and he and his wife Margaret were deeply committed to the care and education of the boys of Cheam School (where corporal punishment was rare, but justice, morality and gardening were the order of the days), until they handed over to their son, in 1777. The Gilpins were now installed at Boldre vicarage in the New Forest (in the presentation of Cheam old boys, the Mitfords of Exbury), which is how Gilpin managed to ride over to Cadland while Lancelot was working there. Boldre was a poor and scattered parish needing much attention, which Gilpin put to use in conjuring up his *Remarks on Forest Scenery and Other Woodland Views (1791)* from his daily journeyings.

A 'tour' to the Wye valley and Wales

Lancelot's journeys of the late 1770s and early 1780s to distant places are poorly documented, for there are no surviving letters home to Biddy describing his night stops or the people he met, and so it is a matter of moving from the known into the unknown. From Berrington Hall and Leominster, he would drive into the south-western view, to Weobley, to find a crossing of the River Wye at Bredwardine or Monnington, and so to Moccas, beside the meanders of the Middle Wye.

At Moccas, Robert Adam was building a red-brick, urban-looking villa on a knoll above the Wye, but the house fails – or at least it does now – in an imaginative relationship to the magnificent river cliff on the opposite bank. It was an ill omen, an early example of the landscape advice coming too late, and Lancelot must have quietly cursed that he was not summoned early enough to do better with the possibilities of the park; the ancient little church, built in the days when people under-stood their native grounds, sat so prettily on its neighbouring hill. Should he have been warned, and walked away? Having come so far, and to this divinely beautiful place, he persevered.

Moccas was an estate of almost 4,000 acres, 'densely inscribed with old features', a baronial deer park with huge pollarded oaks, an ancient British burial ground, the ruins of two castles and a scattering of old buildings, all seemingly made for picnic places, lovers' trysts and eye-catchers. It was so historic and ripe for the picturesque, but as yet this landowner, even on the hallowed Wye, was unconvinced. Sir George Cornewall was a new-come owner, who had acquired his estate and name with his heiress wife, Catherine Cornewall: he seemed torn between being fashionable and his desire to impress his neighbours with his agri-cultural improvements; he was also borrowing to finance his determined expansion of his holdings, which were eventually almost 7,000 acres. John Lambe Davis had surveyed Moccas in 1772, and Lancelot based his proposals of 1778 on this survey. It was a consultant's plan, for which he was paid a neat £100, and Sir George intended to use it as the framework for his developments, or not use it, or modify it, as he pleased. Lancelot had tried for sympathetic guidance. His plan focused on the drive coming from the west at Dorstone and crossing the park, passing the Lawn Pool, which sat within a huge meander of the river, before reaching the house. The present-day surveyor and expert on Brown parks, John Phibbs, suggests that 'the visitor was presumably expected to stop the carriage, and even to walk to a particular viewing station' – Lancelot's purpose being to give pleasurable amusement, but also orien-tation, a sense of unity between resident or visitor with at least part of this complex landscape. But even Phibbs's practised eye admits that 'traces of such walks are seldom found today' at Moccas. Sir George, in confusing Lancelot's careful allotment of pasture or arable, and in juggling field boundaries rather than removing them, negated his £100 worth of advice.

Sir George called in Humphry Repton in the 1790s, but treated him much the same. His neighbours, Uvedale Price from Foxley and Richard Payne Knight from Downton Vale, the loud and controversial doyens of the Picturesque, naturally arrived at Moccas, but also made little effect. Huge amounts of timber were sold from the park and estate – reputedly to the value of £20,000–30,000 before Sir George died in 1819, but the estate forester, Mr Webster, had also planted thousands of young oaks. Moccas became a famous landscape in the nineteenth century, distinguished by the attentions of the pioneering Woolhope Field Club, and by the Rev. Francis Kilvert in his *Diary*: his entry for 22nd April 1876 read, 'I fear those grey old men of Moccas, those grey, gnarled, low-browed . . . misshapen oak men that stand waiting and watching century after century . . . "the trees which the Lord hath planted". They look as if they had been at the beginning and making of the world, and they will probably see its end.' Today, Moccas is a National Nature Reserve. It is only a pity that the legacy of Lancelot Brown, who was constitutionally incapable of destroying a rich habitat, unless he replaced it with a richer one, is not more appreciated.

Lancelot fared better at Dinefwr (Newton House or Dynevor), deep in Carmarthenshire, just outside Llandeilo, in a brief commission carried out for the politician George Rice just prior to his death in 1779. The twelfth-century Dinefwr Castle, steeped in the history of Wales, was already a feature of the park for the seventeenth-century Newton House, the home of the Rice family and ornamental in itself. Lancelot sent plans for an entrance drive and a kitchen garden. The park retains his beech clumps, and the walk to the castle is known as Brown's Walk. It is now owned by the National Trust.

Sir Watkin Williams-Wynn, 4th Baronet, of Wynnstay was a well-known Grand Tourist, patron of Batoni and dapper man about town, for whom Robert Adam built no. 20 St James's Square, and whom Lancelot had surely known of for years, for he frequented Burghley, Castle Ashby and Charlecote amongst many other houses. In 1771, when he was twenty-three, he married, as his second wife, George Grenville's daughter Charlotte, and so it was quite natural that he should commission Lancelot to work at Wynnstay, his home just south of Ruabon, where the park was crossed by the deep and rocky course of the River Belan, before it joined the Dee in the Vale of Llangollen. Lancelot made five journeys to distant Flintshire, with pitiably little result as Sir Watkin was rather volatile in his passions and finances. Loyal John Midgeley was the foreman on the ground, who patiently laboured at plantings around the house and in the pleasure grounds, and was finally allowed to make the series of rocky cascades on the Belan stream, leading to 'a very fine piece of water' held up by a dam. (The cascades and the lake were not finished until 1784 by a local surveyor, John Evans: there was an opening ceremony, 'led by the gamekeeper and two bagpipers, it included 80 colliers, 100 carters, 200 labourers, 20 artificers, 150 gentlemen and farmers, who had helped with their carts, one wagon with a large piece of roast beef, another with a hogshead of beer with a banner *To Moisten the Clay,* Sir Watkin and Lady Williams-Wynn and their daughter in a phaeton drawn by six ponies, Mr Evans on horseback and Mr Midgeley with his levelling staff.')*

Towards an English Picturesque

North-east of Denbigh, at Lleweni Hall on the River Clwyd, Lancelot made one visit to advise Thomas Fitzmaurice, Lord Shelburne's brother, in 1781; it was perhaps a consolation, for at Bowood he had been ousted in favour of the aged Charles Hamilton, creator of Painshill Park in Surrey, though by now a pensioner in Bath. However, Wiltshire was a nest of other possibilities, and they revealed the seeds of the Picturesque to be deeply embedded in the English psyche: Lancelot returned to Wilton in 1779, needing no second bidding to this iconic house, but as so often with famous places his plans for alterations appear to have become overlaid. Farther west was the Beckfords' Fonthill, where he did not go, but a few miles to the south lay the lesser-known hexagonal ruins of the Arundells' Old Wardour, wreathed in stories enough for several Gothic novels. Lord Arundell had long sought Lancelot's advice with politeness and flattery, but had despaired of him being so busy and had called in Richard Woods of Essex. Woods had grumbled that his pay of a guinea a day was not enough:

> to keep myself, horses and servant, considering how many broken days in a year I have, for example take out Sundays, many days ill by getting colds etc., how many days and nights in town at expences, merely to wait on gentlemen without even charging anything for it, how many days in a year are spent at home only in answering letters, and add to that the great expense in a year for postage.

Woods defines well the difficulties of his profession, or is he jealous? A guinea a day, he continues to Lord Arundell, and 'I should soon be

---

* Talacre at Prestatyn, Clwyd, has also been suggested as a Brown site; it was owned by Barbara Mostyn of Kiddington in Oxfordshire.

oblig'd to give over travelling, unless like a Tom Tinker. If the gentleman your Lordship is pleased to mention had done business upon those terms, I know not how he could have raised a fortune at £2,500 per annum.'

Sadly, Lord Arundell chose to spend his money on James Paine's vast new Wardour, for which Lancelot now supplied a landscape plan (1775), but little was carried out. The delights of the old castle ruin, the swan-shaped lake, the castellated banqueting house, and the grotto built later by the doyen of grotto-makers, Josiah Lane of Tisbury, the woods and the views are all considerable, but the apparent confusion between the works of Woods and Lancelot leaves only a muddled understanding.

South of Salisbury is triangular Longford Castle, said to be built with a fortune in silver bars found in a Spanish galleon wrecked off Hurst Castle, and given three towers in honour of the Holy Trinity. It stands immediately beside the River Avon; Jonathan Spyers made a survey in 1778, and Lancelot proposed the park planting and removing the formal flower beds, which he felt cluttered the scene, and which were removed (but subsequently replaced). The grand finale of the Wiltshire Gothic collection is Lacock Abbey, said to be the least-damaged survivor of the medieval houses (in this case a nunnery), because Sir William Sharington acquired it quickly enough after the Dissolution to prevent its damage. Lancelot would have seen more of the lovely timbered Tudor buildings (without their nineteenth-century overlay), but the tranquil walks beside the young River Avon, and the lines of the ha-ha, certainly evoke his presence. No evidence of his working for John Ivory Talbot is certain, but suspicions are growing.

More Picturesque curiosities crowd these late years: a plan of 1779 for pleasure grounds in an old quarry at Whitley Beaumont in West Yorkshire, pre-dating a popular Victorian 'restoration' concept; Byram, also in West Yorkshire, visited in 1782, remains a mystery; haunted Woodchester, in its dramatic 'lost' Cotswold valley near Stonehouse in Gloucestershire, may yet reveal Lancelot's work from 1782; Ickworth in Suffolk, where he submitted plans for the new house, eventually built as a Rotunda in the 1790s, conceals a Brown setting beneath acres of woods and later gardens.

Most spectacular of all was Belvoir Castle, about 5 miles west of the Great North Road just south of Grantham, a road much travelled by Lancelot. Even Arthur Young, who was not easily impressed, and stressed that his road was not by Belvoir but that he went purposely to view it, was overawed: it 'suddenly appears an immense prospect over a prodigiously extensive vale,' Young wrote in his *Six Weeks' Tour through the Southern Counties*. The castle was 'almost in the clouds on the top of a vast hill', almost equally unreachable along a road that was 'dreadfully bad'. Presumably Lancelot's approach was much the same; they saw not the turreted fairytale castle we see today, but a huge square house, with its approach drive spiralling around the mound, snail-fashion, and about one-third of the way up, the mound extends to a huge flat terrace, with walks and pools, from which the stupendous view out over the Vale of Belvoir is taken. Jonathan Spyers made an extensive survey and Lancelot planned his 'alterations', and these were 'made very descriptive, fair and neat' and 'bound into a book', as Lancelot noted in his account book. 'Bound into a book' is the most intriguing phrase, hinting that presenting a scheme in this form was the coming fashion, and not entirely Repton's innovation when he produced his first Red Book a decade later. At Belvoir nothing came of Lancelot's plans because of the death of the 3rd Duke of Rutland in 1779. His heir, his grandson Charles Granby, was a close friend and political ally of the young William Pitt, with other preoccupations.

Return to Croome

After this heavy dose of possibilities, it was a relief to return to well-travelled paths and old friends. Croome was ever there to be visited, and Lancelot had a fatherly affection for the place, for at Croome everything had turned out so happily. George William Coventry was settled with his second wife, Barbara St John, sister to the Dean of Worcester, a more ordinary beauty than the lamented Maria, but with a generous dowry and a real love of country life, gardening and animals. Croome was now sumptuously furnished, with tapestries from the French Royal Gobelin works, a library fitted out by premier carpenters Vile and Cobb, and other fine furnishings masterminded by Robert Adam. Adam had even designed the Coventrys' wedding bed, with fluted spiral bedposts, Corinthian capitals and a carved dome, 'the whole dressed in fresh green linen'.

Croome was a sporting estate: the stable court, completed in a plain solidity reminiscent of Burghley's stables (but to designs submitted by Smith of Warwick some years earlier), now rejoiced in a clock made by Thomas Mudge and an elegant lamp standard set in the centre and surrounded by railings, designed by Adam. On the east hill, near Lancelot's church (with Adam's interior) and his Rotunda, was the new ice house, almost certainly Lancelot's work, with an oval chamber 15 feet across at its widest, sunk 20 feet into the ground and with a thatched roof. It was surrounded by cool shade-planting, but still convenient for the house kitchens. Adam and Lancelot seemed to dovetail easily into their responses to the Countess's ideas, for they had manoeuvred around each other for long enough now, each to know the other's sensitivities. Lancelot must have told the Coventrys about the grotto of love at Hampton Court House being made by Thomas Wright, for, uncharacteristically, he made a grotto at Croome, a modest effort in tufa and rockwork beside the lake, which eventually acquired a nymph, Sabrina fair, the titular deity of the River Severn.

The Temple Greenhouse, Adam's huge columned portico into which frames fitted for winter protection, sited by Lancelot beside the shrubbery, held the nucleus of the Coventrys' collection of exotic plants, brought home from the Indies and Africa by their travelling friends. Adam's ingenuity was responsible for any number of 'follies', although invariably Lancelot had the placing of them and he laid out the circuits – a 3-mile walk and 10-mile ride – for taking the views. Lancelot's water course through the park was now extended northwards to curl in imitation of the Severn and roll out into the new lake. The three-arched bridge was Adam's, but the rockwork Dry Arch was Lancelot's, not to mention his unseen last phase of the drainage to make all this happen.

Lancelot had also relished the challenge of the pleasance at Pirton, the 1,200 acres of the hilly old park of timbered Pirton Court, north of Croome Court's vale. The lamented Maria was buried at Pirton, where the little timber-towered church of St Peter's seems to sit level with the Malverns' tops and presides over the exuberantly dipping fields that sweep up to the cedar-dotted ridge. Though the fields are now mainly arable (and there is the compromising presence of the M5 on the western horizon), it is still evidently Lancelot's landscape, with visible remnants of his scalloped belts and clumps of trees. In the dip to the north the layout is focused on the medieval fishpond, Pirton Pool of legendary expanse, for which Lancelot proposed carefully 'serpentising' the edges and adding two large, planted islands.

A sporting footnote is added to the Croome Park lake by an estate map of 1796, where part of the outline is shown very definitely 'pulled out' at the corners, giving it the shape of an animal pelt pinned to a board. This shape is indicative of a duck decoy, the corner channels screened by woodland and easily fitted with the netting tunnels into which the wildfowl, innocently landed upon the open lake, were lured and captured. Duck made much better eating without being sprinkled with lead shot, which those of bon-viveur tastes felt strongly about. Lancelot was familiar with the decoy at Wotton Underwood and may have played a part in its making: he had twice visited the Aubreys' Boarstall, just a few miles to the west beyond Brill, the home of a seventeenth-century decoy that was in continued use. There was also one at Aynho nearby. Once the distinctive shape of a decoy is learned, it is possible to see them in several places. They were a common feature in the fenland landscape, and Lancelot would have seen them around Boston. At Chillington in Staffordshire, where James Paine had described Lancelot's lake as 'confessedly one of the finest pieces of water' in the country, the 'neck' of water at the south-west corner looks very like the decoy secreted in Big Wood.

Park decoys were set in woodland, so that the business of the decoyman and his dog could be conducted in quiet, the dog 'piper' – traditionally a red setter – working to the subtlest of sound signals, with the decoyman's skills veering towards sorcery as he charmed his tame lure-ducks to tempt the deluded incomers. Decoys were much used in the seventeenth century and were greatly revived for nineteenth-century sport, and so Lancelot's examples helped bridge the gap of knowledge that enabled the art to survive. *The Book of Duck Decoys, their construction, management and history* by Sir Ralph Payne-Gallwey Bt., of Thirkelby Park, Thirsk, published in May 1886, is the celebrated authority. He mentions the Chillington decoy, and those discussed above, and lists decoys at Packington, Oakly, Lowther and Kimpton Hoo amongst Lancelot's parks.

Mrs Montagu's Sandleford Priory

In the summer of 1781 Lancelot was at Sandleford Priory, just south of Newbury. It was familiar country, with the Cravens' Benham in the Kennet valley, where Henry Holland's house had turned out prettily enough, a few miles to the north, and Highclere about the same distance to the south. Could he have resisted calling at Highclere, where he had left his overall proposals for the Herberts' park a decade earlier? He had spent hours riding around the hugely impressive deer park, which had once belonged to the Bishops of Winchester and was still partly protected by its medieval pale, dominated on the south by Sidown and Beacon Hills, while to the north were the fishponds, fed from abundant chalk streams, run by the medieval bishops as commercial fisheries. Robert Sawyer Herbert and his brother, the Architect Earl of Pembroke from Wilton, had done a great deal to the park in the way of avenues and eye-catchers: Lancelot remembered the litany of associations, of places of interest and views, which he had incorporated into the rides he marked out, and the new roads he planned. The fishponds had conjoined into Milford Lake, which took on his outline, and the new Dunsmere was made, moving the Newbury road to the east. Henry Herbert, just become Lord Porchester (in 1780), had so loyally implemented much of Lancelot's plan that Highclere has become known as one of the finest Brown parks, though Lancelot himself had hardly touched it.

Sandleford was a much more domestic place, and though he had not entered the park gate before, it was a kind of homecoming. Lancelot was working for Elizabeth Montagu, at last; they had first met a quarter of a century before, when William Pitt had found himself in love with both Hester Grenville and Mrs Montagu's Hayes in Kent and won both of them, having persuaded Mrs Montagu to part with Hayes. With the Pitts and the Garricks among her close friends, and her much larger social circle, Elizabeth Montagu was certainly aware of Lancelot's progress, but she was constrained – as her life in general was – as an intelligent and educated woman constantly berating herself as to what a woman, or at least a lady, *did not do*. She was a creature of nervous energy, called 'Fidget' as a child, and invariably likened to a chattering bird; her person appeared fragile, and her life had the impression of taking place in a gilded cage. She had been married at twenty-four to the dourly mathematical Edward Montagu, who was fifty; it was a marriage of great affection and loyalty. Montagu had already owned Sandleford, over which the young Elizabeth was ecstatic: 'I think I may say you never saw anything so pretty as the view these gardens command, for my part I would not change the situation for any I ever saw; there is nothing in Nature pretty that they have not. The prospect is allegro'; this suited her philosophy, expressed as 'Mirth with thee I chose to live', and she would have nothing melancholy or of Stygian gloom. The prospect from Sandleford was cheerful:

we have a pretty village on a rising ground just before us – a silver stream washes the foot of the village – Nature has been very indulgent to this country, and has given it enough of wood and water: the first we have in good plenty, and a power of having more of the latter, as improvements are undertaken.

Edward Montagu was a keen fisherman: 'Mr M has just taken some prodigious carp from a fish-pond . . . and was throwing three of the old monks' ponds, or fish-stews, into one large one.' This seems almost the only alteration he made; they planted an oak to celebrate the birth of their son, who died at just over a year old, but his 'Punch's Oak' was to live to a venerable age.

Sandleford became a peaceful retreat: 'my desk and I are placed under the shade of some noble elms,' she wrote, at other times referring to 'my sylvan palace' or the 'arched roofs of twilight groves'. Childless, portrayed by Allan Ramsay in 1762 with huge, kind brown eyes that seem close to tears, Mrs Montagu itemised her life's roles as 'a Critick, a Coal Owner, a Land Steward, a sociable creature'. Her days were divided between her

London literary salon, her bluestocking friends and protégées, their visits to the Montagus' Denton estate and colliery, and Allerton Park in Yorkshire, all of which she managed owing to Edward's declining health, as well as her sociable outings to Bath. She nursed her husband loyally until his death in 1775, when he left her a fortune and set her free: at Sandleford, where the long-established 'Scotch' gardener Thomas Woodhouse and the equally long-serving bailiff also died at about the same time, her cage was indeed opened and she was able to please herself.

Sandleford, the rather battered remains of an Augustinian priory, sat on the south-western corner of the high heath of Greenham Common; the pretty village in the view was Newtown, and the silver stream the Enborne, which flowed southwards from the Common. The soils were Bagshot sands over London clay, and the estate still occupied medieval boundaries. On the east there were paths up to the Common, with a stream flowing down, but most of the acreage was to the west of the Newbury road (then hardly a barrier) towards Wash Common. Mrs Montagu saw herself as a 'farmeress': 'at Sandleford you will find us busy in the care of arable land,' she wrote to her brother in June 1777, 'the meagre condition of the soil forbids me to live in the state of a shepherdess queen which I look upon as the highest rural dignity.' The land west of the road remained this way, but took on the lilting rhythms of Lancelot's definition of boundaries and planting belts.

With her new-found freedom, Mrs Montagu had James Wyatt build her an elliptical, domed drawing room and convert the old chapel ruin into a dining-room, her 'reformed chapel'. Firstly, as she explained to Lancelot, her views from these rooms were not quite elevated enough; he responded 'by removing a good deal of ground and throwing it down below to raise what was too low, while he sunk what was too high [and] has much improved the view to the south'. He further heightened an east window, with a fanlight, 'so that the arch formed by the trees is now visible. These rooms are the most beautiful imaginable. With the shelter the comfort and convenience of walls and roofs you have [a] beautiful passage of the green shade of the grove' – a luminosity brought indoors that was a rare effect.

Lancelot stayed for several days on at least one occasion; we may imagine them sitting and talking over old times, and she enjoyed his company. 'He is an agreeable, pleasant companion, as well as a great genius in his profession. I consider him a great poet.' She felt almost embarrassed that she had spent so much on the 'Demons, Pomp and Vanity' with her much-celebrated new house in Portman Square, and that 'the noble genius of Mr Brown should be restrained by ignoble considerations and circumstances' at Sandleford, but she had a horror of incurring debt, and 'so his improvements must not go beyond what my cash will immediately answer'. Lancelot was all compliance, and they made good progress; 'as fast as time wrinkles my forehead, I smooth the grounds about Sandleford,' she wrote:

> in a little while I shall not see anything belonging to me that is not pretty, except when I behold myself in the looking glass . . . Mr Brown has not neglected any of [Sandleford's] capabilities. He is forming it into a lovely pastoral – a sweet Arcadian scene. In not attempting more, he adapts his scheme to the character of the place and my purse. We shall not erect temples to the gods, build proud bridges over humble rivulets, or do any of the marvellous things suggested by the caprice, and indulged by the wantonness of wealth.

Surely the 'proud bridges over humble rivulets' meant they had talked of Blenheim and other of Lancelot's achievements; did he confess to her that some of his clients spent too much money and that places were spoilt by this, for after all, the lords and their purses came after the *places* with him. Mrs Montagu, so skilled in the arts of conversation, surely drew him out to speak of his lonely profession. On one occasion they walked up to the common and looked at the stream course. 'I am not fond of large pieces of standing water but nothing adds so sweet and so placid an air to a place as a winding river,' she had written earlier. Lancelot proposed a series of ponds and cascades, rather as at Wynnstay, though less dramatically so, and she responded, 'and I am sure all my geese will be swans, when Mr Brown has improved the little river which divides Admiral Derby's territory and mine'. The largest pond became known as Brown's Pond.

In the July of 1782, with work in full swing, Mrs Montagu gave a supper for her workers, and she described it:

> The scene is extremely animated; 20 men at work in the wood and grove, and the fields around are full of haymakers. The persons employed on the work are poor weavers who by the decay of our manufacture at Newbury are void of employment, and not having been trained to the business of agriculture are not dexterous at the rake and pitchfork, but the plain digging and driving wheel barrows they can perform and are very glad to get their daily subsistence.

She also employed the destitute soldiers who roamed the countryside, and made a practice of employing girls who could not get work elsewhere. She must have told Lancelot about her workforce, for in the following October he wrote to her from York, 'honoured with your letter which is an exact Picture of your mind, full of Compassion and good will to all; the Season has been such as I never saw before, and I am doubtfull the consequence of it will be tolerable to the Poor in many places'. He promised to visit Sandleford before she left at the end of October, and if he did, it was their last meeting. But she had given him the blessed habit of self-awareness, and the ability to talk of what he did, even though it was so late: one day in December in the garden at Hampton Court he encountered Mrs Montagu's friend and 'fellow' bluestocking, Hannah More, who was staying at Hampton with the widowed Mrs Garrick. 'Never was such delicious weather!' she wrote:

> I passed two hours in the garden the other day as if it has been April with my friend Mr Brown. I took a very agreeable lecture from him in his art, and he promised to give me taste by inoculation. He illustrates everything he says about gardening by some literary or grammatical allusion. He told me he compared his art to literary composition. 'Now *there*' said he, pointing his finger, 'I make a comma, and there' pointing to another spot, 'where a more decided turn is proper, I make a colon; at another part, where an interruption is desirable to break the view, a parenthesis; now a full stop, and then I begin another subject.

It was a stumbling start, and not kindly received when passed about.

The Christian husband, father, friend

We could wish that Lancelot had had more time to spend with Mrs Montagu and Hannah More, for between them they could well have encouraged him to write his memoirs, or at least his professional *Hints* for posterity. As it was, he was all activity right to the end: in the January of 1783 he made a trip to Suffolk, to Euston, Ickworth and Heveningham. This last was a commission from Sir Gerard Vanneck for his large park in that spectacular but quiet countryside south of Halesworth. Lancelot's scheme was a polished masterpiece, with river-style lake, drive and woodland belt echoing each other's sinuousities across a floating greensward.

At the beginning of February he was spending time in town, staying with his daughter Bridget Holland and her family at their house in Hertford Street in Mayfair. It was an ordinary business trip, which enabled him to visit his clients at their London houses; on the Wednesday evening,

5th February, he dined with Lord Coventry at his house in Piccadilly, and while he was walking the short distance home he collapsed from 'an apoplexy', and the next day he died.

In death Lancelot slipped back into the world from which he came; the King's Master Gardener was no more, and there were no honours, no public orations or life-charting obituaries, no list of those attending his funeral, nor was there any statue erected. His family and those he loved ushered him to his rest at Fenstanton — 'my body I commit to the Earth to be decently buried' — as his Will had stated, and as the curate Thomas Johnson entered in the modest calf-bound register of burials with the date, 16th February.

All his other wishes were faithfully carried out: his last Will was dated 26th March 1779, appointing his son-in-law Henry Holland as an executor instead of John Drummond, who had died in 1774, but otherwise mainly full of those ponderous clauses reciting the rights of male heirs as yet unborn, as Lance, Jack and young Thomas Brown were not as yet married. A final codicil written around midnight after his collapse (5th February changed to the 6th) diverted £2,000 of the £3,000 allocated for Biddy's house to Lance, stipulating that the house could be bought out of 'ready money' — that is, his Drummonds account. Lance Brown was now MP for Totnes, which had cost his father £1,000 (the corporation needed favouring) and presumably they foresaw an expensive progress in politics. The codicil was proved by Henry Holland the elder and the lawyer Edison on 19th February.

The family's belongings at Wilderness House were packed up, and Biddy Brown moved to her new house in Kensington, where Lance, Thomas and Peggy were still with her at various times. Lance had his house in Elsworth, where Peggy liked to spend much of her time in the country. They all made sure that Biddy, though frail, had plenty of society, and one letter she wrote to Peggy (whom she persists in calling Margaret) in the summer of 1784 tells of her visit to the elder Hollands in their new cottage on the Hans Town estate in Chelsea, which the younger Henry was developing. 'My time has been filled up,' she wrote, adding the list of her visitors, who included her Holland grandchildren; Bridget, who acquired her coveted silver candlestick, was now the mother of a young 'Bidy', and of Harry, Mary, Harriet and Lancelot (with Charlotte and Caroline to come).

Biddy Brown died on 26th August 1786, and was buried at Fenstanton. Affections for their mother had kept the family together, but now a division opened; Bridget and Henry Holland were entirely preoccupied with their lives in Chelsea, but the younger Browns all gravitated to Huntingdonshire.

Lance Brown had kept his Totnes seat until the election of 1784, when he surrendered it for the rising star, William Pitt, though Pitt was invited to stand for Cambridge University, a seat he had always wanted, and where he was elected. Lance, rather at the mercy of Lord Sandwich's ebullient control of local politics, was elected for Huntingdon. His House of Commons career was not marked by enthusiasm, he never made a speech, and he voted against Pitt's 1785 proposals for equality of trade with Ireland. Less than a year after his mother's death, in May 1787, Lance lost his seat (through Sandwich's machinations) and went abroad, travelling in Switzerland and northern Italy, where the 'good climate and amusement in seeing the various characters of different countries' suited him, and proved that he was at least in small part his father's son. In 1788, in Lausanne, he married Frances, the daughter of the Rev. Henry Fuller, and sister of John Fuller of Rose Hill in Sussex. The following year, prompted by rumblings of the revolution in Paris, Lance wrote to Lord Sandwich from Toulon, complaining that:

> for a term of years I have consulted your interest more than my own; the best part of my life has been dedicated to your service, and my seats in Parliament all taken at your request, have cost me much money . . . yr Lordship has frequently told me that you had no person whom you wished to push forward in a political line except myself [and] this is the time I should have the greatest expectation.

In the meantime, Peggy Brown seems to have continued living in Lance's house at Elsworth, where she was according to her mother's last letters. Peggy, who had cried on her father's shoulder over the end of her engagement to a Mr Gee in early 1782, had now met a prominent local businessman and partner in a Huntingdon bank, James Rust of Brampton, and they were married in Fenstanton church on 29th September 1788. The signatures of the witnesses at the ceremony were 'Susan Brown' and 'M. E. Cowling' – two new names in our story. Who were they? Susan or Susannah Brown is found easily enough, for she was the daughter of the Rev. Charles Dickins, rector of neighbouring Hemingford Abbots, and had recently married Peggy's younger brother, Thomas Brown. Thomas, now twenty-seven and a 'clerk' or curate, seems to have fulfilled his sunny expectations as Lancelot and Biddy's youngest child; coming down from Oxford in the summer after his father's death, he had settled at Fenstanton. In the year after his marriage, 1789, he was appointed to the living of Conington, an ancient village halfway between Fenstanton and Elsworth, where he served the parish for forty years. Thomas and Susannah had three children: Susan and her brothers named Lancelot and Thomas, who were both ordained priests.

For 'M. E. Cowling' – Mary Elizabeth Cowling – clearly at least a close friend of Peggy's, we have to look a little farther. Mary Elizabeth lived to be ninety, and she died in 1846, and so she was born in 1756, or thereabouts. She was married to Peter Cowling junior, his father of the same name being well known in Fenstanton as a local worthy, a prosperous owner of hostelries that drew their trade from the Great North Road, and a Huntingdon magistrate. Cowling junior had come under the Hinchingbrooke wing of patronage, though in his case it was apparently from the estranged Countess of Sandwich – to whom he dedicated the travel diary he wrote of a European tour taken in his early twenties. He was twenty-five in 1788, recently married, but no record of his marriage to Mary Elizabeth can be found in the Huntingdonshire or Cambridgeshire registers. It is of course possible that Peter Cowling was a friend of Lance Brown, and that the wedding took place abroad. The Cowlings had a son named Peter Lancelot Cowling, who was baptised on 15th October 1790. Was he named for Lance, who could have stood godfather, or was he named for his two grandfathers?

The only clue comes in Mr Inskip Ladds's dotted line! S. Inskip Ladds was the church architect for Fenstanton, and in or around 1910 he was concerned about the state of the Brown monument; he sketched a family tree, a rough sketch, which survives in his papers in the Norris Museum in St Ives, and after recording Lance, Jack, Peggy and Thomas as the surviving children of Lancelot and Biddy, he extended a dotted line to Mary Elizabeth Cowling. Mr Inskip Ladds was much in tune with local life, the Cowlings' niece, Miss Mary Anne Cowling had only died twenty-five or so years before, well within living memory – and living memory clearly informed him that Mary Elizabeth Cowling was Lancelot's natural daughter. Thus the connection between the Cowlings and the Browns, who lie together in their vault beneath Fenstanton's chancel, is explained.

Many other questions come tumbling: where was Lancelot in or about 1756, and where did he stay long enough to forge a relationship and father a child? Was there a connection to his self-confessed twenty-five years 'of happiness' at Burghley – just the kind of great-house community where such a thing could have happened and been treated with discretion? There was Croome, but that has always seemed a 'foreign' country; he was in Cambridgeshire a great deal, or passing through, and the existence of Mary Elizabeth as a sturdy and appealing ten-year-old in need of a secure future surely becomes a powerful reason for his purchase of the Fenstanton estate, which has always seemed an illogical enterprise. Fenstanton, conveniently placed between Cambridge and Stamford (and Burghley) was well away from Hampton Court and London gossips, and from his wife and family, whom he would not have wanted to hurt for the world. And yet Fenstanton was always his secret; it seems most likely that Biddy Brown never went there until she was taken in her coffin.

It is important to add that there is no mention of Mary Elizabeth or anyone connected to her in Lancelot's Wills: the draft of 1769, and the final version, little changed, of 1779. It would have been in character for him to have regularly taken care of her upbringing, perhaps with those useful £100 notes. If, when he was sharing confidences with his daughter Peggy in his last years, he had told her his secret (perhaps Mary Elizabeth's mother had died?), it explains Peggy liking to live in Huntingdonshire; Thomas was perhaps in on the secret too, but Mary Elizabeth does not emerge into family life until after Biddy Brown's death – Lancelot would have been very definite about that. What is certain is that Mary Elizabeth Cowling had a comfortable life in Fenstanton; her husband Peter died in August 1824 at the good age of seventy-one. She was a widow for twenty-one years, living with her son, who became the Rev. Peter Lancelot Cowling, MA.

There is something poignant about the flurry of marriages after Lancelot and Biddy were safely buried. Captain Jack Brown married in 1789, his marriage settlement dated 17th December of that year, and his bride was Mary Linton of Stamford; the witnesses were his brother Thomas and her brother, John Linton of Freiston in Lincolnshire, a marshland village west of Boston. The Lintons owned several properties in south Lincolnshire, and these were joined to the land that Jack had inherited from his mother. Jack's name cannot be found in connection with any ship in the naval records, but he was gazetted as a Rear-Admiral of the Blue on 1st June 1795, and continued to rise steadily after short intervals; he was made a Vice-Admiral of the Red on 9th November 1805, a few weeks after the victory at Trafalgar. Shortly before his death he became a full Admiral of the Blue, and died on 2nd May 1808, making him fifty-seven years old.

Lance's political career had stumbled on: he was elected as a county member for Huntingdonshire in May 1792 to keep the seat warm for Sandwich's heir, the minor Viscount Hinchingbrooke, who came of age two years later. When Lance's nemesis the Earl died in 1792, he found himself appointed executor of his lordship's complex affairs. Lance's wife

Frances died in December of 1792, after less than four years of their marriage, and was buried at Fenstanton. Lance, who suffered much from the disdain of the Huntingdonshire gentry – one anonymously calling him 'a mere mushroom sprung from a dunghill in Stowe gardens' – rose to be a Deputy Lieutenant and was given a minor court appointment as a Gentleman of the Privy Chamber. He used his influence to obtain Thomas his living at Conington, and good brotherly relations were also maintained with Jack, who took over the lease of Stirtloe House, a Georgian house prettily situated on the outskirts of Buckden, on the opposite side of the Great Ouse west of Fenstanton, after Lance's death in 1802.

Their sister Peggy Rust lived comfortably with her husband James in and around Huntingdon; they had four children, and Peggy died in 1806 and was buried at St Mary's, Huntingdon.

Lancelot's loyal friend, executor and business colleague, Henry Holland senior, followed up the outstanding accounts. Work was carried on for a while at Kew, Sandleford, Wynnstay and Nuneham Courtenay, managed by Samuel Lapidge and William Ireland from the yard at Hampton that Lancelot had leased. Lapidge and Ireland later worked for Humphry Repton. The elder Holland died in 1785 and was buried at All Saints church in Fulham, with his wife Mary, who had died a few weeks after Lancelot.

Lancelot gave 100 guineas, 'with all my Drawings with my Sincere Blessing', to his son-in-law, Henry Holland. Holland's architectural career had prospered on its own merits: his house in St James's for Brooks's club was much admired, and when the Prince of Wales became a member of the club in 1783 it led to Holland's appointment as architect at Carlton House; this in turn led to him working at the Royal Pavilion at Brighton, Woburn Abbey, Althorp and other prestigious places. As well as being a stylish architect, Henry Holland had his father's good business sense as a developer, and his ambitious Hans Town development off London's Sloane Street included a house in large grounds for himself, Bridget and their family, where Lancelot had designed a small lake. Bridget Holland was rather like her mother, with her own quiet dignity, and Henry was of the same retiring character, grumbling that he found himself 'more an object of public notice than suits me'. He was not interested in landscapes, and it is shocking to see his sketched proposals for gardens round the houses at the Spencers' Althorp and at Southill in Bedfordshire, and even for Brighton Pavilion, which exhibit the stilted spottiness that later marked the Victorian formal revivals; fortunately he worked with Humphry Repton. Henry Holland died in 1806, and Bridget survived him, in very comfortable circumstances, until 1823. They were both buried in All Saints churchyard at Fulham, with Henry's parents, and a tablet in the church records Bridget as the daughter of Lancelot.

Neither of Henry and Bridget's sons followed their father's or grandfather's professions; Henry (1775–1855) became a prosperous sail-maker in Aberdeen, and Lancelot (1781–1859) became a professional soldier, and a colonel in the Coldstream Guards. Colonel Lancelot Holland and his wife Charlotte Peters (1788–1876) had fifteen children, most of whom married and had large families of their own. The most intriguing was their daughter Henrietta (1829–1912), who married a farmer named Henry Wise, and it seems they realised that they were both descended from royal gardeners.

Lancelot's proudly held title as the King's Master Gardener at Hampton Court died with him. It was fortunate that he probably never knew of the rumblings of official disapproval of his prosperous private practice, and the instigation of a review, which proposed the appointment of a Surveyor-General or Comptroller of royal gardens. This eminence, though 'bred a gardener' and responsible for the production of vast amounts of fruit, vegetables and flowers, was on a par with the royal surveyors of the Office of Works (buildings) and of Woods & Forests. At Hampton Court the Head Gardener continued to live in Wilderness House for another hundred years, until it was converted to a grace-and-favour apartment. At Kew, the distinguished Superintendent William Aiton died in 1793, and was succeeded by his elder son, William Townsend Aiton, as 'Gardener to His Majesty' with responsibility for Kew and Richmond, and soon for Kensington and St James's. The younger Aiton, John, was appointed 'Foreman' at Windsor in 1804, with a vastly extended territory (as Lancelot had imagined all those years before) and a salary of £2,000 a year. W. T. Aiton became a great favourite of the Prince Regent, later George IV, and was appointed 'Director-General of the Royal Gardens' in 1827. William IV abolished the post.

However, it was another of the Prince Regent's favourites, the architect John Nash, who most nearly succeeded Lancelot in a practical way. Nash designed Regent's Park and the ceremonial way, Regent Street, and when George IV decided to turn the Queen's House into his Buckingham Palace, it was Nash (with a little help from Director-General Aiton) who revamped (and vulgarised) Lancelot's layout of 1762, and did the same with his St James's Park.

Henry Holland's stout defence of his father-in-law – that 'no man under-

Lancelot's eldest child, Bridget Holland, from a miniature, c.1775, and her husband Henry Holland by John Opie.

stood so well what was necessary for the habitation of all ranks and degrees of society' – was written to Humphry Repton in the summer of 1788. Repton seems to have looked for a talisman, some sort of connection with Lancelot (whom he never met), to carry him into his new career as a *landscape gardener*, the term he had just invented. Repton was thirty-six, and he had led a life of sudden inspirations and mixed fortunes; he now 'boldly ventured forth once more, and with renewed energy and hope push[ed] off my little bark into a sea unknown'. He compared himself to Lancelot beginning at Hammersmith at much the same age. Holland sent Repton 'the maps of the greatest works in which his late father [in-law] had been consulted, both in their original and improved status'.

These drawings have never been found, but it is worth considering what they might have been. They would not have been for any of the places – Berrington, Cadland, Claremont or Broadlands, for instance – in which Holland had an interest on his own account. 'Original and improved status' implies the surveys and the overlays with Lancelot's designs, but were they only the office copies and of workaday quality? Watercoloured surveys on vellum or heavy paper were expensive and precious, and most of these remained in their respective estate offices; Lancelot's overlay, finished by Spyers or Lapidge, would have gone to the client. Was Repton simply looking for contacts? He was such a modern man; instead of Lancelot's imperative and exhausting galloping over half of England looking for work, Repton had written a circular letter offering his services. Whereas Lancelot's headstrong naïvety over geography sent him dashing from one side of the country to another, Repton began close to his home; he had settled at Hare Street in Essex and concentrated upon East Anglia and the Home Counties. Of Lancelot's places, Repton's list of commissions includes (* indicates the drawings that Holland may have sent): Brocklesby* and Holkham* (by 1791), Redgrave*, Heveningham*, Thorndon and Belhus, Tewin, Panshanger, Ashridge, Taplow, Wycombe Abbey, Stoke Park, Aynho* and Nuneham Courtenay*. Repton made specific forays that appear Lancelot-inspired, to Himley*, Ingestre* and Shugborough in Staffordshire, and to Longleat*, Bowood* and Corsham* in Wiltshire. He saw Harewood*, and Wimpole* and even far-away Moccas* on the Wye.

Repton did not rely on plans, he only ever drew small layouts, and as he was a talented and practised watercolourist, his method was to sketch the scene. As well as coining the friendly term 'landscape gardener', he developed the idea of a bound set of proposals (as Lancelot had provided for Belvoir), which he called his Red Books. Each Red Book had 'before' and 'after' sketches, and an 'open letter' to the client, full of optimism and flattery, which inspired confidence.

Repton's character was both sympathetic and generous, and he was careful of the good name of his profession, which implied respect for his forebears, including Lancelot; Lancelot became a landscape gardener in retrospect. Repton worked on a different scale: for instance, at Ashridge where Lancelot had planted the sweeping beech woods of the Golden Valley, Repton's contribution was the ornamental sequence of gardens (including the Monk's Garden, with the gardeners robed as monks) ranged around Wyatt's Gothick palace. Repton did well out of two families that would not employ Lancelot: the Bedfords at Woburn and Endsleigh in Devon, and the Portlands at Bulstrode and Welbeck. (In his book on Repton, Stephen Daniels suggests that Lancelot did go to Bulstrode; if so, it would have been under Mrs Montagu's late influence.) Otherwise Repton's clients owned much smaller properties, which he cleverly organised into clusters, within commuting distance of London, Bristol, Leeds, Norwich and Ipswich. Repton was not a contractor, he was anxious not to soil his hands, but rather to keep a professional distance and avoid tiring supervisory visits. Even so, after a few years he found the travelling too exhausting and – modern man that he was – decided to write his memoirs. In doing so, as Dame Sylvia Crowe has observed, he 'codified' the art of landscape design for his successors. Sir Geoffrey Jellicoe thought that 'Repton humanised Brown's conception of landscape', though 'he compromised it as a work of art'.

Jellicoe hit the mark: Repton's 'common-sense approach and his ingenious method of the presentation of ideas' were easily applied in education, they were 'media-friendly'. Repton's books, *Sketches and Hints on Landscape Gardening* (1795), *Observations on the Theory and Practice of Landscape Gardening* (1803) and finally *Fragments* of 1816 passed on the grail, even if it was a lesser chalice. Repton felt he had to apologise for Lancelot's lack of education and the fact that he did not draw; he did not criticise Lancelot's work, but then he did not praise his achievements. Repton had troubles enough of his own: his unhappy, brief partnership with Nash, his debts and ill health, the vain hope of commissions (and of the patronage of William Pitt the Younger) and difficulties over his publications; he died suddenly, of a heart attack, at his home in Hare Street in March 1818. But Repton was fortunate in his sons, John Adey and George Stanley Repton, who guarded their father's legacy.

AFTERPIECE

This tree is planted in memory of
Lancelot 'Capability' Brown 1716–83
Lord of this Manor
Who planted a million others
Notice on Hilton Green, near Fenstanton, Huntingdonshire

THE AVUNCULAR PRESENCE OF THE King's Master Gardener had always attracted attention, and with his death his absence left an emptiness, a momentary silence, in hundreds of villages and gardens and country communities. In thirty-five years of hard work he had transformed thousands of acres of landscape, but the reality of his everydays was to give employment to men and women – often of the lowliest labouring kind – for whom his schemes were a means of survival. It has been said that 'architecture is the art of organising a mob of craftsmen' which leaves park-making as the art of organising a noisy crowd of the unskilled; much of Lancelot's success was that he was a superb 'man' manager, though there were also many women, boys and girls employed on lighter tasks. The loyalties of his foremen, and his known record – from his concern over Christmas payments at Stowe to his sympathy for Mrs Montagu's philanthropy amongst her workers at Sandleford – suggest that he was a fair and considerate taskmaster. His was not a fleeting presence and time and again his heavy tread would be heard at the garden door or on the estate office step – as at Burton Constable every September during the 1770s – and once a place was gathered into his network it was never forgotten, and he would always call in, if passing, to see how things were. Up and down the country roads of Britain Lancelot had become a familiar figure, at the inns and posting houses along his regular routes, at gate lodges and keepers' cottages and amongst tenant farmers. The foresters and woodsmen, the charcoal burners, the blacksmiths and wheelwrights, the lime-burners and brick-makers – all such scattered countrymen were familiar with his arrivals, for invariably he brought them work. But lodge-keepers and blacksmiths are not the historians of their times.

Without Lancelot, his trees continued to grow; his lakes evolved into rich habitats for wading birds and water rats, for eels, chub, dace and grayling, as well as trout, carp and the lazy, shovel-mouthed pike. Fish were attracted to the active water around his dams and cascades, and literally thousands of country fishermen spent happy days on lake and river banks.

For perhaps fifty years his parks served the contented state of mind of the country sportsmen, who revelled in a challenging pastime and nothing more. Lancelot's clumps and coverts were home to deer, badger, fox and hare (rabbits were not yet running amok) and a balance was maintained. 'How happy was the lot of the old-fashioned sportsman,' wrote Ralph Nevill in *Sporting Days and Sporting Ways* (1910):

> in September there was partridge shooting . . . steadily pursued till came the pheasant shooting, from its shining beauty, on the first of October, to its happiest variety in November; woodcock, till frost had driven both the sportsman and the birds from the woods; snipe, while the bogs were wet and when the rippling spring still ran through sparkling icicles.

Finally, the wildfowl, 'most exciting of sports, when the spirits were buoyant and the eye clear'. This was a golden age, 'the conscious pride of art,' writes Nevill, in matching the instincts of a trained dog 'against the finer instinct of the bird', and vastly different from the mass slaughter of 'battue' and shooting-flying that was to come with the mid-nineteenth century.

Behind their walls Lancelot's kitchen gardens thrived, and nearer the house his lawns grew into flower-rich carpets, banquets for bees and butterflies. His lawns hosted the first cricket matches and gave space for the modern passions for archery, tennis and golf and other outdoor games to grow.* Some of his clients called in William Emes or Humphry Repton to continue the 'improving', but most left Lancelot's work to mature, before the next heir and the next fashion – the early-Victorian revival of formal flower terraces – arrived.

And yet, it was true that he worked for the narrowest elite of society in pursuit of an esoteric taste. 'Voguish philosophies did little' for the great oracle of Lancelot's age, Samuel Johnson, who dealt swiftly with

---

* Lawn-tennis courts, croquet and miniature golf lawns were not designed into gardens and public parks until the late nineteenth century, and were the outcome of improved lawn-seed mixes by Suttons and other seedsmen.

estates and the mania for tulips as fashionable luxuries, in his *Dictionary*. Not one landscape nerve seemed to find a place in Johnson's mighty brain: he had visited Lancelot's Luton Hoo on 4th June 1781, by coincidence the royal birthday, James Boswell having obtained a ticket for entry and crowing over his friendship with Lord Mountstuart. The conversation went:

B: I shall probably be much at this place.
J: Don't you be too sure of that.
B: [shows him the botanical garden]
J: Is not *every* garden a botanical garden?
B: The shrubbery extends for several miles!
J: That is making a very foolish use of the ground; a little of it
      is very well.
B. Shall we walk on the pleasure-grounds?
J: Don't let us fatigue ourselves. Why should we walk there?
      Here's a fine tree, let's get to the top of it.

Johnson did, slightly, relent, concluding that Luton Hoo was 'one of the places I do not regret having come to see', and then they adjourned to drink the King's health in an inn in Luton.

Irrelevance was an awful fate, but the world was turning away from the English countryside and all that it represented. At Kew, Lancelot's lovely riverside gardens for the King and Queen had been subsumed into Sir Joseph Banks's Royal Botanic Garden, now devoted to economic botany; Banks, the great panjandrum of all things scientific and horticultural, had returned from the other side of the world, his dreams peopled with hibiscus-draped Tahitian girls, his ambitions directed towards the commercial production and trading of tea, cotton, coffee and opium. Within weeks of Lancelot's death, Banks was receiving reports from Benjamin Franklin, the American Ambassador in France, that the Montgolfier brothers had successfully flown their hot-air balloon and 'opened a Road in the Air', as Banks observed. If Franklin was the advance guard of newborn America finding its way in the world, then he was soon joined by his countryman, Thomas Jefferson, on shuttle diplomacy between France and England. Few people, and certainly not Banks, would have suggested to Jefferson that he should see Brown parks on his brief tour of this country, but Jefferson was keen on architecture and landscape design as a bellwether of his new country's status, and he had admired Lord Chatham. Jefferson visited Pitt's former South Lodge on Enfield Chace, noting in his diary, 'the water very fine'; he saw Moor

Park, Stowe and Wotton Underwood, where he admired Lancelot's
L-shaped water, which 'affords 200 brace of carp a year'; he found
Caversham 'well disposed', and much to admire at Blenheim: 'the water
here is very beautiful, and very grand. The cascade from the lake a fine
one'. Jefferson was a stern critic, and made some harsh comments on
the standards of maintenance, but it is pertinent that he spent most of
his time looking at Lancelot's works. At home in Virginia, his house and
gardens at Monticello were an intended blueprint for American tastes,
and – with the extension of his groves and walks into the grounds of
the University of Virginia – became a far-reaching influence on campus
and park design in nineteenth-century America.

Lancelot's influence also slipped into Europe. During the 1770s and into
the 1780s Georges-Louis Le Rouge published a series of pattern-books
– called *cahiers* – showing *Nouveaux jardins à la mode,* in the irregular or
natural style. He illustrated Stowe, Claremont and Lancelot's Kew, but
most interestingly also rather bowdlerised layouts of the Queen's House
and Lord Holderness's Sion Hill. Lancelot's 'edge of the cornfield' effect,
of a path winding through woodland, but allowing glimpses of a sunny
field of corn or grasses, was much in evidence. (Le Rouge's later editions
adopted the title *Jardins anglo-chinois,* William Chambers having persuaded
him of the Chinese love of their native landscape as the origin of the
natural style.) Naturalism found favour in France, with exiles returning
to ruined gardens after the Revolution as well as with republicans who
wanted nothing to do with the *ancien régime* of Versailles-like formality.
The term *le jardin anglais,* quickly applied to any patch of naturalism, owed
much to Lancelot's style, but also something to the Empress of Russia,
Catherine the Great's passion: 'I am at present madly in love with English
gardens,' she had written to Voltaire in 1772, 'with curved lines, gentle
slopes, lakes formed from swamps, and archipelagoes of solid earth'. She
added that she hated straight lines and fountains that tortured water.
Evidence of her passion was demonstrated at her country estate, Tsarskoe
Selo, where she employed British gardeners, and in her commission to
Josiah Wedgwood for her Imperial Russian dinner service, usually known
as the 'Frog Service' from its emblem, with more than 900 pieces deco-
rated with English scenes. Lancelot's places that were pictured include
Alnwick Castle, Audley End, Blenheim, Burghley, Chatsworth, Claremont,
Harewood, St James's Park, Milton Abbas, Roche Abbey, Sherborne, Stowe,
Syon, Trentham, Warwick Castle, Wrest and Wimpole Hall (this last with
views of Lancelot's lake painted by Lady Amabel Polwarth).

★   ★   ★

At home, the literary associations multiplied, and so many were wrong-headed; one of Lancelot's last jobs was for the 2nd Earl Harcourt at Nuneham Courtenay near Oxford. Harcourt had written to William Mason:

> Poor Brown! I have really been much concerned & hurt at his unexpected death; for, exclusive of the admiration I naturally feel for true genius in every art, I respected the man's private character, & ever found him obliging, good-humoured, & accommodating in the highest degree; while I felt an affection for him, and liked his company, in spite of his puns.

Lancelot's work there fell foul of a mistaken belief that Nuneham was the 'Sweet Auburn', the deserted village of Oliver Goldsmith's much-loved lament of the same name. *The Deserted Village* was first published in 1770 when Goldsmith was just over forty; he was brought up and educated in Ireland and on the Continent, and had only arrived in London, destitute, some fourteen years earlier, to toil at hack journalism and reviewing. He had hardly seen England until, during the 1760s, he began to travel about, and certain places were impressed upon his mind. One of them was Nuneham, and no wonder, for it occupies an undulating green ground, high on a river cliff of the Thames, looking out over the plain of Radley towards Foxcombe and Boar's Hills. But it was not so much 'the loveliest village of the plain' (hardly an apt geographical description) that Goldsmith remembered as the fact that Simon Harcourt was building his new village to rehouse forty families out of their hovels in the hilly park, and was also rebuilding the 'ruinous' old church 'that topp'd the neighbouring hill'. Harcourt's modernisation somehow sparked a memory in the poet's mind – though Harcourt's was certainly not the 'tyrant's hand' that Goldsmith blamed, for he was a soft-hearted man who died in 1777 in rescuing his dog from a well. Goldsmith was, of course, aiming for another target:

> Ill fares the land, to hastening ills a prey,
> Where wealth accumulates, and men decay,

and in remembering, in poignant line after poignant line, the playfellows of his youth, he was seeing his beloved 'plantationed' Ireland through 'the softening and beautifying mist of years'. (Both Scott and Macaulay later carefully identified the features of 'Auburn' in Goldsmith's home, Lissoy, County Westmeath.)

However, Lancelot's gentle works at Nuneham, deftly levelling, planting and displanting the hilly park to organise the views, were derided as destroying the evidence of *The Deserted Village.*

In reality, the threesome of Lord Harcourt, William Mason – whose flower garden was being made (and has been restored) – at Nuneham and their poetical friend, William Whitehead, seemed to be having too much fun to notice. Whitehead composed a satire in which Dame Nature and Lancelot compete for the beauties of Nuneham, and she eventually concedes to Lancelot, curtseying and blushing, but murmuring as she leaves:

> I may have my revenge on this fellow at last
> For a lucky conjecture comes into my head,
> That, whate'er he has done, and whate'er he has said,
> The world's little malice will balk his design:
> Each fault they'll call his, and each excellence mine.

Two years after Lancelot's death William Cowper's epic *The Task* was published. Cowper was sickly and depressive; he had once lived in Huntingdon, and was now at Olney, not far from Stowe, and must have known what Lancelot was like. Book III of *The Task* is called 'The Garden' and finds the poet 'a stricken deer that has left the herd', viewing the world from the safety of his garden (where he is ruthless with his pruning knife) and bemoaning the rural landscape's surrender to city values and gamblers' wiles:

> Were England now
> What England was, plain hospitable and kind,
> And undebauch'd.

He despises improvement, or seems to, introducing 'The omnipotent magician, Brown' as a villain; but then it is Cowper himself who is spellbound:

> He speaks. The lake in front becomes a lawn,
> Woods vanish, hills subside, and valleys rise,
> And streams, as if created for his use,
> Pursue the track of his directing wand,
> Sinuous or straight, now rapid and now slow,
> Now murmuring soft, now roaring in cascades,
> Even as he bids.

There is ambiguity here: Brown the destroyer of nature, or her wondrous dresser? Cowper's denouement is that the vain lord who has spent all his money on improvement has to leave for the City and political patronage, or even go into the army to recoup his fortunes, but becomes prey to the shark, the leech and the sycophant. Lancelot's works are the ruin of England?

There was plenty of the world's malice in what was called the 'Picturesque Controversy' of the 1790s, most of it directed towards Repton; the arguments were mainly over pictorial composition, as if a landscape's prime user was the painter at his easel with his static view, rather than everyone else passing through, for whom the picture composed and recomposed – the 'moving picture'. In 1794 Thomas Hearne illustrated Richard Payne Knight's poem *The Landscape* with a rather childish insult to Brown, contrasting the bare slopes and naked water of a Brownian park with the lush greenery of the Picturesque version, the house shrouded in bushes, the water course sprouting rocks and greenery. Knight expressed the Picturesque people's hatred of Brown's lawns, and how the goddess Nature:

> wrap't all o'er in everlasting green,
> Makes one dull, vapid, smooth, unvaried scene.

But he reserved his most malicious couplets for Lancelot's lakes, turned into symbols of oppression:

> As the dull, stagnant pool, that's mantled o'er
> With the green weeds of its own muddy shore,
> No bright reflections on its surface shows,
> Nor murmuring surge, nor foaming ripple knows;
> But ever peaceful, motionless, and dead,
> In one smooth sheet its torpid waters spread:
> So by oppression's iron hand confined,
> In calm and peaceful torpor sleep mankind;
> Unfelt the rays of genius, that inflame
> The free-born soul, and bid it pant for fame.*

The response to Knight was swift, in Uvedale Price's *An Essay on the Picturesque*, published by Robson of New Bond Street, also in 1794. But

---

* Knight was a follower of Charles James Fox and those who supported the beginnings of the revolution in France, until the reports of brutality and bloodshed changed their minds.

Price was equally mean to Lancelot: he compared Claude, who began life as a pastry cook, to 'Mr Brown the gardener' who 'formed his style upon the model of a parterre & transferred its minute beauties, its little clumps, knots & patches of flowers, the oval belt that surrounds it & all its twists & crincum crancums to the great scale of nature'. Did Claude's pastry edges appear in the scenes he painted, asked Knight? And, seemingly contradicting himself, he condemns spacious lawns:

> To improve an old family seat,
> By lawning a hundred good acres of wheat.

It was Price who wrote of Lancelot, 'this fellow crawls like a snail all over the grounds and leaves his cursed slime behind him wherever he goes'.

Oddly, it was William Mason's innovatory flower garden at Nuneham that was 'little clumps, knots & patches of flowers', and was to become so popular an expression of the Picturesque. There were many confused notions; but it would appear that Lancelot's name and legacy were saved by controversy, there being no such thing as bad publicity.

And, all the time, there was a thin stream of appreciation: the good William Mason did not let him down, in his late sonnet of 1797, 'To a Gravel Walk':

> Smooth, simple Path! Whose undulating line,
> With sidelong tufts of flow'ring fragrance crown'd,
> Plain, in its neatness, spans my garden ground;
> . . .
> Liberal though limited, restrain'd though free,
> Fearless of dew, or dirt, or dust I rove,
> And own those comforts all deriv'd from thee!
> Take then, smooth Path, this tribute of my love,
> Thou emblem pure of legal liberty!

Here is remembrance of Frances Irwin and Lancelot's path at Temple Newsam, which kept her slippers out of the mud, and all his other serpentine, domed, gravelled garden paths, symbols of liberty.

Also in 1797 the fourth edition of Dr William Mavor's *New Description of Blenheim* sported a refreshing wisdom:

[Brown] saw the deformity of perverted beauty with keener optics than
 Kent, he viewed nature with the enthusiasm of a lover; and though it
 cannot be denied that he sometimes tricked her out in meretricious

ornaments, and patched her with too refined an art, he never lost sight
of her prominent charms; and his worst errors can only be considered
as minute pimples on a beautiful face.

The trouble, according to Dr Mavor, was that Brown – 'originally bred
a gardener' – had given 'every person who can superintend a kitchen-
garden, or handle a spade' the idea to 'quit his sphere and attempt design',
regardless of possessing 'a particle' of Lancelot's genius. This of course
was to be the disease of decades to come.

That shrewd observer, Arthur Young, found time to appreciate both
Croome and Rothley: at Croome (in *Annals of Agriculture*, 1801) he felt
the Malverns themselves to be so deliberately placed as to complete the
scene, the house was 'excellent' and the serpentine sheet of water that
wound through the park 'one of the most perfect pieces of garden scenery',
and clearly the means of effective drainage. He admired Lancelot's 80-
foot cedar, a birch and Turkey oak beside the water, and went on in his
praises for the horticultural delights that the Coventrys had added, the
shrubberies, greenhouses and hothouses, the orangery and the American
borders: 'nothing too crowded', nor jumbled – all is nature, 'not a thistle
or a weed can be seen, not a single tree or shrub is out of its proper
place'. At Rothley, Young had found Lancelot's 'very fine new made lake'
some years earlier (in volume 3 of his *Tour*, 1771): 'the bends and curves
of the bank are bold and natural, & when the trees get up, the whole
spot will be remarkably beautiful'. (Young found the Wallington estate
roads, made by George Brown, 'a piece of magnificence which cannot
be too much praised' and the new hedges 'remarkably good'; the kitchen
garden was 'admirable', and Wallington was 'the only place I have viewed,
as a stranger, where no fees were taken'.)

There was one other 'bred a gardener' whose career in the nineteenth
century has interesting parallels to Lancelot's, and that was Joseph Paxton:
there are similarities between the twenty-five-year-old Lancelot ringing
the bell for admittance on his arrival at Stowe and the nervous Paxton,
aged twenty-three, presenting himself at Chatsworth early one morning in
1826, seventy-five years later. At Chatsworth, Paxton found Lancelot's techniques of drainage, land-sculpture and drive-layout waiting for him, as practical demonstrations; undoubtedly the 6th Duke of Devonshire had to stay
Paxton's hand and preserve Brown's Chatsworth, but he encouraged Paxton
in other ways: to the construction of rock-works, the remaking of the
Emperor Fountain and the Cascade, and the building of his glass and stove
houses – these being Paxton's apprenticeship for the Crystal Palace of the
1851 Great Exhibition. Paxton worked for the Rothschild family, and in

1853 at the Château de Ferrières (about 20 miles east of Paris) he dammed a stream and created a 'Brownian' lake, 'planting trees in subtle groups on the banks'. He also transferred the 'Brownian' techniques to his design for Birkenhead Park, Liverpool's resort across the Mersey and the first public park. The site was swampy, needing drainage and lakes, with landforms and a serpentine path system, as well as varied planting, to make it both interesting and enjoyable. Paxton was blessed with better health than Lancelot, and with catholic ambitions – he was a journalist, author, magazine proprietor, railway promoter and a Member of Parliament; when he died in 1865 he was a very rich man, with a knighthood.

Birkenhead Park, in the making, was seen by a young visitor from America, Frederick Law Olmsted, who had landed at Liverpool at the end of May in 1850. Olmsted also saw Lancelot's Wynnstay and Eaton Hall, and then he and his companions headed for London, by way of the Wye valley, Bath, the Isle of Wight and Portsmouth, 'more than three hundred miles, most of it on foot, in twenty-three days at the cost of seventy-one cents a day per man'. Wales and England in June – eulogised by Olmsted as 'Dear old mother England' and met face to face, and found to be 'a better garden-republic' than his own country, fired Olmsted's ambition to design landscapes. Birkenhead Park influenced his designs for Central Park in New York.

Olmsted was a loyal republican with little sympathy for the landed aristocrats, but on leaving the Grosvenors' park at Eaton he made a note in his diary: 'What artist, so noble . . . as he who, with far-reaching conception of beauty and designing power, sketches the outline, writes the colors, and directs the shadows of a picture so great that Nature shall be employed upon it for generations, before the work he has arranged for her shall realise his intentions.' His note was to himself, a reminder of what he might achieve, but it must have been prompted by seeing, or being told of, Lancelot's £800 worth of landscape plan that was being put in hand on the Grosvenor estate. On a subsequent visit to England, Olmsted saw Trentham and Charlecote. When, after his harrowing experiences as a medic in the Civil War, which ended in 1865, and his campaign to save the giant-redwood forests of Yosemite, Olmsted finally settled to park-making, his landscape practice became the largest and most influential in America and trained a whole generation of landscape architects. In the serene expanses of meadow and lake in Prospect Park in Brooklyn, in the woodland drives through housing along the Des Moines River at Riverside, on the outskirts of Chicago and in miles of scenic parkways, Lancelot Brown's methods were reborn into the exhilarating New World.

★   ★   ★

In Lancelot's home country the second half of the nineteenth century was a low time for the appreciation of his parks, if not quite the lowest. Victorian architects and horticulturists actively disliked the image of a Palladian villa floating in a sea of grass, and the most extreme solution was to rebuild the 'villa' in the neo-Gothic style, with added formal gardens. Some of Lancelot's most famous parks found themselves distanced from their houses by stupendous terrace constructions or acres of balustraded flower gardens: notably Coombe Abbey, Trentham, Harewood, Castle Ashby, Bowood, Luton Hoo and Blenheim, although there were many smaller examples. Sometimes – as at Coombe Abbey and Trentham – these flower terraces were made in the name of restoration, from the old gardens that Lancelot had supposedly swept away. (At this remove in time, supposition – the hazy recall of some aged gardener – was adequate evidence in itself, and no one bothered to find out the truth.) In the worst cases the whole relationship between the house and its landscape was confused and disorientated; at best the new terraces, with their spreads of coloured gravels cut into curlicues, ribbon-bordered hearts and ovals, monograms in box, vases, statues and water-spouts, were so greedy of labour and resources that the parks were left in peace.

A semblance of peace remained throughout the Edwardian era of great shooting parties, when the parks were planted, with rhododendrons and other evergreen 'coverts'. Many estates surrendered the woods that Lancelot had planted in the name of a patriotic duty for the Great War effort. After the war, the deaths of the young as well as the old, and taxes, brought the country society that had paid for – and worked for – Lancelot to its knees. The Twenties were a nadir for the great houses and their estates, and many were carved into lots, stripped of their valuables and sold, even that 'Work to wonder at': Lancelot's Stowe. For many of his parks their future was to be ploughed up, built over or excavated for gravel – the luckier ones fell into institutional or public ownership. Land and land-scape may theoretically be indestructible, but their spirit can be broken.

The rest of the twentieth-century story is fairly briefly told: Christopher Hussey's *The Picturesque: Studies in a Point of View* of 1927 was a reminder of the seemingly lost world of the eighteenth century. Hussey wrote from the high-Victorian library of his home, Scotney Castle at Lamberhurst in Kent, which had its own ruined castle and fern-fringed quarry in a garden of rhododendrons. In his quest for the origins of Picturesque taste, he lifted the heavy velvet drapes of Victoriana that had obscured the past. Others were only too aware of London's eighteenth-century streets and buildings at risk, and after a campaign against the proposed demolition of Nash's Carlton House Terrace, the Georgian Group was formed in

1937 with an avowal to champion the conservation of eighteenth-century buildings, including country houses.

Then came another war: with every country house of any size requisitioned into war use, their lawns covered with Nissen huts, their woods concealing tanks or ammunition dumps (which so frequently exploded), the longing for serenity – dimly positioned in the life of the houses in an England 'that was' – became far wider than the lot of a few architectural historians. Evelyn Waugh's *Brideshead Revisited,* published in December 1944, was a subtle propaganda to divert any sympathy for the decline of the eccentric Flytes towards the much greater pending tragedy, the loss of their house – imagined as Castle Howard – its architecture, art and contents and the gardens and park, these values entrusted to the character of Charles Ryder. War on the home front not only introduced thousands of soldiers, nurses and evacuated schoolchildren to the fragile beauties of these houses and their landscapes, but inspired a widespread dream of a restoration of their peace.

It was into this post-war longing that Dorothy Stroud published her *Capability Brown* in 1950, her researches held up by her own war work. Her cataloguing and locating of more than 200 of his works was a revelation, and a source for a thousand references, especially because, with the Festival of Britain in 1951, there was an official desire to find places of interest for visitors from overseas. Thus it was that the heirs to Lancelot's parks revealed that they were not finished yet; the opening of country houses to visitors really saved Lancelot Brown's legacy, beginning with Lord Bath at Longleat. Though there had been paying visitors as long as there had been country houses, the efficiency with which this was picked up from the haphazard 'shillings in the bucket' method of the 1930s was astounding. Very soon there was a scramble to add the line 'Park by Capability Brown' to the houses' listings, for it was a real 'feather in the cap'. A 1960 guide, price 3s. 6d., to 500 *Historic Houses and Castles* open to the public contains no fewer than thirty-four of Lancelot's parks. A recent edition of *Hudson's Historic Houses & Gardens,* now so weighty, has sixty Brown places. At least another dozen of his parks are publicly owned and open, and others can most likely be seen upon request. (The National Trust has fourteen, and these include Berrington, Charlecote, Clandon, Croome, Dinefwr, Petworth, Stowe and Wimpole).

In the 1970s the scourge of Dutch Elm disease led to the death and destruction of the elms that Lancelot had loved to plant. In 1987 and again in 1990 the Great Storm and its successor, which swept across southern England when the trees were in full leaf, felled whole swathes of his woodlands, especially the shallow-rooted beech trees. But the storm of October 1987 was the proverbial 'ill wind', for the traumatic effects of its passage galvanised English Heritage's process of surveying and assessing the designed parks, and produced government funds for their restoration. Of course, funding and even quangos are transient, and diseases and storms are inevitable, but the Register of the parks and their descriptions is a solid safeguard. Those that are open – and many have free access and are enjoyed for weekend leisure pursuits – are firmly embedded in the affections of the nation.

However, in Britain, the heirs to Lancelot's profession have had a longer struggle than in America, for there has been no equivalent of the messianic Fred Olmsted, nor do we have such exhilarating expanses of space to fill. The Institute of Landscape Architects was founded in 1929, but on rather Reptonian, 'gardenesque' principles, confined to exquisite layouts for public parks, playgrounds and small housing developments. It was only in the late 1950s that people's perceptions awoke to an increase in the scale of living – it was as if our individual human scale had been multiplied by four – and the new unit was the load of a family car. New towns, new roads, new power stations and water supplies were needed, and for this alien scale of design Lancelot Brown's methods were resurrected and used. The landscape architect Sylvia Crowe, who was a consultant to the Ministry of Transport, the Forestry Commission and the power undertakings, and who designed Rutland Water, wrote:

> It is particularly necessary to be able to handle contours when artificial lakes are to be made. Capability Brown was a master of this, as he was of all problems of contouring. His critics' complaints that his slopes were too smooth for a natural effect may surely be discounted, when we see how the easy, graceful sweeps and slopes have stood the test of time, in a way that a picturesquely crumbling bank could never have done. His sheets of water lie naturally within the land-form. If there is a headland, the slight swell on the ground suggests it as a natural formation, if the water widens out, it does so into a gentle basin.

If you have the opportunity to travel the road between Stamford and Oakham, along the north bank of Rutland Water, the truth of these words will be vividly illustrated; the Oakham to Stamford, west–east views are perhaps even more exhilarating, and all are infinitely variable at different times of day or seasons. If you have time for a closer acquaintance with Rutland Water, as the signs repeatedly invite you to, you will realise its capacity to delight sailors, walkers, fishermen, bird-watchers, cyclists and picnic parties – and that it is the pride of this small county. But there are many other evidences of the extrapolation of Mr Brown's skills into the service of our twenty-first-century landscape – the satisfactory 'roll-out' of views from a newer (free-running) motorway (the M40 is a fine example), the redeeming green slopes of restorations of old coal or mineral workings, and the lifting of the deadening green blanket of coniferous planting from beautiful bare mountains. These things are often so subtle that we take them for granted; Sylvia Crowe and her landscape colleagues and successors have been only too aware that, when they have done their job properly, no one realises they have done anything at all. For, like Lancelot Brown and all his flirtations with Dame Nature, she will have the last word:

> The world's little malice will balk his design:
> Each fault they'll call his, and each excellence mine.

NOTES AND SOURCES

Notes

One-off references are given in full; for abbreviated references, please see full details in the list of Sources on p.358.

Prologue

2 **'this planet, Earth'**: Colvin, pp.2–4
2 **'the visual degradation'**: ibid.
2 **'The choice then'**: Fairbrother, pp.7–8
2 **'It was in the eighteenth century'**: Colvin, pp.59–60
2 **'whose name was'**: Stroud, Foreword, 1975. 1984 edn used throughout.
4 **'Your Dryads'**: Stroud, 1984, p.201
4 **'With one Lost Paradise'**: Stroud, 1984, p.202/Walpole and Mason, p.329
4 **'genius/good spirits'**: Stroud, 1984, p.202
4 **'Now Mellicant'**: Hinde, p.204
4 *Newcastle Courant*: 15th February 1783
5 **'Le Brun'**: Stroud, 1984, p.205
5 **'finished England'**: Stroud, 1984, p.202
6 **'Ye Sons of Elegance'**: upon close examination this is a puzzling monument, almost certainly constructed some considerable time after Lancelot's death. The epitaph is shallowly cut in a curious hand, and the lettering – now painted in Roman red – is contorted to fit the centre of three panels, suggesting that the slab, with delicate Gothic decoration, had a previous life. The names of Lancelot, his 'relict' (unconventionally given as *Mrs* Bridget Brown), their sons Lancelot and John, and John's wife Mary (née Linton), who did not die until 1834, are all engraved in the same hand; the younger Lancelot's inscription has been spaced to compensate for the absence of the name of his wife, Frances (née Fuller), who died in 1792, and who has a fine tablet with a veiled figure and an urn by John

Bacon the Younger nearby. In 1910 the church architect, S. Inskip Ladds, whose papers are in the Norris Museum in St Ives, noted the poor condition of the Brown monument but could find no relative willing to take responsibility for repairs. Outside the north-chancel wall is a gravestone for Mary Anne Cowling (d.1884), who is also remembered in the adjacent and very fine stained-glass window. It appears that the Browns and the Cowlings, twelve of them in all, lie in a sealed vault below this north-chancel wall. A modern stone commemorating Lancelot has been placed near the spot (see Family Tree, p. xiii).

6   **'with dirges due'**: Thomas Gray, *Elegy Written in a Country Churchyard*, 1750

1 Northern Perspective

The material for this chapter was gathered from places in the Northumberland landscape that Lancelot knew; I rented a cottage in a farmsteading that dated from his time, and spent my days haunting Kirkharle, Wallington, Cambo, Rothley, Rothbury, Alnwick, Redesdale and Coquetdale. Morpeth Library has a comprehensive local collection, and all the parish registers and major histories are at the Northumberland Collections (Archives) at Woodhorn: www.northumberland.gov.uk/collections.

John and Kitty Anderson's Kirkharle Courtyard – presiding deity, one Lancelot Brown – is a welcome source of creature comforts.

8   **'high-boned faces'**: Colley, p.16

8   **'fyrebrande'**: George Macdonald Fraser, *The Steel Bonnets, the Story of the Anglo-Scottish Border Reivers*, 1971 1986, p.321ff.

9   **'fause-hearted Ha's'**: see Wedgwood, p.72; Reed, pp.110–18 (The Ballad of Parcy Reed)

11   **Joyous Gard/Lancelot**: Alcock, *Arthur's Britain*, p.67; Christina Hardyment, *Malory, The Life & Times of King Arthur's Chronicler*, 2005

12   **'Tillage'**: Welford, p.78

13   **Robert Loraine**: inscription taken from the stone at Kirkharle

15   **'marquess or duke'**: Wedgwood, p.72

15   **Merchant Venturers**: Reed, p.110

15   **'misterie of Gardening'**: Jennifer Potter, *Strange Blooms, The Curious Lives and Adventures of the John Tradescants*, 2006, p.245

15   **'Forest-trees'**: Welford, p.78

16   **Loraine arms**: Hodgson, p.246

16   **'faultless arithmetic'**: Lisa Jardine, *The Curious Life of Robert Hooke*, 2003, p.146

17   **Evelyn, *Sylva***: quoted in Campbell–Culver, spreading oak, p.66; elm, tree of comfort, p.78; glittering beech leaves, p.81; enigmatic ash, p.89

17   **'happiness would be the lot'**: Stephen Switzer, *Ichnographia Rustica*, quoted in Hunt and Willis 1975, pp.151–8

20   **'honour in his own hand'**: Raleigh, Wallington guide 1994, p.37

20   **Daniel Garrett**: see Peter Leach, 'Designs from a Practical Man, the Architecture of Daniel Garrett', *Country Life*, 12th September 1974; 'A Pioneer of Rococo Decoration', 19th September 1974; 'In the Gothic Vein', 26th September 1974

22   **Knowlton**: see Blanche Henrey, *No Ordinary Gardener: Thomas Knowlton 1691–1781*, ed. A. O. Chater, 1986

23   **'proper instruments'**: *Newcastle Courant*, 15th January 1737

23   **theodolite**: see Wallington archives, Letter Book, 1764–76, NRO Woodhorn 672/2/48, 10th October 1769

23   **Hesleyside**: see Brian Hackett, 'A Formal Landscape at Hesleyside in Northumberland', *Archeologia Aeliana*, Newcastle upon Tyne, MCMLX [1960]; see also Barbara Charlton, *Recollections of a Northumbrian Lady 1815–66*, Stocksfield, 1989, p.123

24   **'pleasant and romantic'**: the Woodland Trust leaflet on Hartburn Glebe Woods (available at the site)

2 *Cherchez la femme*, or Lancelot's Bride

A skeletal framework of facts prompted this chapter: that Lancelot had introductions to the Smiths in Buckinghamshire and the Vyners (see Steffie Shields in *Garden History*, 34:2), in Lincolnshire, and that John Penn giving the date of 1739 for the lake at Kiddington in Oxfordshire confirms that Lancelot came south that year; the Langton letter of December 1739 places him in Lincolnshire, emphasising just how inconvenient it was that he fell in love with Bridget Wayet of Boston, which really upset his plans, as his best prospects were miles away in middle England; they married at Stowe in 1744. The rest is geography: the order of his gruelling rides to keep in touch with Bridget, and the undoubted appeal of the country-side back from Boston; the lovely 'Spilsby Crescent' country of the southern wolds, where he might have settled, had there been someone – perhaps William Banks of Revesby (father of Joseph, born in 1743) – with the wit to employ him. Finding the Wayet monuments in St Botolph's church was a comfort; the family continued to prosper and become ever more prominent, though they called themselves Waite in the nineteenth century: see *The Personal and Professional Recollections by the late Sir George Gilbert Scott, R.A.,* ed. G. Gilbert Scott, FSA, 1879.

27   **'The Brides of Enderby'**: this is so evocative of Bridget's background that I could not resist using it; the legends and realities of
those devastating high tides were strong in Boston life, the tragedies
of 1571 long remembered. Jean Ingelow used that memory, along
with those of the 1810 disaster, in which Dinah Craik was drowned
whilst milking her father's cows, in her poem, published in
Poems, 1863. See Roger Norburn, 'Jean Ingelow and her Poetry,' in
All Things Lincolnshire, ed. Jean Howard and David Start, 2007.

27   **'at Gateshead'**: Harvey, p.68

28   **Woodman correspondence**: see Harvey, p.68 and App. VII

28   **'organizer, draughtsman'**: Jill Lever and Margaret Richardson,
The Art of the Architect, 1984, p.50

30   **'of respected memory'**: Thompson, p.101, n.2; also Boston
Guildhall, list of Mayors kindly supplied by Polly Stanley

30   **lantern tower**: Thompson, pp.96–7

31   **Mareham**: Rev. Langton to Banks, quoted in *Lincolnshire Country
Houses & Their Families*, Part 1, p.30

33   **Vyners**: see Steffie Shields 'Mr Brown Engineer, Lancelot Brown's
Early Work at Grimsthorpe Castle and Stowe' in *Garden History*,
34:2, Winter 2006

34   **Mostyn**: John Penn, *An historical & descriptive account of Stoke Park
in Buckinghamshire*, 1813, p.34 (the British Library copy belonged
to Thomas Grenville of Wotton Underwood)

35   **'Kiddington still looks'**: Hinde, p.18

35   **John Taverner**: *Certaine Experiments Concerning Fish and Fruite*, 1600
(reprinted 1928, Manchester, with an introduction by Eric Parker),
quoted in G. M. Binnie, *Early Dam Builders in Britain*, 1987, pp.36–8

36   **extensive garden**: Jacques, p.19

38   **'able to converse'**: Penn, pp.34–5

3 The Kingdom of Stowe

My visits to Stowe have been several in the last thirty-five years or so.
Perhaps it should be a principality, but whatever the title, Stowe is still
to be wondered at – a fabled, haunted landscape; it is much more than
a garden, and yet it must head the list of the 'great' gardens of England.
Its heyday lasted for just 200 years; Dr Clarke notes that it gained 'a
national reputation' in 1724, and in 1924 it was broken up and sold. The
following year a vast collection of Stowe Papers was sold to Henry E.
Huntington for his library in California. For most of the rest of the twentieth century the landscape led a sheltered, fugitive life, surrounded by
the activities of Stowe School. The school saved the landscape, and the

list of saviours includes the architect, Clough Williams-Ellis (who funded the purchase of the land covered by the Buckingham Avenue), the glass engraver Lawrence Whistler, and Dr George Clarke, whose Paper No. 26 for the Buckinghamshire Record Society, *Descriptions of Lord Cobham's Gardens at Stowe (1700–1750)*, provides the backbone for this chapter. Even across 6,000 miles, the Stowe Papers have been continuously analysed and, now that the garden is in their care, the National Trust continues this work; there could well be treasures illuminating Lancelot's decade – the 1740s – still to be found, but enough has become known to construct this chapter and the next.

This chapter is dedicated to Dexter the Doggerel Dog and his *Paws in Arcadia* guide to Stowe (2007, with Anthony Meredith), because his amusing antics made up for the rule that kept my identical Norfolk terrier, Bertie, in the car, although he later enjoyed gallops to the Obelisk.

39   **Congreve:** Clarke, pp.24–7

41   **Pope:** Clarke, pp.30–1

42   **Addison:** *Spectator*, No. 414, 25th June 1712, (Hunt and Willis, pp.141–3)

42   **'managing director':** Stowe School, *The Stoic*, July 1968, 'The Early Life of Richard Temple'

42   **'pretty high':** Celia Fiennes, *From London to Oxford and Thence into Sussex*, c.1694, p.47

43   **Namur:** see Ian Campbell Ross, *Laurence Sterne, A Life*, 2002, p.28

43   **Malplaquet:** Blanning, p.554

43   **'inferior rank':** Brown, 2006, p.37

44   **the military garden:** see Brown, 1999, Ch.3, for an outline history of this taste

44   **'Mr Kent's notion':** Jacques, p.32: see also Mowl, p.216

44   **'Narrow Visto':** anonymous description of Lord Cobham's gardens, 1738, in Clarke, p.67

46   **'about 2 hours':** ibid.

46   **Elysium:** National Trust, Stowe guide, p.35

46   **new gardener's bills:** Shields, in *Garden History*, 34:2; Huntington Library, Stowe Volumes, V. 167, pp.8, 9

47   **William Roberts:** Hinde, pp.23–4

47   **'not charg'd Christmas':** note in accounts, December 1742; Stowe School, *The Stoic,* December 1971, 'Lancelot Brown', pp.17–22

48   **'courteous, moderate':** Friedman, p.20

48   **5 per cent:** Friedman, pp.327–9

48   **'useful Knowledge':** Friedman, pp.31–3

49   **'to the Liberty':** National Trust, Stowe guide, p.37

50 **'Shell-work'**: National Trust, Stowe guide, p.42, quoting Seeley's 1748 guide

50 **'Scene of Magnificence'**: Samuel Richardson (ed.), Defoe's *Tour*, 3rd edition 1742, in Clarke p.79

50 **'were white washed'**: Michael Bevington, Stowe Church guide, 2001, p.6. The marriage and the engraved signatures are noted on p.16.

50 **'habitable House'**: Defoe/Richardson in Clarke, p.81

51 **'Faithful Companion'**: Gilbert West, 1732, in Clarke, p.51

52 **'Modern Xtians'**: Clarke, p.74 (anon)

52 **Garden descriptions**: all from Gilbert West's 'Stowe', in Clarke, pp.36–51, but see also David R. Coffin, 'Venus in the Eighteenth-Century English Garden', *Garden History*, 28:2, 2000, pp.173–93

53 **Signor Fido**: Defoe/Richardson in Clarke, p.91

53 **'O Pitt!'**: James Thompson, The Seasons, 'Autumn'

53 **Hammond**: National Trust, Stowe guide, p.63

53 **Whitehead**: ibid.

54 **'commanding-looking'**: Ayling, p.49; Ayling's Chapter 7, 'The Pitt Style', captures the elusive Pitt as well as anyone: 'Some part of his compulsive power lay in his physical presence. Though his invalidism became chronic, he was tall, elegant, and upright in carriage; his voice was clear and musical; his gestures studied and graceful; his general appearance commanding', p.106

54 **'cockatrice brood'**: Ayling, p.30

54 **'a little paradise'**: Ayling, p.104

55 **'with the rebels'**: Hinde, p.37, quoting *Verney Letters of the Eighteenth Century*, 1930, Vol. 2, p.200

55 **'not Taste or Judgment?'**: Jemima, Marchioness Grey (1748) in Clarke, p.185

56 **'Oval' letter from Brown**: 24th February 1747, in *The Stoic*, December 1971

56 **Chiswick**: see Harris, 1994, p.250

57 **'the plan of the Long Room'**: The Stoic, December 1971

57 **'Noble Apartments'**: Sophia, Lady Newdigate, *Journal 1748*, in Clarke, pp.176–7

58 **'going on Improvements'**: Marchioness Grey, in Clarke, p.185

58 **'the Wind has'**: Lancelot to George Bowes, October 1750, in Hinde, pp.42–3, quoting Strathmore Coll., D/St 347/37, Durham CRO. Lancelot also wrote, 'The scaffolding of buildings of this kind is the greatest arte in the whole, after the foundations'; and in 1754, Reinhold Angerstein saw and sketched the column being built (see

p.58). Lancelot told Bowes that he would have 'a double pleasure' in building at Gibside and in his 'native country', but things turned out differently.

59 **'so disposed'**: Turner, p.179

59 **'my Lady Cobham'**: Anne Grenville to Richard Grenville, 1750, BL Add. MS. 57806. f.76, in Clarke, pp.186–7

60 **'if architectural historians'**: John Harris, 'A Garden of the Mason School, Stoke Park, Buckinghamshire', *Country Life*, 3rd October 1985, pp.940–42

4 Surveying His Future – Lancelot's Great Ride

Jennifer Meir's revelatory researches on Sanderson Miller, collected into her book *Sanderson Miller and His Landscapes* (2006), have provided the clues – to Lancelot's meeting Miller at Stowe and the consequent associations and visits – that we know led to the commission for Croome. After spending several days following Lancelot's complicated progress from Stowe to Croome Court, by car, I returned exhausted, conscious that he *had done the journey on horseback*, which took stamina and determination, and that this journey was crucial in dictating the pattern of his future career. It is difficult to overemphasise the importance of his capacity for hard riding, and the unsung heroic companions of his life were undoubtedly several nameless saddle-horses, of sturdy build and faithful temperament. He kept a saddle-horse (one is mentioned in his draft Will of 1769) even though he had a carriage, which suggests that he enjoyed riding, though his cross-country journeys of as much as 25–30 miles a day were probably confined to his earlier years.

61 **Boyse**: in Clarke, pp.94–111

61 **'that the author of the *Elegy*'**: Mack, p.415

61 **'The Long Story'**: Mack, p.417

62 **Newnham Paddox**: in Hinde, pp.29–31, referring to the Newnham Building Book in Warwickshire Record Office

63 **'Walking in the Garden'**: Jennifer Meir, 'Development of a natural style in designed landscapes between 1730 and 1760: The English Midlands and the work of Sanderson Miller and Lancelot Brown', *Garden History*, Spring 2002, 30:1 pp.24–48. Two of Miller's diaries survive, for October 1749–September 1750 and April 1756–January 1757, in the Warwickshire Record Office

64 **'irregularities'**: Jennifer Meir, 'Sanderson Miller and the Landscaping of Wroxton Abbey, Farnborough Hall and Honington Hall', *Garden History*, Summer 1997, 25:1, pp.81–106

64 **'happy and devout'**: see Peter D. G. Thomas, *Lord North*, 1976, p.4

64 **'Pox take Bumstead'**: Meir op. cit., Summer 1997, p.167, and National Trust, Upton House guide, pp.68–9

65 **'tawny brown carapace'**: see Alex Clifton-Taylor and A. S. Ireson, *English Stone Building*, 1983, p.23

65 **'had dined here'**: Meir op. cit., Spring 2002, pp.24–48

65 **Jago**: Meir op. cit., Summer 1997, pp.81–106

66 **'rode with him'**: Meir op. cit., Spring 2002

66 **'In sturdy Troops'**: ibid.; see also National Trust, Farnborough guide, 1999.

68 **Charlecote 'deserted on every side'**: National Trust, Charlecote Park guide, 2007, p.34, quoting John Foxe (*Foxe's Booke of Martyrs*), who was tutor to Thomas Lucy

68 **'simple shrewdness'**: Fairfax-Lucy, p.190

68 **'abhorred marriage'**: ibid.

68 **'an excellent widow'**: Fairfax-Lucy, p.192

69 **'Fowls' and 'Fish'**: Fairfax-Lucy, p.194, all Mrs Hayes' comments quoted from her Memorandum Book in Warwickshire Record Office

69 **'the best stone-carver'**: Brown, 2006, p.166

69 **'The view'**: Hinde, p.38, quoting *Correspondence of Horace Walpole* ed. Lewis and Brown, 1941, Vol. IX, p.121

69 **Gopsall sketches**: these are in the British Architectural Library/RIBA Collection, at the Victoria & Albert Museum, and also in Brown, *The Art & Architecture of English Gardens*, 1989, pp.49–51

70 **'unhappy, Black day'**: Gordon, p.85

71 **'I am so shocked'**: Gordon, p.84

71 **'Lord Deerhurst'**: Edward Turner, August 1748, in Dickins and Stanton (eds), p.160

71 **'it has always been an Inn'**: Dickins and Stanton (eds), p.162

71 **'drawing a plan'**: Meir, p.41, n.62

72 **'totally changed'**: Stroud, p.69

72 **Medmenham 'friars'**: see Evelyn Lord, *The Hell-Fire Clubs*, 2008, pp.137–48

72 **'peculiar skill'**: Stroud, p.208

73 **'of a Mortification'**: Mowl, p.245

73 **'dog'/fox**: see Hunt, 1987, p.112; also Richard Hewlings, 'Wakefield Lodge and Other Houses of the Second Duke of Grafton', *Georgian Group Journal 3*, 1993, p.48

73 Wakefield Lawn accounts etc. are in The Grafton Papers in Northampton Record Office.

75   **'courting the Muse'**: Thomson quoted in Cousins, p.46

75   **''Tis Nature'**: Brown, 2006, p.157

75   **'grave young lord's**: Gordon, Ch. VII, 'The Grave Young Lord and His Grand Design'

5 Hammersmith, a Stage for Mr Brown

Present-day Hammersmith Broadway is hardly the place to stand and stare into the past, searching for signs of the village that the Brown family knew as their home for thirteen years, from 1751 to 1764. There are a few quiet back streets that have an antique air, St Paul's church survives, though much enlarged from the brick chapel that they knew, and the Mall and the Thames are still geographically, if not atmospherically, in the same places. But really the Browns' Hammersmith of strawberry fields and nursery gardens, and the river busy with all the paraphernalia of sail-boats and fish wives, is gone for ever. Hammersmith dates its self-important bustle from the completion of the first suspension bridge in 1827, engineered by W. Tierney Clark, who was born the year that Lancelot died, 1783. After the bridge came the railways, the tramways and the Underground, and most recently the Great West Road Flyover, which dominates the Broadway. The Hammersmith & Fulham Archives – www.lbhf.gov.uk – smartly housed in the Lilla Huset Professional Centre, tucked beneath the flyover in Talgarth Road – admittedly have very little on the lost world of eighteenth-century Hammersmith. My day was saved with their *History of Hammersmith based upon that of Thomas Faulkner in 1839*, ed. Philip D. Whitting, 1965 (1990 reprint), which gives much of the background for this chapter and the next. I have long blessed the name of Miss Eleanor J. Willson for her *Nurserymen to the World* (1989) on the nursery gardens of the Surrey sands, and now I find that she was formerly Hon. Secretary to the Fulham and Hammersmith Historical Society, as well as the author of *James Lee and the Vineyard Nursery* (1961) and *West London Nursery Gardens* (1982); she has also contributed a chapter entitled 'Farming, Nursery and Market Gardening' to the *History of Hammersmith*, which has been invaluable.

77   **'Danube, Seine or Po'/'late years'**: Defoe, Letter 2, p.174

79   **'Servant to Mr London'**: Whistler, p.62

79   **'when Vanbrugh'**: Whistler, pp.30–1

79   **'most beautiful'/'never fail'**: Harvey, p.79

80   **'as fresh and Lively'**: Brown, *Tales of the Rose Tree*, Ch. 3, 'The King's Botanist's Tale'

81   **'almost manic activity'**: Laird, p.70

81   **'black Virginian walnut-tree'**: see *A Walk Round Fulham Palace*

and Its Garden, Sibylla Jane Flower & Friends of Fulham Palace, 3rd edn 1995

81   **'Apricock Boats'**: *Mr Spectator*, Monday 11th August 1712, in *The Spectator*, ed. Donald F. Bond, 1965, Vol. iv, p.98ff.

81   **vines**: Willson in *History of Hammersmith*, p.95

81   **Lee and Kennedy**: Willson in *History of Hammersmith*, pp.92–3

81   **Hitt**: Harvey, p.83

84   **'Whatever merits'**: Gordon, p.105

85   **'designing'**: Gomme, p.3

88   **'a good deal altered'**: Gordon, p.105

89   **'Mansion Mourns'**: Gordon, p.97

89   **'a few ideas'**: Hinde, p.38, quoting Lewis and Brown (eds), *Walpole Correspondence*, Vol. ix, p.121

89   **'It may look natural'**: see Warwick Castle guide, 2002, p.48

90   **'I have undone'/'family beside it'**: Hinde, p.39

91   **'I must say'**: ibid.

91   **'a little burrough'**: Stroud, 1984, p.61, quoting *Correspondence of Thomas Gray*, ed. P. Toynbee and L. Whibley, 1935, 1971, Letter 192

92   **'a dramatic long sheet'**: Meir, pp.128–9

92   **'a Dunghill of Chalk'**: Dacre to Miller, January 1748, in Dickins and Stanton, p.135

93   **'with its elbows to the town'**: Defoe, Vol. 1, *South-eastern Counties*, Letter 2, p.148

93   **'to reduce'**: Laird, p.136

93   **planting details**: Laird, pp.136–7

94   **'siege to life'**: Boswell, Vol. iii, p.288

97   **'in great style'**: Bolitho and Peel, p.48

97   **'I am sorry'**: Admiral Anson's letter of 26th September 1753 is the first [f.1] of the 'Pakenham Correspondence' series acquired by Dorothy Stroud and later presented by her to the British Library. They are now catalogued as BL Add. Mss. 69795 and given folio numbers in date order.

98   **'white Palladian palace'**: Buchan, p.8

98   **'sharpness of the edge'**: Tom Williamson, 'The Age of the Landscape Park', in *The Parks and Gardens of West Hertfordshire*, T. Williamson, Anne Mallinson and Anne Rowe, 2000, p.43

98   **'artificial molehills'**: ibid, p.42, quoting *Walpole Correspondence*, ed. Lewis and Brown, Vol. ix, p.285, letter to George Montagu of 4th July 1760

98   **'hillocks'**: ibid, p.43, quoting Whateley's *Observations on Modern Gardening*

98   **'dullish piece'**: Buchan, p.8

98   **'Brown has been here'**: Dickins and Stanton, p.226

99   **'The alteration of Burleigh'**: Dickins and Stanton, pp.334–5

99   **'twenty-five years pleasure'**: letter to Lord Harcourt, Harcourt Papers, ed. E. W. Harcourt, 1880–1905, Vol. viii, p.266

100   **'the plums'**: E. C. Till, *A Family Affair*, 1990, p.41

100   **'sett the house dry'/'sore work'**: see E. C. Till, 'The Development of the Park and Gardens at Burghley, *Garden History*, Vol. 19, No. 2, Autumn 1991, pp.128–45, quoting Steward Peter Kemp's reports of the 1560s

100   **'bluff, blunt-featured'**: Inglis-Jones, p.48

100   **'peaceful potentate'**: ibid.

101   **'the Home Manors'**: Till, *A Family Affair*, pp.6–7

101   **'ran his estate'**: ibid, p.8.

102   **'the old Hall'**: Dickins and Stanton, pp.334–5

102   **Osterley Park**: see Iain Browning, *Palmyra*, 1979, p.91

102   **'short notes'**: see Victoria Leatham, *Burghley, The Life of a Great House*, 1992, on the 9th Earl and Lancelot

103   **'matchless vale'**: Thomson, *The Seasons*, 'Summer'

104   **'Belhouse'/'ten acre pool'**: Dacre to Miller, in Dickins and Stanton, p.226

6 Lancelot and 'The Great Commoner'

This chapter came as a great surprise to me, and I resisted its need to exist for a long time. Michael Symes's paper 'William Pitt the Elder: The Grant Mago of landscape gardening' (in *Garden History*, 24:1) suggested Pitt's passion – but on Pitt's side, his political biographers failed to grasp that gardening had any status as a life-force at all, even in the eighteenth century. Once I started to connect the politics to the garden history, and to Lancelot's activities, the evidence for this relationship became a flood. Pitt's was an unfathomable personality netted in class loyalties and patriotism, and only his love for Hester Grenville humanised him. I now feel that he was the puppeteer who made Lancelot's career possible, and that, in his heart, Lancelot knew this.

105   **'My House!'**: Sanderson Miller's ditty is given by Barbara Jones in *Follies & Grottoes*, 1974 edn, pp.398–9; also in Dickins and Stanton, p.348

105   **'to the astonishment'**: Hague, p.11

106   **South Lodge/'wandering Scythian life'**: Ayling, p.103. Pitt acquired the lease of South Lodge with 65 acres from Lady Charlotte Edwin in 1747, and sold it in 1753 to a Mr Sharpe;

see Basil Williams, *The Life of William Pitt*, 2 vols, 1913, vol. I, pp.192–4

106 **'It vexes me'**: Cousins, p.21

106 **'your verdant hills'**: Ayling p.105

106 **'a company of gypsies'**: Ayling, p.136

107 **'continual rains'**: Ayling, p.144

107 **'well cobbled'**: ibid.

107 **'beautiful rural scene'**: Ayling, p.106

108 **'pleasure grounds'**: John Ehrman, *The Younger Pitt, The Years of Acclaim*, 1969, pp.7–8, quoting Christie's Sale Catalogue of 7th May 1789, in Kent County Archives, Till Mss. U.468, Q5/1

108 **'ever passionate husband'**: Ayling, p.168

108 **'through ye Laurels'**: Laird, p.136

108 **'Half Moon Wood'**: Stroud, p.68

108 **'digged right downe'**: John Taverner quoted in Binnie, pp.37–8

109 **'Pittian'**: Hague, pp.9–10

109 **'hold no common ground'**: Leslie Mitchell, *The Whig World 1760–1837*, 2007, p.1

109 **Fox letter**: BL Add. Mss. 69795 f.2

109 **'vain toad'**: Tillyard, p.51

110 **Rhodes's survey**: see Caroline Dakers, *The Holland Park Circle*, 1999, p.25

110 **ill 'on the Road'**: see correspondence with Sir John Hynde Cotton, October–November 1756, etc., Cotton Papers, 588/E26 1–4, Cambridgeshire Archives

111 **contract**: ibid., November 16th 1756

111–12 **'systematic'/'truest taste'**: Gerald Wellesley, 7th Duke of Wellington, *Collected Works*, 1990, p.144

112 **'gentle Hertford'**: see Brown, 2006, and Helen Sard Hughes, *The Gentle Hertford, Her Life and Letters*, New York, 1940. Frances Hertford's letters are in Alnwick Castle Archives.

113 **'a landscape of lawns'**: Laird, pp.141–2

113 **'a wild lane'**: see Brown, 2006, pp.144–5

116 **'a fine lawn'**: *Capability Brown and the Northern Landscape*, comp. Gill Hedley, Newcastle, 1983, p.19

117 **'Protestant and Anglophone'**: Colley, p.101

117 **'heaven-born general'**: Ayling, p.262

117 **'well-wishers'**: Stroud, p.121

118 **Ragley**: Stroud, 1984, p.237; Turner, p.186

118 **'Dutch style'/'Newbury cabbages'**: John Harris, 'Le Rouge's

Sion Hill: A Garden by Brown', in *The London Gardener or The Gardener's Intelligencer,* No. 5, 1999–2000, pp.24–8

118 **'a rope & a border'**: ibid.

119 **Enville**: the archives held at Enville Hall have been catalogued online for the Historical Manuscripts Commission (ref. GB-2184-Grey) and are extensive. Harry Grey, 4th Earl of Stamford, lived at Enville until his death in 1768 and there are boxes of estate correspondence, day-books and accounts, etc., which may yield evidence of Lancelot's work.

119 **'ever-warm and victorious'**: Ayling, pp.262–3, quoting Walpole, 21st October 1759

119 **Marchioness Grey**: her papers are in Bedfordshire & Luton Archives (L.30, etc.); see also Joyce Godber, 'Marchioness Grey of Wrest Park' in *Bedfordshire Historical Record Society,* Vol. XLVII, 1968; and English Heritage, Wrest Park guide

120 **'the canals'**: Godber op. cit., p.62

7 'The One Great Argument of the Landscape Gardener'

By now it has become clear that Lancelot's great passion was for water engineering, and that the provision of a lake was his trump card. For some reason this has recently been regarded as a vice, a systematic imposition upon the landscape by one short of imagination. Our eyes, sated with flooded gravel pits and reservoirs, have to close – and open upon an eighteenth-century landscape with hardly any stretches of water in lowland England large enough to be called lakes, and furthermore upon many great houses at risk in their waterlogged parks. That the nineteenth- and twentieth-century agriculturists overdid the drainage of meadows and marshes is not a crime to be attributed to Lancelot.

121 **'The one great argument'**: Sacheverell Sitwell on Blenheim's lake in *British Architects and Craftsmen,* quoted by David Green in *Blenheim Palace* guide, published by the Estate Office, 1950, p.3

121 **'And now for the *Water'***: Izaak Walton and Charles Cotton, *The Compleat Angler,* ed. John Buxton, p.32

121 **'Gravely inquiring'**: ibid., Foreword p.xxx

122 **'Landscape = habitat'**: Fairbrother, p.4

122 **Wilson/Farington**: see Leslie Parris, *Landscape in Britain c.1750–1850,* Tate Gallery, 1973, p.32. This theme can be pursued; Wilson painted Tabley House (1774) looking like a Brown landscape, though as far as we know it was not, and George Barret painted the lake at Burton Constable even as Lancelot was making it.

122 **'study of the folk-heart'**: *The Compleat Angler op. cit.,* Introduction

122   **'in the pastoral tradition'**: ibid., Editor's foreword, p.xxv
122   **'amiable'/'ruined his health'**: Foreman, pp.14–15
123   **'vast extended moor'/'beautiful palace'**: Defoe, pp.476–7
124   **'very high mountain'**: ibid.
124   **'found building so delightful'**: *Chatsworth*, ed. Charles H. Wood, 1973, p.30
125   **'making vast plantations'**: Stroud, 1984, p.104, quoting Walpole, *Visits to Country Seat*, Walpole Society, Vol. XVI, p.28; see also Tom Williamson, 'Chatsworth', *Garden History*, 29:1, Summer 2001, pp.82–90
125   **'crowning the long hill'**: Duchess of Devonshire, pp.148–9
125   **'foolish waterworks'**: Walpole, quoted by Tom Williamson, 'Chatsworth' op. cit., p.86
125   **'serpentised not at all'**: Duchess of Devonshire, p.148
125   **'ugly ponds'**: *Chatsworth*, ed. Wood op. cit., p.30
125   **'I am ever thankful'**: Duchess of Devonshire, p.148
126   **'a patch of rushes'**: Duchess of Devonshire, p.173; the new guide, *Explore the Gardens at Chatsworth*, ed. Simon Seligman, Chatsworth House Trust, 2005, has an explanatory two-page spread (pp.14–15) on the water works
126   **Mrs Travis**: Duchess of Devonshire, pp.152–3
127   **'His Grace's waggon'**: 1757–8 facsimile page of accounts, in Duchess of Devonshire, p.77
127   **'To the Revd Mr Barker'**: Duchess of Devonshire, p.151
127   **letter of 2nd January 1765**: Stroud, 1984, p.126
128   **Gray on Chatsworth**: Mack, pp.543–4
128   **'a fayre house'**: Olivia Staughton and Jeanne Upton (eds), *Latimer, A History of the Village*, 1999, p.4
129   **'procured' the view**: Stroud, 1984, p.231, quoting George Johnson's *History of English Gardening*, 1829
129   **'little paradise'**: quoted in Staughton and Upton op. cit., p.15ff., but see also Sir G. G. Scott, *Recollections* 1879.
129   **'a little decorated'**: Fairfax-Lucy, pp.201–2
130   **'Wellsborn Brook'**: 29th September 1757, Mrs Hayes, quoted in Fairfax-Lucy, p.213
130   **'smooth flaxen sheets'**: Fairfax-Lucy, p.195
130   **contract articles**: Fairfax-Lucy, pp.213–15, with a note to the effect that the original contract has been lost, but Mary Elizabeth Lucy (1803–90) quoted it in her journal and 'though she was often careless, there is no reason to suppose she did not record the substance of it'
131   **'£100 note'**: Fairfax-Lucy, p.213

131 **'of a much sweeter'/'cold in Winter'**: *The Compleat Angler* op. cit., pp.212–13

133 **'a long serpentine'**: Williams, pp.86–7

133 **'a number of Expences'**: Lord Dacre to San Miller, see Laird, p.149

134 **'as much in the mud'**: George Grenville to Miller, 1758 (eds), Dickins and Stanton, p.214

134 **'deep shades'**: Ayling, p.181

134 **'most affectionate grandfather'/'good dancing'**: in Brown, 2006, p.52

135 **'50,000 acres'**: Thynn, pp.26–7

135 **'debt and disrepair'**: Thynn, p.34

135 **'*the gardens are no more!*'**: Mary Delany, quoted in Ruth Hayden, *Mrs Delany and her flower collages*, 1992 edn, p.81; see also David Burnett, *Longleat, The Story of an English Country House*, Wimborne Minster, 2009

136 **'catamaran'**: for the Petty fortune, see P. G. Dale, *Sir W.P. of Romsey*, Romsey, 1987

136 **displaced locals**: see *The Independent* online, 20 July 2007, on the mystery of Mannings Hill and local press reports about the underwater archaeology of the Bowood lake, blaming Lancelot (of course) for drowning a 'lost city', although only remnants of one garden or field wall were found!

136 **'What wou'd you give'**: Hinde, p.85, quoting the Earl of Kerry, 'Bowood Park', *Wiltshire Archaeological and Natural History Magazine*, XLII, December 1924

137 **'I am persuaded'**: ibid., see also Stroud, p.90

137 **'Making the great Walks'**: Stroud, p.87, from Corsham Archives

137 **'My health'**: ibid.

139 **'exceeding great tumble'**: Hinde, p.83

140 **Charlotte's arrival, etc.**: see Claire Tomalin, *Mrs Jordan's Profession*, 1995, pp.12–14

140 **'only three CROWNS'**: Brown, 2004, p.13. The Yale Center for British Art, Dept of Prints and Drawings, has a plan of the scheme for St James's Park, B 1975.2.485

142 **election to Society of Arts, etc.**: recorded in Ms Subscription Book 1754–63 in the library of the Royal Society of Arts (RSA), John Adam Street, London

142 **Colonel Clive**: *Diary of a Duchess*, ed. James Greig, 1926, Tuesday 15th July 1760

143 **'for mezzotints'**: see Minute book 1759–60, f. 142, RSA Library

143 **'an unimaginative schoolmaster'**: J. Steven Watson, *The Reign of George III*, Oxford History, England, 1960, p.96

144 **Marlborough, 29th June 1763**: BL Add. Mss. 69795 f.4

144 **'the chief is Thamisis'**: *The Compleat Angler* op. cit., p.208

145 **Aynho papers**: Northamptonshire Record Office, Aynho C(A) 6273 and 6274, and ML 1310, Accounts of Francis Burton 1758–70

145 **'a truly monumental structure'**: David Green, 'Blenheim: The Palace and Gardens under Vanbrugh, Hawksmoor and Wise', in *Blenheim, Landscape for a Palace*, ed. Bond and Tiller, 1995, pp.76–7

146 **'Mr Vanbrugh my enemy'**: ibid., p.3; Bond and Tiller, p.77

146 **constant disputes**: Vanbrugh v. the Duchess Sarah is documented by David Green op. cit.; see also Lawrence Whistler, *The Imagination of Vanbrugh and his Fellow Artists*, 1954, p.122ff.; Frances Harris, *A Passion for Government, the Life of Sarah, Duchess of Marlborough*, 1991; and Ophelia Field, *The Favourite, Sarah, Duchess of Marlborough*, 2002

146 **'Survey . . . before Mr Brown's works'**: this is discussed in David W. Booth, 'Blenheim Park on the eve of Mr Brown's improvement', *Journal of Garden History, 15:2*, Summer 1995, pp.107ff. The drawing is in the Canadian Centre for Architecture, Montreal, Acc. no. DR 1985:0416.

146 **'he was an old man'**: Green, p.101ff.

146 **'colossal polygon'**: ibid., see also Brown, 1999, chapter on the Military Garden, pp.93–4

146 **'ranks of rifle green'**: Green, pp.101ff.

147 **'cascade/swans & all such sort'**: David Green, *Blenheim Park & Gardens*, 1972, p.10.

148 **Stukeley sketch**: reproduced in Booth, *Journal of Garden History* op. cit.; Bodleian Library, Oxford, Top. Gen. D. 14, f.14

148 **'The minnows'**: David Green, *Blenheim Palace*, 1950, p.3

148 **1961 aerial survey**: in Bond and Tiller, p.83

150 **'On Lord Holland's Seat'**: Mack, pp.588–9; Barbara Jones, *Follies & Grottoes*, p.351; see also Hugh Honour, 'An Epic in Ruin Building', *Country Life*, 10th December 1953

151 **'had Bute been true'**: Bute and Shelburne were Lancelot's clients, but Richard Rigby was not; John Calcraft, possibly Fox's natural son, lived a colourful life and a prosperous one, but 'defected' to be Pitt's right-hand man; Lancelot visited Calcraft at Ingress Abbey, dramatically sited on the Thames at Greenhithe, between Dartford and Gravesend, and he also went to see Leeds Abbey, in the village of Leeds near Leeds Castle, which Calcraft bought shortly before

his death. He died at Ingress on 23rd August 1772, before anything was done in either place. For Ingress, see Anthea Taigel, 'Obituary for Ingress', in *The London Gardener*, Vol. 4, 1998–9.

8 The King's Master Gardener at Hampton Court

It has always been assumed that the Duke of Newcastle arranged Lancelot's royal appointment, but an odd reference led to the location of Lancelot's letter of June 1764 in the Grenville Papers: the Duke was a Thomas Greening man, with little time for Lancelot, and he must have rolled in his tomb when Lancelot came to rebuild his beloved Claremont for Robert Clive. On the other hand, George Grenville, Pitt's brother-in-law, stepped into the role of Lancelot's benefactor during his timely elevation as First Lord of the Treasury from April 1763 until July 1765. Otherwise, I confess to a certain breathlessness in this chapter in trying to keep up with Lancelot's phenomenal pace of work and travelling: for my reader's sake, jobs have to be accomplished in one or two continuous passages, whereas in reality he was dodging backwards and forwards across England, spending half a day here, then two hours there, in a chaotic progress that was often in complete disregard of geography.

152   **'But your Great artist'**: now known to be by Sidney Swinney and addressed to Viscount Irwin in 1767, quoted in Hedley, *Capability Brown and the Northern Landscape*, 1983, p.32 (West Yorkshire Archives, Temple Newsam Mss)

152   **'You, I am sure'**: Supplement to the Grenville Papers, BL Add. Mss. 57822–57828, f.155, 22nd June 1764

153   **'raising pineapples' etc.**: Stroud, 1984, p.122

153   **'supplying Horse Dung'**: Green, p.62

154   **'The whole project'**: BL Add. Mss. 57822, f.155

154   **'every contiguous spot'**: Jane Roberts, *Royal Landscape*, 1997, p.61

155   **Pitt on Eton**: Ayling, p.23

156   **'Capey'**: *The Eton College Register 1753–90*, ed. R. A. Austen-Leigh, 1921, notes Lance's entry on 7th September 1761, fee two guineas, boarding with Mrs Mary Young at the Manor House, Eton; Lance left in 1765 for Trinity College, Oxford; Jack apparently entered Eton College in 1762, leaving in 1765 for the navy.

156   **'afflicted with an Asthma'**: Heath, p.86

157   **'rich and brilliant glaze'**: Berg, pp.132–3

158   **'grace and favour'**: Thurley, p.317ff.

158   **Great Fountain Garden**: Green, p.72

158   **Evelyn 'near perfected'**: Green, p.62

159   **'planting all ye trees'**: Green, p.63

159 **'Grate Avenew'**: ibid.

159 **'Chestnut Sunday'**: ibid.

159 **The account book**: this is in the Royal Horticultural Society's Lindley Library in Vincent Square, London

164 **James Wood at Huntingdon**: see John Drake, *Wood & Ingram: A Huntingdon Nursery 1742–1950*, 2008; these unique nursery records (yet to be fully analysed) show orders for Burghley and Wimpole whilst Lancelot was working there, and further vividly illustrate the gardening enthusiasms of the countryside around Huntingdon and Fenstanton, which perhaps attracted him to purchase the Manor of Fenstanton

165 **'your Lordship has taken William Ireland'**: Stroud, 1984, pp.133–4, quoting a letter of 11th March 1767 to Lord Bute, BL Add. Mss. 5726, f.72. The landscape architect David Brown has researched the foremen, see 'Lancelot Brown and his Associates', *Garden History*, 29:1, Summer 2001, pp.2–11; see also David Brown, 'Nathaniel Richmond, one of the first Ornamental Gardeners, and the London Network in the mid-Georgian period', *The London Gardener*, 1998–9, No. 4, pp.37–9

165 **'Milliken I sent for you'**: Stroud, pp.126–8

165 **'by whose attention'/'keeping them'**: BL Add. Mss. 69795, f.13

166 **Princess of Wales's garden**: 11th March 1767, BL Add. Mss. 5726, f.72

166 **'very fine beeches'**: Young, Vol. 1 (of 4), 1771, pp.24–5

167 **'morning air'**: Switzer, quoted in Susan Campbell, *Charleston Kedding, A History of Kitchen Gardening*, 1996, p.49, etc. Further descriptions from 'A Brief History of the Luton Hoo Walled Garden' (which is being restored), see: www.lutonhoowalledgarden.org.uk

167 **'unspoiled old English land'**: Williams, p.154

167 **'Kew Cart'**: see M. Baxter Brown, *History of the Royal Deer Park*, 1985, p.110

168 **Audley End**: this is beautifully put into context in *Littlebury, A Parish History*, 2005, for the History Group of the Parish of Littlebury Millennium Society; see also English Heritage, Audley End guide

169 **'the common brick bridge'**: in *Littlebury*, p.102

169 **contract details**: Turner, p.97

171 **'was very backward'**: Hinde, p.90

171 **'by a gentleman's agreement'**: I have tried to calm the heated descriptions of the Audley End affair by gathering evidence from several sources, including Lancelot's account records, *Littlebury*, Dorothy Stroud (1984) and Thomas Hinde (who gives the fairest

treatment). The arguments pale into insignificance at Audley End itself, an exquisite Brownian miniature.

171 **'none so blind'**: Hinde, p.92

171 **'whole incident is a strange one'**: ibid.

173 **'Mrs Serle'**: Stroud, 1984, p.242. The Serle family, merchants of Leghorn, had owned Testwood since 1695 and there are fine memorials in Eling church. They were also connected to Weston Corbett near Basingstoke and to Chilworth near Southampton, so Lancelot perhaps had hopes of their patronage. However, they seem to have been extraordinarily warm-hearted people – he would have loved the Test waterscape around Testwood – although no work materialised.

173 **'water house'/'the Mold and Soyle'**: Fiennes, p.73

173 **'giving away'**: Stroud, 1984, p.137

174 **'only settled the plans'**: Turner, p.108

174 **Middleton, Exeter and Totnes**: contemporary descriptions of the industries of these towns are given in R. R. Angerstein's *Illustrated Travel Diary 1753–55*, translated by T. and P. Berg, 2001

177 **''Tis yours, My Lord'**: Turner, p.148

178 **'russet-coloured' hair**: Foreman, p.7

178 **John Spencer's marriage**: Charles Spencer, *The Spencer Family*, 1999, p.111

179 **Althorp**: on 24th January 1780 the Countess Spencer wrote, 'Mr Brown has been giving some very excellent advice about this place . . . and I think all his ideas are good. He is against removing your Barns' (probably the dominant Roger Morris stables of 1732–3), see Stroud, 1984, p.214. Henry Holland extended and reorganized the house for £20,257, but Lancelot never worked there. It was Althorp's great loss, for the gardens and the Round Oval pool were laid out by W. M. Teulon in the 1860s and are very disappointing.

179 **'stood close'**: Stroud, 1984, p.135. The survey plan by an unknown hand for the work done at Wimbledon by Lancelot shows 1,200 acres of the park with paths, belts of trees, clumps, water courses and the dam for the large lake; the house and village church are on the south of the site, with an older kitchen garden, and roads and neighbouring properties neatly labelled. Canadian Centre for Architecture, Montreal, Acc. no. DR1985:0415

9 Brownifications! (Hampton Court 1765–7)

'Brownifications' is a term invented by Viscountess Irwin for Lancelot's doings at Temple Newsam; a great deal of mud was usually involved. His work pace was still frenetic; it is worth noting that he had no secretary or assistant at home to manage his expeditions, and occasionally he wrote ahead to make appointments or sometimes made a date verbally when meeting his client in London. More often he just turned up, and his sudden appearances became the mark of his celebrity. In his early days he approached via the walled kitchen garden, the gardeners' entrance, but as the King's Master Gardener he would have called at the Estate Office, and gradually – as his fame increased – at some houses he would have been received at the front door!

180 **'While from the Thames'**: Sidney Swinney, quoted in Gill Hedley, *Capability Brown and the Northern Landscape*, 1983, p.32

181 **'real mortification'**: 6 March 1765, Tottenham correspondence for Brown's work; Wiltshire and Swindon Archives, Ailesbury Papers, 1300/1910 quoted in Hinde, p.108.

181 **'in a storm of snow'**: ibid., p.110

181 **'a miniature Holkham'**: see Harris, 1994, p.87ff

181 **'tolerably favourable'/'alter my route'**: Tottenham correspondence op. cit.

182 **'Brown was'/'Canal Age'**: Hal Moggridge, '"Capability" Brown at Blenheim', Ch. 8 in Bond and Tiller, pp.90–114, offers a brilliant analysis of his technical achievements

182 **'Park Farm'**: ibid., p.104

182 **Fawsley in Northamptonshire**: the survey by George Nunns, 1741 (a hand-painted masterpiece of cartography), is in the County Archives, ref. Map 853. Maurice Beresford, *History on the Ground*, 1984, identifies Fawsley's deserted village, and led the vilification of Lancelot with such sentences as: 'The church's setting in the deer park makes it perhaps the most scenic of all the Midland deserted villages for those who like their landscape tamed in the Capability Brown manner', even though he affirms that depopulation took place 'just before 1485' (p.111), and Nunns's survey confirms the shape of the landscape prior to Lancelot's work. In Beresford's *The Lost Villages of England*, 1998 edn, many more Brown parks are 'targeted' – Stowe, Burton Constable, Wotton Underwood, Harewood, Wimpole, Nuneham Courtenay, Milton Abbas, Coombe, Compton Verney among them; in many cases Professor Beresford confirms a much earlier date for depopulation, but merely by association he has provided ammunition for Lancelot's detractors. Some cases I have been able to defend, but the 'lost village' literature is now so vast that it would need another book to state the positions properly. I hope to have shown enough of Lancelot's character to make it clear that he would never have evicted a family from their

cottage, unless giving them a better one, for he understood too well what hardship that caused.

183 **'Mr Brown'**: Stroud, 1984, p.91

183 **'nearer to every day'**: ibid.

183 **'in perfect order'/'satisfy yourself'**: Tottenham correspondence op. cit.

184 **'how the passion'**: Ayling, pp.333–4

184 **'of his demands'**: ibid.

184 **'I called at'**: Chatham Papers, PRO/30/8/24/ f.137, 10th September 1765

185 **'I have been'/'very unpleasant'**: Tottenham correspondence op. cit.

186 **'Mr Brown complained'/'narrow avenue'**: ibid.

186 **'In Lancashire'/'greater connection'**: in Anthony Burton, *The Canal Builders*, 1972, pp.24–5

187 **Ashridge**: see Kay N. Sanecki, *Ashridge: A Living History*, 1996

188 **Shugborough**: see Corinne Daniela Caddy, *Shugborough, The Complete Working Historic*, Estate guide, 2008

188 **Ingestre pavilion**: this is a Landmark Trust property available for holiday lets, and a few days spent there enable exploration of this quiet countryside: see www.landmarktrust.org. There is probably a book in Lancelot's adventures at Shugborough, Ingestre and Tixall and their connections, if only the evidence could be found!

189 **'occhilor survey'**: Uglow, p.109

189 **'He knew Water'**: James Brindley, online Wikipedia entry

190 **'*one line of grace*'**: Saunders, p.94

190 **'Trent, so called'**: *The Compleat Angler* op. cit., p.209, also quoting Michael Drayton's, *Idea's Mirrour*, 1594

191 **'lowering the hill'**: Stroud, 1984, pp.148–9

191 **'confessedly one'**: Stroud, 1984, p.147, quoting James Paine in *Plans of Noblemen's and Gentlemen's Houses*, 1767

191 **'Brownifications'**: 'you will find us very dirty for we are over head and heels in Brownifications, and a little rain with a good many carts makes mires but a great deal which we have had lately makes a *quagmire*'; Frances, Viscountess Irwin, to Susan Countess Gower, Granville Mss, PRO 30/29/4/2 corres., f.25

191 **'We have had a long continuance'**: ibid., 7th October 1765

191 **'good-looking'/'deeply smitten'**: James Lomax, 'Temple Newsam: A Woman's Domain', in *Maids & Mistresses, Celebrating 300 Years of Women and the Yorkshire Country House*, ed. Ruth M. Larsen,

York, 2004, pp.89–105; see also Adrian Budge, 'Temple Newsam and the Good Shepheards', *Leeds Arts Calendar* 98, 1986

192 **'the most expeditious way'**: Stroud, p.116

192 **Sidney Swinney**: quoted in Hedley op. cit.

192 **'I am out of doors'**: Francis Irwin, PRO 30/29/4/2 f.20, 8th April 1766

192 **'a deal has been done**: ibid., f.21, 26th July 1766

192 **Brownifying**: ibid., 5th February 1767

193 **'my little Horsham business'**: Lomax op. cit., p.99, quoting PRO, undated letter 1780

193 **'with my girls'**: ibid., p.98, quoting PRO, undated letter

193 **Swinney's verse**: quoted in Hedley op. cit.

193 **'I apply myself'**: Lomax op. cit., pp.98–9

194 **'to extricate'**: Ayling, pp.349–50. Was the relationship between George III and Pitt coloured by the remembrance that Pitt had witnessed George's marriage to Hannah Lightfoot at St Anne's Chapel in Kew in April 1759 and there were three children from the 'marriage'? See David Blomfield, *Kew Past*, 1994, p.40.

194 **'of advanced taste'**: see Batoni's portrait of the young 7th Earl in Edgar P. Bowron and Peter B. Kerber, *Pompeo Batoni, Prince of Painters in Eighteenth-century Rome*, Houston and London, 2008, p.61

194 **'that you and Mr Drummond'**: Hinde, p.137ff., which deals with Castle Ashby in detail

195 **'I had the pleasure'/'in perfect union'**: letter to Lady Chatham, Chatham Papers, PRO/30/8/24, f.139, 10th April 1767

195 **'given me your answer'**: Hinde, p.137

195 **'defer my journey'**: ibid.

196 **'his health to mention'**: Chatham Papers, PRO/30/8/24, f.142, 7th June 1767

196 **'mentally shipwrecked'**: Ayling, p.368

196 **'up into his head'**: ibid.

196 **'enfeebled state'**: Ayling, p.369

196 **'devoted to Lord Chatham'**: in Chatham Papers, PRO/30/8/24, f.143, 7th August 1767

196 **'bewildered'**: Ayling, pp.368–72, gives a detailed account of Pitt's collapse

197 **'much out of order'**: Hinde, p.138, who was able to research in the Compton Archives at Castle Ashby, which are no longer accessible. The catalogue of the Compton Documents, Vol. V, in Northamptonshire Record Office, gives a general description and details of plans.

197 **'I hope in God'**: Chatham Papers, PRO/30/8/24, f.145, 10th September 1767

197 **'in exchange for it'**: Stroud, 1984, p.109; Hinde, p.138

198 **Lancelot's draft Will of 1769**: this is in Huntingdonshire Record Office

199 **'Break off. Break off'**: Grey papers, Luton and Bedfordshire Archives, L30/9a/9/f.124, 19 Sept 1769

200 **'Complimts of the season'**: BL Add. Mss. 69795 f.20

10 Return to the North

The question arises: did Lancelot grow so grand and successful that he forgot his origins? It was not in his affectionate and loyal nature to do so, but up until now his work and travelling and his young family seem to have taken all his time, and at Stowe and Hammersmith there would have been few opportunities to break away from his preoccupations. He went as far north as Harewood near Harrogate in 1758, and all the way to Lowther near Penrith in 1763, and surely called at Kirkharle on that occasion. It appears that contacts with Biddy's family at Boston were more frequent, as they were easier. After his brother John's death in 1766 and the purchase of Fenstanton the following year, which gave him a base on the road to the North, Lancelot travelled that way more frequently, and his working visits to Kirkharle, Wallington and Alnwick in 1769 and 1770 were in celebratory mood, albeit tinged with some social inflexibilities.

201 **'When You bid Me'**: *The Letters of David Garrick*, ed. D. M. Little and G. M. Kahrl, 1963, col. II, letter no. 600

201 **'great alterations'**: Stroud, 1984, p.123

202 **'Amsterdam design'**: see Susan Campbell, *Charleston Kedding*, p.154ff. and Ch. 11 on the Vinery

202 **Hampton houses**: see Heath, Hampton Court, 2000

203 **'David Garrick'**: he was born in Hereford, at the Angel Inn, by the accident of his parents visiting the town, though he regarded Lichfield as his home; see Robin Haig, *A History of Theatres & Performers in Herefordshire*, Logaston, 2002, p.16

203 **'Garrick picked up'**: Benedetti, p.188

203 **'quit his own mind'**: Benedetti, p.192

203 **'frozen by terror'**: Uglow, *Hogarth*, 1997, pp.399–400

204 **'I shall content Myself'**: Garrick, *Letters* nos 134 and 137 n.4

204 **'Home, seeing the tunnel'**: Stroud, 1984, p.81

204 **Ice houses**: see Tim Buxbaum, *Icehouses*, 2008; also Sylvia Beamon and Susan Roaf, *The Icehouses of Britain*, 1990

205 **Lord Chalkstone**: quoted in Michael Symes, 'David Garrick and landscape gardening', *Journal of Garden History*, 6:1, pp.34–49; Laird, p.163

205 *The Clandestine Marriage*: Symes op. cit., p.48

206 **Edward Lovibond**: Lovibond (1724–75) lived at Elm Lodge or The Elms, High Street, Hampton, from 1748; a gentleman of leisure, poet and contributor to *The World*, he was also interested in the 'rural economy'; see Twickenham Local History Society, Paper no. 67, *The Fashioned Reed*, by Brian Louis Pearce, 1992

206 **'A Grotto this'**: Michael Symes, *The English Rococo Garden*, 1991, pp.66–8; also Heath, pp.74–5

207 **'Till a lawn'**: Hunt, 1987, p.49, cat. nos 48 and 49, designs for Euston Hall

207 **'not really up to the job'**: Jeremy Black, *George III, America's Last King*, 2008, p.93

208 **George Stubbs**: see Robin Blake, *George Stubbs and the Wide Creation*, 2005

211 **'he will be missed'**: Wallington Estate Letterbook, 1764–76, Northumberland Record Office, NRO 672/2/48, March 1766

211 **John Brown and the Portland estates**: Letters from 1762 (Pw F 1730) to 1767 (Pw F 1835) in the (online) Catalogue of Papers of William Henry Cavendish-Bentinck, 3rd Duke of Portland, Part 4, University of Nottingham Library. Subsequent letters to 1782 detail Richard Brown's career as agent.

211 **'charitable benefaction'**: John Brown to 3rd Duke of Portland, 15th January 1763 ibid.

212 **'4 Isle of Skye cows'**: John Brown, 20th October 1764 ibid.

212 **'unwearied diligence'**: Richard Brown, 24th March 1767 ibid.

213 **'knowledge and skill'**: Colin Shrimpton, *A History of Alnwick Parks and Pleasure Grounds*, 2006, p.36

214 **'upon herself the role'**: ibid., p.37

214 **'made to feel at home'**: Bertram Hylton Davis, *Thomas Percy, A scholar-cleric in the age of Johnson*, Philadelphia, 1989, p.142

214 **'deep sequestered Valley'**: Thomas Percy, *A Letter describing the ride to Hulne Abbey from Alnwick etc.* (5th August 1765), University Library, Cambridge

215 **'principal estate servant'**: Shrimpton op. cit., p.37ff.

216 **'Look about you'**: ibid., p.49

217 **'Lady Loraine'**: Wallington Letterbook 672/2/48, October 1769

217 **'that he would have'**: ibid., 3rd March 1770

217 **'a vast ruin'd Castle'**: Hedley, op.cit., 1983, p.27

217 **'a very fine'**: Young, 1771, Vol.3, p.94

218 **exhibition in Newcastle**: *Capability Brown and the Northern Landscape*, Tyne and Wear County Council Museums and the North East Chapter of the Landscape Institute, Laing Art Gallery, Newcastle, June–July 1983, and Bowes Museum, Temple Newsam and Cleveland Gallery, Middlesbrough

219 **'desiring me to'**: Wallington Estate Letterbook, NRO 672/2/48, 18th September 1770, to Mr Lancelot Brown at Lady Loraine's at Kirkharle

220 **Stubbs 'shooting pictures'**: Blake, pp.172–3

220 **'and gives me some direction'**: Wallington Letterbook, NRO 672/2/48, 18th September 1770

220 **'the impropriety'**: Wallington Letterbook, NRO 672/2/48, 30th September 1770, to 'Mon. Blackett' in Paris

220 **'If you have five Minutes'**: BL Add. Mss. 69795 f.116

222 **'Their Majestys'**: Stroud, 1984, p.124

222 **'not in so good a condition'**: Stroud, 1984, pp.124–5; PRO Works ¼, pp.86–7, letters dated 29th October and 5th November 1770

11 'All Over Estates and Diamonds'

Meant as an insult, this quote is Horace Walpole on Robert Clive (from Maya Jasanoff, *Edge of Empire*, 2006, p. 32), in disdain of the latter's flashy wealth, made up of jewels and gold given to him by Indian princes. Diamonds turn out to be *de rigueur* the basis of Indian fortunes, including that of the Pitt family and of the Pigots of Patshull. George Durant of Tong was one of the clients with an overtly West Indian sugar and spice fortune, which involved slave labour. Attempts have been made to tarnish Lancelot for working for tainted money, but this was not a concept that applied during his lifetime. William Cowper wrote of slavery in *The Task* (1785): the first Quaker moves calling for abolition came after Lancelot's death, and it was in December 1785 that William Wilberforce confessed to the younger Pitt that his sudden conversion to evangelical Christianity had made him susceptible to social evils (see Hague, pp.216–18; the Wilberforce shipping fortune came from trading between the West Indies and Russia). The effects of enclosures and the 'Captain Swing' riots were not felt until well after Lancelot's death, either; it might be argued that he was working on the coat-tails of the 'flowering of rural England' that Professor Hoskins once assured us was a Georgian reality. Rather late in the day, I realised that Lancelot's story could be told almost entirely in the context of the works of Gray, Fielding and Sterne and their contemporaries, whose worlds he did inhabit. Lancelot was always concerned for the welfare of his workers, there are endless evidences of this, and it was quite possible that he exercised his own unspoken censorship, working only for landowners who felt the same, notably Lord Exeter, the Duke of Devonshire, the Duke of Marlborough, Lord Coventry and others, most of whose (old) money came from their landed estates. What was perhaps most remarkable was that the ownership of a green park, and a park dressed by Lancelot Brown, had outstripped all other luxuries, to become the ultimate in aspirational jewels.

225   **'No man that'**: Henry Holland to Humphry Repton, see Kedrun Laurie in G. Carter, P. Goode and K. Laurie (eds), *Humphry Repton catalogue*, 1982, Norwich, p.11, quoting Repton's *Sketches and Hints*, 1794, p.30. Repton apparently paid additional homage to Brown by studying forest scenery in Hainault Forest in Essex (as Lancelot had done) – the information coming from Samuel Knight, who was Repton's friend and a connection of the younger Browns in Huntingdonshire.

225   **'The nomination'**: Lord Sandwich to Sir John Hynde Cotton, March 1764, in Stazicker, p.92

226   **'county dignity'**: see Sidney and Beatrice Webb, 'The Parish and the County' chapter, in *English Local Government*, 1906 (reprinted 1963)

226   **'hence a sort of tacit'**: ibid.

226   **'Brown should be relieved'**: N. A. M. Rodger, *The Insatiable Earl, the 4th Earl of Sandwich*, 1993, p.88, quoting PRO 30/29/1/14 ff.6–16, November 1769

226   **'I remember hearing'**: Uvedale Price, *Essay on the Picturesque*, 1794, p.192. Rare Books, Cambridge University Library.

227   **'Permit me to hope'**: William Constable, BL Add. Mss. 69795 f.31, 22nd July 1772

228   **'400 or 500 acres'**: Deborah Turnbull, 'The Making of the Burton Constable Landscape', in *Burton Constable Hall: The Eighteenth and Nineteenth Centuries*, East Yorkshire Local History Society, 1998, p.10

228   **'the Management'**: Burton Constable Hall guide, revised by Gerardine Mulcahy, Burton Constable Foundation, 2008, p.2

228   **'2 stoves with'**: Turnbull op. cit., p.11

228   **'hollies and laurels'**: ibid., p.13

228   **Thomas White**: see Deborah Turnbull, *Thomas White 1739–1811: Eighteenth-Century Landscape Designer and Arboriculturist*, Ph.D. thesis, University of Hull, 1990

229   **'after the manner of Rousseau'/'bit of a Vertu'**: Burton Constable Hall guide, p.2

229 **'How to Clump my Avenues'**: William Constable, BL Add. Mss. 69795 f.31; Elisabeth Hall, 'Mr Brown's Directions, Capability Brown's landscaping at Burton Constable 1767–82', in *Garden History*, 23:2, Winter 1995, pp.145–74

230 **'Trench the ground'**: Hall op. cit., 8th September 1772

231 **'by breaking the side'**: ibid., 4th September 1773, p.156

232 **'the lawn before'**: ibid.

232 **'lower the surface'**: ibid., 30th September 1775

232 **'make a clay wall'**: ibid.

232 **'the islands to be'**: ibid., 3rd August 1776

232 **'Mr Brown will send'**: ibid.

232 **'in levelling and uniting'**: ibid.

233 **'to a Christmas gambol'**: Lord Coventry from Croome, BL Add. Mss. 69795 f.42

233 **Knowsley Park**: Lancelot was paid £100 in 1775 for 'A General Plan' and visited Knowsley again in 1776, just after the death of the 11th Earl of Derby, to plan the 'New Kitchen Garden' and grounds around the house, and was paid £84. These plans (which are not at Knowsley) were 'most probably' carried out by estate workmen; the formal pools were not loosened until 1796, and then Richard Yarnell, formerly a gardener at Hampton Court, became Head Gardener. Information sent to the author by Edward Perry at Knowsley, 29th October 2008.

233 **'fortunate swain'**: James Jodrell, BL Add. Mss. 69795 f.46, 21st December 1772

233 **'that my lord has enjoyed'**: Lady Chatham, 'Exact copy to Mr Brown', 17th October 1772, Chatham Papers, op.cit., f.147

233 **'the family at Hampton'**: BL Add. Mss. 69795 f.48, 4th January 1773

233 **'old friend Mr Brown'**: ibid., f.27, 4th January 1773

234 **'a piece of hung beef'**: George Brown, ibid., f.55

234 **note from Drummonds**: ibid., f.58, 5th March 1773

235 **Lord North**: ibid., f.40, 5th October 1772

235 **'I have made the'**: William St Quentin, ibid., f.57, 2nd March 1773

235 **Edward Hussey Montagu**: ibid., f.60

235 **'regards to Mrs Brown'**: ibid., f.61, 12th April 1773

235 **'going on very properly'**: Lord Sandwich, ibid., f.69

235 **'you can possibly spare'**: Lord Craven, ibid., f.67, 8th June 1773

236 **Clive in India**: see Maya Jasanoff, *Edge of Empire*, New York, 2006, p.32ff., see also Lawrence James, *The Rise and Fall of the British*

Empire, 1995, p.125ff.; Lucy Sutherland, *The East India Company in 18th-century politics*, 1952; Robert Harvey, *Clive, The Life and Death of a British Emperor*, 1998

236 **a 'small box'**: Laurence Whistler, 'Newly Discovered Vanbrugh Designs for Claremont', *Country Life*, 25th February 1949, p.426; see also Whistler, 1954, on Claremont; and the National Trust guide to Claremont Landscape Garden, 1989

238 **'Liberal Brooks'**: Stroud, 1966, p.50

238 **'that the great wicked Lord'**: Phyllis M. Cooper, *The Story of Claremont*, 7th edn, 1979, p.17

239 **'always ye Greatest'**: Lambert, BL Add. Mss. 69795 f.73, 4th November 1773. Brown's payment for Claremont has been much exaggerated mainly because of Repton's assertion in his *Fragments* that house and grounds cost £100,000 (Cooper op. cit., p.17); Lancelot's account book shows £30,612. 16s. 11d. received from January 1771 to June 1776, with an additional £3,000 paid in March 1778 and the account balance received – an unstipulated amount – in 1780. As this letter from Lambert reveals, Lancelot was responsible for the lavish interior fittings to the house, and so all these expenses went through his hands. Most was passed on to Henry Holland and the craftsmen suppliers.

240 **golden guineas**: see Cooper op. cit., p.18

240 **'once had full of gold'**: Boswell, Vol. 3, p.58

241 **'Two of Lord Clive's sisters'**: BL Add. Mss. 69795 f.38, 21st August 1772

241 **'several specimens'**: Lord Arundell, ibid., f.71, 16th August 1773

241 **'I should be glad'**: Lord Lisburne, 17th August 1772, Stroud, 1984, pp.97–8

242 **'sorry to find you'**: Lord Dacre, BL Add. Mss. 69795 f.75, 7th November 1773

242 **'which may be material'**: Lord Lisburne, ibid., f.77, 7th November 1773

242 **'that the amendment'**: Lord Howe, ibid., f.81, 18th December 1773

243 **'affectionate Friend'**: Lancelot, ibid., f.83, 20th March 1774

243 **'I have now lived'**: David P. Miller, 'My favourite studdys, Lord Bute as a Naturalist,' p.230 in *Lord Bute: Essays in Re-interpretation*, ed. K.W. Schweizer, Leicester, 1988, pp.213–39

243 **'but spend the poor remains'**: ibid.

244 **'[Lord Bute] is sorry'**: ibid.

244 **'the dreaded East'**: *The Correspondence of Horace Walpole, Earl of*

Orford and the Rev. William Mason, ed. Rev. J. Mitford, 2 vols, 1851, Vol. 1, 9th May 1772

244 **'I have read Chambers's book'**: ibid., 25th May 1772

244 **'In England'**: Chambers, *Dissertation*, 1772, Rare Books, Cambridge Unviversity Library

245 **'liked that Country best'**: Nikolaus Pevsner, *The Englishness of English Art*, 1956, pp.173–4; see also John Harris, 1970

245 **'regular professors'**: Chambers, *Dissertation*, 1772, Rare Books, Cambridge Unviversity Library

245 **'whole woods have been'**: ibid.

246 **'waters for sailing'**: ibid.

246 **'Come then, prolific Art'**: Rev. William Mason, *An Heroic Epistle*, 1773, see Jacques, p.108

247 **'Haste, bid you livelong terrace'**: ibid.

248 **Berrington Foreman's notes**: kindly given to me at Berrington Hall

249 **'which was rather too much'**: Lancelot, BL Add. Mss. 69795 f.91, 11th December 1775

250 **'very much upon'**: ibid., f.91

250 **John Byng**: quoted in Robin Moore, *A History of Coombe Abbey*, Coventry, 1983, p.64

251 **'I shall leave'**: Stroud, 1950, p.170

251 **'the famous man'**: *The Beautiful Lady Craven, The Original Memoirs of Elizabeth Baroness Craven, etc.*, ed. A. M. Broadley and Lewis Melville, 2 vols, 1914, Vol. 2, p.100

251 **'with the finest trees'**: Mowl and Barre p.180

251 **'the approach road'**: ibid., p.181

252 **Anne Seymour Conway**: see Percy Noble, *A Woman of Art and Fashion 1748–1828*, 1908; and Angelica Goodden, *Miss Angel, The Art and World of Angelica Kauffman*, 2005

254 **1769** For the demolition of Middleton, see *Milton Abbas, Dorset*, an illustrated guide by C. H. R. Fookes, 8th edn, 2004; maps and plans of the Milton estate are in Dorset Record Office

254 **'unmannerly, imperious Lord'**: see Harris, 1970, p.237

254 **'the layout of the village'**: ibid., p.238

254 **'had given plans'**: Stroud, 1984, p.119

256 **'with great difficulty'**: Janet Waymark, 'Sherborne, Dorset', *Garden History*, 29:1, 2001, pp.64–81 (Architectural Association Diploma thesis, 1996), quoting Sherborne Castle Estate Archives, Game Book, 1771–84

257 **'Mr Brown came'**: ibid., see also Sherborne Castle guide by Ann Smith, Sherborne Castle Estates, 2007

12 Treading the Enchanted Ground

This phrase is taken from Jemima, Marchioness Grey's description of her exploration of Wimpole Park with Lancelot; combined with the opening quotation from her well-schooled daughter, Lady Amabel Polwarth, on the visit of a 'great Man' – which ('as happens sometimes with great Men) has ended in very little' – it subscribes to Lancelot's elevation to somebody approaching a mythical magician. To many people he is no longer a mere gardener, even a royal one, but a worker of miracles.

261 **'Now I must request'**: Lady Amabel Polwarth, 19th November 1778, Luton & Bedfordshire Archives

262 **'I will not fail'**: Lord Chatham to Lady Stanhope, 1777, Stroud, 1984, p.186; see also *Chatham Correspondence*, ed. W. S. Taylor and J. H. Pringle, 1838–40, Vol. iv, p.430

262 **'My dear Sir'**: *Garrick, Letters*, Vol. 3, 5th February 1776, letter 980

263 **'The eagerness of the people'**: Benedetti, p.223

263 **'My Wife is resolv'd'**: Garrick to Lancelot, *Letters*, op.cit., fn. to letter 980

263 **Jack Brown from Boston**: BL Add. Mss. 69795 f.89

263 **'though in a wretched condition'**: ibid.

264 **'as he has lived'**: Black, p.99

265 **'the oldest new place'**: the Rev. William Gilpin, in *Remarks on Forest Scenery*, 1791, wrote of the first Cadland that the 'abundance of old timber gives the house, tho' lately built, so much the air and dignity of an ancient mansion that Mr Brown, the ingenious improver of it, used to say "It was the oldest new place he knew in England". The clumps he has managed 'with great judgment.' Stroud, 1984, p.178

266 **'I find you added'**: Stroud, 1984, p.178

266 **'Today, and indeed'**: Lancelot to Lady Chatham, Chatham Papers; Stroud, 1984, p.187

267 **'It is impossible'**: Lady Chatham, BL Add. Mss. 69795 f.99, 13th November 1777

267 **'From the Stamp Act'**: Lady Chatham, ibid., 1777

267 **'a rugged and awful crisis'**: Ayling, pp.420–1

268 **'The sentiments of'**: 13th November ibid.

268 **'to deprive the royal offspring'**: Ayling, pp.424–5

268 **Lancelot from Trentham**: BL Add. Mss. 69795 f.101, 15th April 1778

268 **'she likes them'**: Lancelot to Peggy, from Wisbech, BL Add. Mss. 69795 f.103

269 **'I am just returned'**: Lancelot from Hampton Court, Chatham Papers/PRO/30/8/24 f.154, 9th May 1778

269 **Pitt's funeral**: see Hague, Prologue

269 **death of Thomas Linley**: Valerie Purton, 'A Lost Lincolnshire Link', in *All Things Lincolnshire*, ed. Jean Howard and David Start, Lincoln, 2007, pp.170–3

271 **'Make the lake'**: see Hall, 'Mr Brown's Directions', *Garden History*, 23:2, Winter 1995, pp.145–74

271 **'a Godforsaken place'**: Sykes, p.10

272 **'Mr Perfect likes'**: Sykes, pp.15–16

272 **'his primary interest'**: Sykes, p.38

272 **'The Great Brown'**: Sykes, p.49

272 **'small holes made'**: Sykes, p.49

273 **'built fourteen'**: Sykes, p.53

273 **'a veritable orgy'**: Sykes, p.54

274 **'devoted to horticulture'**: Jane Brown, *Trinity College: A Garden History*, 2002, pp.25, 27

275 **'and no very great funds'**: St John's College archives

276 **'do wonders'**: Brown op. cit., p.29

276 **'the eye would'**: ibid, p.31

278 **'Mr Brown has'**: Marchioness Grey quoted in D. Adshead, *Wimpole, 278 Drawings* etc., 2009, p.47

282 **'a Pencil & Paper'**: Lady Amabel Polwarth, quoting Lancelot, letter 19 November 1778, Luton & Bedfordshire Archives L30/13/12/52

13 The Omnipotent Magician

This chapter was intended to be my finale, but Lancelot showed no sign of giving up; nor could I let him die. He mellowed, he allowed himself time to sit and talk, and it was as if he softened his landscapes, fitting them into the fashion that we call the 'Picturesque'. He did this on his own terms, and from his own dealings with the Rev. William Gilpin, whom he had known for many years. Throughout these pages I have purposely refused to foist fashionable intellectual theories upon him from the benefit of hindsight, even though they appeared in books published in his time: it was not his way to rush home to consult Hogarth's *The Analysis of Beauty* or Edmund Burke's *Enquiry into the Origin of our Ideas of the Sublime and the Beautiful*, or any other luminary's words, though he may have imbibed their sentiments from his own conversations.

281 **'If Jack is'**: BL Add. Mss. 69795 f.107

282 **'I will give'**: ibid.

282 **'very sober'/'There Remains'**: letter to 2nd Viscount Palmerston,

17th November 1779, Broadlands Papers, Hartley Library
(Special Collections), University of Southampton, MS 62/BR
103/18/7

283 **Henry Cecil and Sally Hoggins**: see Elisabeth Inglis-Jones, *The
Lord of Burghley*, 1964

283 **'boxed and coxed'**: Doreen Yarwood, *Robert Adam*, 1970, p.126,
and the whole of Ch. 4 on Adam's 'Glorious Decade', when most
of his sites were also Lancelot's

283 **'I have always said'**: Stroud, 1984, p.106

283 **Appuldurcombe House**: see L. O. J. Boynton, English Heritage
guide, 2005 edn; Sir Richard Worsley, *The History of the Isle of Wight*,
1781; Hallie Rubenhold, *Lady Worsley's Whim, An Eighteenth-Century
Tale of Sex, Scandal and Divorce*, 2009

284 **'diligently overseen'**: 7th Earl of Harewood, introduction to the
Harewood guide by Richard Buckle, Derby, n.d. The Norris
Museum in St Ives, Cambridgeshire (Gertrude Peet Collection)
has a copy of a letter from the Fenstanton Women's Institute that
accompanied a flower basket sent to H.R.H. The Princess Mary
in 1922 on the occasion of her marriage to the 6th Earl of Harewood
and in recognition of their Lord of the Manor's designs for
Harewood.

284 **'If Tom Girtin had lived'**: J. M. W. Turner, quoted by Richard
Buckle in Harewood guide, 1970, p.16

284 **'dashed down'**: ibid.

285 **'To finish all the Valley'**: for the 1774 contract, see Roger Turner,
p.133

286 **'he has finished'**: quoted in Roger Turner, p.134; see also Peter
Fergusson, *Roche Abbey*, English Heritage guide, 2006 edn

286 **'the springtime'/'men of feeling'**: Christopher Woodward, *In
Ruins*, 2001, pp.124–5

288 **'densely inscribed'/'Sir George Cornewall'**: see *Moccas: An
English Deer Park*, ed. Paul T. Harding and Tom Wall, English Nature,
c.1999, Ch. 2, 'Historical Context'

288 **'the visitor was'**: John Phibbs, 'Reading the Landscape', in *Moccas*,
p.72

289 **'I fear those'**: Rev. Francis Kilvert, quoted in *Moccas*, opposite title
page, from Kilvert's *Diary*, 22nd April 1876

289 **Wynnstay**: Paul Sandby, who was working at Wynnstay, notes a visit
to Mr Brown at Hampton Court on Sir Watkin's behalf on 2nd
June 1771, a most definite connection; see *Paul Sandby: Picturing
Britain*, ed. John Bonehill and Stephen Daniels, 2009, p.218

290 **'a very fine'/'led by the gamekeeper'**: Hinde, pp.193–5

290 **'to keep myself'/'£2,500 per annum'**: Richard Woods to Lord Arundell, quoted in Hinde, p.164.

291 **'suddenly appears'**: Young, 1772, p.93

292 **'fresh green linen'**: Gordon, p.113

293 **Pirton**: the plan for Pirton Park and Pool, *c.*1763, and John Snape's map of the Croome Estate, 1796, were seen while on temporary exhibition at Kelmarsh Hall; they belong to the Croome Estate Trustees Archive

295 **'I think I may say'**: Elizabeth Montagu's letters were originally edited by her nephew, Matthew Montagu, and published in 1809, 1813 and 1817. See also *Elizabeth Montagu: The Queen of the Bluestockings, Correspondence 1720–61*, ed. E. J. Climenson, 2 vols, 1906; R. Blunt, *Mrs Montagu, Queen of the Blues, her letters and friendships from 1762–80*, 2 vols, 1923. My quotations are from the landscape architect Sybil Wade's statement at the Newbury District Local Plan Inquiry, September 1997 into development affecting Sandleford (St Gabriel's School)

295 **'we have a pretty village'/'Mr M has just taken'**: Climenson, 1906, letter after her marriage, *c.* 1742

295 **'Punch's Oak'**: Punch was born on 11th May 1743 and the oak soon planted

295 **'my desk and I'**: Blunt op. cit., Summer 1752

296 **'at Sandleford you will find'**: Blunt, 1923, 9th June 1777

296 **'reformed chapel'**: Stroud, 1984, p.195

296 **'by removing a good deal'**: 9th July 1782 in Blunt, 1923

296 **'He is an agreeable'**: Stroud, 1984, p.195

296 **'Demons, Pomp'**: Montagu to Mrs Elizabeth Carter, Blunt 1923, n.d. but 1781

297 **'as fast as time'**: ibid.; there is a 1781 Survey of the Estate at Sandleford in Berkshire Record Office (BRO: D/ELM T19/2/13), which Matthew Montagu identified as by 'Mr Speers' – i.e. Jonathan Spyers. No overlay of Lancelot's scheme has been found, but this may be with the estate papers, which are in America.

297 **'I am not fond'**: letter to Mrs Elizabeth Carter, *c.*1765, in Blunt op. cit.

297 **'The scene is extremely'**: Stroud, 1984, p.196

298 **'I passed two hours'**: December 1782, Stroud, 1950, p.201; R. B. Johnson, *The Letters of Hannah More*, 1925

299 **'My time has been'**: Biddy Brown to her daughter Peggy

(Margaret), in BL Add. Mss. 69795, ff.110, 112, 114 (the intervening pages are cover sheets)

300 **'for a term'**: Lance Brown to Lord Sandwich, 17 February 1789, in Sir L. Namier and J. Brooke, *History of Parliament, House of Commons 1754–90*, Vol II, 1964, pp. 122–3

301 **Rev. Thomas Brown**: he served the parish of Conington for forty years, and a tablet on the chancel wall (beside the organ) commemorates this

303 **'more an object of'**: Henry Holland, Oxford *Dictionary of National Biography* entry

304 **Henry and Bridget's son Lancelot**: he married Charlotte Peters and, of their fifteen children, twelve married and had large families, and the name Lancelot has persisted down the generations to the present

304 **'Gardener to His Majesty'**: see Jane Roberts, *Royal Landscape*, 1997, p.65

306 **'boldly ventured forth'**: G. Carter, P. Goode and K. Laurie, *Humphry Repton*, 1983, 'First Years', p.5

306 **'the maps of'**: ibid., p.11

306 **Repton's gazetteer**: see Stephen Daniels, *Humphry Repton and the Geography of Georgian England*, 1999, pp.256–70

307 **'codified'**: Sylvia Crowe in Carter, Goode and Laurie op. cit., p.128

307 **Geoffrey Jellicoe**: ibid.

Afterpiece

308 **'architecture is the art'**: Geoffrey Scott, *The Architecture of Humanism: A Study in the History of Taste*, 1980 edn, p.41

309 **'How happy was the lot'**: Ralph Nevill, *Sporting Days and Sporting Ways*, 1910, pp.238–9

310 **James Boswell**: *The Life of Samuel Johnson*, Vol. 3, p.184, 4th June 1781

310 **'opened a Road'**: Richard Holmes, *The Age of Wonder*, 2009, pp.126–7

310 **'the water very fine'/'a fine one'**: Thomas Jefferson, 'Notes of a Tour of English Gardens', March and April 1786

311 **'I am at present'**: G. Jellicoe, S. Jellicoe, P. Goode, M. Lancaster (eds)., *The Oxford Companion to Gardens*, 1986, p.490.

311 **'Frog Service'**: the places illustrated are listed in Ray Desmond, *Bibliography of British Gardens*, 1984, Appendix, p.313; see also *The Green Frog Service, Wedgwood and Bentley's Imperial Russian Service*, ed. M. Raeburn, L. Voronikhina, A. Nurnberg, London,

1995, commemorative volume illustrating the entire service in colour. The Frog Service is in the Hermitage Museum, St Petersburg

312 **'Poor Brown!'**: Lord Harcourt's letter in Walpole and Mason, Vol. 2, p.406 n.

312 **'Ill fares the land'**: see William Black, *Goldsmith*, English Men of Letters series, 1880, Ch. 14, 'The Deserted Village'

313 **'I may have my revenge'**: Jacques, p.122

313 **'Were England now'**: William Cowper, *The Task*, Book 3, 'The Garden'

314 **'wrap't all o'er'**: Richard Payne Knight, *The Landscape* quoted in Turner, 1999, p.164

315 **'Mr Brown the gardener'**: Uvedale Price, *An Essay on the Picturesque as Compared with the Sublime and the Beautiful*, etc., 1794, p.188

315 **'To improve'**: ibid. on lawns

315 **'this fellow crawls'**: ibid.

315 **'To a Gravel Walk'**: quoted in Stephen Bending, 'William Mason's *An Essay on the arrangement of Flowers in Pleasure-Grounds'*, *Journal of Garden History*, 9:4, 1989, pp.217–20

315 **'saw the deformity'**: Dr Mavor on Blenheim, quoted in Green, p.191

316 **Paxton**: see Kate Colquhoun, *A Thing in Disguise, the Visionary Life of Joseph Paxton*, 2003

317 **'more than three hundred miles'**: Laura Wood Roper, *FLO: A Biography of Frederick Law Olmsted*, 1973, p.68

317 **'What artist, so noble'**: ibid., p.71. Olmsted identified the question so often asked of Lancelot's work these days: how did he know what his planting would look like in 250 years' time? It is interesting that this observation came from an American, from a country with only an infantile concern then for husbandry, after an orgy of raping the land. Olmsted saw himself as saving the threatened wild beauty (e.g. Yosemite) and repairing the ravages of the slave economy, as restoring the living conditions that fostered liberty and self-improvement to 'the slave, the savage, the maniac, the criminal, and the peasant . . . as with the child' (Roper op. cit., p.69).

Lancelot, on the other hand, knew nothing but a countryside of ancient practices governed by the seasons; he knew how trees grew because he was aware of them at all stages of their development, and they grew with him. The moving of well-grown trees was standard practice then, illustrated by the 'Great Duke' of Marlborough's request to Henry Wise for large trees, because he was an old man and had not time to wait for effect; by mixing mature trees with fast-growing 'nurse' trees, Lancelot's effects were soon created in, say, fifteen or twenty years, or even less on good soils. He knew also that good woodland management, taking out the poor and damaged trees to allow space for the young hardwoods to develop, was an essential part of the rural economy, generating interim profits and job opportunities. Lancelot had no need to explain forward management or write maintenance regimes. This much – a mine of collective understanding of trees and woods – we have lost. We have, in old Europe, returned to the 'infantile' state of misunderstanding of the young United States of America.

319   **Dorothy Stroud**: Stroud (1910–87), the daughter of a working mother (her father having left after Dorothy's birth), finished her education at Edgbaston High School, and in January 1930 she joined *Country Life* Books, where she met Christopher Hussey who inspired her researches on Brown. At the beginning of the war she worked for John Summerson on the National Monuments Record survey of London, along with her voluntary war work, and then moved with Summerson on his appointment as Curator of Sir John Soane's Museum in Lincoln's Inn Fields. Dorothy was appointed Inspectress at the Soane in 1946 – *she was the Soane* – until her retirement in 1984. After *Capability Brown*, (1950), she wrote *Henry Holland* (1966) and other books. She always lived in London; after her death her ashes were interred beside Lancelot's lake at Croome Court, where there is a memorial.

320   **'it is particularly necessary'**: Sylvia Crowe on land-form, *Garden Design*, 1965 edn, p.103

Sources

Eighteenth- and nineteenth-century sources

Boswell, James, *The Life of Samuel Johnson*, 3 vols, 1901, ed. Arnold Glover

British Library, Add. Mss. 69795: the former 'Pakenham' letters presented by Dorothy Stroud, letters to and from Lancelot Brown and his family, 1753–84

Brown, John, Lancelot and Richard, *Correspondence to the 3rd Duke of Portland*, 1762–7, Papers of W. H. Cavendish-Bentinck, 3rd Duke of Portland, University of Nottingham Library

Chambers, Sir William, *Dissertation on Oriental Gardening*, 1772. Rare Books, Cambridge University Library

Cotton Papers, 588/E26 1–4, Cambridgeshire Archives Shire Hall, Cambridge

Cowper, William, *The Task*, Book 3, 'The Garden', 1785, in *The Poetical Works of William Cowper*, 1875 edn

Defoe, Daniel, *A Tour Through the Whole Island of Great Britain*, 1724–6, Penguin Classics edn, ed. Pat Rogers, 1986

Dickins, Lillian and Stanton, Mary (eds) *An Eighteenth-Century Correspondence* (mainly letters to Sanderson Miller from his friends) 1910

Fiennes, Celia, *The Journeys of Celia Fiennes*, ed. John Hillaby, 1983

Garrick, David, *Letters*, ed. D. M. Little and G. M. Kahrle, 1963

Gray, Thomas, *Correspondence*, ed. P. Toynbee and L. Whibley (and H. W. Starr), 3 vols, 1935, 1971

Grey Papers, Marchioness (Jemima), Bedfordshire & Luton Archives, Bedford, L. 30, etc.

Harcourt, E. W. (ed.) *The Harcourt Papers*, 1880–1905

Hodgson, Rev. John, *A History of Northumberland*, Part II, vol. I *Redesdale and Morpeth Deanery Parishes*, 1827, facsimile 1973

Irwin, Viscountess, *Correspondence to Susan, Countess Gower*, Public Record Office, PRO 30/29/4/2 etc.

Loraine, Sir Lambton, *Pedigree and Memoirs of the Family of Loraine of Kirkharle*, 1902

Montagu, Elizabeth, *Mrs Montagu, Queen of the Blues, her letters and friendships from 1762–80*, ed. R. Blunt, 2 vols, 1923

More, Hannah, *Letters*, ed. R. B. Johnson, 1925

Penn, John, *An Historical & Descriptive Account of Stoke Park in Buckinghamshire*, 1813

Percy, Thomas, *A Letter describing the ride to Hulne Abbey from Alnwick in Northumberland etc.*, 1765. Rare Books, Cambridge University Library

Pitt, William, Earl of Chatham, *Correspondence*, ed. W. S. Taylor and J. H. Pringle, 1838–40

Pitt, William, Earl of Chatham, Pitt Papers, Public Record Office, PRO 30/8 etc.

Price, Uvedale, *An Essay on the Picturesque*, 1794. Rare Books, Cambridge University Library

The Stoic, Journal in Stowe School Library

Thomson, James, *The Seasons*, pub. in parts 1726–30

Thompson, Pishey, *History and Antiquities of Boston*, 1856

Scott, *Personal and Professional Recollections by the late Sir George Gilbert Scott, R.A.*, edited by his son G. G. Scott, 1879

Wallington Estate Letter Book 1764–76, Northumberland Archives, Woodhorn, ref. 672/2/48

Walpole, Horace, *Correspondence with George Montagu*, ed. W. S. Lewis and
    R. S. Brown, vol. 9 of the 10 volume Yale University Press edn, 1940
Walpole, Horace and Mason, Rev. William, *Correspondence*, ed. Rev. J.
    Mitford, 2 vols, 1851
Welford, Richard, *Men of Mark 'Twixt Tyne and Tweed*, 1895
Young, Arthur, *Six Months' Tour through the North of England*, 1770, 1771 edn
Young, Arthur, *A Six Weeks' Tour through the Southern Counties of England
    and Wales*, 3rd edn, 1772

Modern published sources

All published in London, unless otherwise stated.

Adshead, David, *Wimpole, Architectural Drawings and Topographical Views,
    illustrated catalogue with CD*, 2007.
Angerstein, R.R., *Illustrated Travel Diary 1753–1755*, trans T. and P. Berg,
    2001
Ayling, Stanley, *The Elder Pitt, Earl of Chatham*, 1976
Benedetti, Jean, *David Garrick and the Birth of the Modern Theatre*, 2001
Berg, Maxine, *Luxury & Pleasure in Eighteenth-Century Britain*, Oxford,
    2005/2007
Binnie, G. M., *Early Dam Builders in Britain*, 1989
Black, Jeremy, *George III: America's Last King*, 2006/2008
Blake, Robin, *George Stubbs and the Wide Creation*, 2005/2006
Blanning, Tim, *The Pursuit of Glory, Europe 1648–1815*, 2007/2008
Blomfield, David, *Kew Past*, Chichester, 1994
Bolitho, Hector and Peel, Derek, *The Drummonds of Charing Cross*,
    1967
Bond, James and Tiller, Kate, *Blenheim, Landscape for a Park*, 1995
Brown, Jane, *The Pursuit of Paradise, A Social History of Gardening*, 1999
Brown, Jane, *The Garden at Buckingham Palace, An Illustrated History* with
    photographs by Christopher Simon Sykes, 2004
Brown, Jane, *My Darling Heriott, A Life of Henrietta Luxborough 1699–1756*,
    2006
Buchan, Alice, *A Scrap Screen*, 1979
Burnett, David, *Longleat: The Story of an English Country House*, Wimborne
    Minster, 2009
Campbell-Culver, Maggie, *A Passion for Trees, the Legacy of John Evelyn*, 2006
Carter, George, Goode, Patrick and Laurie, Kedrun, *Humphry Repton
    Landscape Gardener 1752–1818*, University of East Anglia, Norwich, 1983
Clarke, George B. (ed.), *Descriptions of Lord Cobham's Gardens at Stowe
    1700–1750*, Buckinghamshire Record Society, 1990

Colley, Linda, *Britons Forging the Nation 1707–1837*, 1992

Colvin, Brenda, *Land and Landscape*, 1970

Cousins, Michael, Hagley Park, vol. 35, Supp. 1, *Garden History*, 2007

Daniels, Stephen, *Humphry Repton: Landscape Gardening and the Geography of Georgian England*, 1999

Devonshire, The Duchess of, *The Estate, A View from Chatsworth*, 1990

Fairbrother, Nan, *New Lives, New Landscapes*, 1970

Fairfax-Lucy, Alice, *Charlecote and the Lucys: The Chronicle of an English Family*, revised edn, 1990

Foreman, Amanda, *Georgiana, Duchess of Devonshire*, 1998

Friedman, Terry, *James Gibbs*, 1984

Gomme, Andor, *Smith of Warwick: Francis Smith, Architect and Master-Builder*, Stamford, 2000

Gordon, Catherine, *The Coventrys of Croome*, Chichester, 2000

Green, David, *Gardener to Queen Anne, Henry Wise and the Formal Garden*, 1956

Hague, William, *William Pitt the Younger*, 2004/2005

Harris, John, *Sir William Chambers, Knight of the Polar Star*, 1970

Harris, John, *The Palladian Revival: Lord Burlington, His Villa and Garden at Chiswick*, 1994

Harvey, John, *Early Nurserymen*, Chichester, 1974

Heath, Gerald, *Hampton Court, the Story of a Village*, ed. K. White and J. Heath, The Hampton Court Association, 2000

Hedley, G., comp., *Capability Brown and the Northern House*, Landscape Trust, 1983

Hinde, Thomas, *Capability Brown: The Story of a Master Gardener*, 1986

Holmes, Richard, *The Age of Wonder, How the Romantic Generation Discovered the Beauty and Terror of Science*, 2008/2009

Howard, Jean and Start, David, *All Things Lincolnshire*, The Society for Lincolnshire History and Archaeology, Lincoln, 2007

Hunt, John Dixon, *William Kent, Landscape Garden Designer*, 1987

Hunt, John Dixon, *The Picturesque Garden in Europe*, 2003/2004

Hunt, John Dixon and Willis, Peter, *The Genius of the Place: The English Landscape Garden 1620–1820*, 1975

Jacques, David, *Georgian Gardens, The Reign of Nature*, 1983

Laird, Mark, *The Flowering of the English Landscape Garden, English Pleasure Grounds 1720–1800*, Philadelphia, 1999

Littlebury: A Parish History, ed. Lizzie Sanders and Gillian Williamson, Littlebury, 2005

Lunn, Angus, *Northumberland*, New Naturalist Series, 2004

Mack, Robert L., *Thomas Gray: A Life*, 2000

Meir, Jennifer, *Sanderson Miller and His Landscapes*, 2006

Mowl, Timothy, *William Kent: Architect, Designer, Opportunist*, 2006

Mowl, Timothy and Barre, Dianne, *Staffordshire, The Historic Gardens of England*, Bristol, 2009

Reed, James, *The Border Ballads*, 1973

Roberts, Jane, *Royal Landscape, The Gardens and Parks of Windsor*, 1997

Saunders, Edward, *Joseph Pickford of Derby, A Georgian Architect*, Stroud, 1993

Stazicker, Elizabeth, *The Sheriffs of Cambridgeshire and Huntingdonshire, a brief history*, Cambridge, 2007

Stroud, Dorothy, *Capability Brown*, 1950, 1975, 1984

Stroud, Dorothy, *Henry Holland: His Life and Architecture*, 1966

Sykes, Christopher Simon, *The Big House: The Story of a Country House and its Family* (Sledmere), 2004

Thurley, Simon, *Hampton Court: A Social and Architectural History*, 2003

Thynn, Alexander, Marquess of Bath, *Strictly Private to Public Exposure, The Early Years*, 2002

Turner, Roger, *Capability Brown and the Eighteenth-Century English Landscape*, Chichester, 1985, 1999

Uglow, Jenny, *The Lunar Men: The Friends Who Made the Future*, 2002/2003

Wedgwood, Iris, *Northumberland and Durham*, 1932

Whistler, Laurence, *The Imagination of Vanbrugh and His Fellow Artists*, 1954

Williams, Guy, *The Royal Parks of London*, Chicago, 1978

Williamson, Tom, *Polite Landscapes Gardens & Society in Eighteenth-Century England*, Stroud, 1998

Willis, Peter, *Charles Bridgeman and the English Landscape Garden*, 1977, reprinted Newcastle upon Tyne, 2002

ACKNOWLEDGEMENTS

My first thanks go to the producers of the Wentworth Wooden Jigsaw puzzle of Burghley House's portrait of Lancelot Brown, which hangs in the Pagoda Room; his enigmatic face in fragments on the table before me were the prompting to try to put his life together.

My grateful acknowledgements go to those who have published distinguished works touching on Lancelot's career, in alphabetical order they are David Brown, George Clarke, Elisabeth Hall, John Harris, Thomas Hinde, David Jacques, Mark Laird, Jennifer Meir, Timothy Mowl, John Phibbs, Steffie Shields, Dorothy Stroud (of course), Michael Symes, Deborah Turnbull, Roger Turner, Janet Waymark, Tom Williamson and Peter Willis. I want to acknowledge particularly the opening up of estate archives by such as David Burnett (Longleat), the 11th Duchess of Devonshire (Chatsworth), Catherine Gordon (Croome), David Green (Blenheim), Colin Shrimpton (Alnwick), and Christopher Simon Sykes (Sledmere), as also the late Andor Gomme's *Smith of Warwick* for revealing so much of the working lives of Georgian builders and craftsmen. I have endeavoured to credit all these works, as well as other I have consulted, justly and accurately.

For helping me personally my thanks go to John and Kitty Anderson, Jeanne Battye, Jane Bolesworth, Julia and Derek Brown, Judith Christie, Fiona Colbert (St John's College, Cambridge), Dominic Cole, Rod Conlon, David Cousins, Lesley Denton, Hugh Dixon, John Drake, Gilly Drummond, Harry Willis Fleming, Bridget Flanagan, Edward and Polly Hutchison, Carole Jones, Jonathan Lovie, George and Susan Lowes, Michael Morrice, Miles Williamson-Noble, Nick Owen, Christopher Vane Percy, Edward Perry, John Phibbs, Crispin Powell (Northamptonshire Record Office), Heather Robertson, Sybil Wade and Lance Wise. In addition, my appreciations go to my family, friends and neighbours who have answered outlandish questions or been sent on wild goose chases in Mr Brown's cause.

My agent, Caradoc King, found a home for this book at Chatto & Windus, and my gratitude to my editor Jenny Uglow, and her colleagues, is boundless. Particular thanks go to my copy editor Mandy Greenfield, to Vera Brice and Leslie Robinson for drawing the plans, and to Douglas Matthews for the index.

The Omnipotent Magician now goes on his own way; I am bereft, but thank him for his company, and can only wish him 'God speed'.

Jane Brown
October 2010

INDEX

Burroughs, Rev. Benjamin, 129
Burroughs, Rev. William, 129
Burton Constable, East Yorkshire, 227–32, 241, 271, 308
Burton Dassett, 66
Burton, Francis, 145
Burton Pynsent, Somerset: tower (Burton Steeple), 17n, 184–5, 197; bequeathed to Chatham, 177–8, 194, 252; Lady Chatham sells land, 196; Chatham's life at, 233
Bush, John: nursery, 80–1
Bute, John Stuart, 3rd Earl of: and Medmenham 'friars', 72; Bartram's boxes sent to, 80; and improvement to St James's Park, 130; influence on George III, 139; trustee for Queen's House purchase, 141; LB hopes for commission from, 143; in LB's account book, 159–60; and William Ireland, 165; advanced agricultural methods, 166; as Ranger of Richmond Park, 167; fall from grace, 243–4; LB visits, 243, 249; death, 243; seeks office with Chatham, 268
Byng, Admiral John, 117
Byng, Hon. John (diarist), 250
Byram, West Yorkshire, 213, 268, 291

Cadland House, Hampshire, 248, 265–6, 282
Cadogan, Charles, 2nd Baron, 165
Cadogan, Charles Sloane Cadogan, 3rd Baron and 1st Earl, 165
Cadogan, Elizabeth, Lady (née Sloane), 165, 264
Call, Thomas, 215–16
Cam (or Granta), River (Cambridgeshire), 168–9, 172
Cambo, Northumberland, 14, 20, 24
Cambridge: Botanic Gardens, 274; St John's College, 275; development, 294–7
Cambridge, Richard Owen, 201, 206, 208
Camden, William: Britannia, 25
Campbell, Colin: Vitruvius Britannicus, 148
Canaletto (Giovanni Antonio Canal), 113, 215
canals (waterways), 186–90
Capability Brown and the Northern Landscape (exhibition, Newcastle, 1983), 3
Capheaton Hall, Northumberland, 23
Cardiff Castle, 244
Carlton House Terrace, London, 318

Caroline, Queen of George II, 133, 140, 221
Carpenter, Stephen, 252
Carr, John, 176, 273, 283
Carton, Co. Kildare, 5
Cartwright, Elizabeth (née Dormer), 144
Cartwright, Thomas, 145
Cartwright, William, 144–5
Castle Ashby, Northamptonshire, 161, 194–5, 197, 230
Castle Howard, Yorkshire, 28, 36, 319
Catherine II (the Great), Empress of Russia, 215n, 311
Cavendish, Sir William, 123
Caversham Park, Reading, 165
Cecil, Emma (née Vernon), 282
cedar of Lebanon (Cedrus libani): as LB's signature tree, 79–80; at Warwick Castle, 91; at Sherborne Castle, 257
Centurion, HMS, 98
Chambers, Sir William: in Society for Encouragement of Arts, 142–3; as architect for Office of Works, 221; enmity towards LB, 223; lays out Richmond Park and Kew Gardens, 224; works on Clive's London house, 238; Swedish knighthood, 244; Lord Milton quarrels with, 252, 254; supplies plan for Milton Abbas, 254; Harewood plans rejected, 283; influence on Le Rouge, 311; A Dissertation on Oriental Gardening, 244–6
Charlecote, Warwickshire, 67–8, 70, 120, 129–32, 317
Charles II, King, 158, 245
Charlotte Sophia, Queen of George III, 139–41, 154–5, 220
Charlton, Barbara: Recollections of a Northumbrian Lady 1815–66, 24n
Charlton, William, 23
Chatham, Hester, Countess of (née Grenville), 107, 134, 143, 194–7, 233, 267, 268, 295
Chatham, William Pitt, 1st Earl of: and Burton Pynsent Tower, 17n; forms government (1766), 19; family, 35, 54; LB meets at Stowe, 54; ramblings, 54, 106–7; and Seven Years War (1756–63), 57n, 117, 119, 143; indifference to money, 105; political career, 105; buys and improves Hayes Place, 107–8, 295; marriage and children, 107–8; LB's political allegiance to, 109; joint ministry with Devonshire (1756–7), 117, 122; petitions for royal appointment and